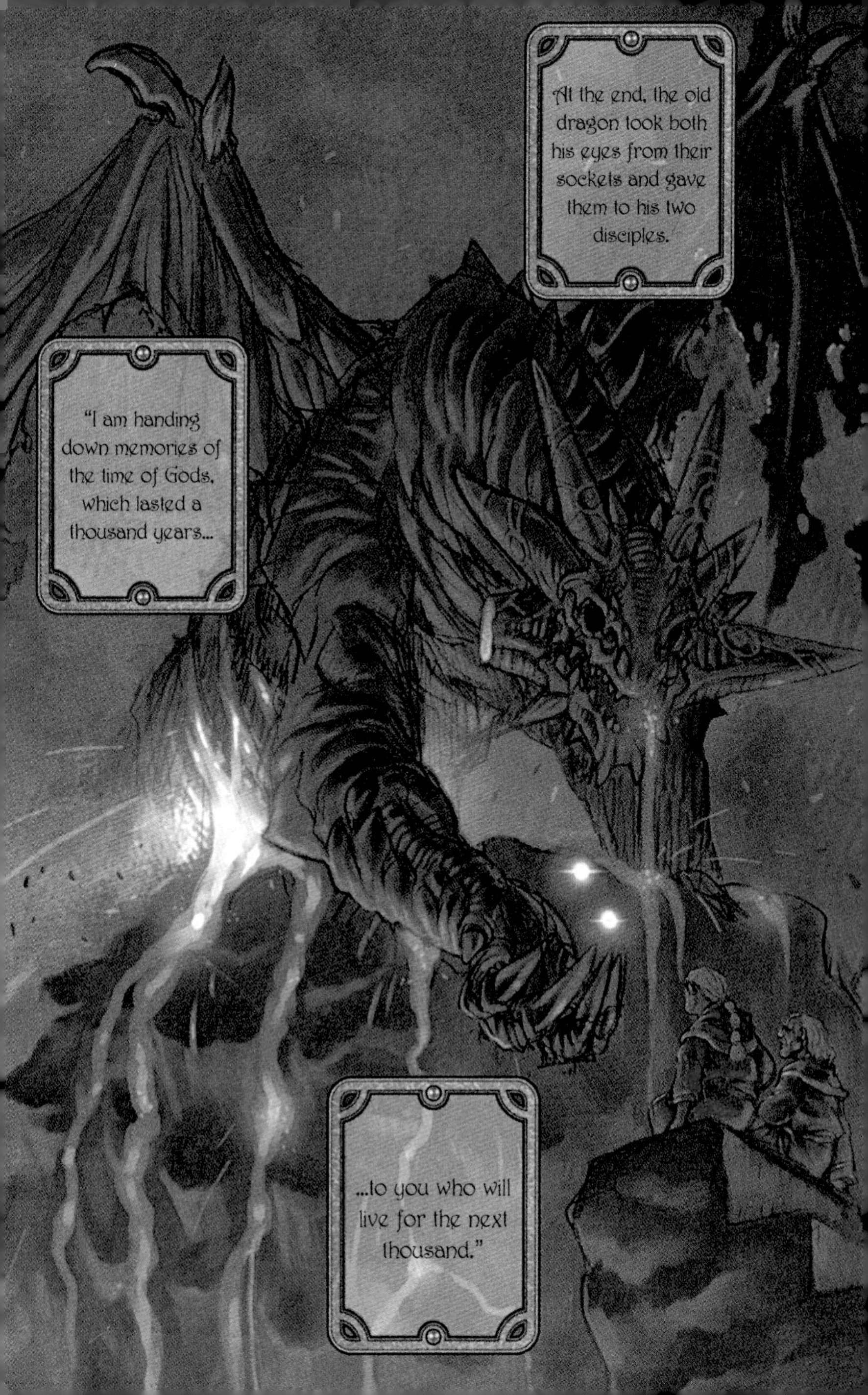
At the end, the old dragon took both his eyes from their sockets and gave them to his two disciples.
"I am handing down memories of the time of Gods, which lasted a thousand years...
...to you who will live for the next thousand."

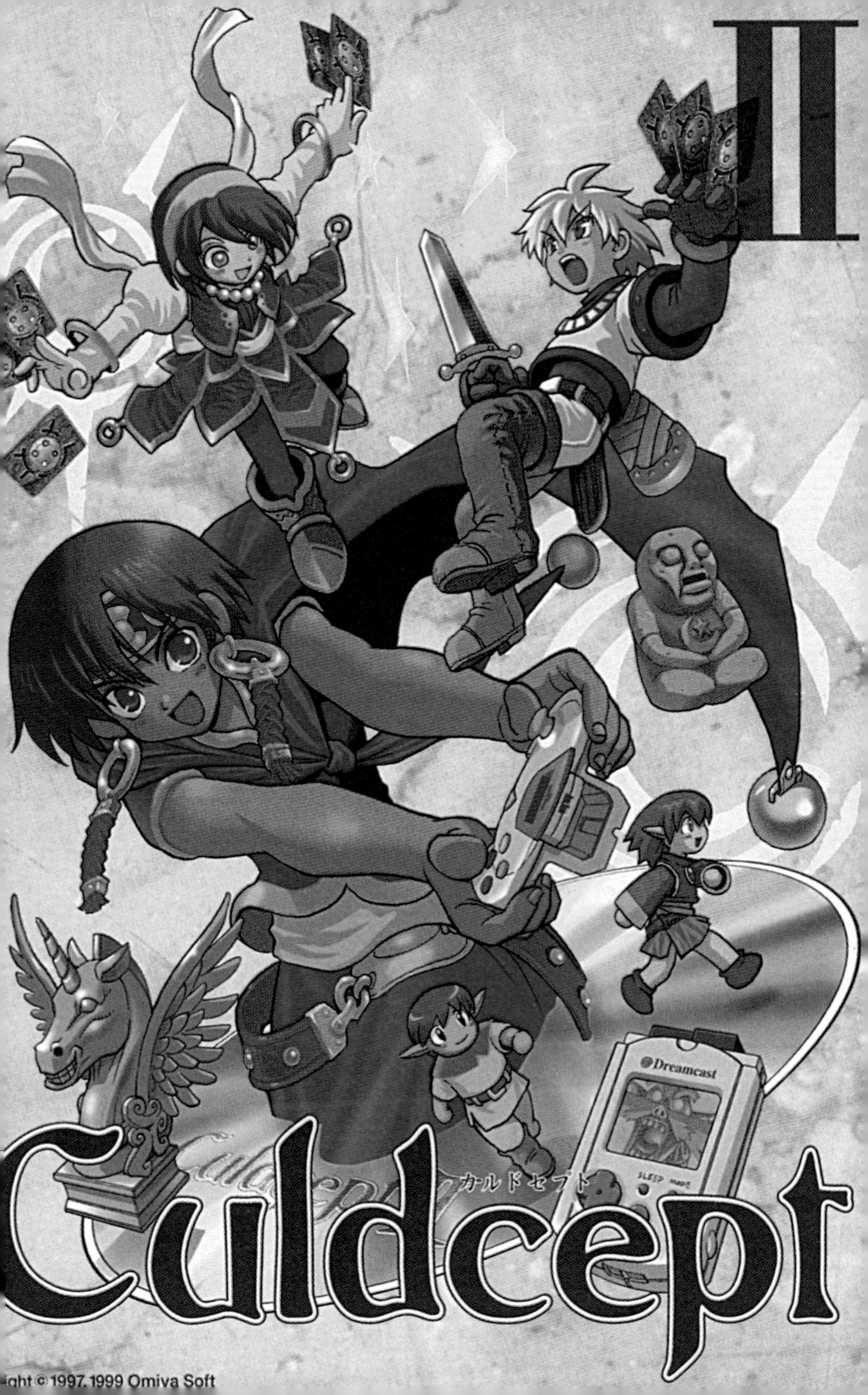
III
Culdcept
カルドセプト
Dreamcast
SLEEP
MODE
ight © 1997, 1999 Omiya Soft

Culdcept

VOLUME 2
by
Shinya Kaneko

Editorial Supervison:
Omiya Soft

HAMBURG // LONDON // LOS ANGELES // TOKYO

Culdcept Vol. 2
Created by Shinya Kaneko
Editorial supervision: Omiya Soft

Translation - Takae Brewer
English Adaptation - Jay Antani
Copy Editor - Hope Donovan
Retouch and Lettering - Haruko Furukawa
Production Artist - James Dashiell
Cover Design - Patrick Hook

Editor - Paul Morrissey
Digital Imaging Manager - Chris Buford
Pre-Press Manager - Antonio DePietro
Production Managers - Jennifer Miller and Mutsumi Miyazaki
Art Director - Matt Alford
Managing Editor - Jill Freshney
VP of Production - Ron Klamert
President and C.O.O. - John Parker
Publisher and C.E.O. - Stuart Levy

A  Manga

TOKYOPOP Inc.
5900 Wilshire Blvd. Suite 2000
Los Angeles, CA 90036

E-mail: info@TOKYOPOP.com
Come visit us online at www.TOKYOPOP.com

ISBN: 1-59182-783-3

First TOKYOPOP printing: October 2004
10 9 8 7 6 5 4 3 2 1
Printed in the USA

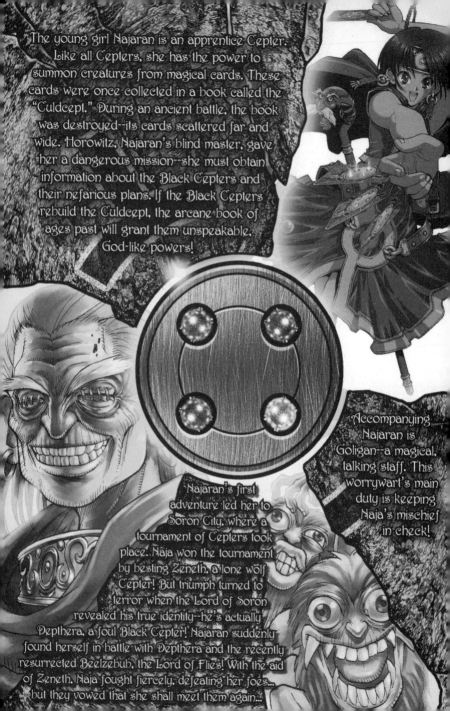

The young girl Najaran is an apprentice Cepter. Like all Cepters, she has the power to summon creatures from magical cards. These cards were once collected in a book called the "Culdcept." During an ancient battle, the book was destroyed--its cards scattered far and wide. Horowitz, Najaran's blind master, gave her a dangerous mission--she must obtain information about the Black Cepters and their nefarious plans. If the Black Cepters rebuild the Culdcept, the arcane book of ages past will grant them unspeakable, God-like powers!

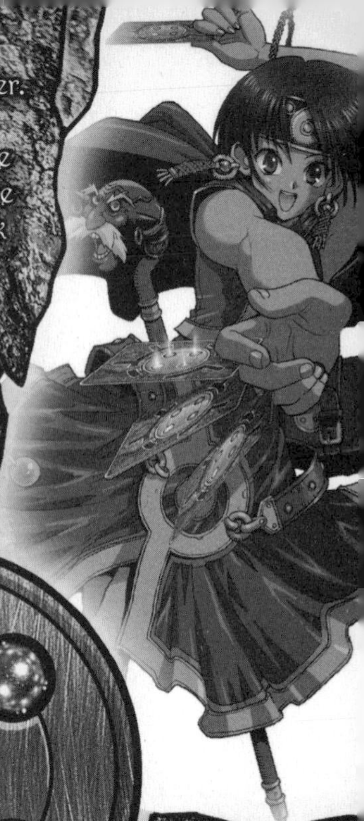

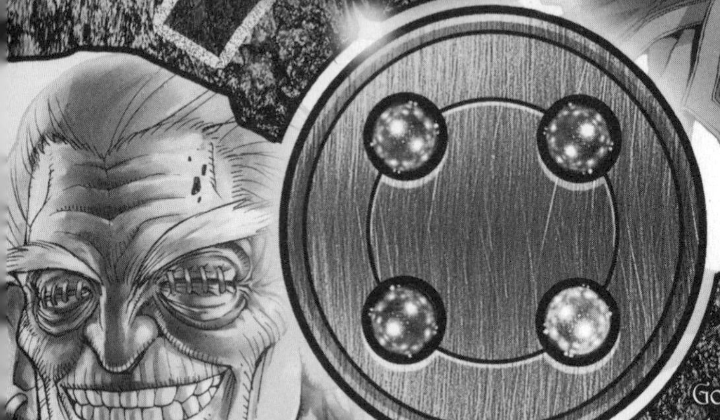

Accompanying Najaran is Goligan--a magical, talking staff. This worrywart's main duty is keeping Naja's mischief in check!

Najaran's first adventure led her to Soron City, where a tournament of Cepters took place. Naja won the tournament by besting Zeneth, a lone wolf Cepter! But triumph turned to terror when the Lord of Soron revealed his true identity--he's actually Depthera, a foul Black Cepter! Najaran suddenly found herself in battle with Depthera and the recently resurrected Beelzebub, the Lord of Flies! With the aid of Zeneth, Naja fought fiercely, defeating her foes... but they vowed that she shall meet them again...

CONTENTS

Culdcept

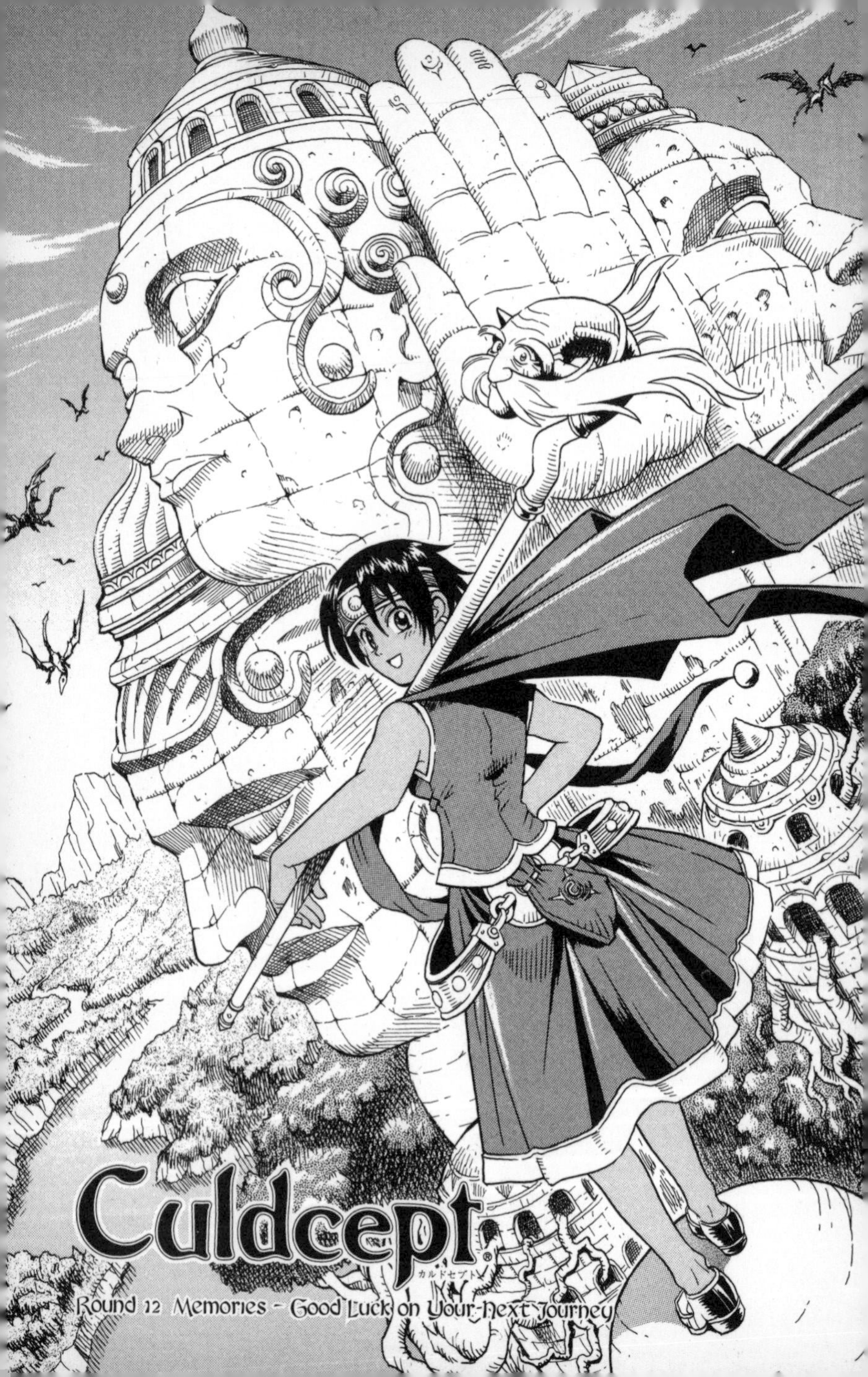
Culdcept
カルドセプト
Round 12 Memories - Good Luck on Your Next Journey

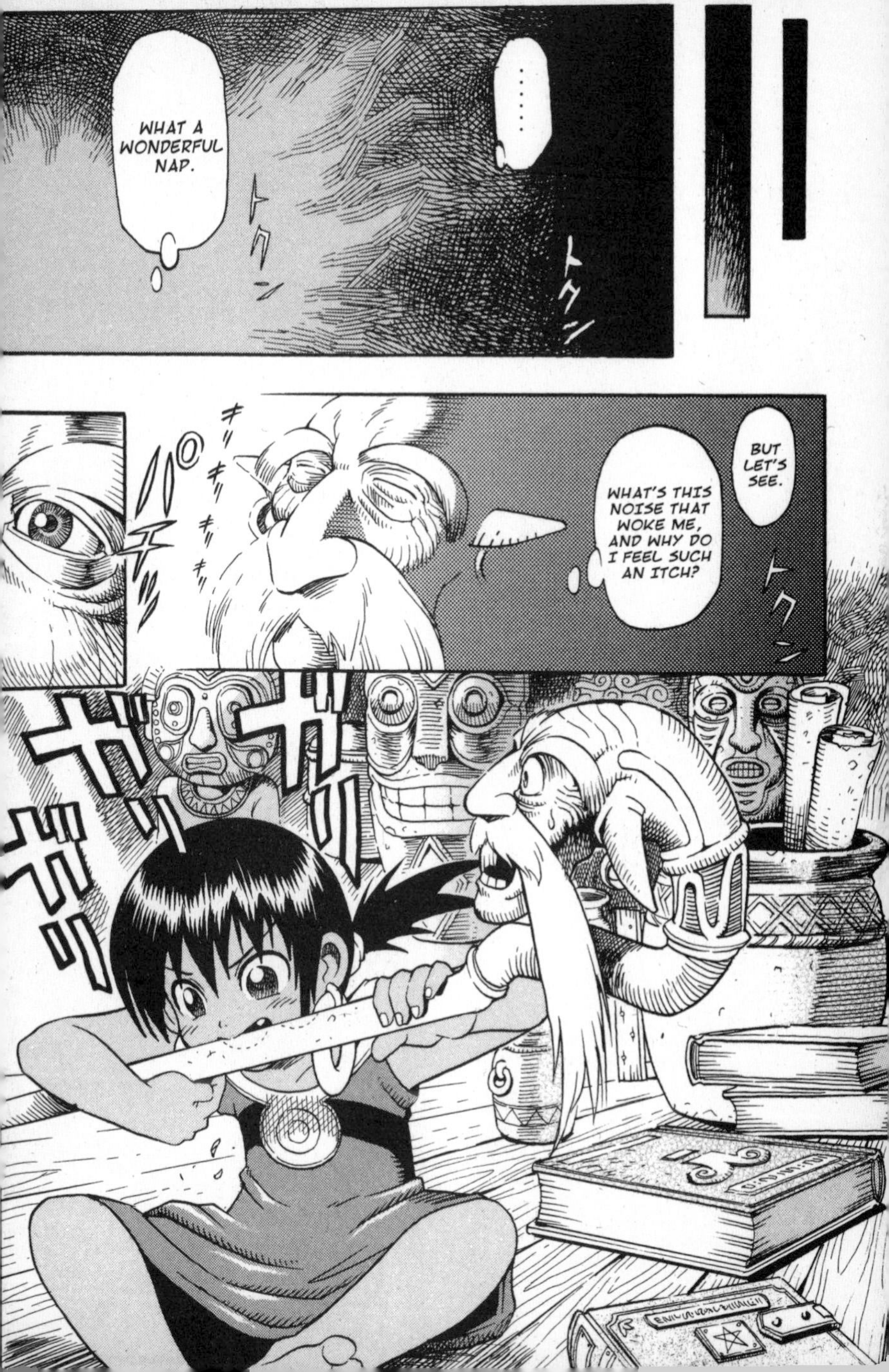

トクン
. . . . .
トクン
WHAT A WONDERFUL NAP.
BUT LET'S SEE.
WHAT'S THIS NOISE THAT WOKE ME, AND WHY DO I FEEL SUCH AN ITCH?
トクン

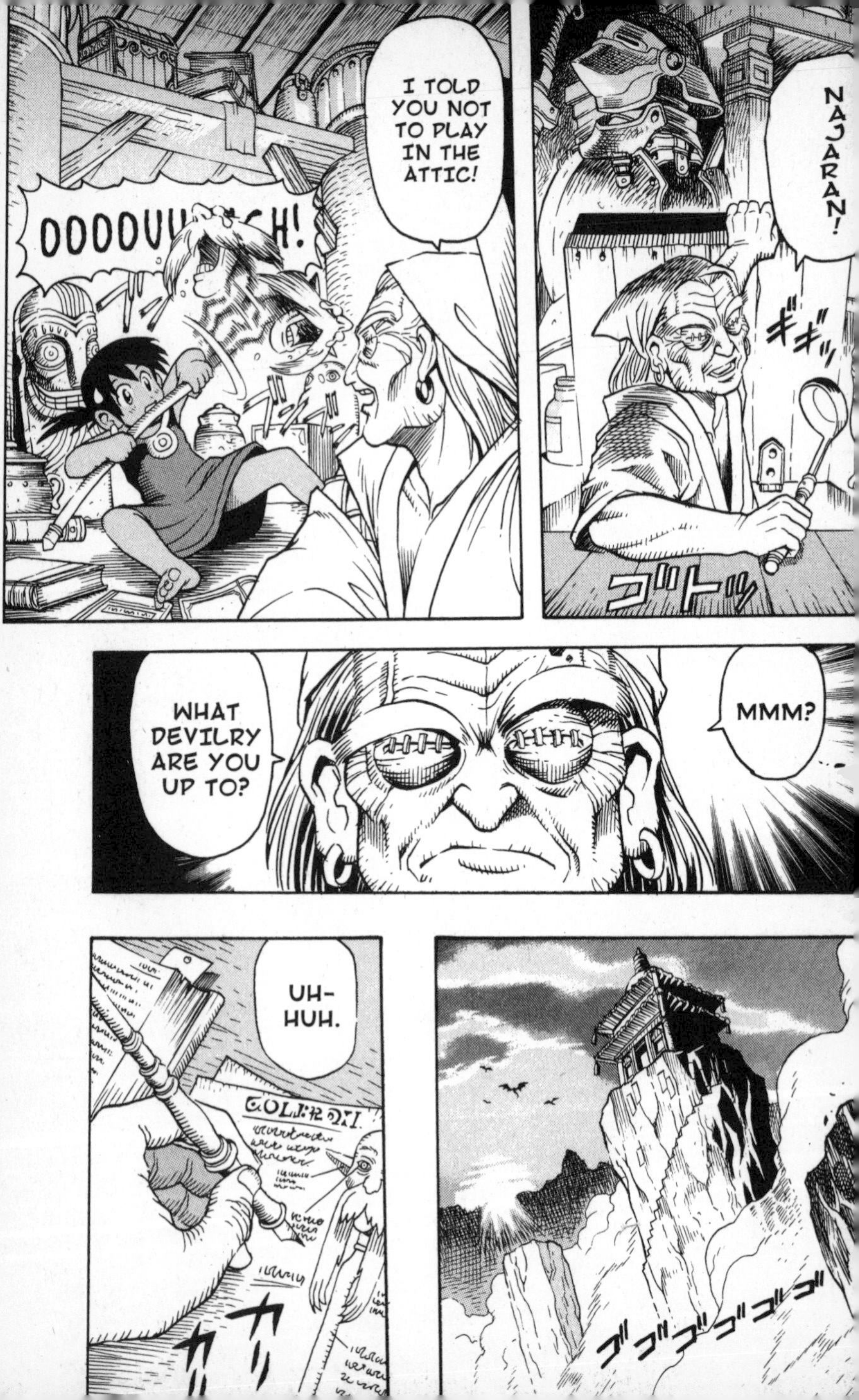
NAJARAN!
ギギッ
ゴトッ
I TOLD YOU NOT TO PLAY IN THE ATTIC!
OOOOUUCH!
MMM?
WHAT DEVILRY ARE YOU UP TO?
ゴゴゴゴゴ
UH-HUH.
カリ

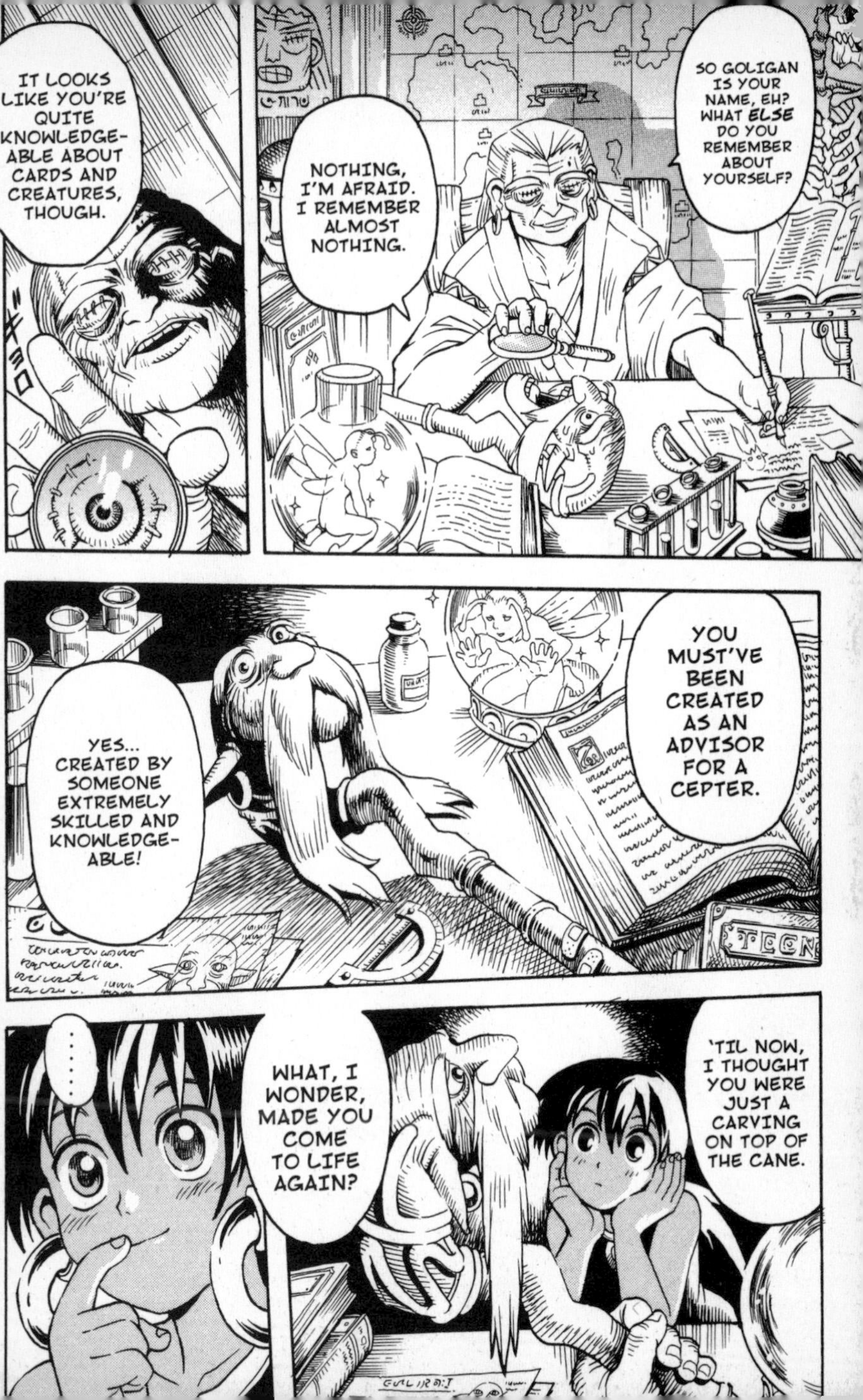
SO GOLIGAN IS YOUR NAME, EH? WHAT ELSE DO YOU REMEMBER ABOUT YOURSELF?
NOTHING, I'M AFRAID. I REMEMBER ALMOST NOTHING.
IT LOOKS LIKE YOU'RE QUITE KNOWLEDGE-ABLE ABOUT CARDS AND CREATURES, THOUGH.
ギョロ
YOU MUST'VE BEEN CREATED AS AN ADVISOR FOR A CEPTER.
YES... CREATED BY SOMEONE EXTREMELY SKILLED AND KNOWLEDGE-ABLE!
'TIL NOW, I THOUGHT YOU WERE JUST A CARVING ON TOP OF THE CANE.
WHAT, I WONDER, MADE YOU COME TO LIFE AGAIN?
......

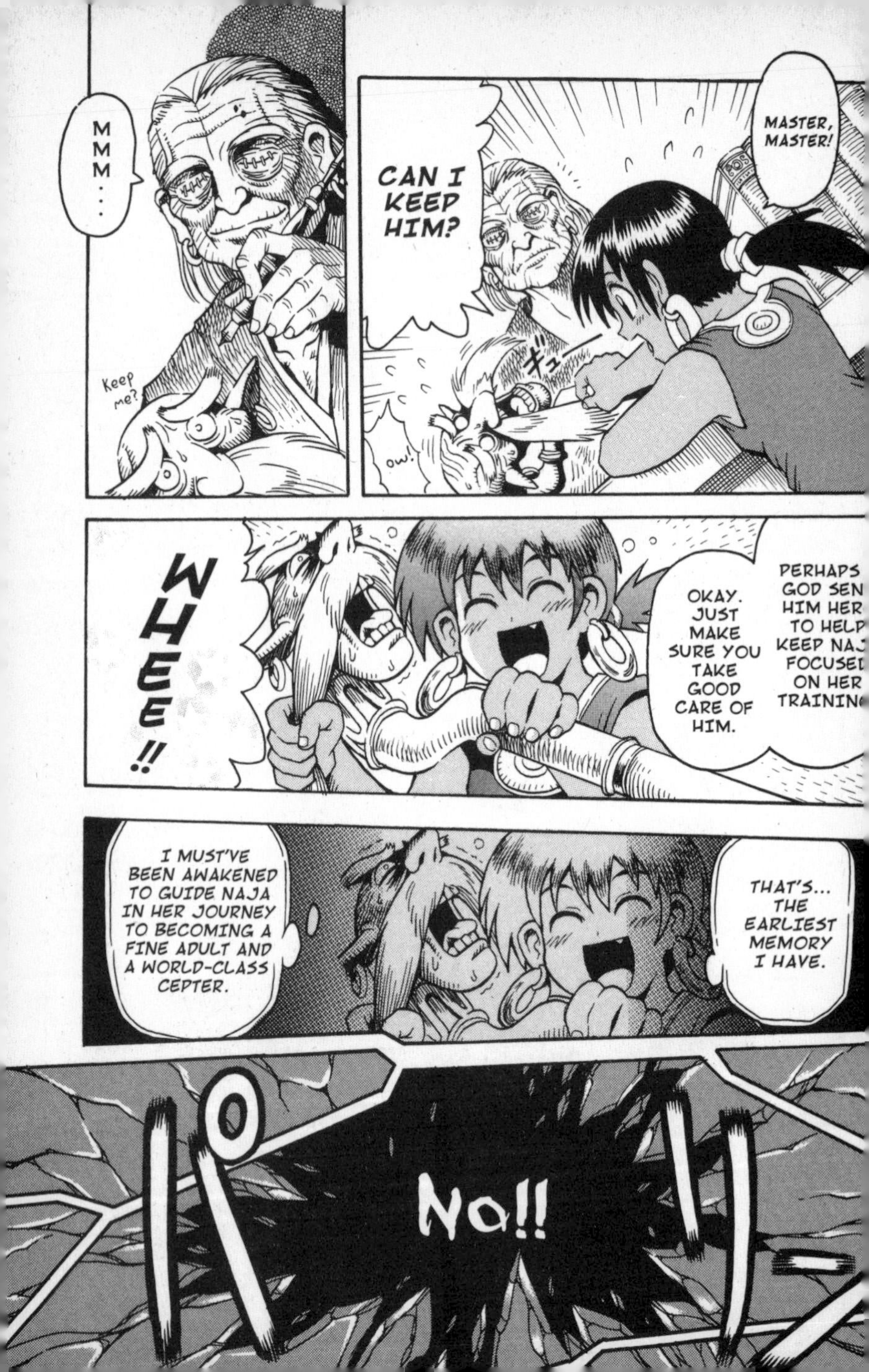
MASTER, MASTER!
CAN I KEEP HIM?
ギュー
ow!
MMM...
Keep me?
PERHAPS GOD SEN HIM HER TO HELP KEEP NAJ FOCUSED ON HER TRAININ
OKAY. JUST MAKE SURE YOU TAKE GOOD CARE OF HIM.
WHEE!!
THAT'S... THE EARLIEST MEMORY I HAVE.
I MUST'VE BEEN AWAKENED TO GUIDE NAJA IN HER JOURNEY TO BECOMING A FINE ADULT AND A WORLD-CLASS CEPTER.
No!!

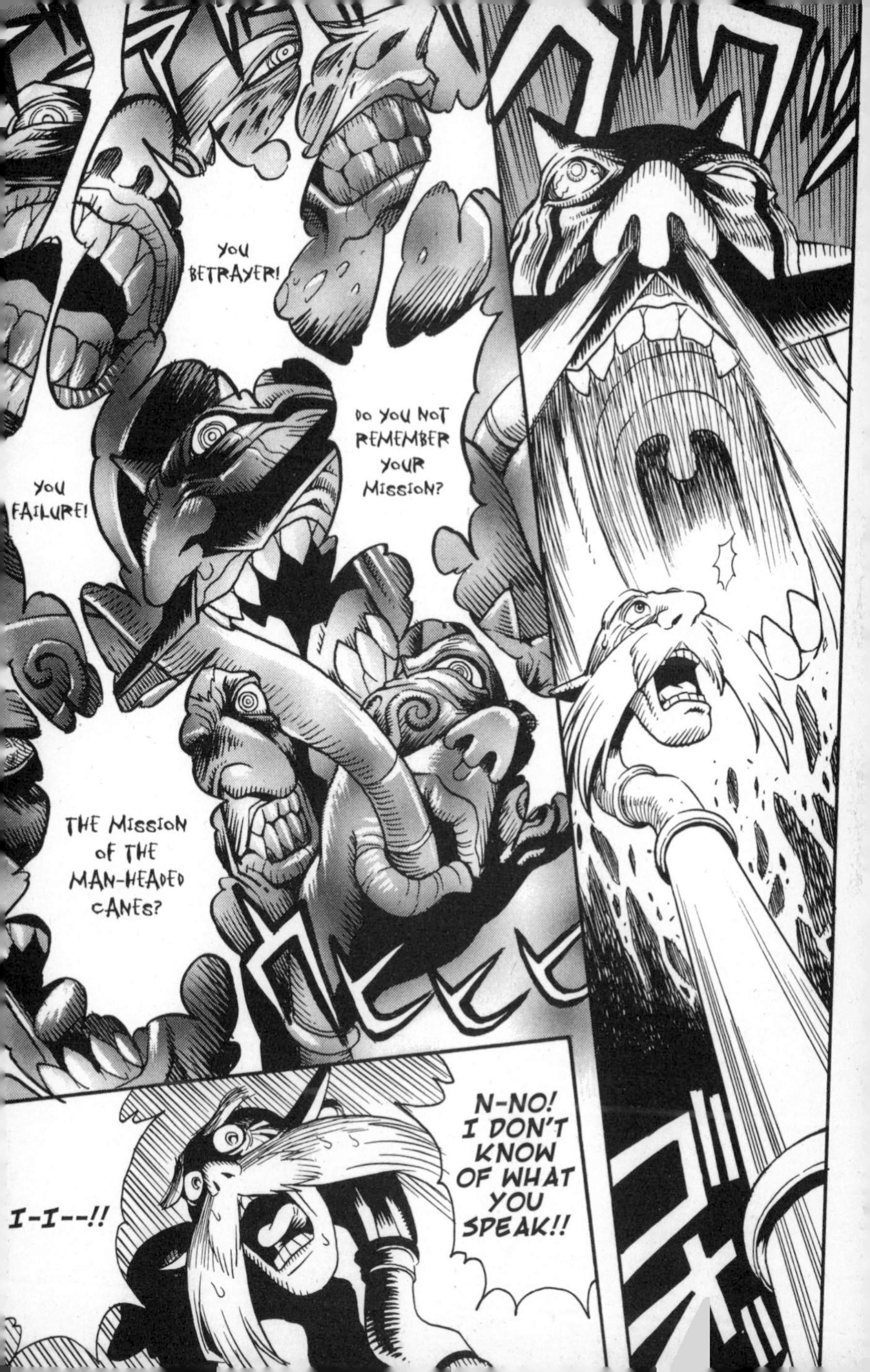
YOU BETRAYER!
DO YOU NOT REMEMBER YOUR MISSION?
YOU FAILURE!
THE MISSION OF THE MAN-HEADED CANES?
N-NO! I DON'T KNOW OF WHAT YOU SPEAK!!
I-I--!!

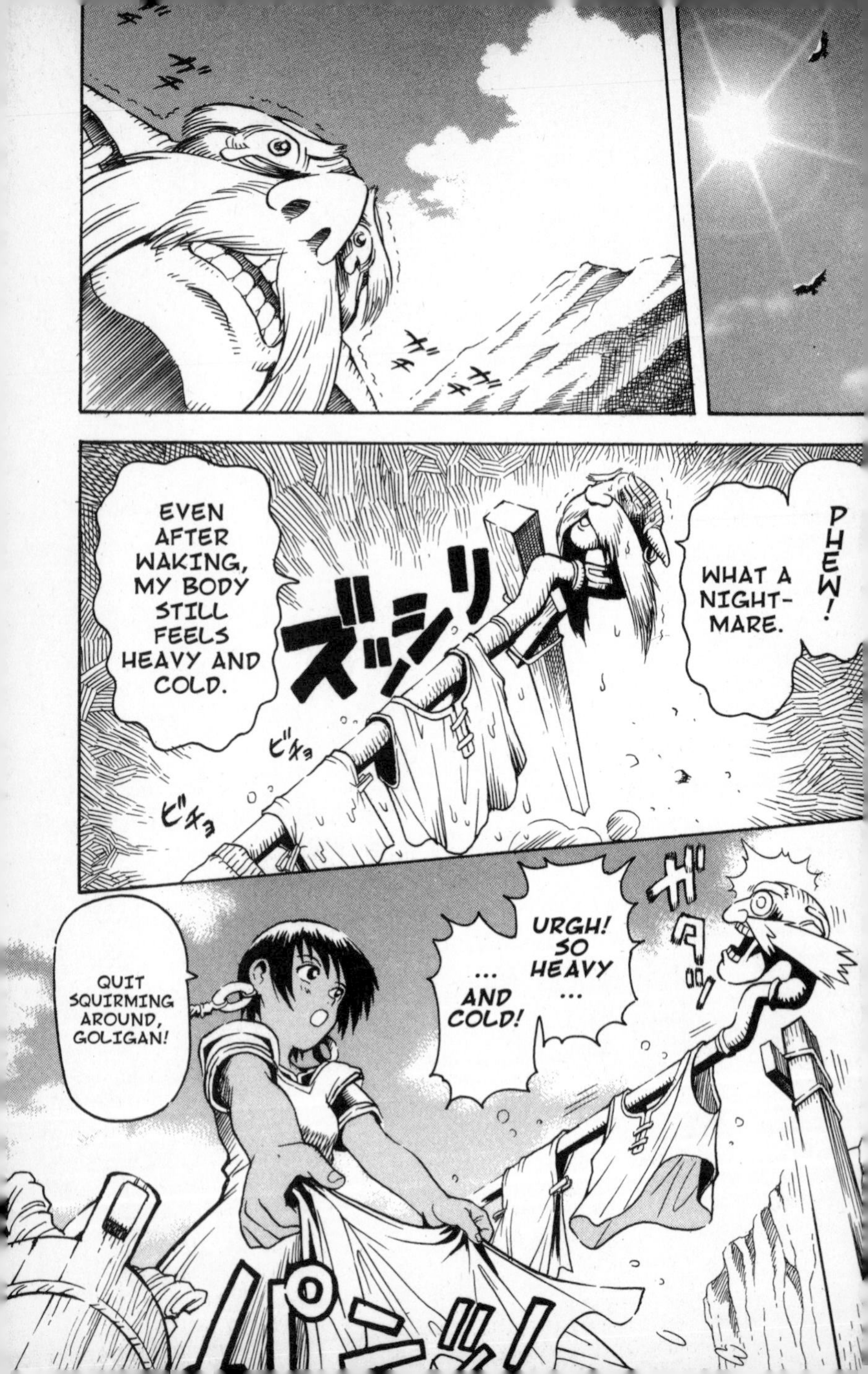
PHEW!
WHAT A NIGHT-MARE.
EVEN AFTER WAKING, MY BODY STILL FEELS HEAVY AND COLD.
ズッシリ
URGH! SO HEAVY ...
... AND COLD!
QUIT SQUIRMING AROUND, GOLIGAN!

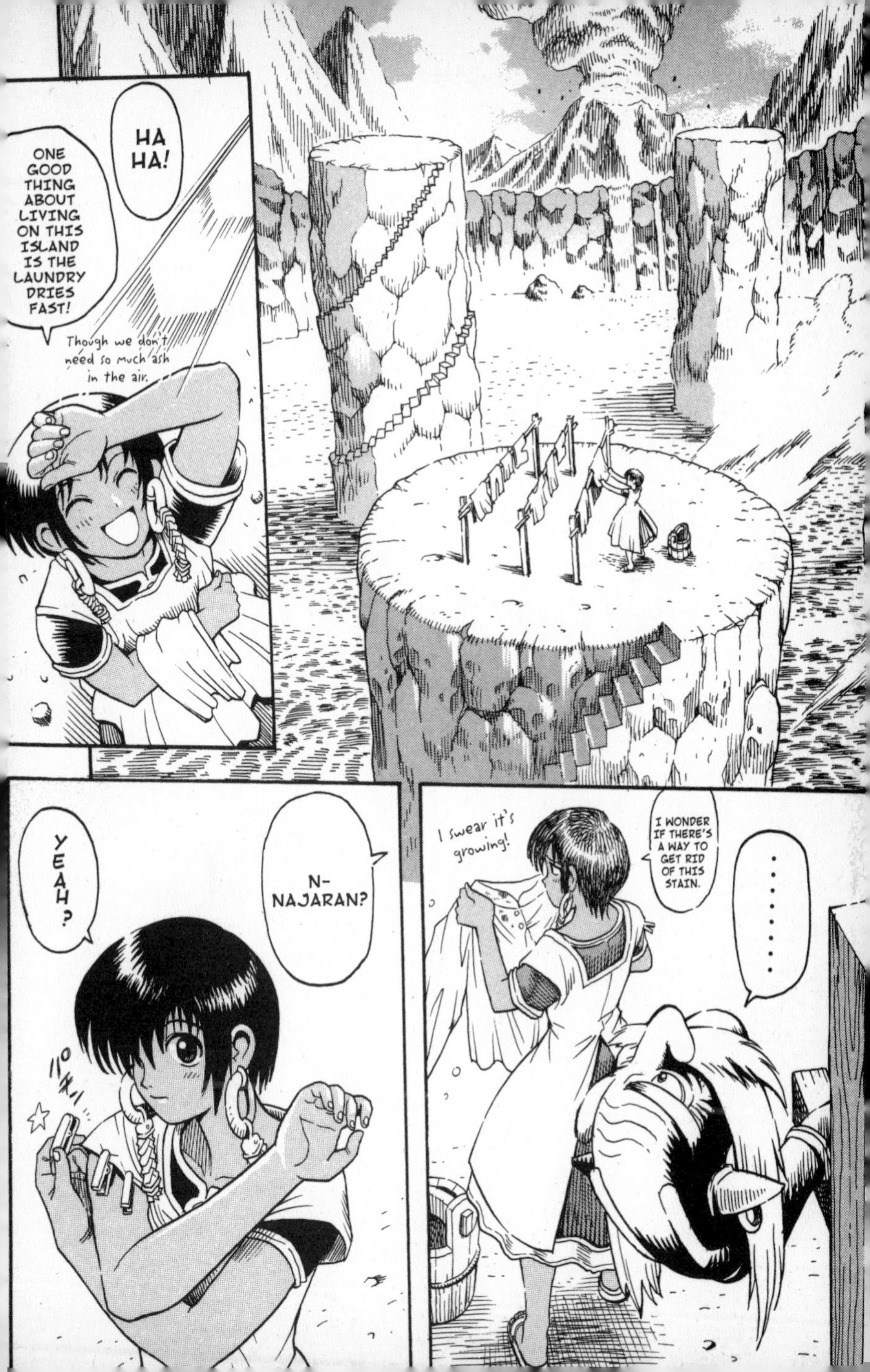
HA HA!
ONE GOOD THING ABOUT LIVING ON THIS ISLAND IS THE LAUNDRY DRIES FAST!
Though we don't need so much ash in the air.
......
I WONDER IF THERE'S A WAY TO GET RID OF THIS STAIN.
I swear it's growing!
N-NAJARAN?
YEAH?

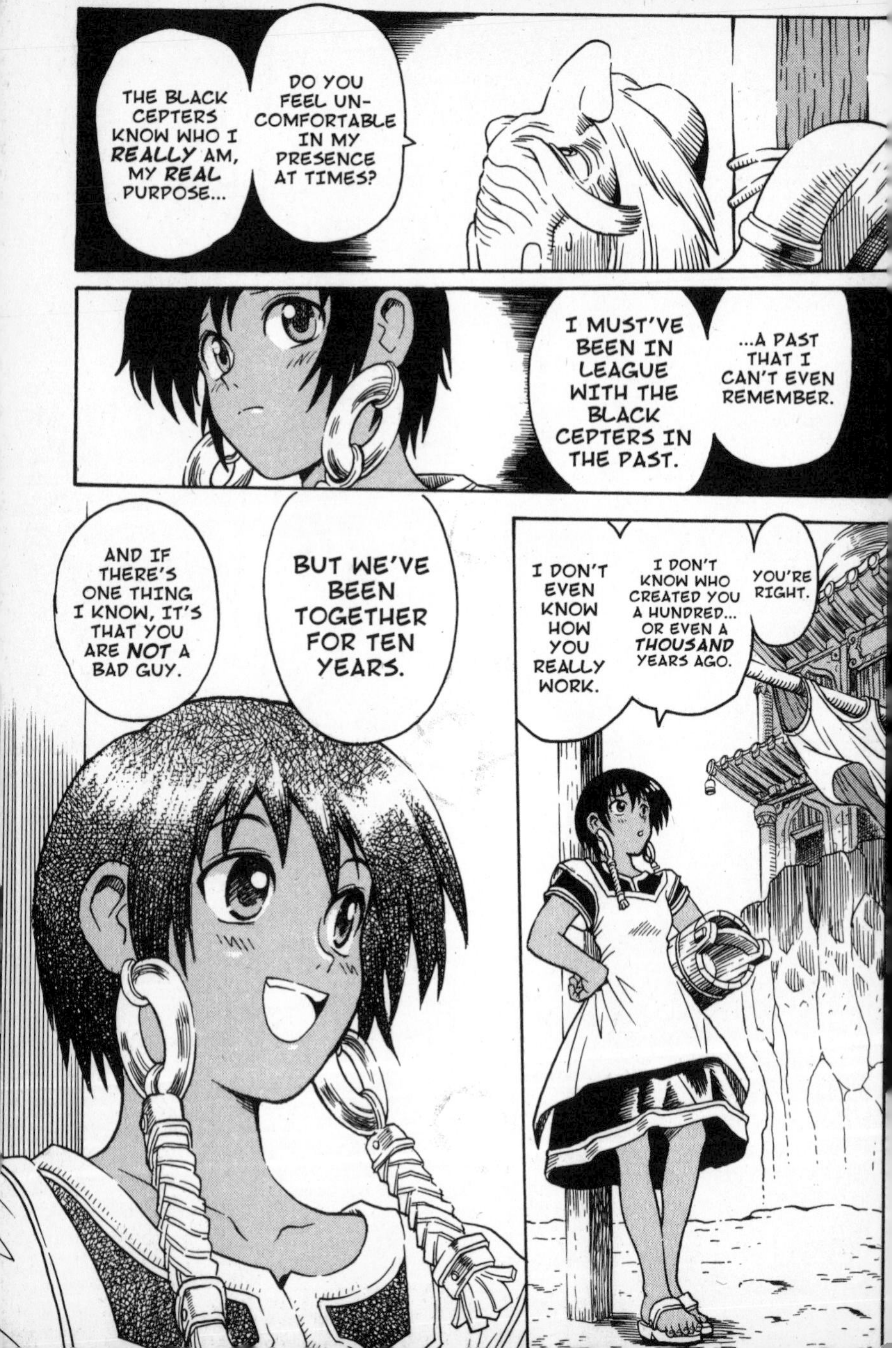
DO YOU FEEL UN-COMFORTABLE IN MY PRESENCE AT TIMES?
THE BLACK CEPTERS KNOW WHO I REALLY AM, MY REAL PURPOSE...
...A PAST THAT I CAN'T EVEN REMEMBER.
I MUST'VE BEEN IN LEAGUE WITH THE BLACK CEPTERS IN THE PAST.
YOU'RE RIGHT.
I DON'T KNOW WHO CREATED YOU A HUNDRED... OR EVEN A THOUSAND YEARS AGO.
I DON'T EVEN KNOW HOW YOU REALLY WORK.
BUT WE'VE BEEN TOGETHER FOR TEN YEARS.
AND IF THERE'S ONE THING I KNOW, IT'S THAT YOU ARE NOT A BAD GUY.

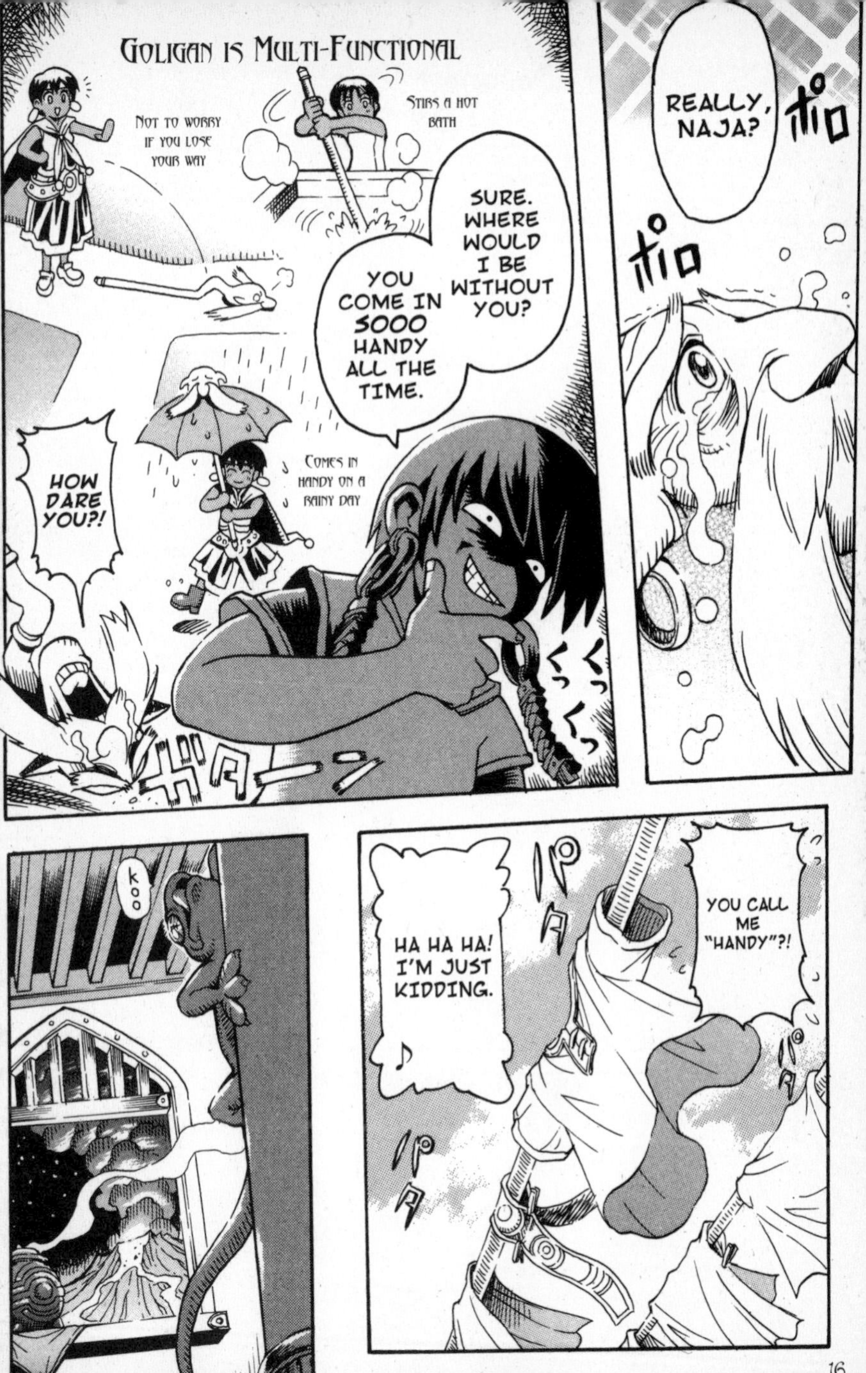
REALLY, NAJA?
Goligan is Multi-Functional
Not to worry if you lose your way
Stirs a hot bath
Comes in handy on a rainy day
SURE. WHERE WOULD I BE WITHOUT YOU?
YOU COME IN SOOO HANDY ALL THE TIME.
HOW DARE YOU?!
YOU CALL ME "HANDY"?!
HA HA HA! I'M JUST KIDDING. ♪
koo

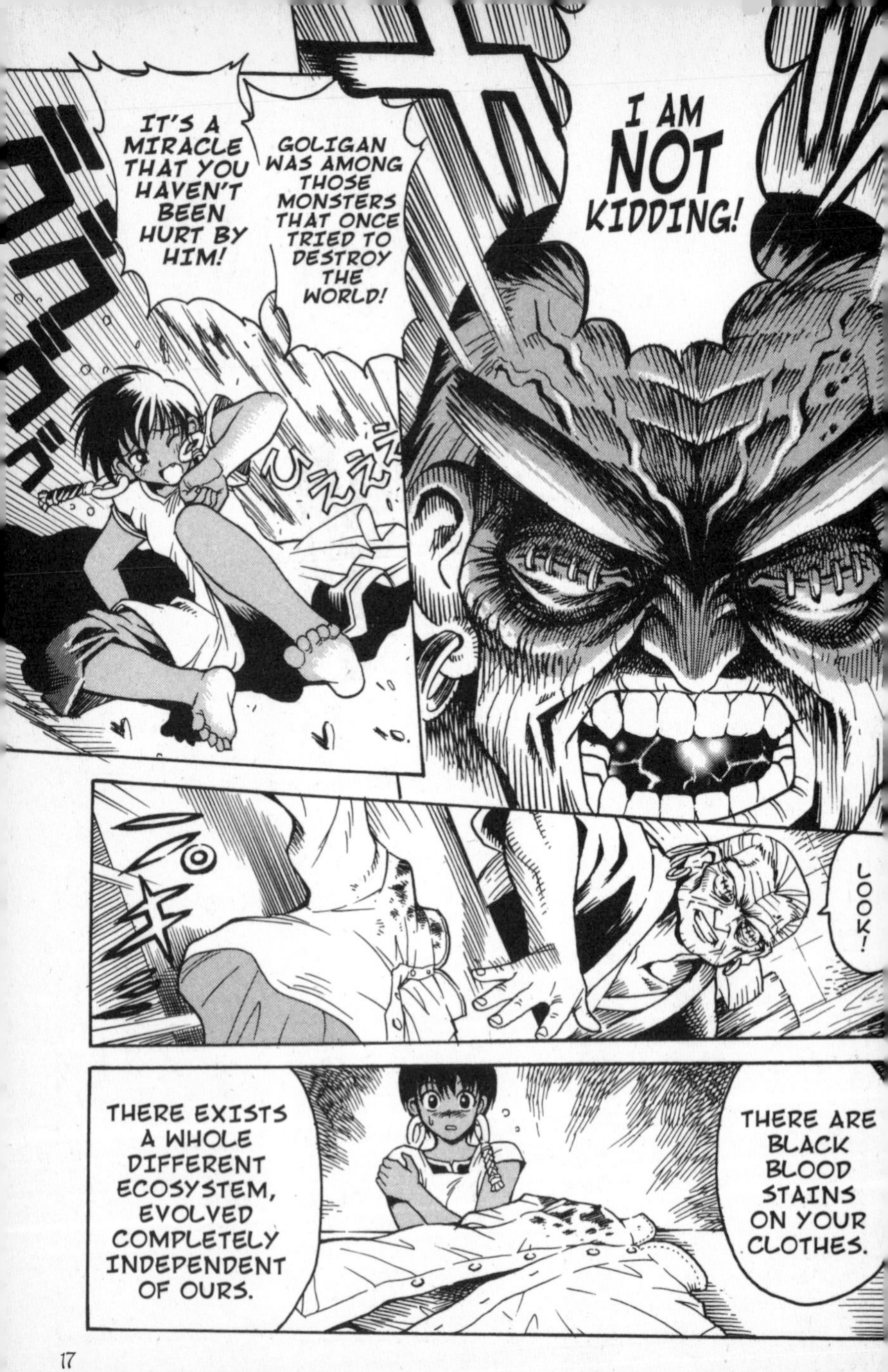
I AM NOT KIDDING!
GOLIGAN WAS AMONG THOSE MONSTERS THAT ONCE TRIED TO DESTROY THE WORLD!
IT'S A MIRACLE THAT YOU HAVEN'T BEEN HURT BY HIM!
LOOK!
THERE ARE BLACK BLOOD STAINS ON YOUR CLOTHES.
THERE EXISTS A WHOLE DIFFERENT ECOSYSTEM, EVOLVED COMPLETELY INDEPENDENT OF OURS.

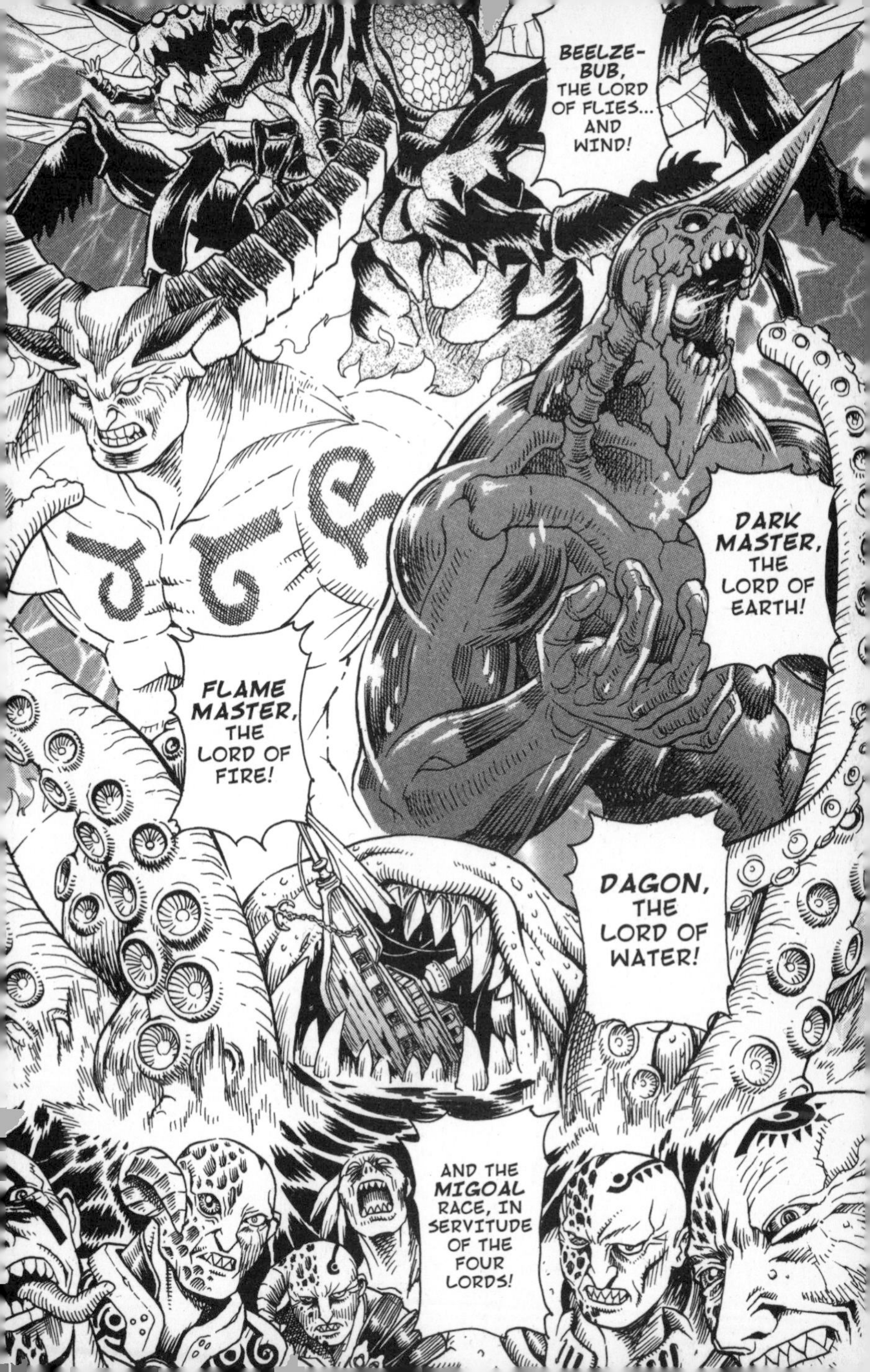
BEELZE-BUB, THE LORD OF FLIES... AND WIND!
DARK MASTER, THE LORD OF EARTH!
FLAME MASTER, THE LORD OF FIRE!
DAGON, THE LORD OF WATER!
AND THE MIGOAL RACE, IN SERVITUDE OF THE FOUR LORDS!

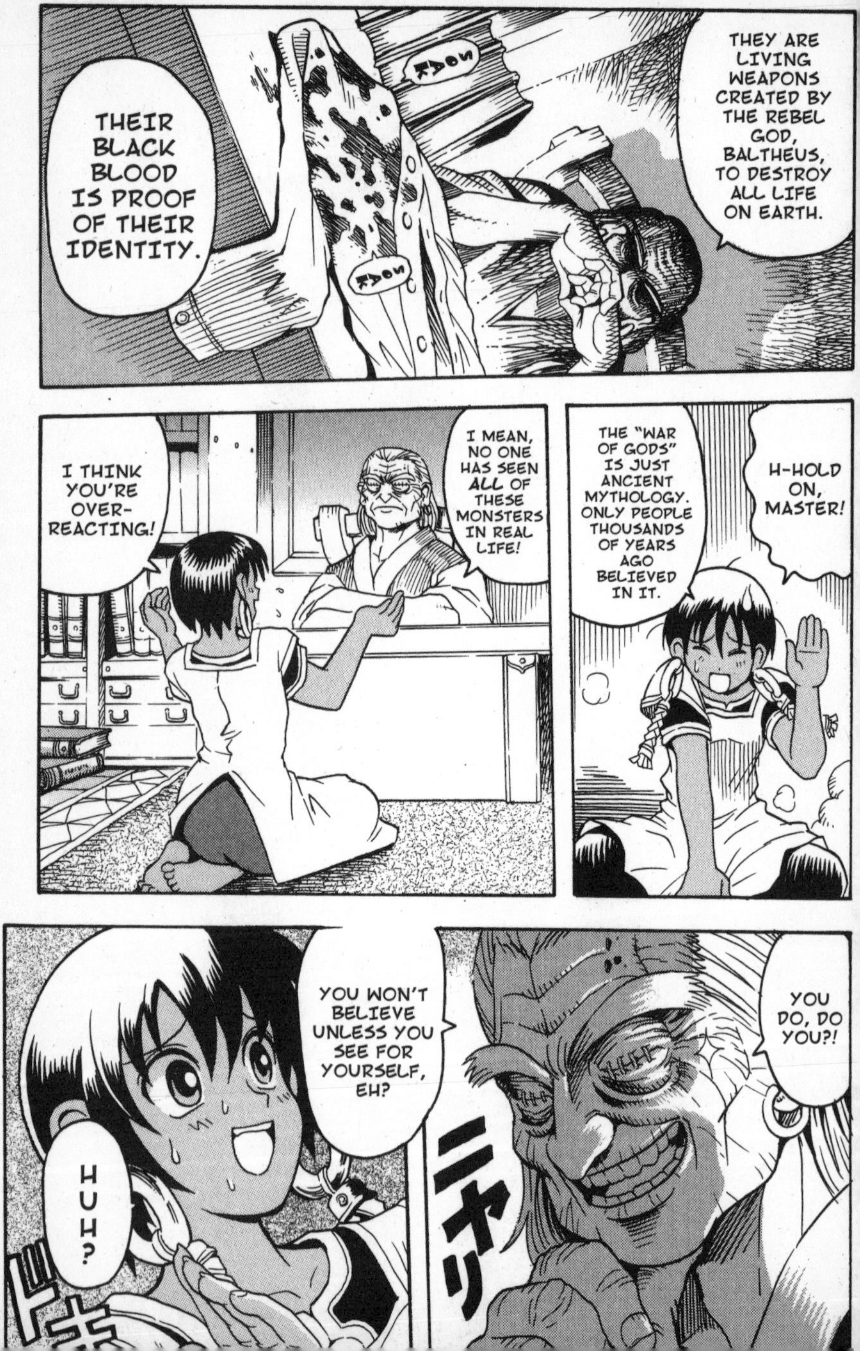
THEY ARE LIVING WEAPONS CREATED BY THE REBEL GOD, BALTHEUS, TO DESTROY ALL LIFE ON EARTH.
THEIR BLACK BLOOD IS PROOF OF THEIR IDENTITY.
H-HOLD ON, MASTER!
THE "WAR OF GODS" IS JUST ANCIENT MYTHOLOGY. ONLY PEOPLE THOUSANDS OF YEARS AGO BELIEVED IN IT.
I MEAN, NO ONE HAS SEEN ALL OF THESE MONSTERS IN REAL LIFE!
I THINK YOU'RE OVER-REACTING!
YOU DO, DO YOU?!
YOU WON'T BELIEVE UNLESS YOU SEE FOR YOURSELF, EH?
ニヤリ
HUH?

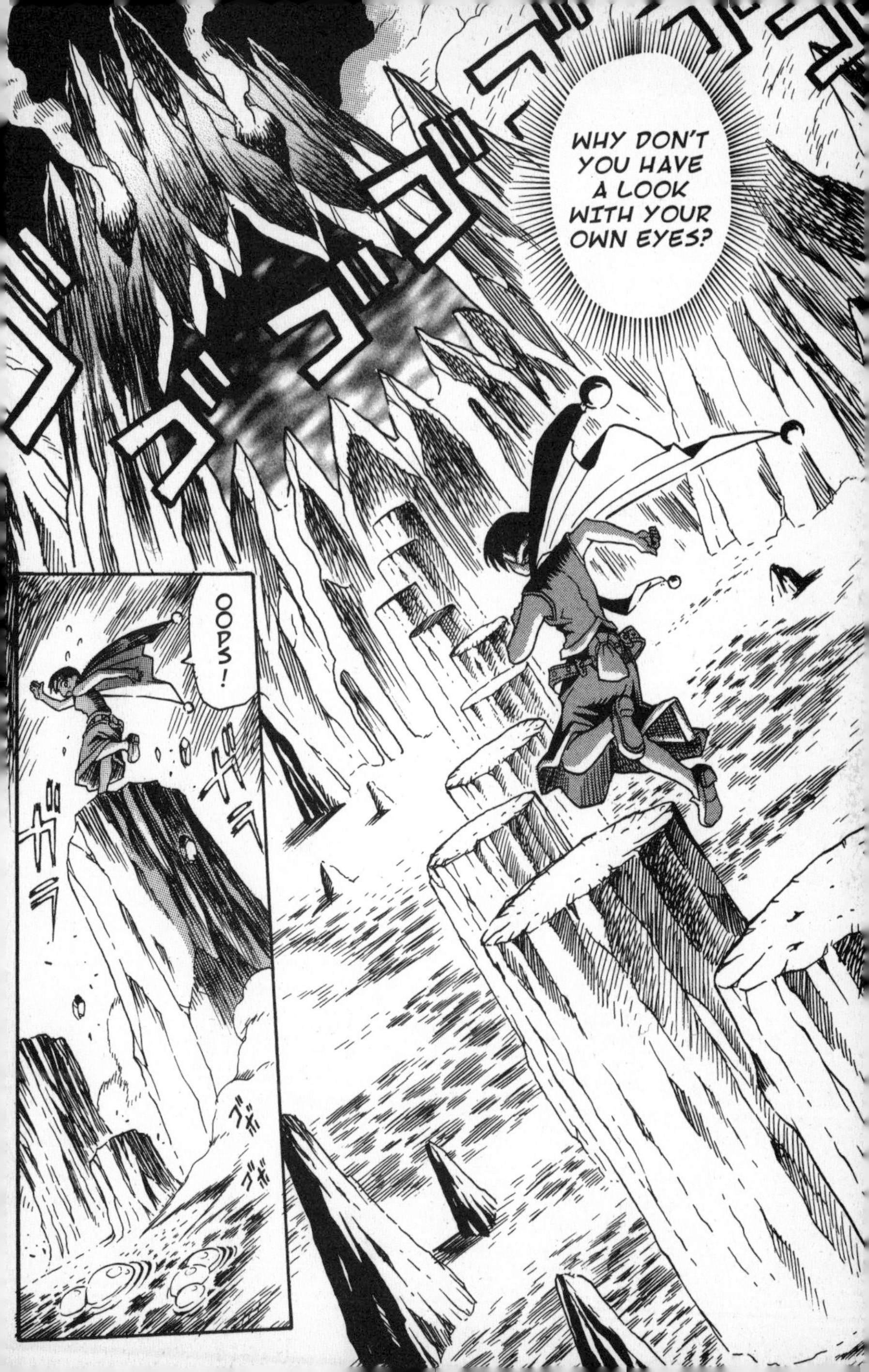
WHY DON'T YOU HAVE A LOOK WITH YOUR OWN EYES?
OOPS!

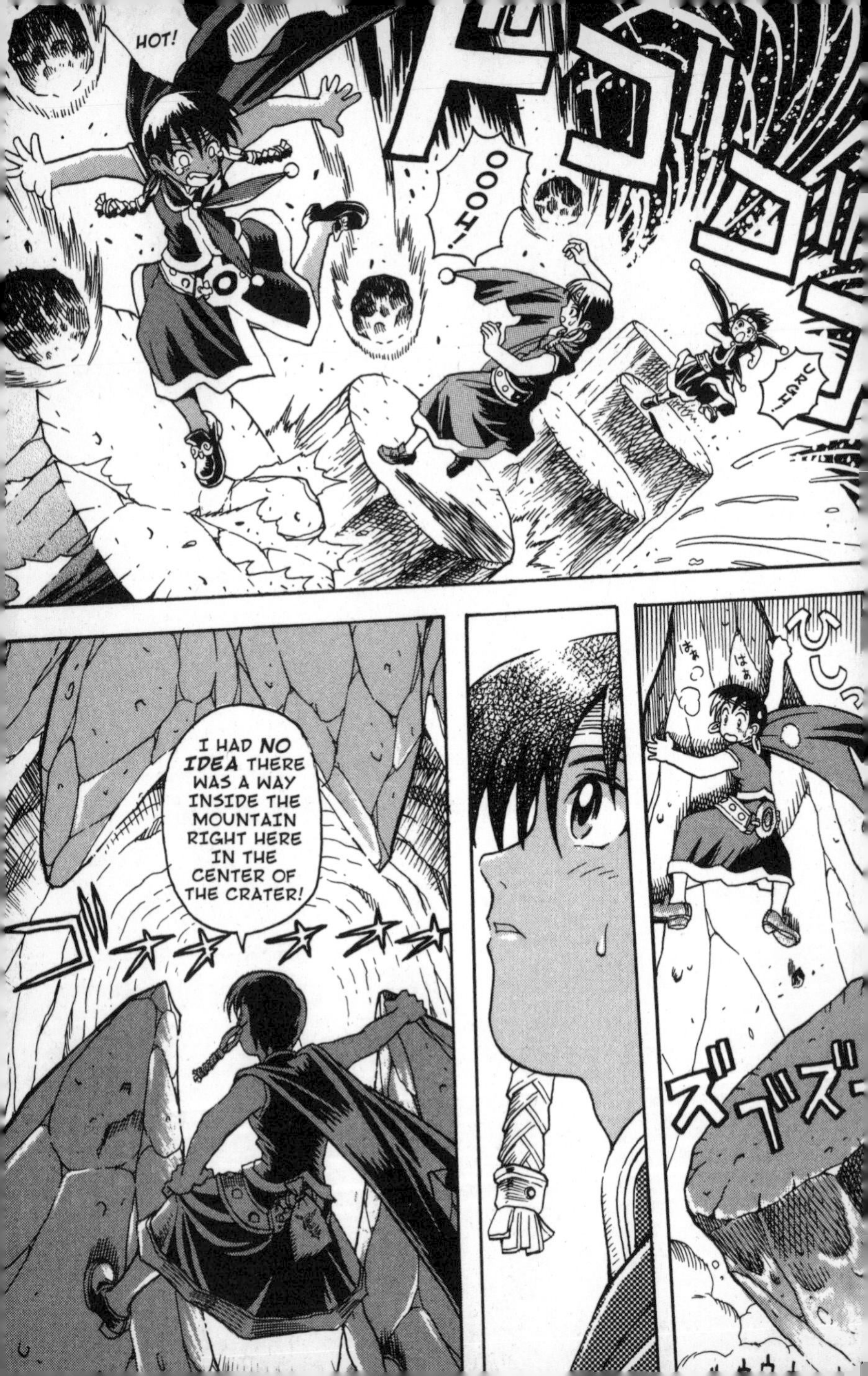
URGH...!
OOOOH!
HOT!
はぁ
はぁ
ひしっ
ズブズー
I HAD **NO IDEA** THERE WAS A WAY INSIDE THE MOUNTAIN RIGHT HERE IN THE CENTER OF THE CRATER!

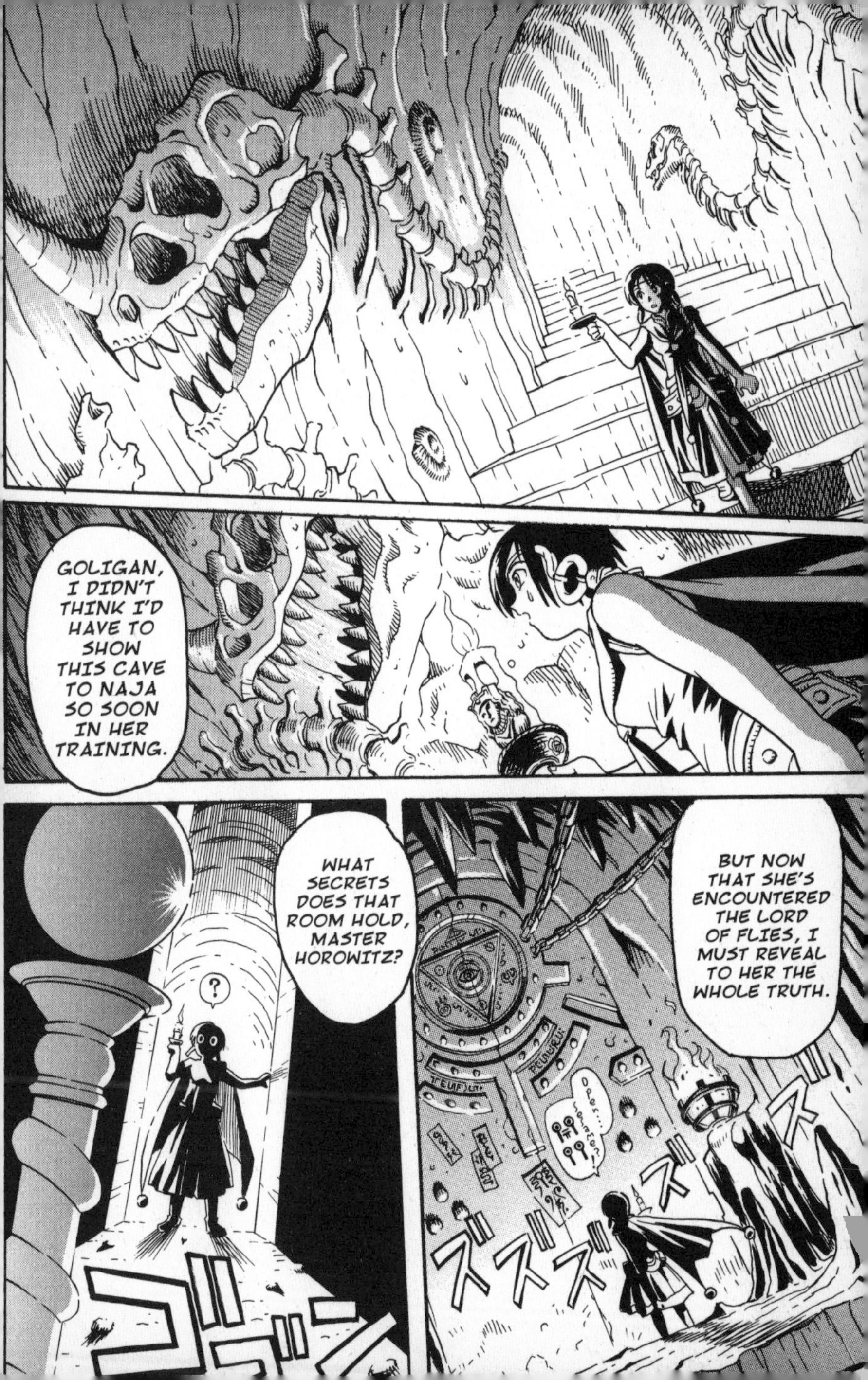
GOLIGAN, I DIDN'T THINK I'D HAVE TO SHOW THIS CAVE TO NAJA SO SOON IN HER TRAINING.
BUT NOW THAT SHE'S ENCOUNTERED THE LORD OF FLIES, I MUST REVEAL TO HER THE WHOLE TRUTH.
WHAT SECRETS DOES THAT ROOM HOLD, MASTER HOROWITZ?
?

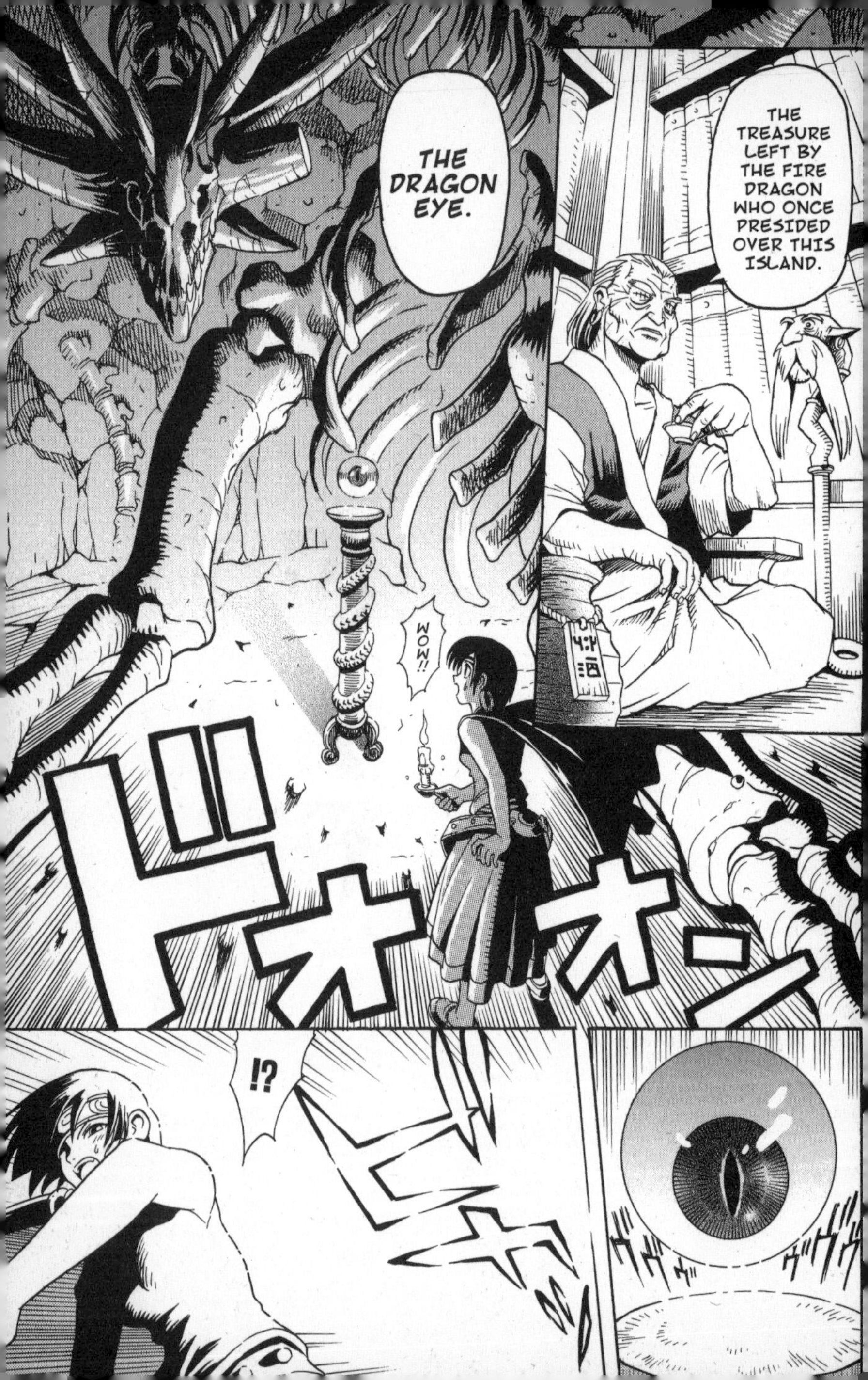
THE TREASURE LEFT BY THE FIRE DRAGON WHO ONCE PRESIDED OVER THIS ISLAND.
THE DRAGON EYE.
WOW!!
!?

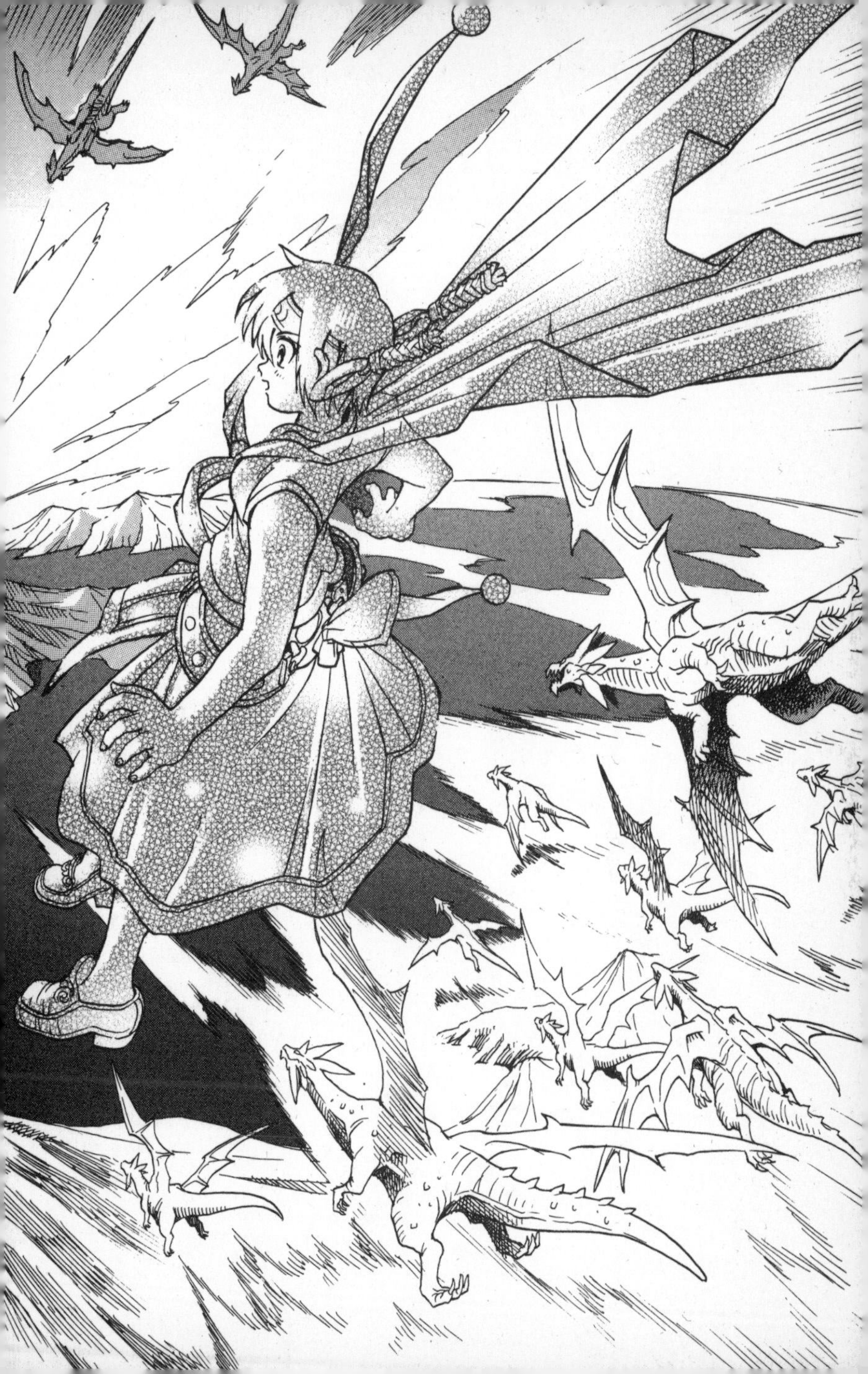

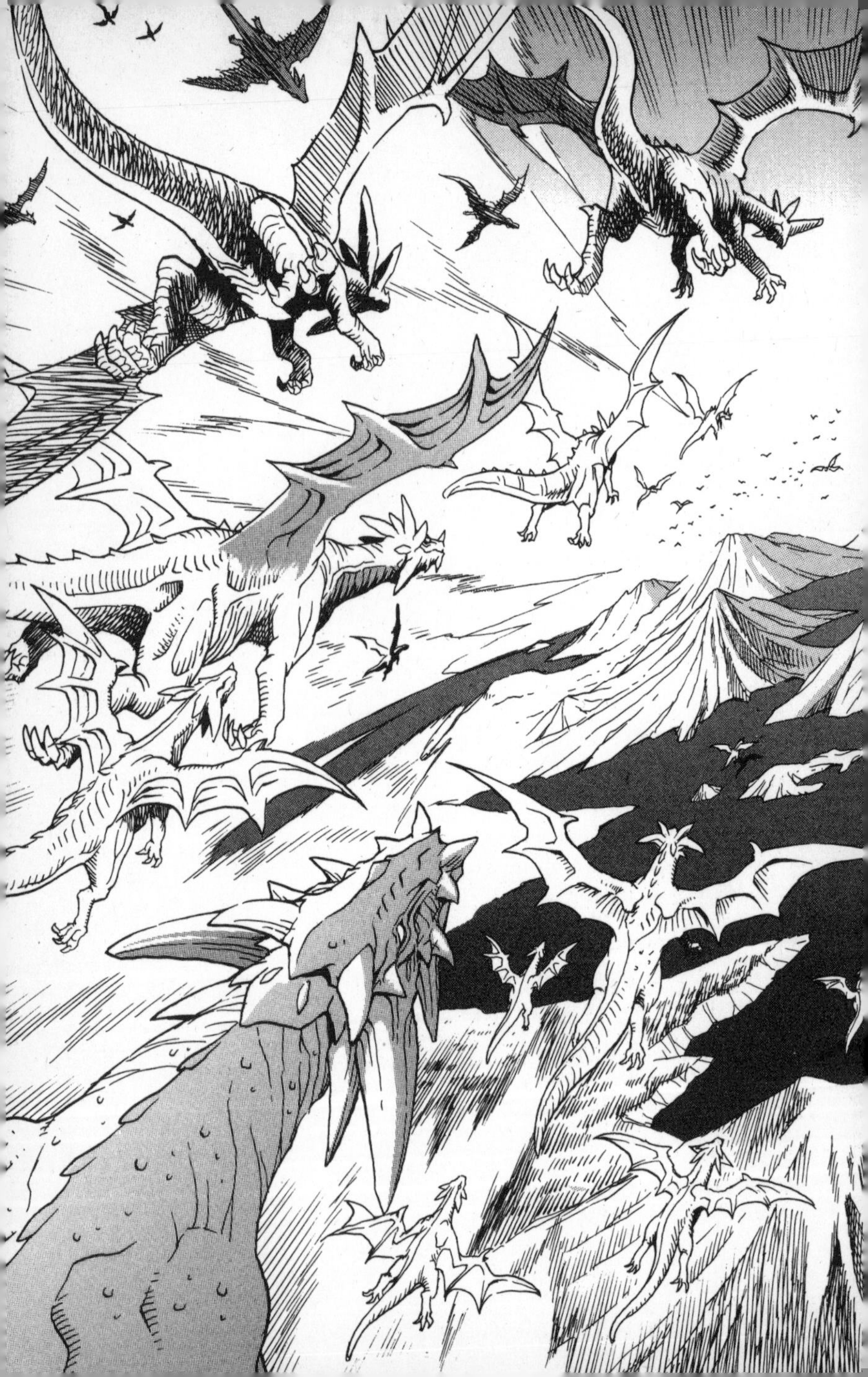

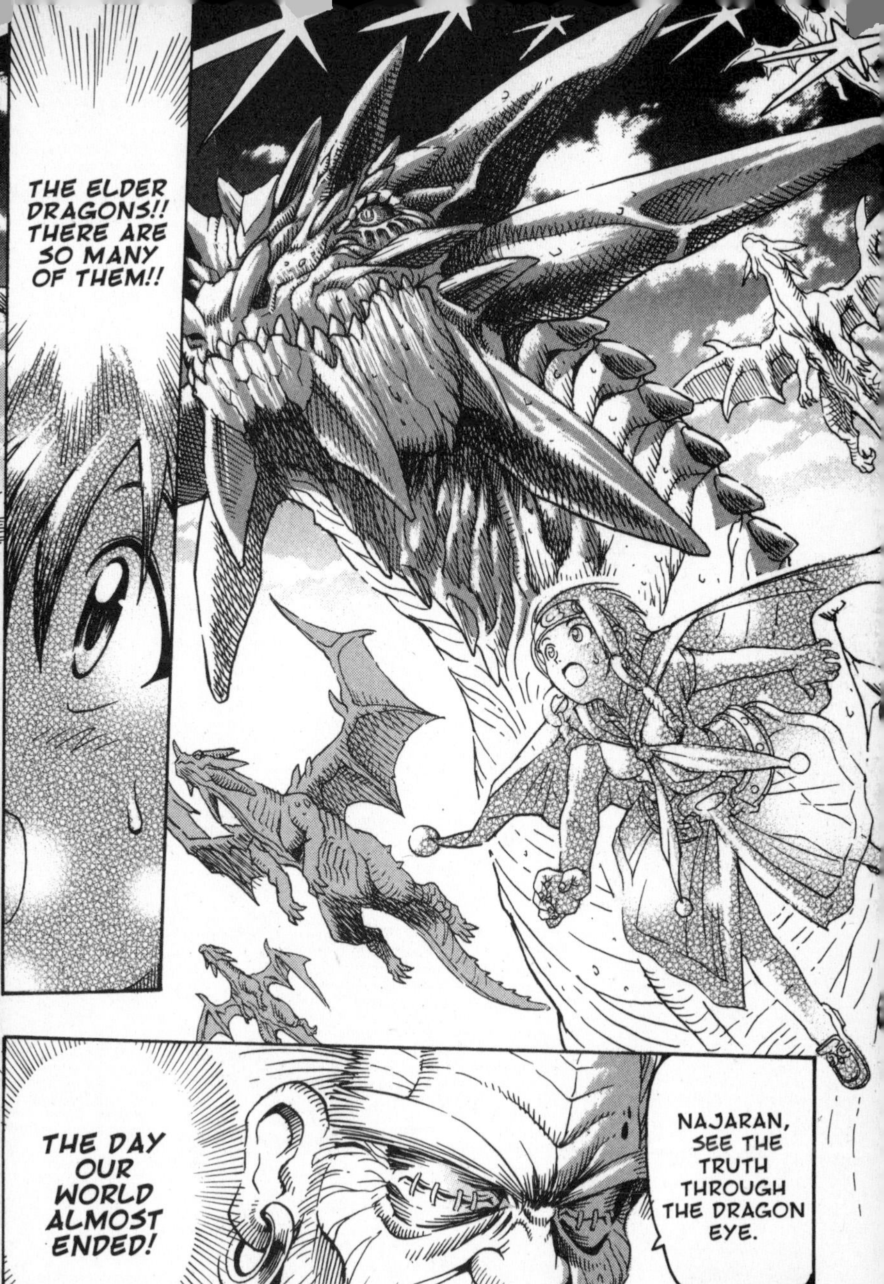
THE ELDER DRAGONS!! THERE ARE SO MANY OF THEM!!
NAJARAN, SEE THE TRUTH THROUGH THE DRAGON EYE.
THE DAY OUR WORLD ALMOST ENDED!

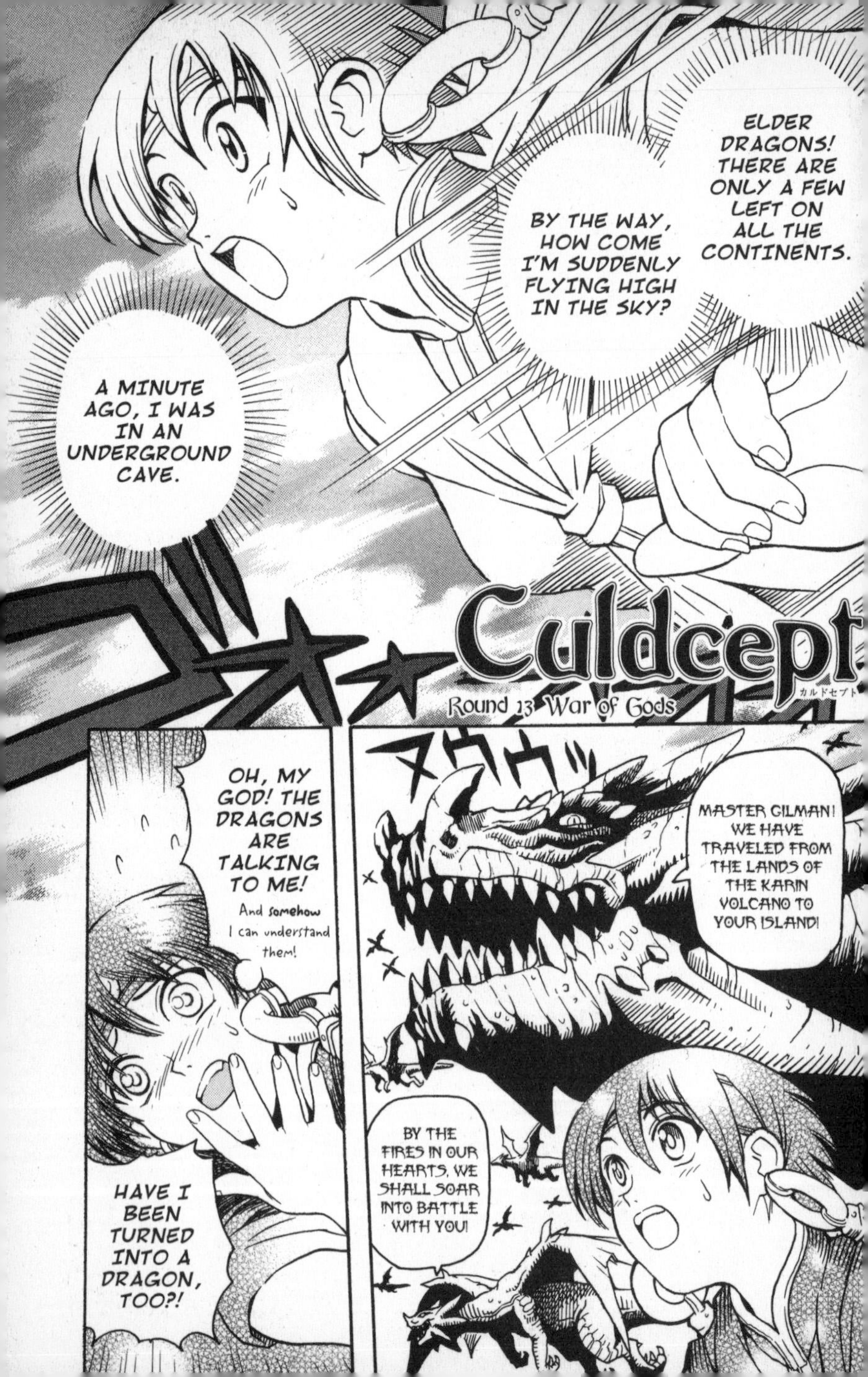
ELDER DRAGONS! THERE ARE ONLY A FEW LEFT ON ALL THE CONTINENTS.
BY THE WAY, HOW COME I'M SUDDENLY FLYING HIGH IN THE SKY?
A MINUTE AGO, I WAS IN AN UNDERGROUND CAVE.
Culdcept
カルドセプト
Round 13 War of Gods
MASTER GILMAN! WE HAVE TRAVELED FROM THE LANDS OF THE KARIN VOLCANO TO YOUR ISLAND!
BY THE FIRES IN OUR HEARTS, WE SHALL SOAR INTO BATTLE WITH YOU!
OH, MY GOD! THE DRAGONS ARE TALKING TO ME!
And somehow I can understand them!
HAVE I BEEN TURNED INTO A DRAGON, TOO?!

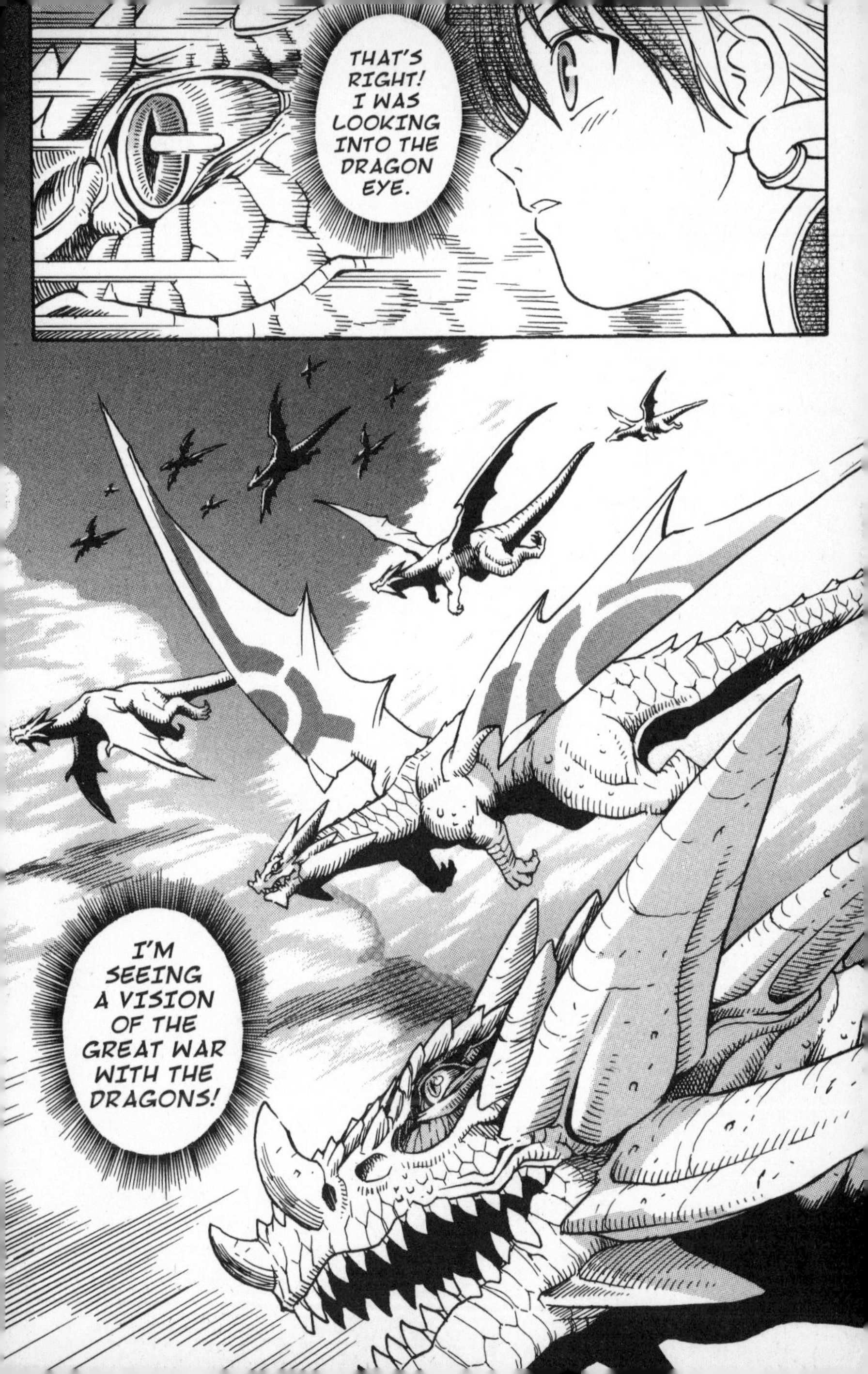
THAT'S RIGHT! I WAS LOOKING INTO THE DRAGON EYE.
I'M SEEING A VISION OF THE GREAT WAR WITH THE DRAGONS!

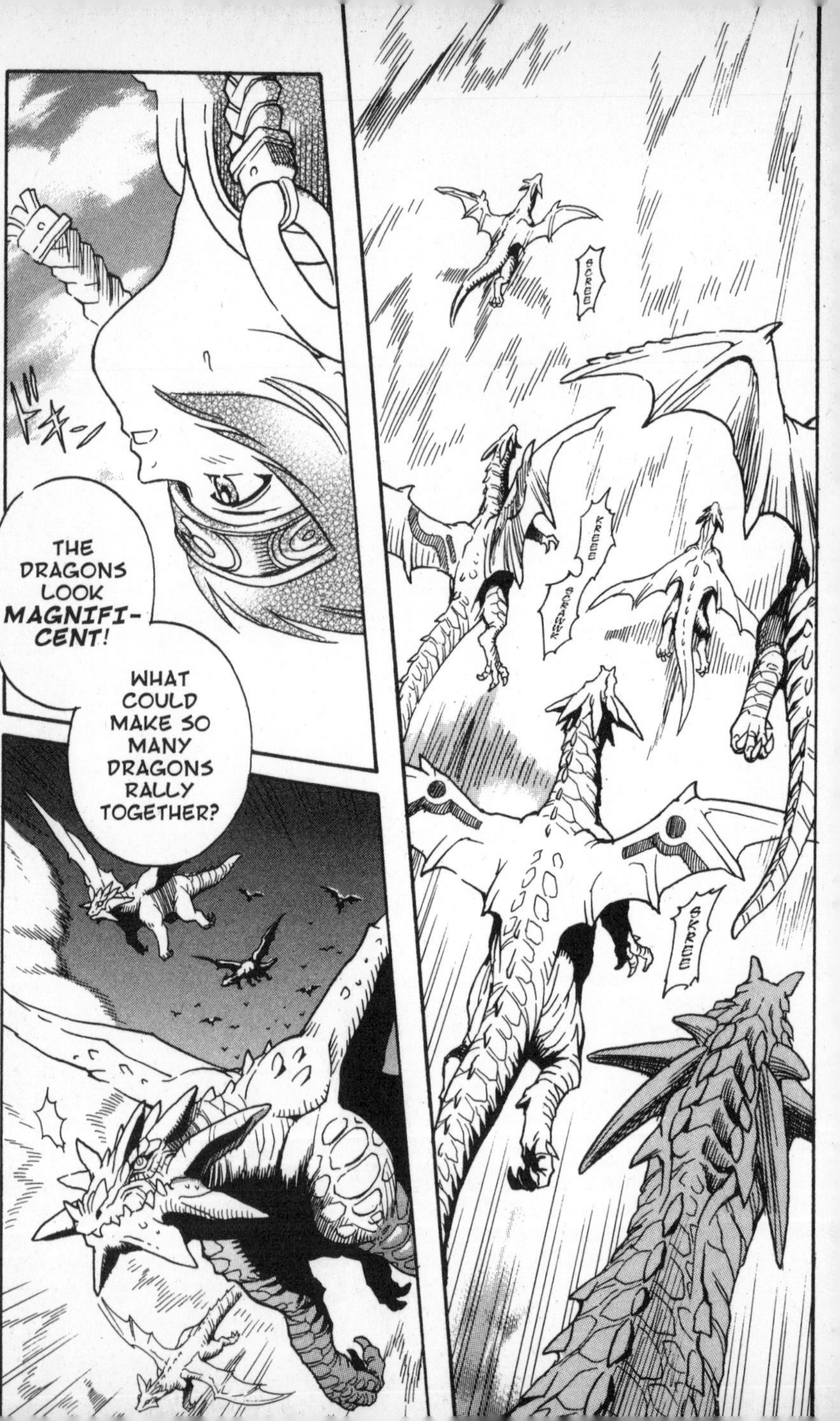
SCREE
KREEE
SCRAWK
SKREEE
ドキーン
THE DRAGONS LOOK MAGNIFI-CENT!
WHAT COULD MAKE SO MANY DRAGONS RALLY TOGETHER?

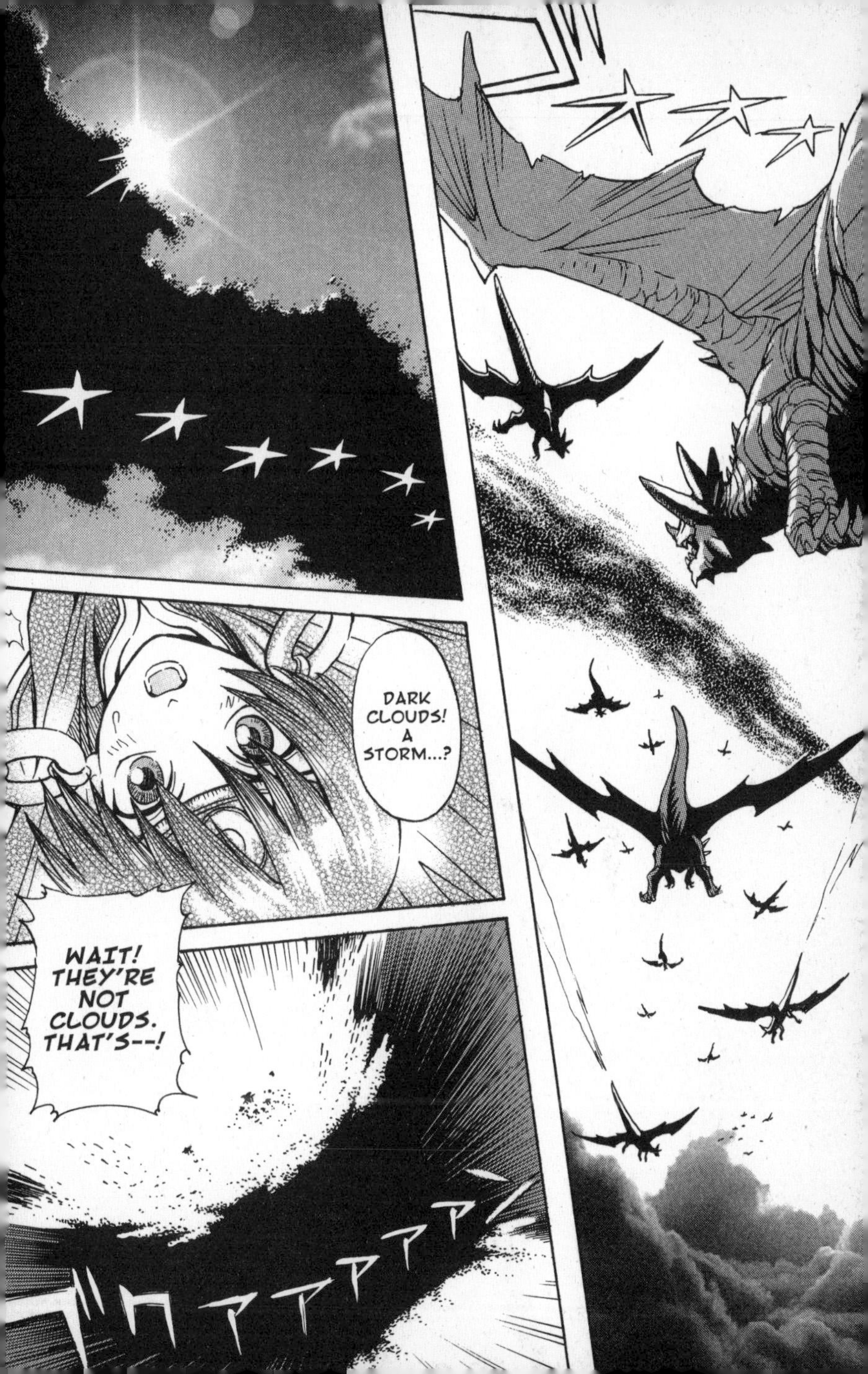
DARK CLOUDS! A STORM...?
WAIT! THEY'RE NOT CLOUDS. THAT'S--!

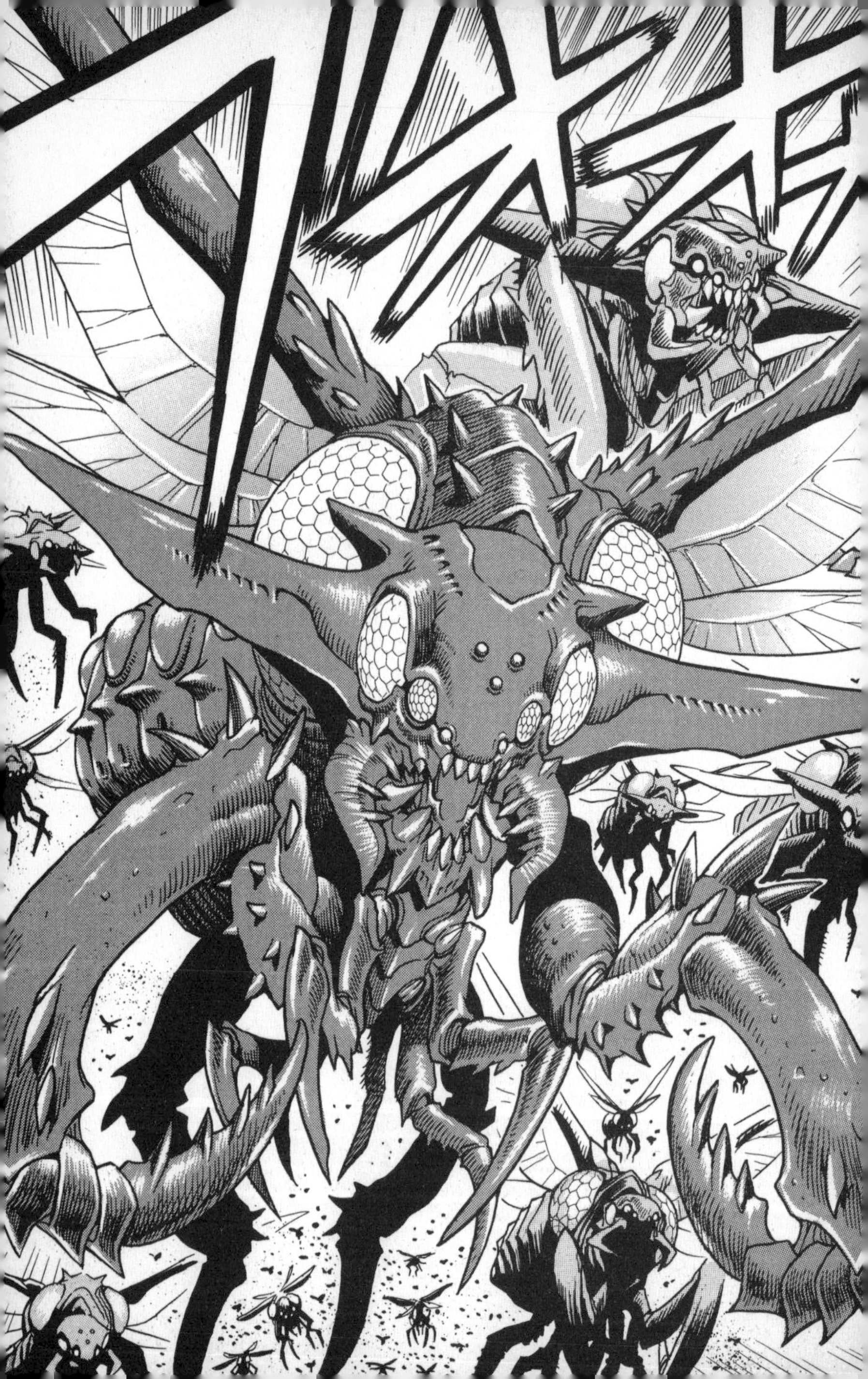

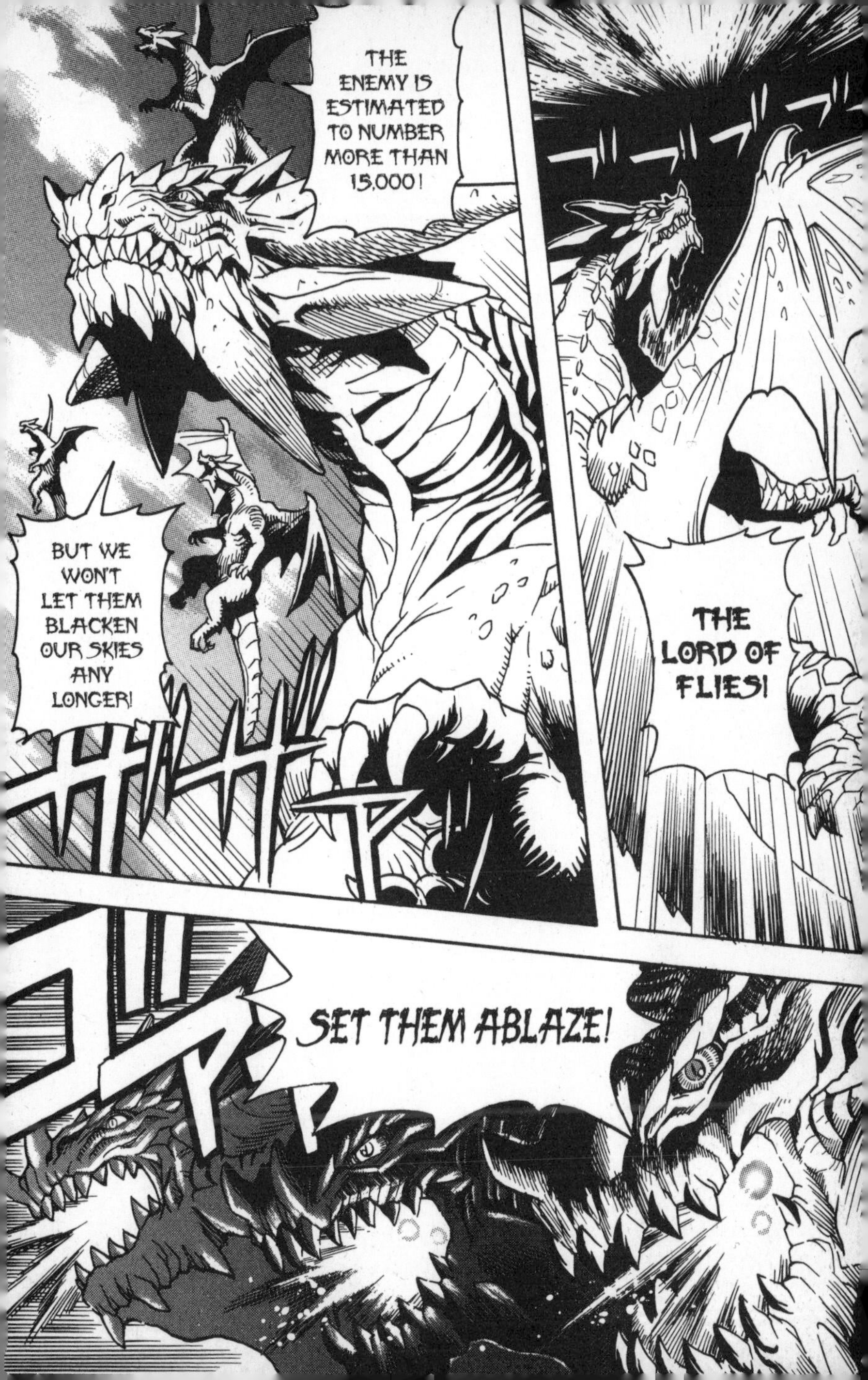
THE LORD OF FLIES!
THE ENEMY IS ESTIMATED TO NUMBER MORE THAN 15,000!
BUT WE WON'T LET THEM BLACKEN OUR SKIES ANY LONGER!
SET THEM ABLAZE!

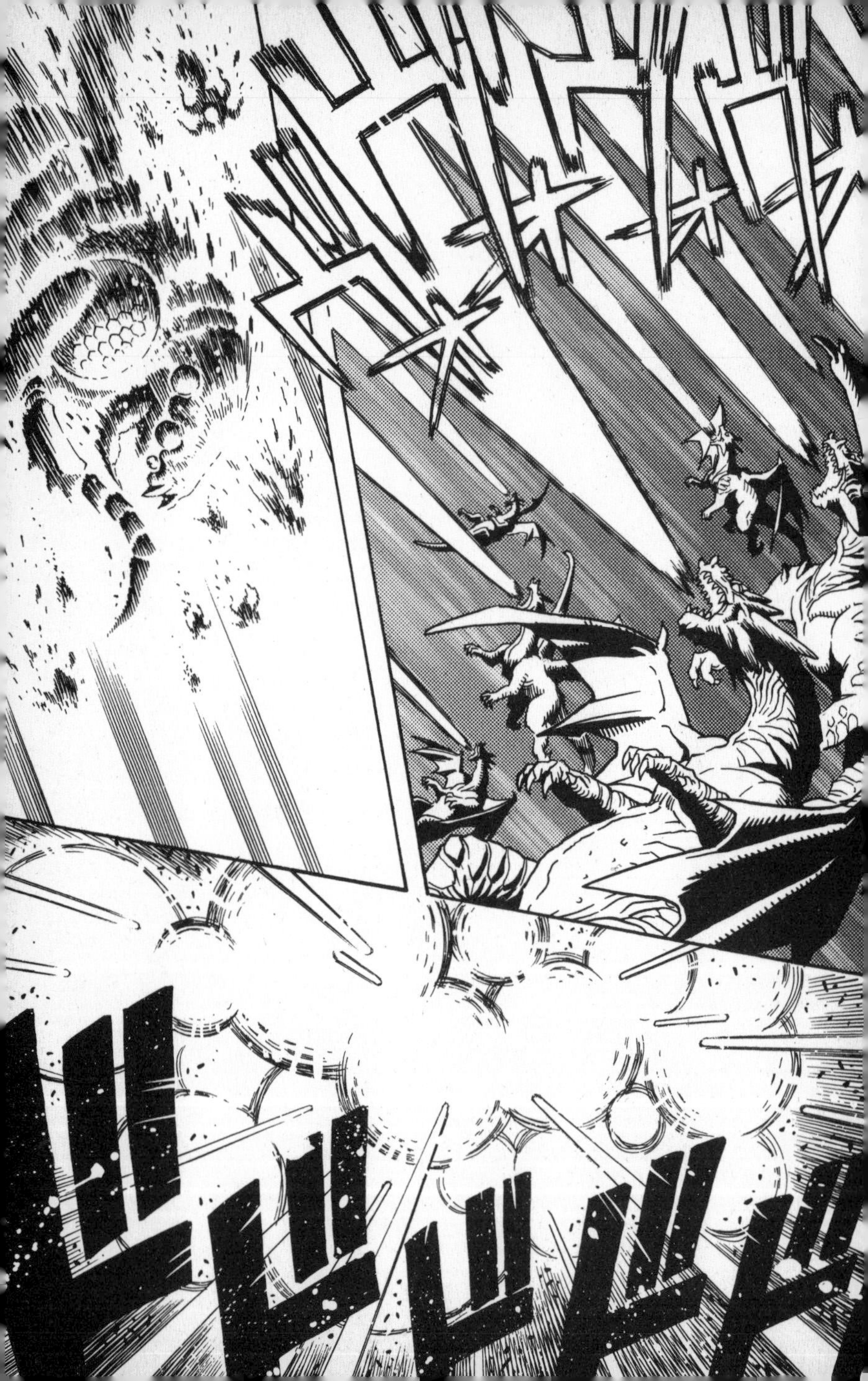

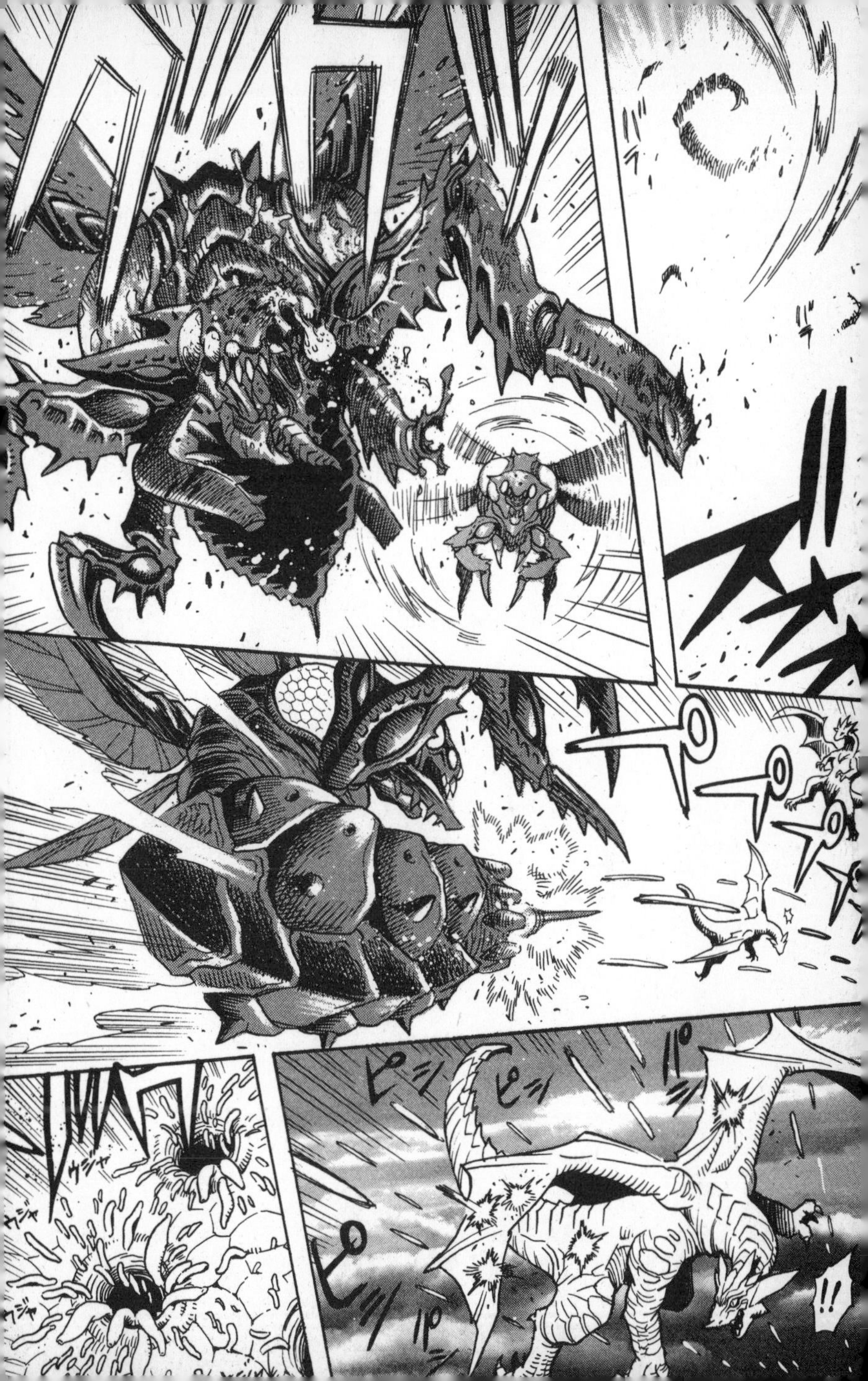

パ
ピシ
ピシ
パ
!!
ウジャ
ウジャ
ウジャ

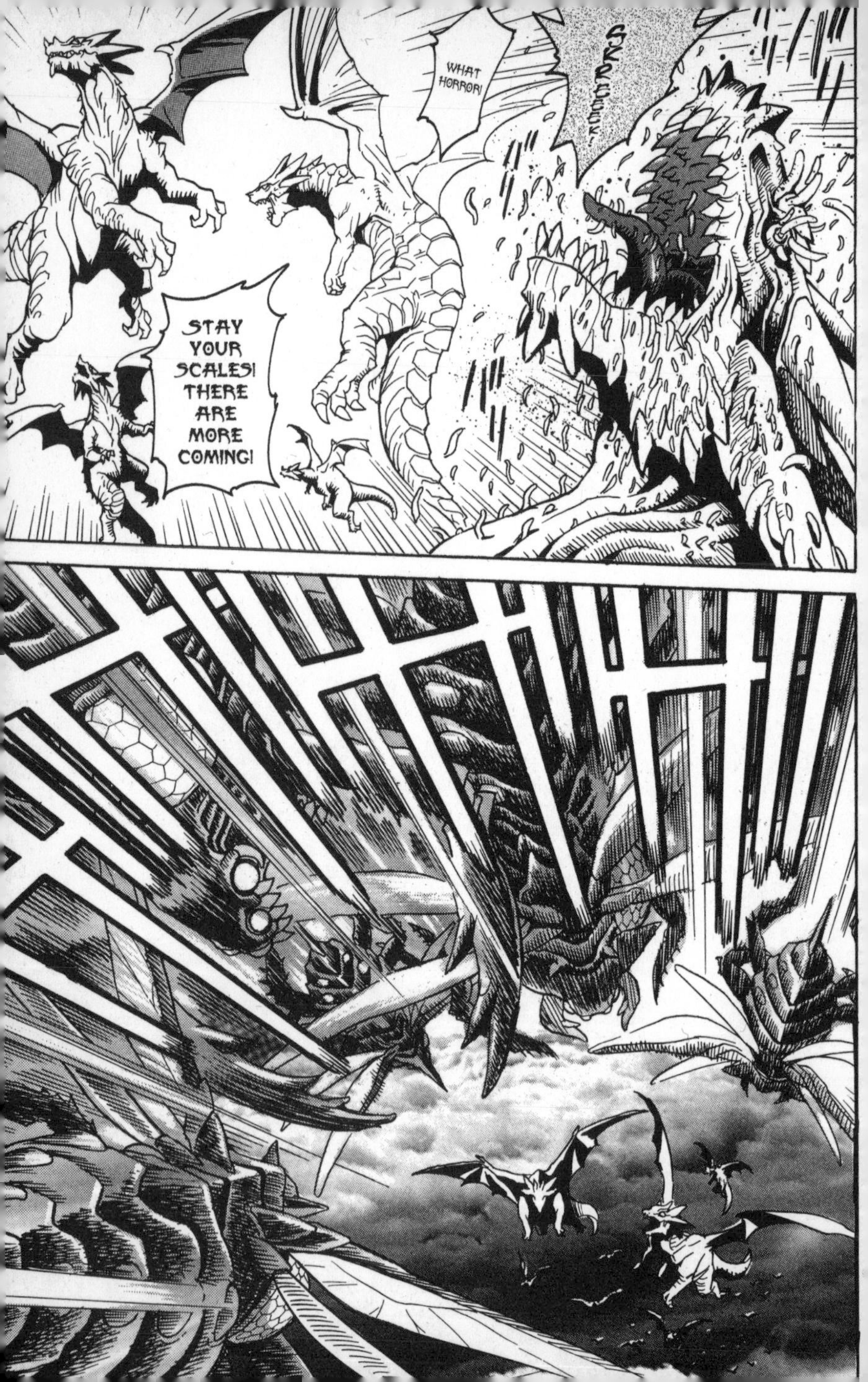
SKREEEEK!
WHAT HORROR!
STAY YOUR SCALES! THERE ARE MORE COMING!

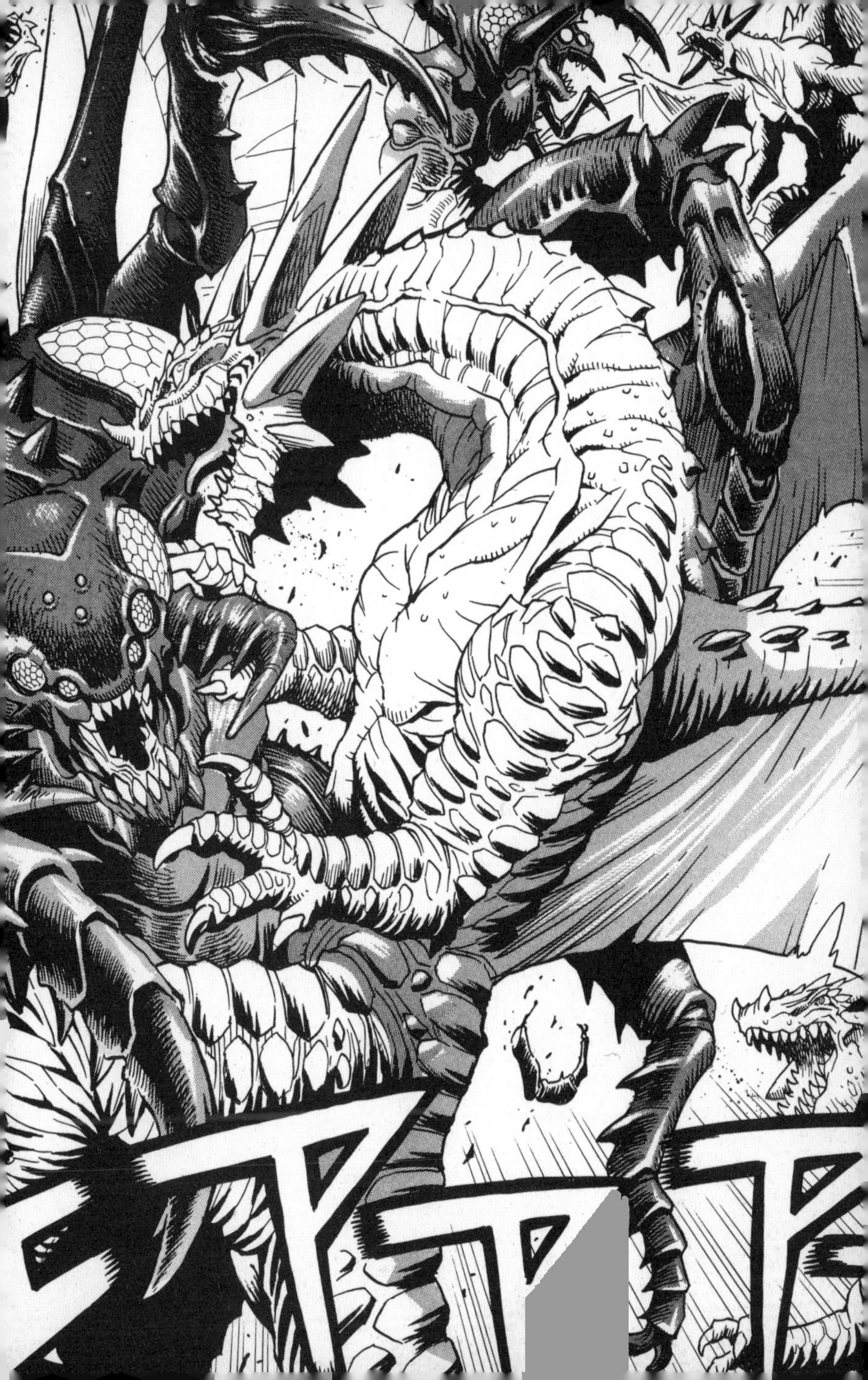

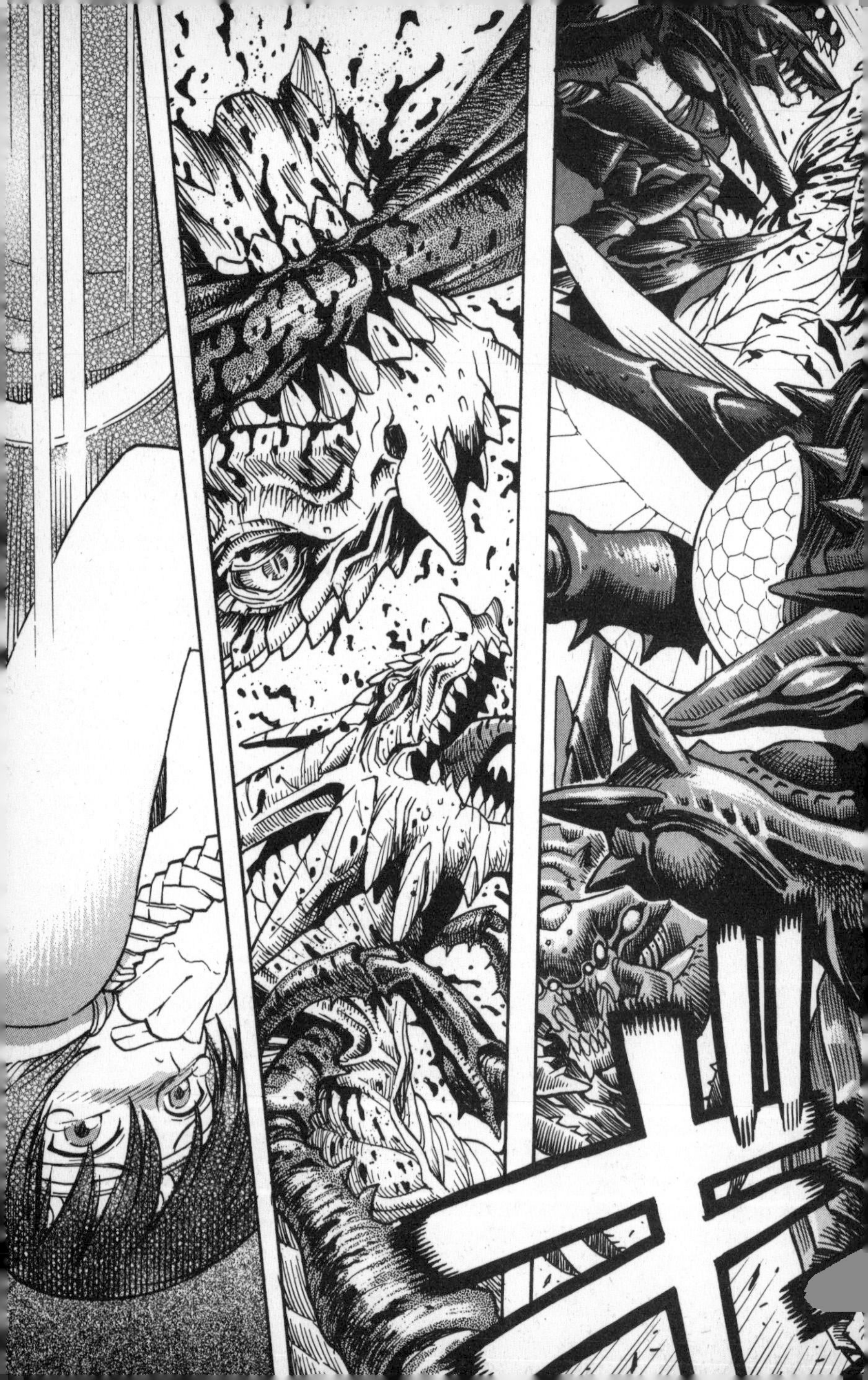

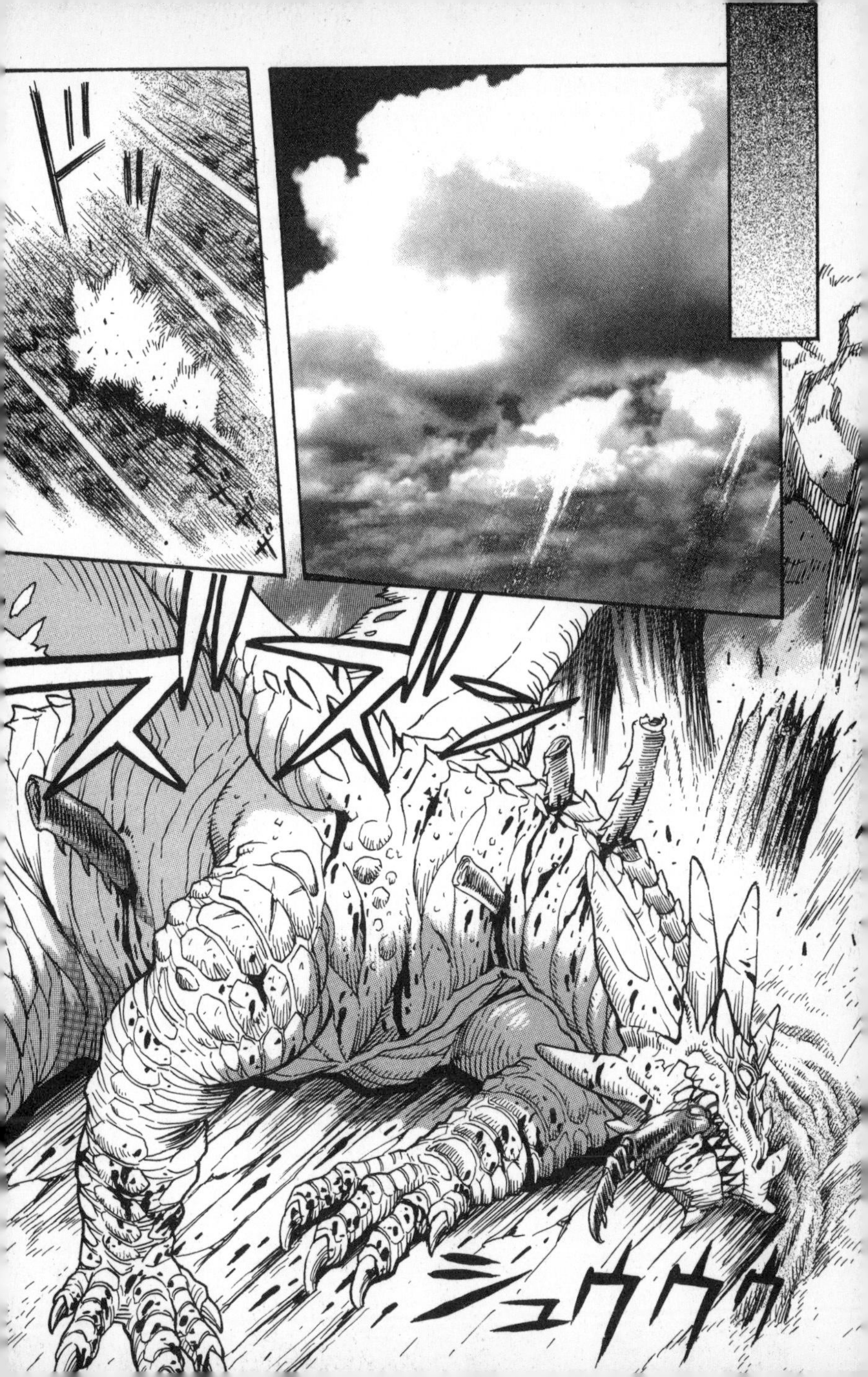
ドッ
ザザザザ
ズズ
シュウウウ

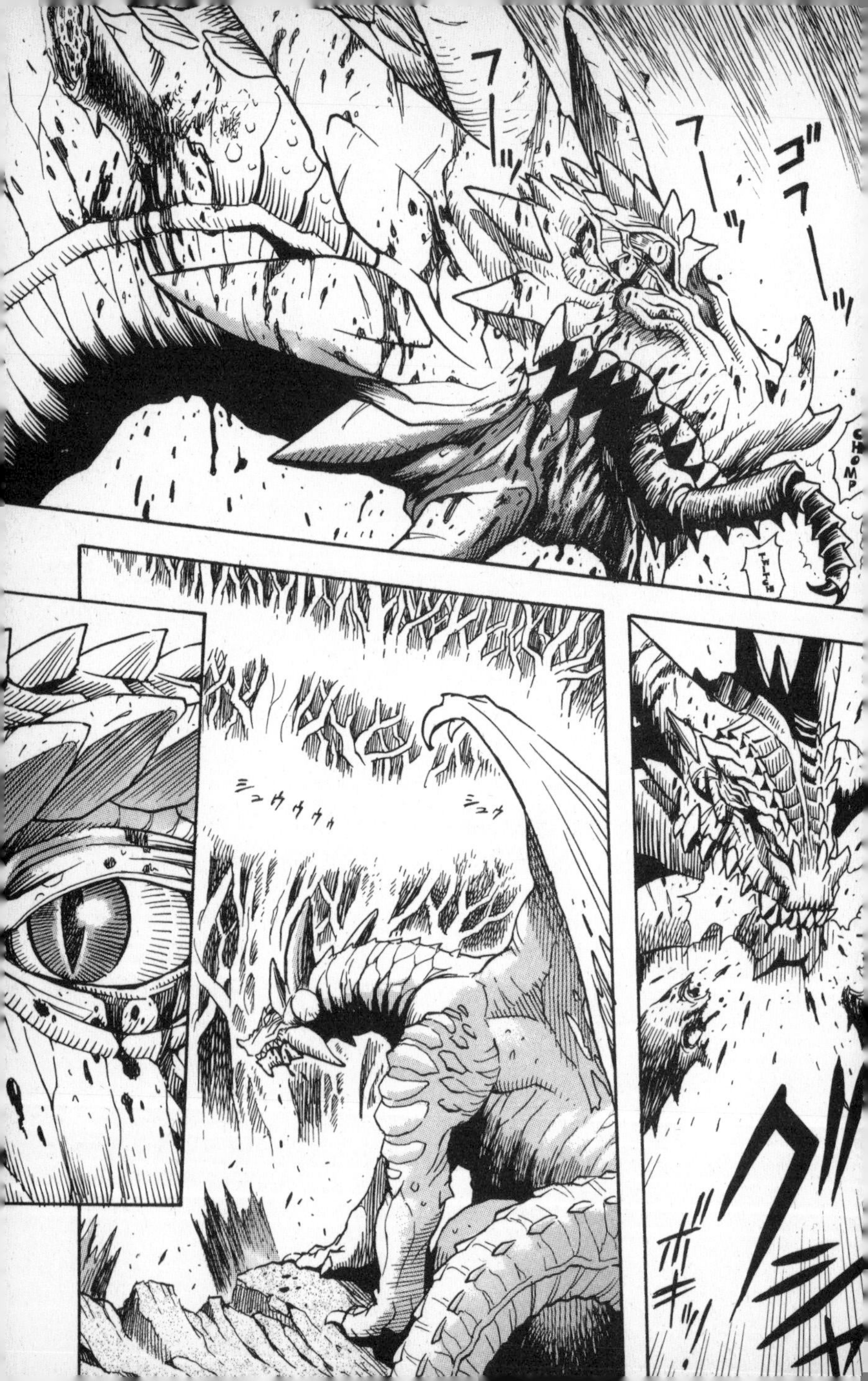
ゴフーーッ
フーーッ
フーッ
CHOMP
TWITCH
グシャ
ボキッ
シュウ
シュウウウゥ

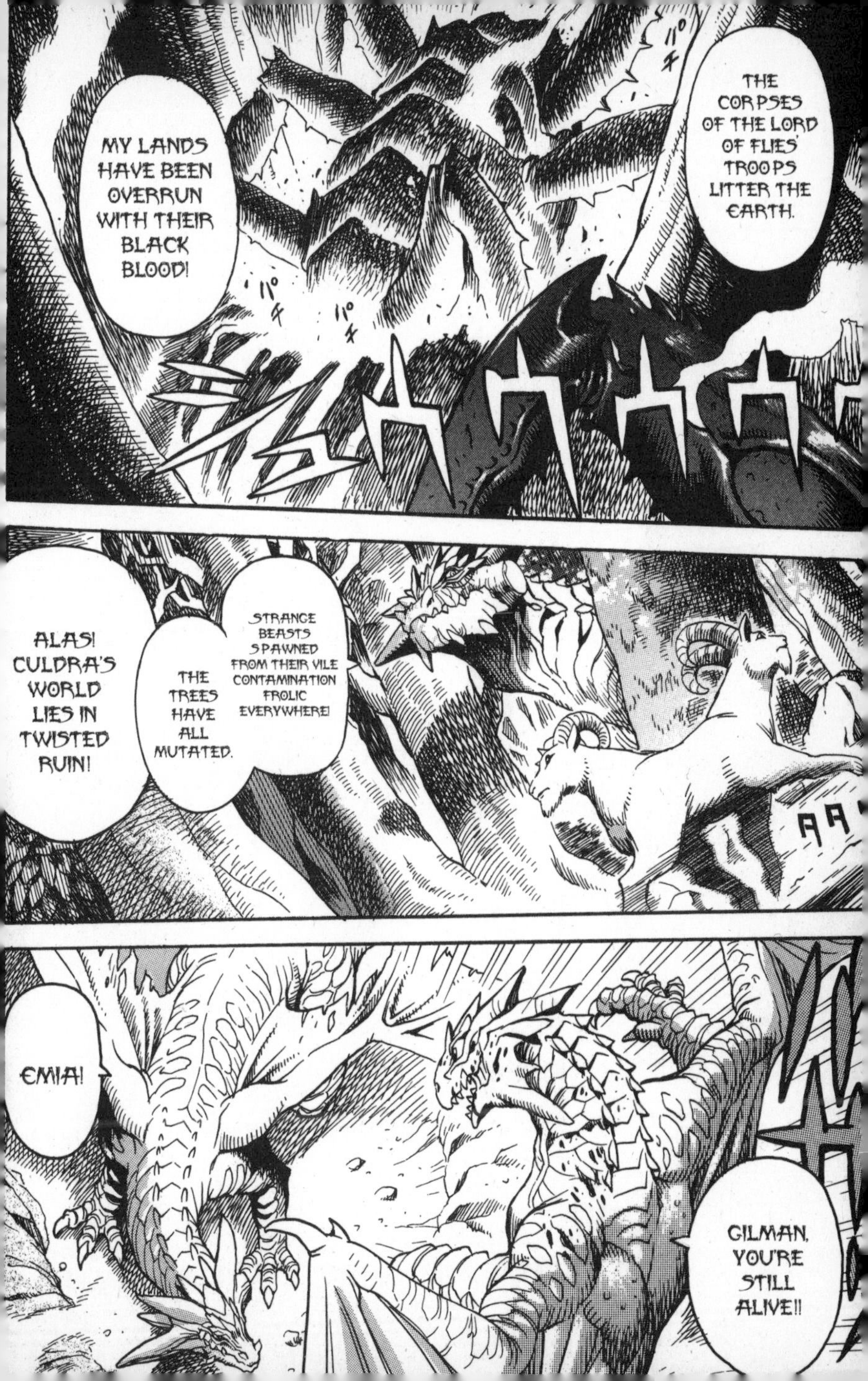
THE CORPSES OF THE LORD OF FLIES' TROOPS LITTER THE EARTH.
MY LANDS HAVE BEEN OVERRUN WITH THEIR BLACK BLOOD!
STRANGE BEASTS SPAWNED FROM THEIR VILE CONTAMINATION FROLIC EVERYWHERE!
THE TREES HAVE ALL MUTATED.
ALAS! CULDRA'S WORLD LIES IN TWISTED RUIN!
GILMAN, YOU'RE STILL ALIVE!!
EMIA!

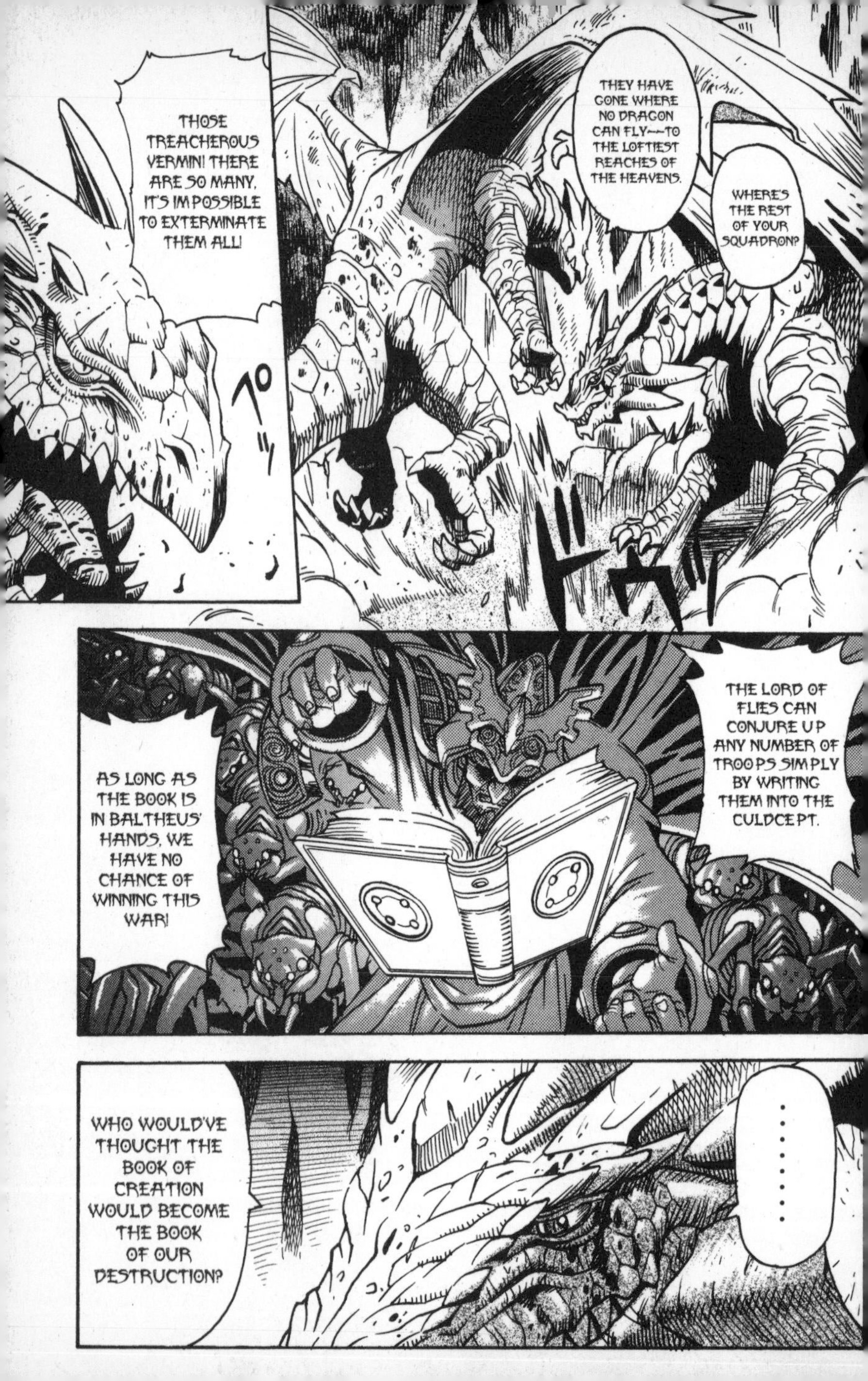
WHERE'S THE REST OF YOUR SQUADRON?
THEY HAVE GONE WHERE NO DRAGON CAN FLY---TO THE LOFTIEST REACHES OF THE HEAVENS.
THOSE TREACHEROUS VERMIN! THERE ARE SO MANY, IT'S IMPOSSIBLE TO EXTERMINATE THEM ALL!
THE LORD OF FLIES CAN CONJURE UP ANY NUMBER OF TROOPS SIMPLY BY WRITING THEM INTO THE CULDCEPT.
AS LONG AS THE BOOK IS IN BALTHEUS' HANDS, WE HAVE NO CHANCE OF WINNING THIS WAR!
......
WHO WOULD'VE THOUGHT THE BOOK OF CREATION WOULD BECOME THE BOOK OF OUR DESTRUCTION?

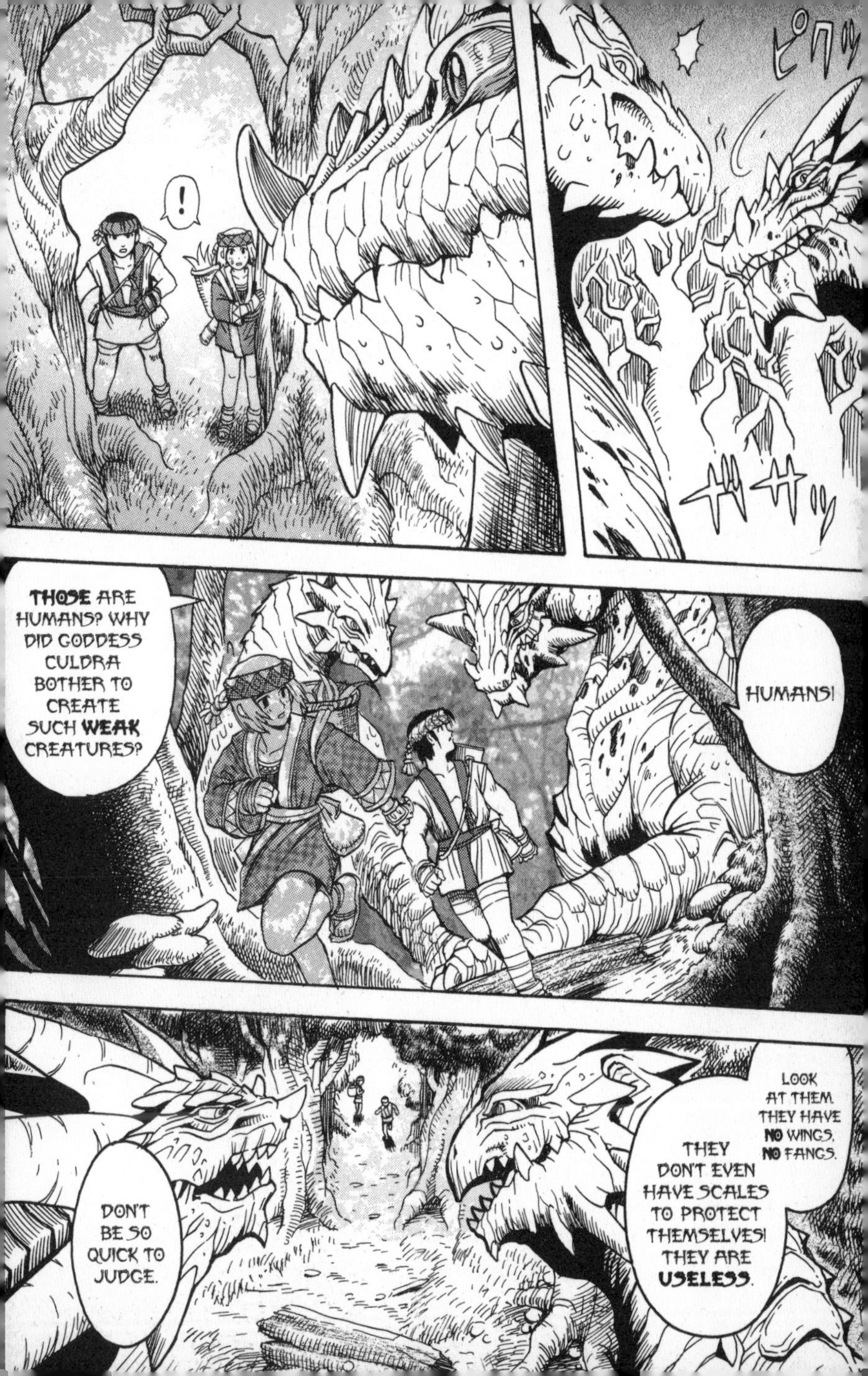
ピクッ
ザザッ
!
HUMANS!
THOSE ARE HUMANS? WHY DID GODDESS CULDRA BOTHER TO CREATE SUCH **WEAK** CREATURES?
LOOK AT THEM. THEY HAVE **NO** WINGS, **NO** FANGS.
THEY DON'T EVEN HAVE SCALES TO PROTECT THEMSELVES! THEY ARE **USELESS**.
DON'T BE SO QUICK TO JUDGE.

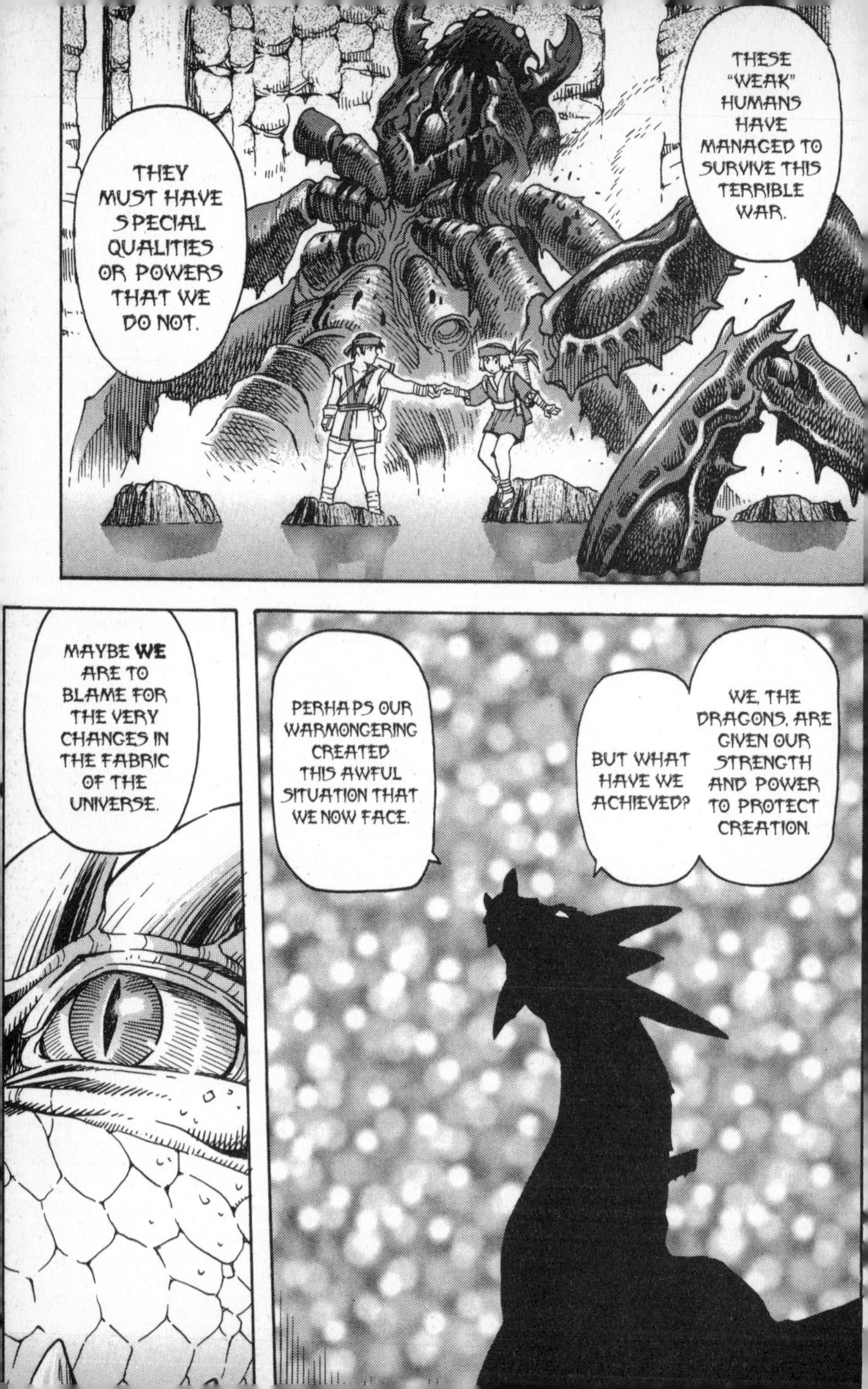
THESE "WEAK" HUMANS HAVE MANAGED TO SURVIVE THIS TERRIBLE WAR.
THEY MUST HAVE SPECIAL QUALITIES OR POWERS THAT WE DO NOT.
WE, THE DRAGONS, ARE GIVEN OUR STRENGTH AND POWER TO PROTECT CREATION.
BUT WHAT HAVE WE ACHIEVED?
PERHAPS OUR WARMONGERING CREATED THIS AWFUL SITUATION THAT WE NOW FACE.
MAYBE **WE** ARE TO BLAME FOR THE VERY CHANGES IN THE FABRIC OF THE UNIVERSE.

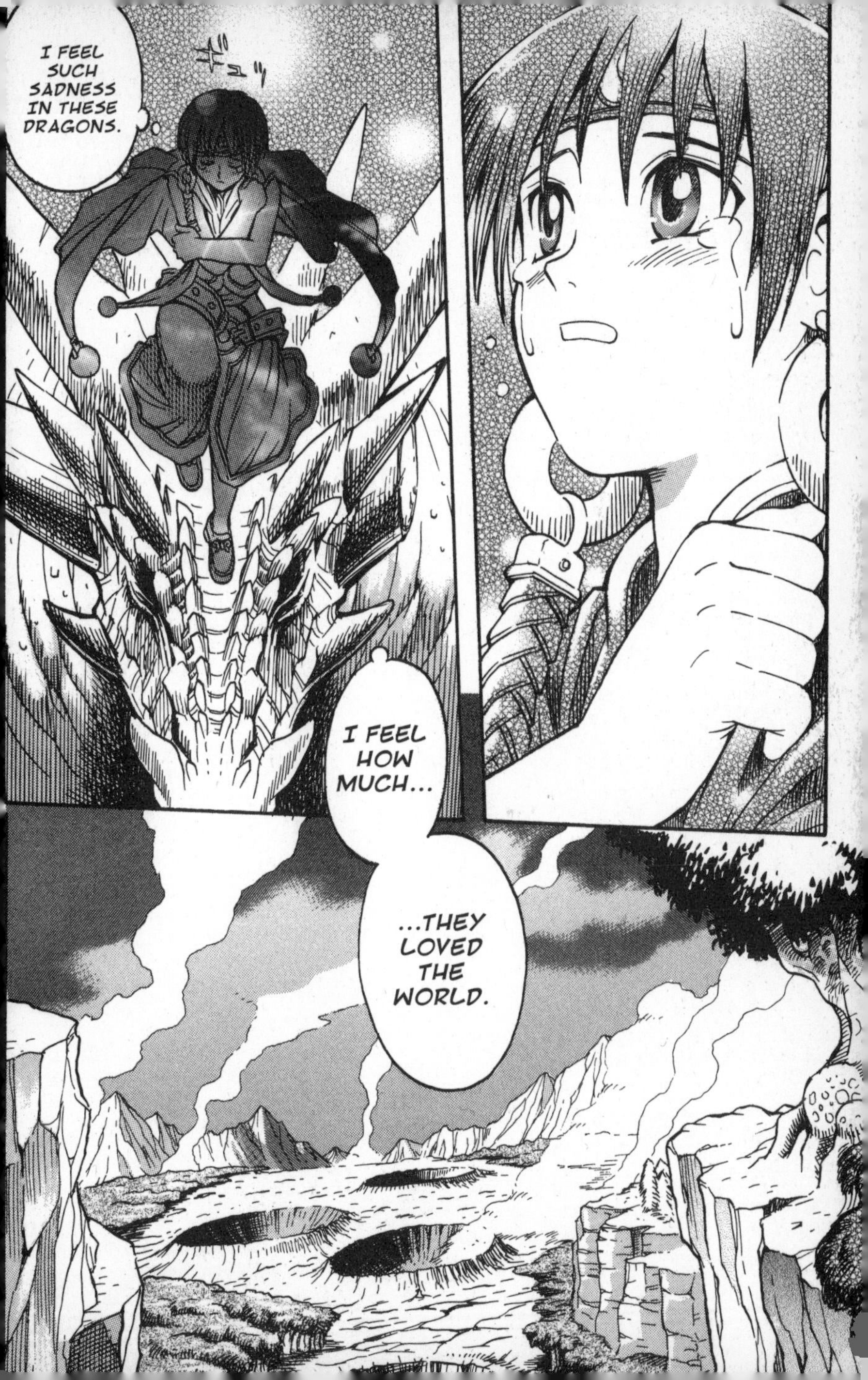
ギュッ
I FEEL SUCH SADNESS IN THESE DRAGONS.
I FEEL HOW MUCH...
...THEY LOVED THE WORLD.

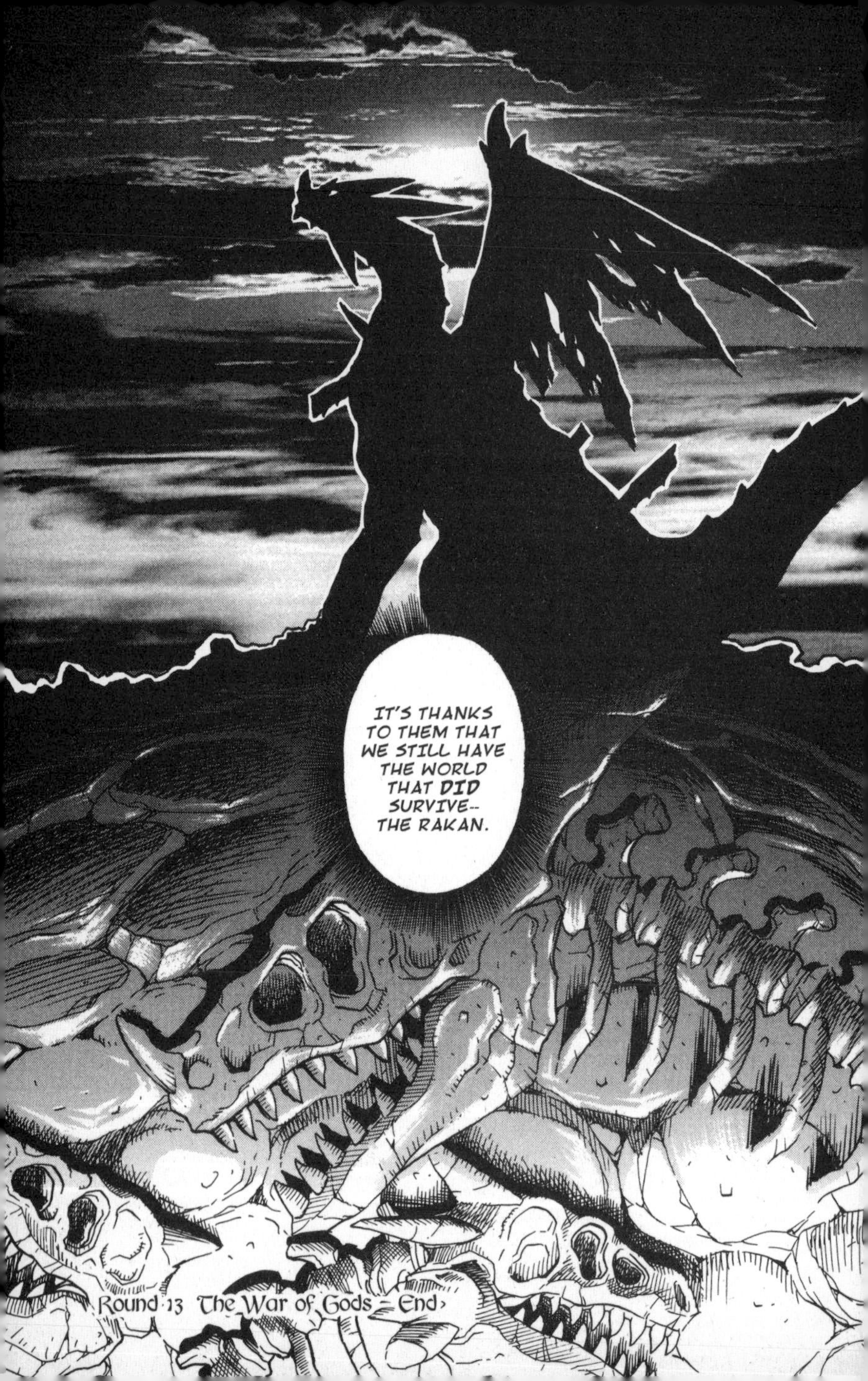
IT'S THANKS TO THEM THAT WE STILL HAVE THE WORLD THAT DID SURVIVE-- THE RAKAN.
Round 13 The War of Gods - End

THE WAR OF GODS
CREATURES LOST TO TIME

MANY POWERFUL CREATURES LIVED DURING THE WAR BETWEEN THE GODDESS CULDRA AND THE REBEL GOD BALTHEUS. MOST PEOPLE BELIEVE THAT THESE CREATURES NO LONGER EXIST.

MASTER HOROWITZ

BEEZLEBUB, THE LORD OF FLIES [AIR]

Attack Points	70
Defense Points	70
Summon Cost	160
Summon Condition	Wind x2
Special Abilites	Increase attack power in all Air creatures.

AN AIR CREATURE CREATED BY BALTHEUS TO FIGHT AGAINST CULDRA'S FOUR PILLAR GODS. HE IS AN EVIL MONSTER WHO CAN FLY AS MUCH AS 10,000 METERS ABOVE GROUND LEVEL.

MIGOALS [AIR]

Attack Points	40
Defense Points	40
Summon Cost	100
Summon Condition	Sacrifices
Special Abilites	Powerful attacks against Water and Neutral. Blocks Fire and Air.

THEY WERE CREATED TO SERVE THE FOUR LORDS. THEY ARE SUPERIOR TO THE CREATURES OF ALL FOUR CATEGORIES: NEUTRAL, FIRE, AIR AND WATER. DRAGONS' FIRE AND NYMPHS' ARROWS CAN HARM THEM.

ELDER DRAGON [FIRE]

Attack Points	60
Defense Points	80
Summon Cost	180
Summon Condition	None
Special Abilites	Draconic creatures gain +10 attack.

THE OLDEST SPECIES IN RAKAN. THE ELDER DRAGONS RULE ALL OTHER DRAGON RACES. THEY ARE CERTAINLY AMONG GODDESS CULDRA'S MOST POWERFUL ALLIES. IF YOU ARE LUCKY ENOUGH TO MEET ONE OF THE FEW SURVIVING ELDER DRAGONS, YOU MIGHT WANT TO ASK FOR SOME SAGE ADVICE.

NYMPH [AIR]

Attack Points	30
Defense Points	30
Summon Cost	85
Summon Condition	Wind x2
Special Abilites	Suprise attacks.

A RACE OF NYMPHS ALLIED WITH THE DRAGONS IN THE WAR OF GODS. THE NYMPH IS WEAKER THAN THE DRAGON IN TERMS OF ATTACK POINTS, BUT THEIR AMAZING SPEED COMPENSATES FOR THAT. A SMALL NUMBER OF NYMPHS SURVIVED THE WAR AND CURRENTLY LIVE DEEP IN THE FOREST. THEY SAY NYMPHS TEND TO HIDE FROM PEOPLE.

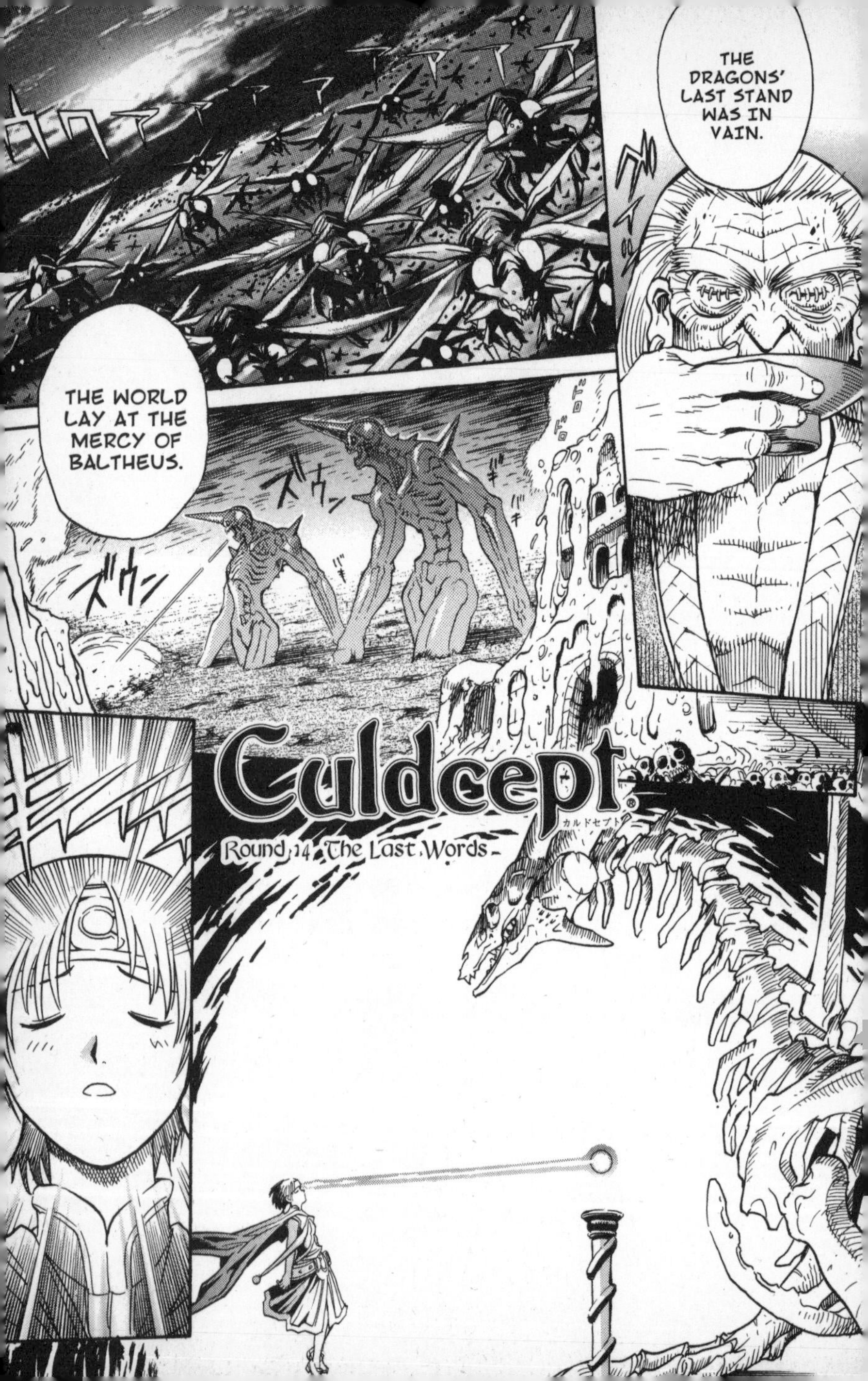
THE DRAGONS' LAST STAND WAS IN VAIN.
THE WORLD LAY AT THE MERCY OF BALTHEUS.
ズウン
ズウン
Culdcept®
カルドセプト
Round 14 The Last Words

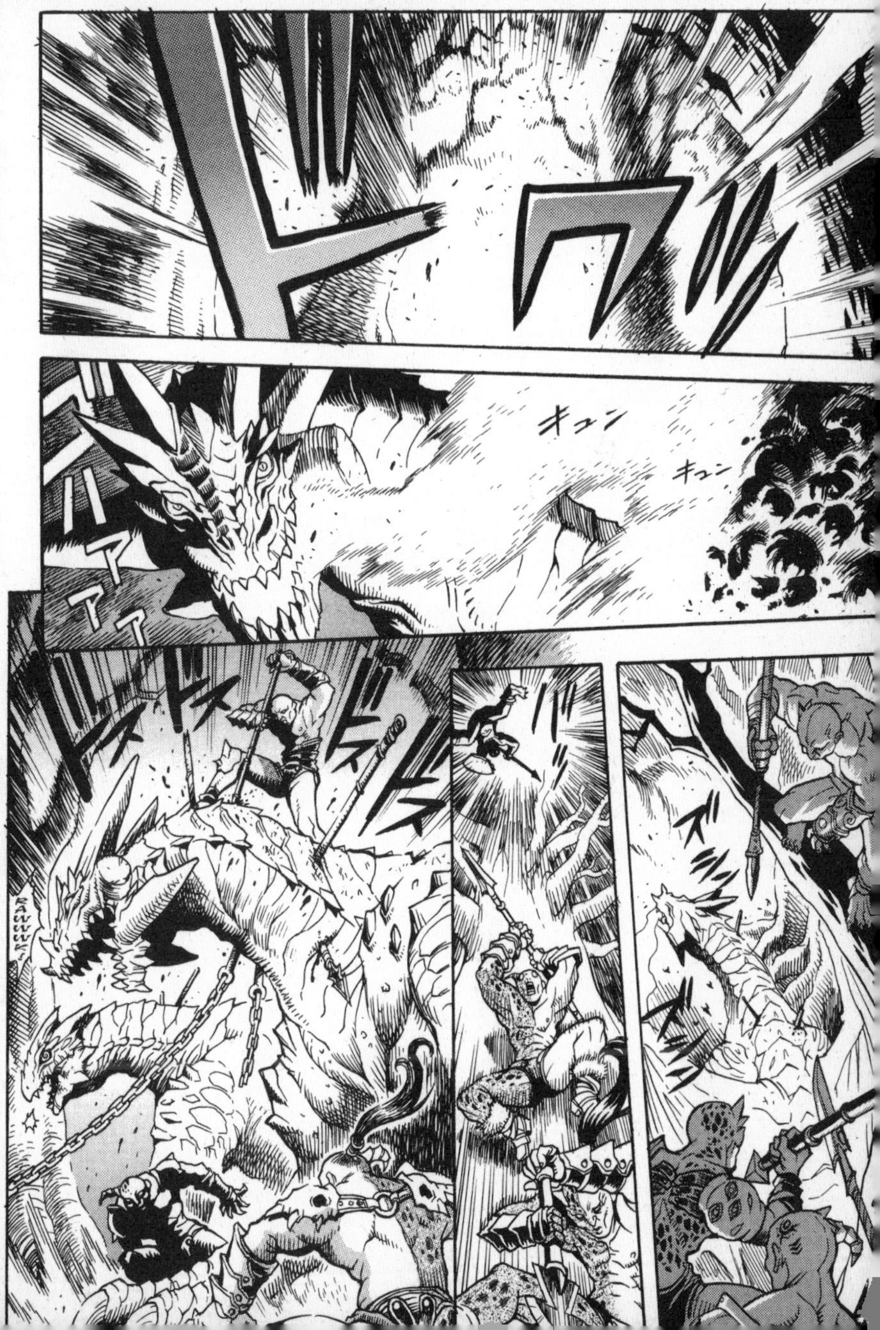

ドワッ
キュン
キュン
ハァァ
ドス
ドス
ドス
RAWWWK!

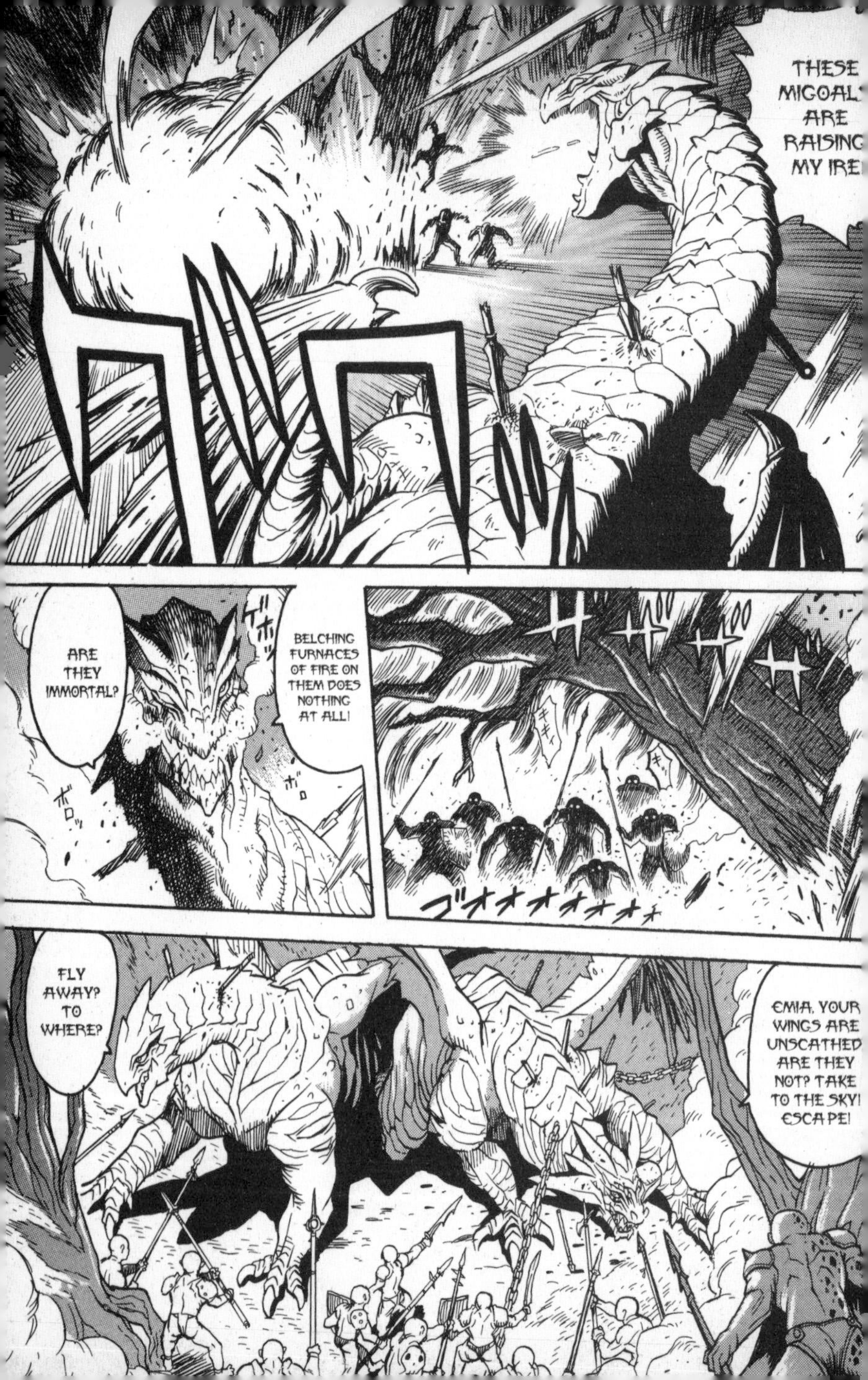
THESE MIGOALS ARE RAISING MY IRE!
BELCHING FURNACES OF FIRE ON THEM DOES NOTHING AT ALL!
ARE THEY IMMORTAL?
EMIA, YOUR WINGS ARE UNSCATHED ARE THEY NOT? TAKE TO THE SKY! ESCAPE!
FLY AWAY? TO WHERE?

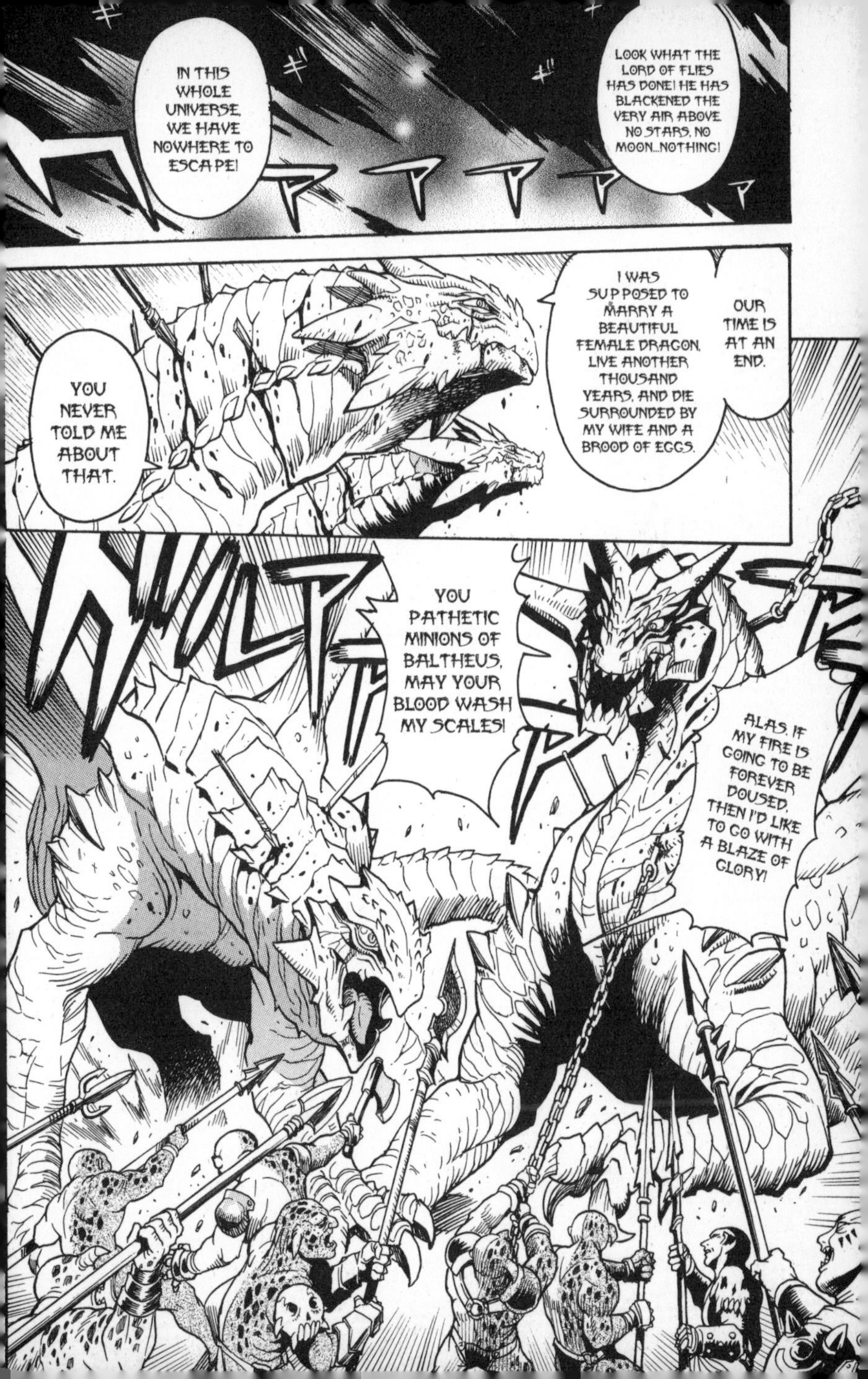
LOOK WHAT THE LORD OF FLIES HAS DONE! HE HAS BLACKENED THE VERY AIR ABOVE. NO STARS, NO MOON...NOTHING!
IN THIS WHOLE UNIVERSE, WE HAVE NOWHERE TO ESCAPE!
OUR TIME IS AT AN END.
I WAS SUPPOSED TO MARRY A BEAUTIFUL FEMALE DRAGON, LIVE ANOTHER THOUSAND YEARS, AND DIE SURROUNDED BY MY WIFE AND A BROOD OF EGGS.
YOU NEVER TOLD ME ABOUT THAT.
ALAS. IF MY FIRE IS GOING TO BE FOREVER DOUSED, THEN I'D LIKE TO GO WITH A BLAZE OF GLORY!
YOU PATHETIC MINIONS OF BALTHEUS, MAY YOUR BLOOD WASH MY SCALES!

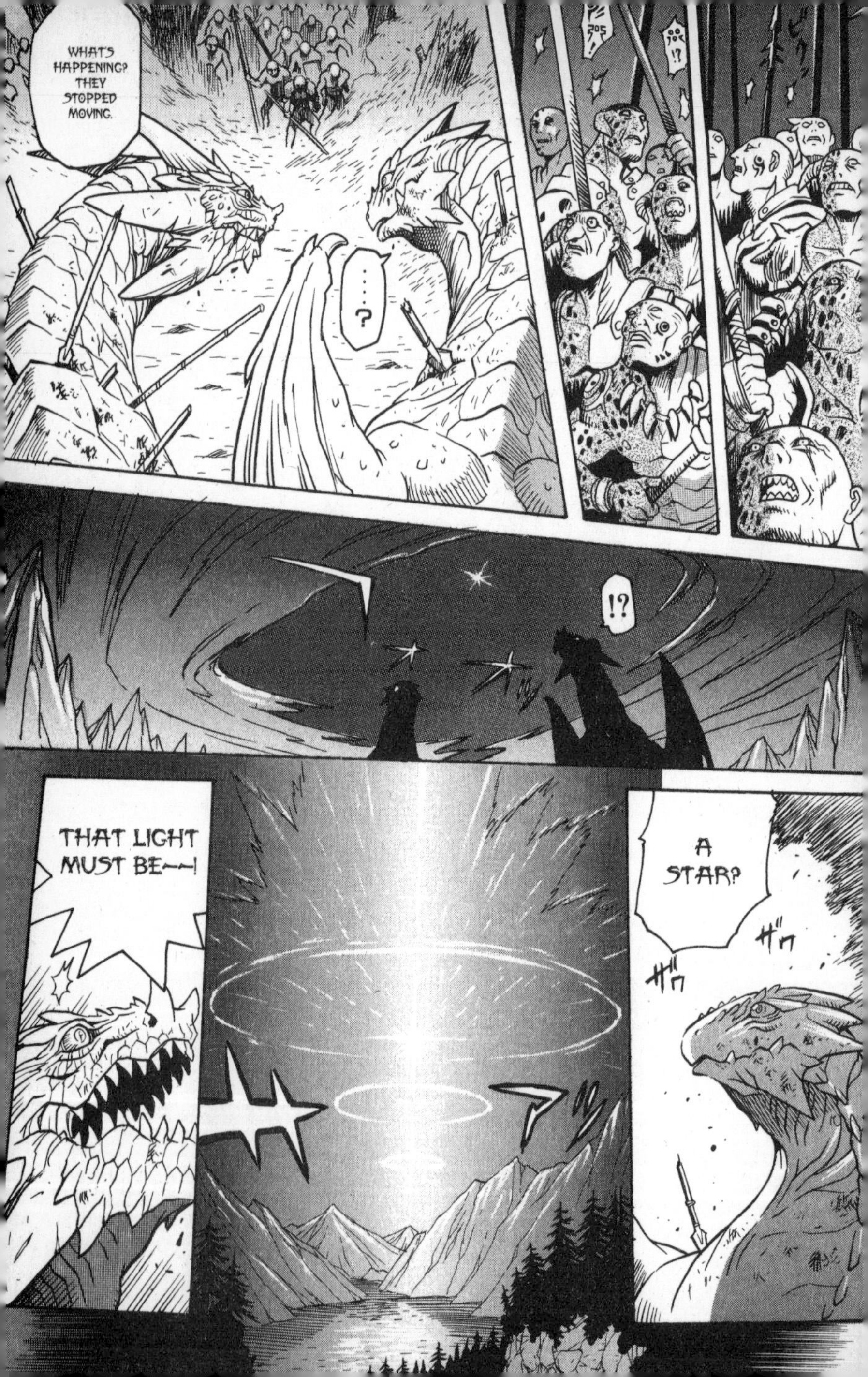
!?
WHAT'S HAPPENING? THEY STOPPED MOVING.
.....?
!?
A STAR?
THAT LIGHT MUST BE—!

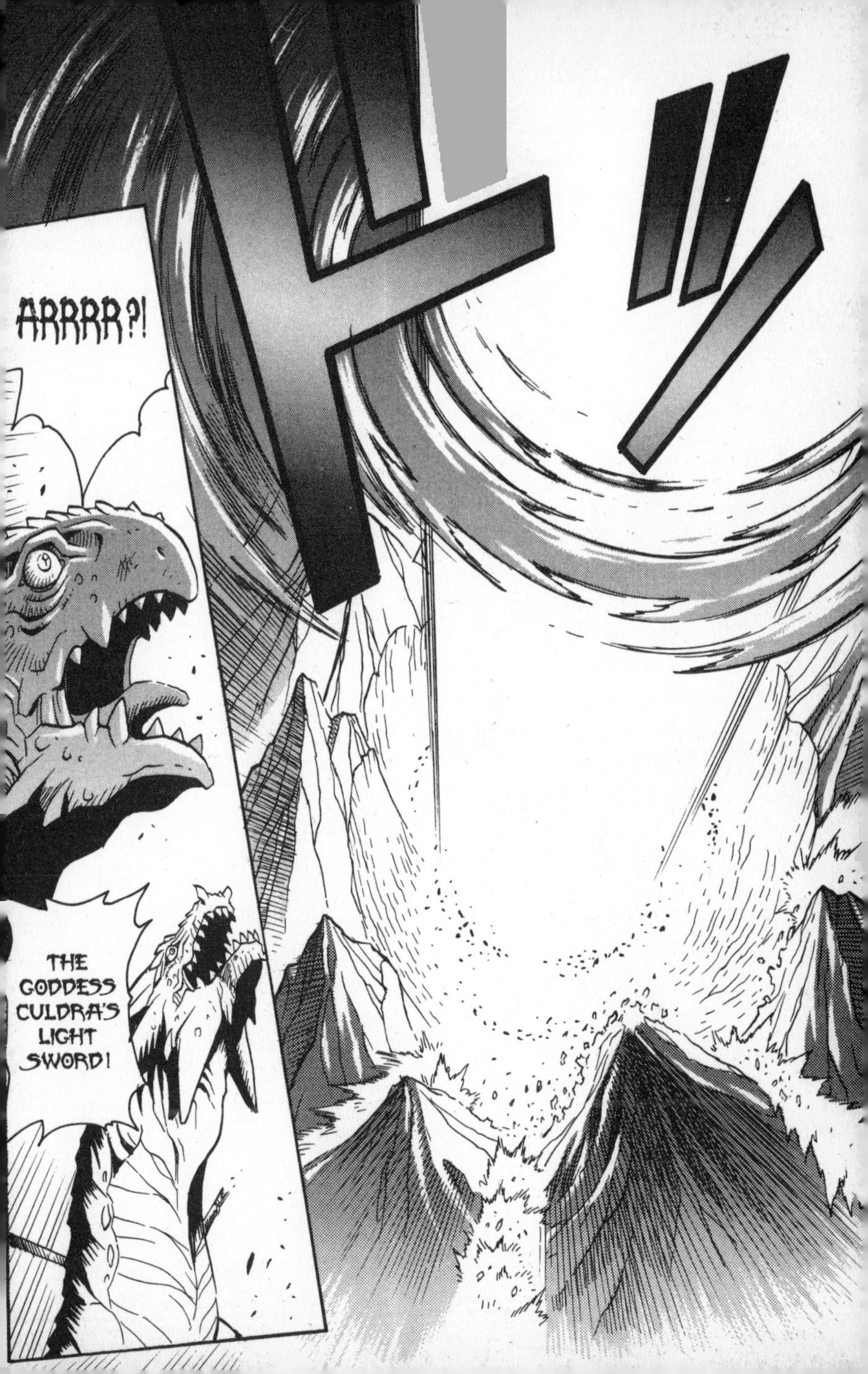
ARRRR?!
THE GODDESS CULDRA'S LIGHT SWORD!

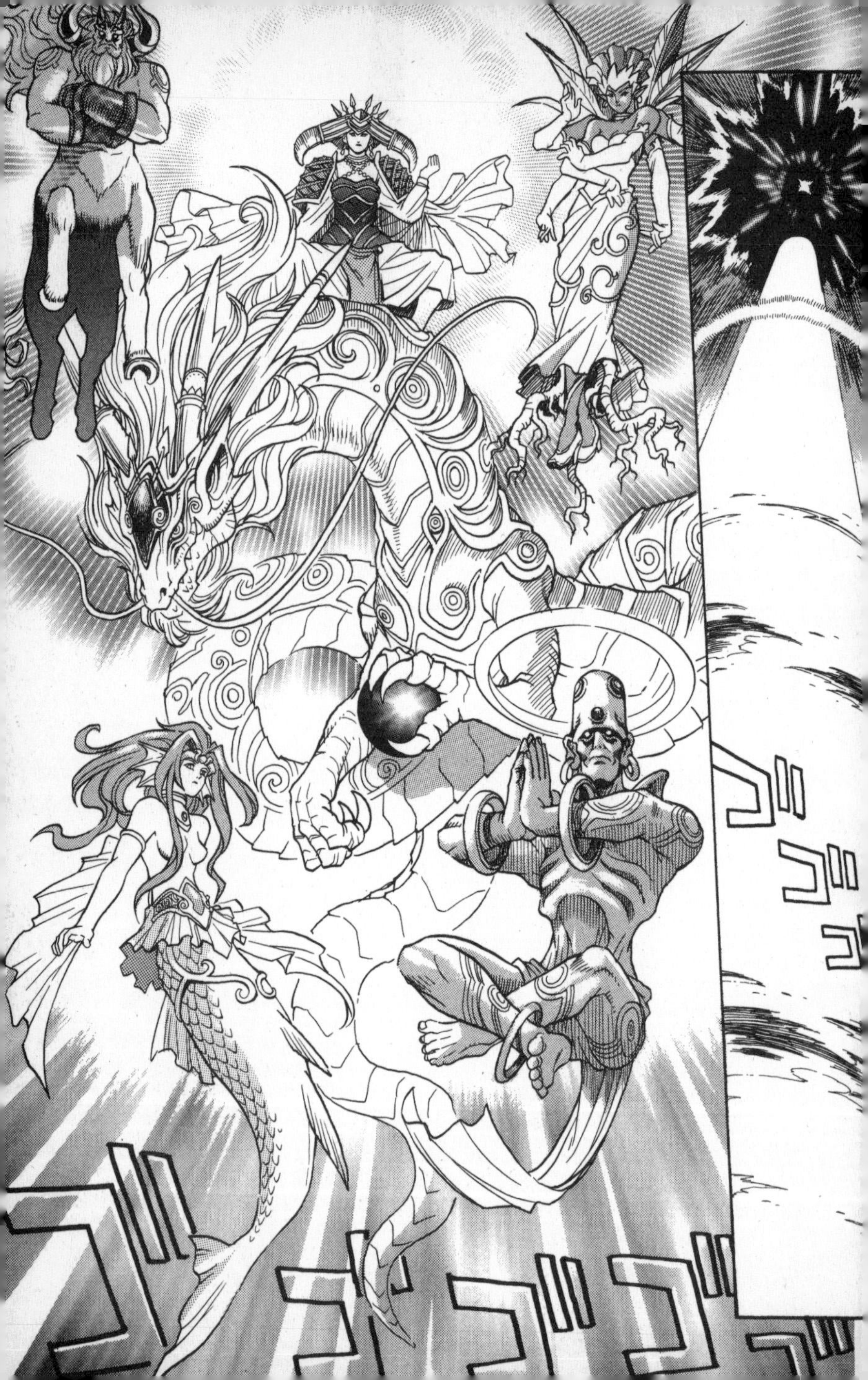
ゴゴゴ
ゴゴゴゴゴ

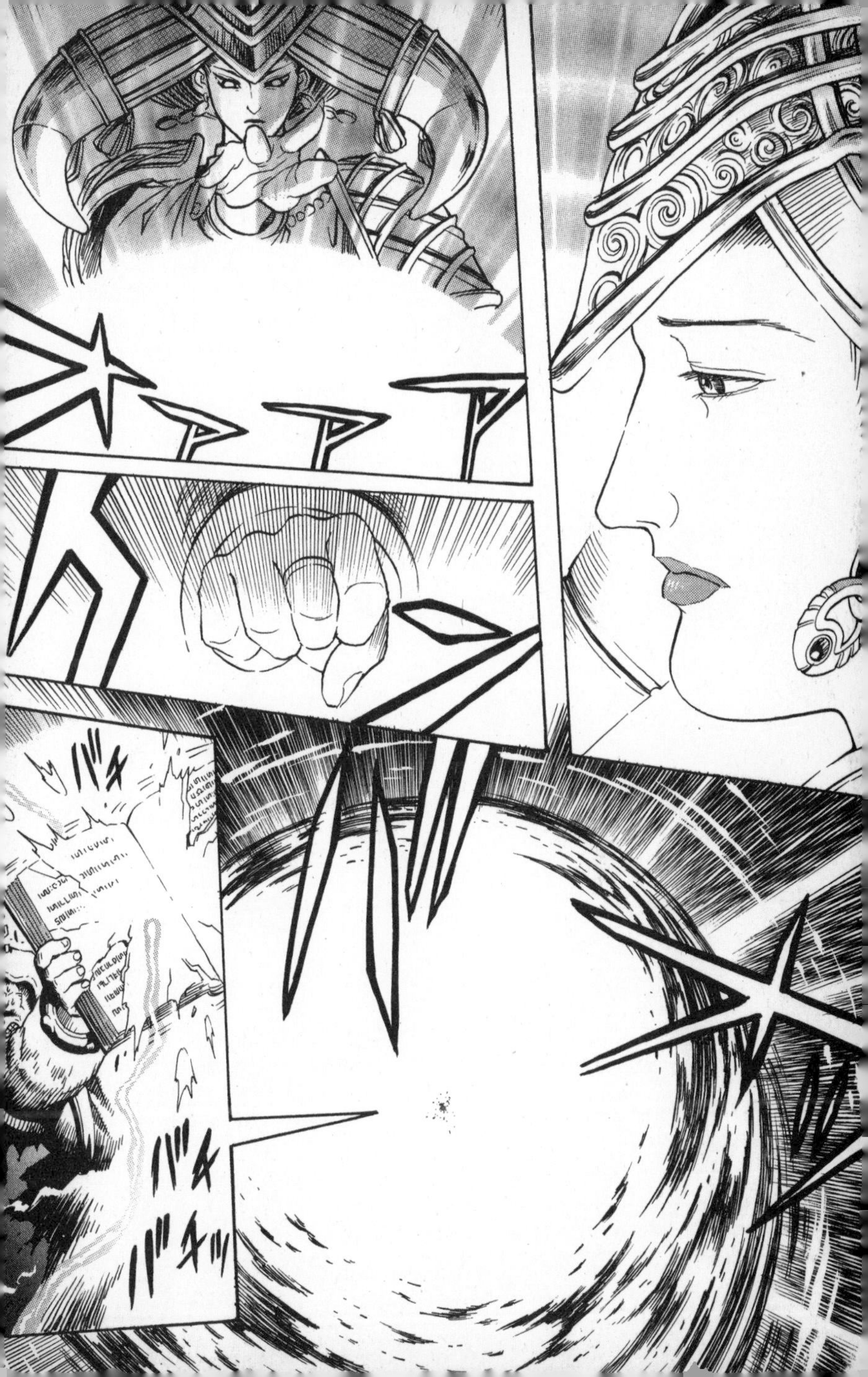
バチ
バチ
バチッ

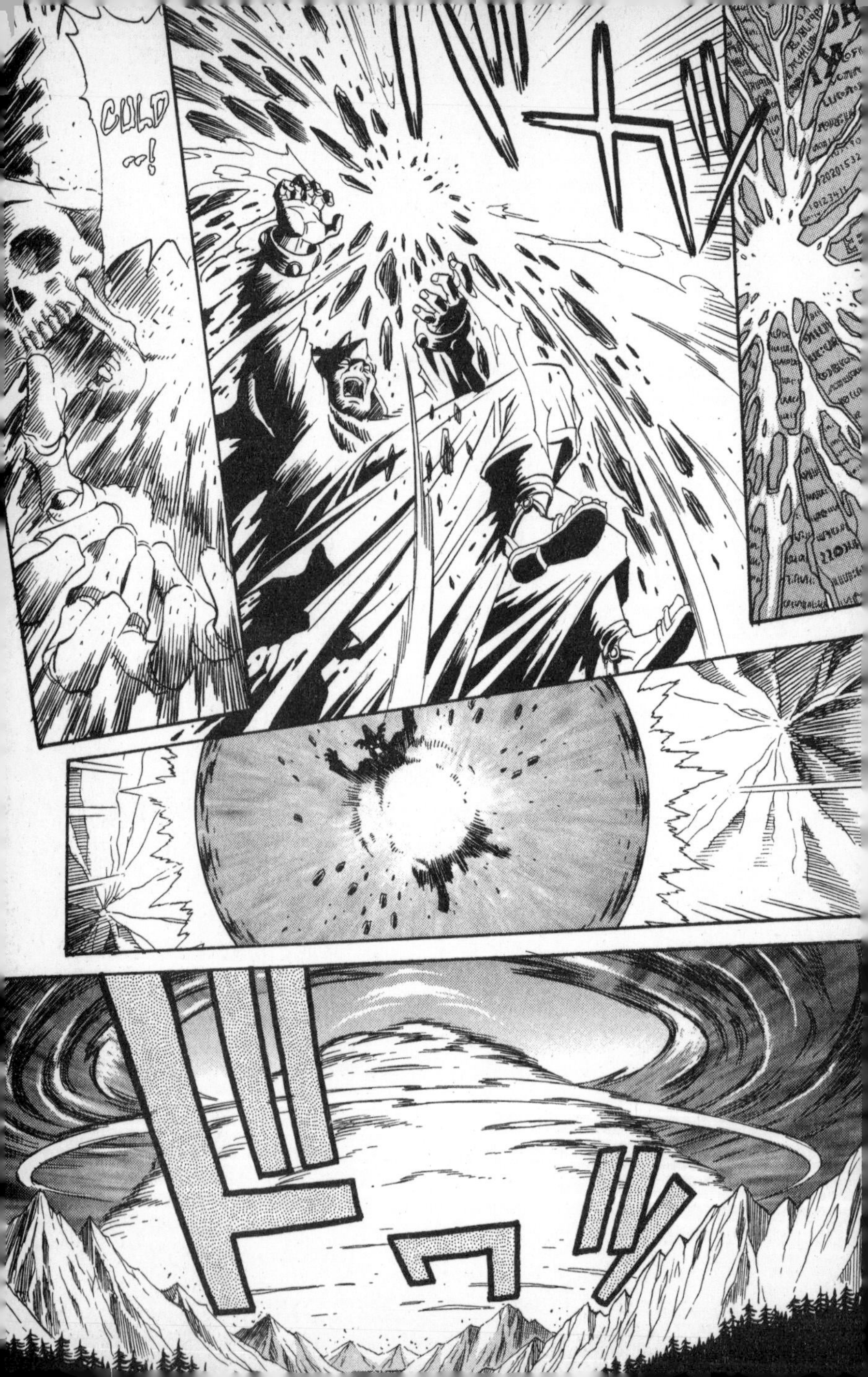
CULD
--!

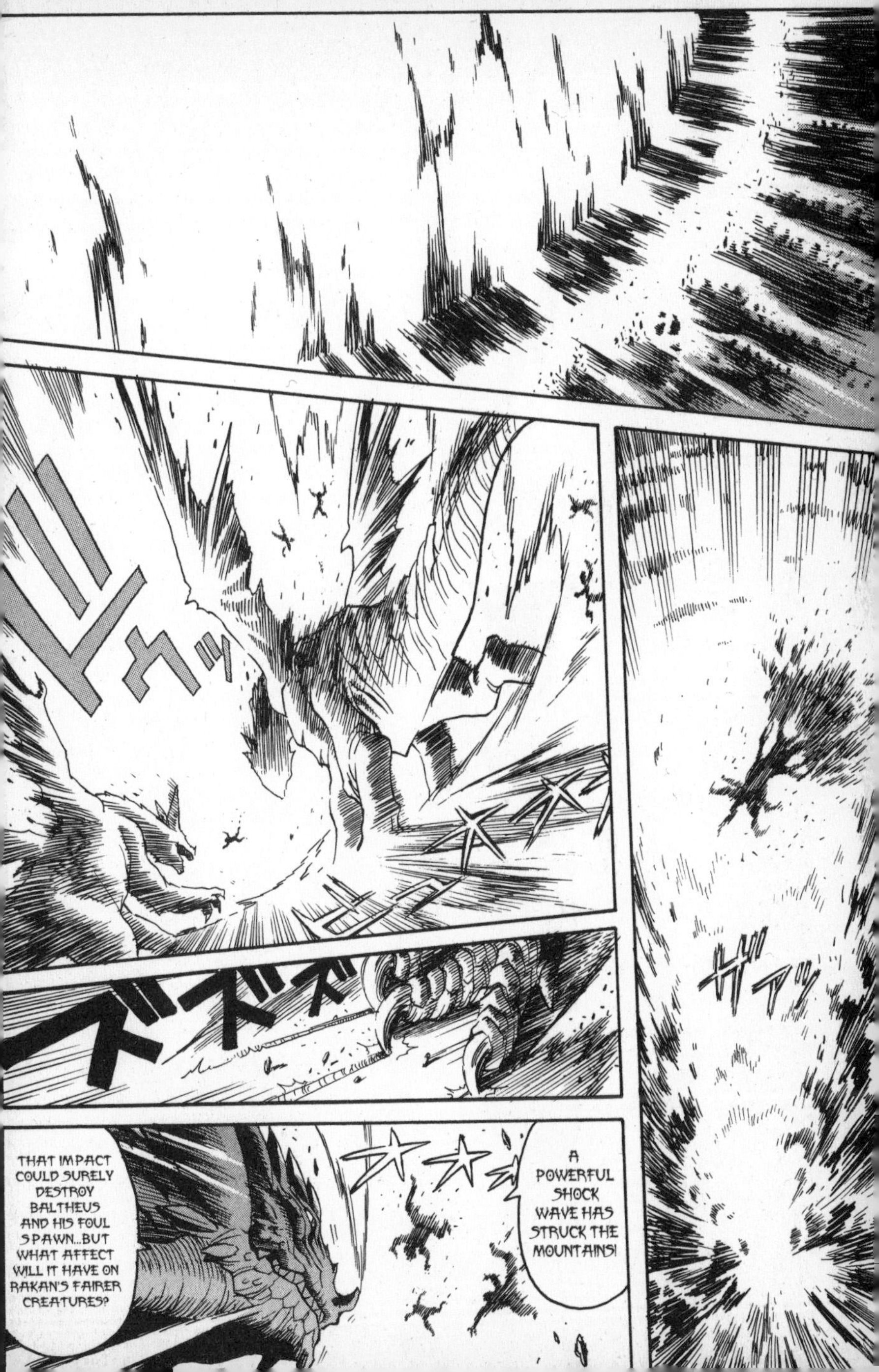
A POWERFUL SHOCK WAVE HAS STRUCK THE MOUNTAINS!
THAT IMPACT COULD SURELY DESTROY BALTHEUS AND HIS FOUL SPAWN...BUT WHAT AFFECT WILL IT HAVE ON RAKAN'S FAIRER CREATURES?

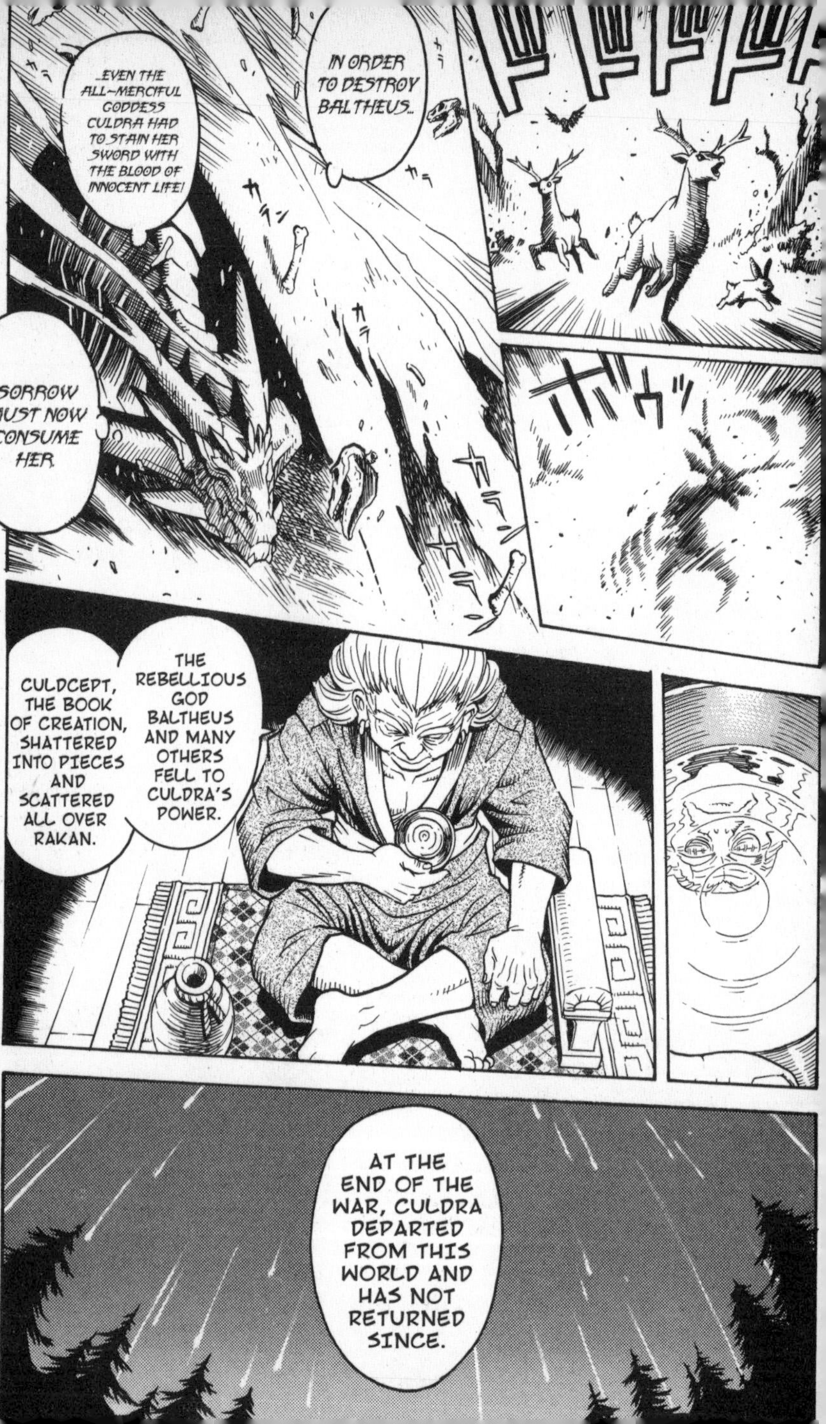
IN ORDER TO DESTROY BALTHEUS...
...EVEN THE ALL-MERCIFUL GODDESS CULDRA HAD TO STAIN HER SWORD WITH THE BLOOD OF INNOCENT LIFE!
SORROW MUST NOW CONSUME HER.
THE REBELLIOUS GOD BALTHEUS AND MANY OTHERS FELL TO CULDRA'S POWER.
CULDCEPT, THE BOOK OF CREATION, SHATTERED INTO PIECES AND SCATTERED ALL OVER RAKAN.
AT THE END OF THE WAR, CULDRA DEPARTED FROM THIS WORLD AND HAS NOT RETURNED SINCE.

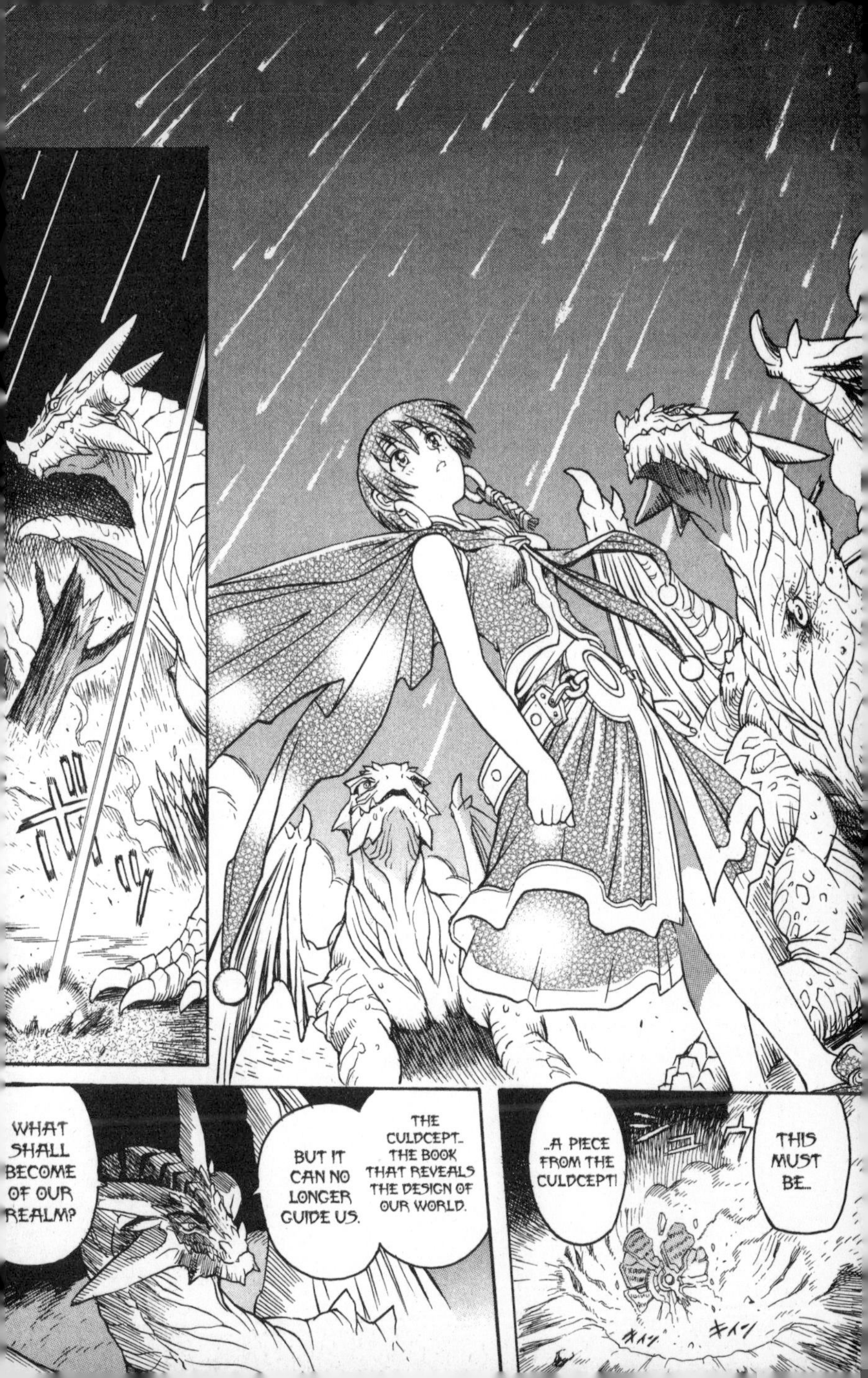
THIS MUST BE...
...A PIECE FROM THE CULDCEPT!
THE CULDCEPT... THE BOOK THAT REVEALS THE DESIGN OF OUR WORLD.
BUT IT CAN NO LONGER GUIDE US.
WHAT SHALL BECOME OF OUR REALM?

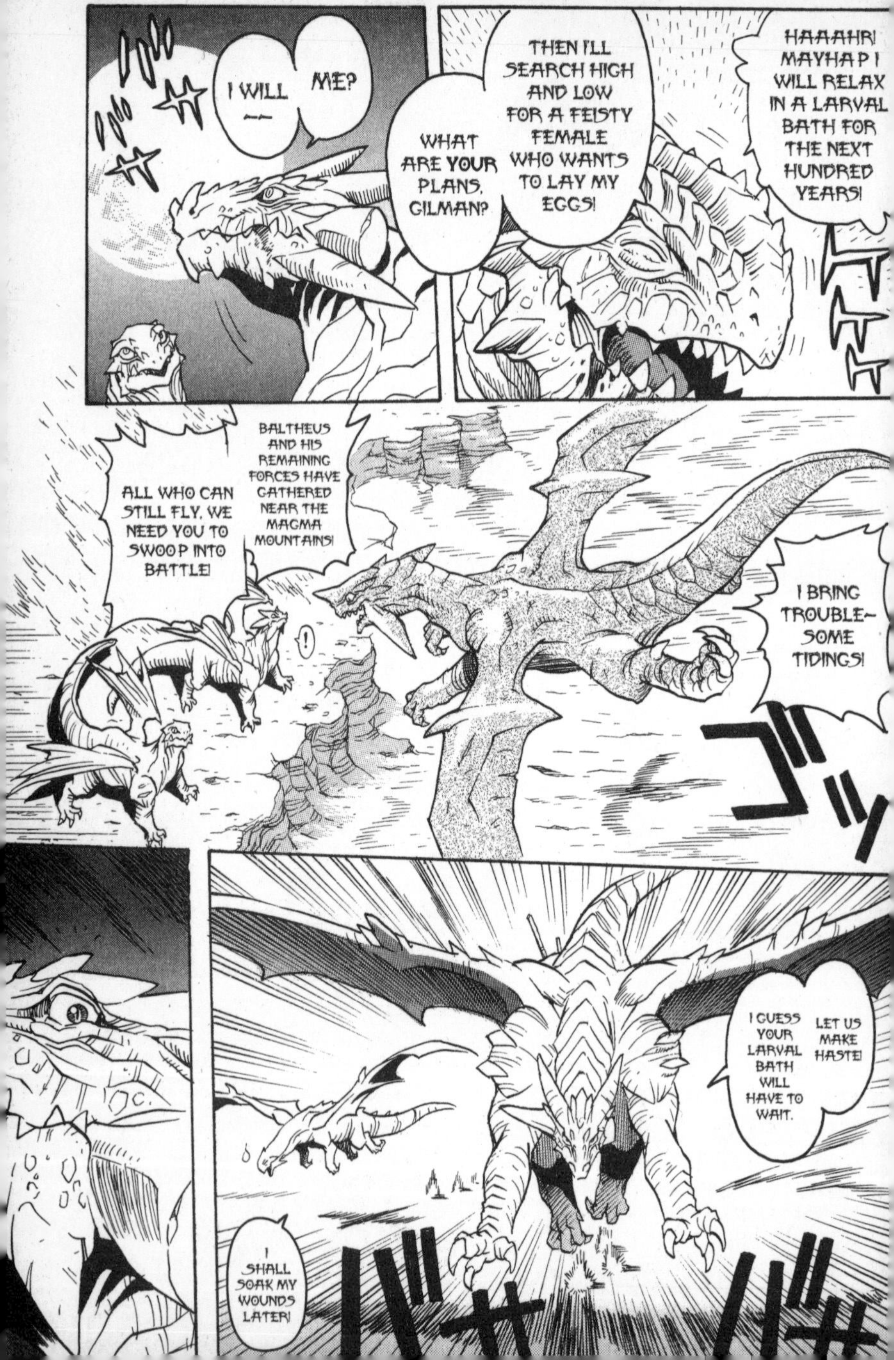
HAAAHR! MAYHAP I WILL RELAX IN A LARVAL BATH FOR THE NEXT HUNDRED YEARS!
THEN I'LL SEARCH HIGH AND LOW FOR A FEISTY FEMALE WHO WANTS TO LAY MY EGGS!
WHAT ARE **YOUR** PLANS, GILMAN?
ME?
I WILL --
I BRING TROUBLE-SOME TIDINGS!
BALTHEUS AND HIS REMAINING FORCES HAVE GATHERED NEAR THE MAGMA MOUNTAINS!
ALL WHO CAN STILL FLY, WE NEED YOU TO SWOOP INTO BATTLE!
!
LET US MAKE HASTE!
I GUESS YOUR LARVAL BATH WILL HAVE TO WAIT.
I SHALL SOAK MY WOUNDS LATER!

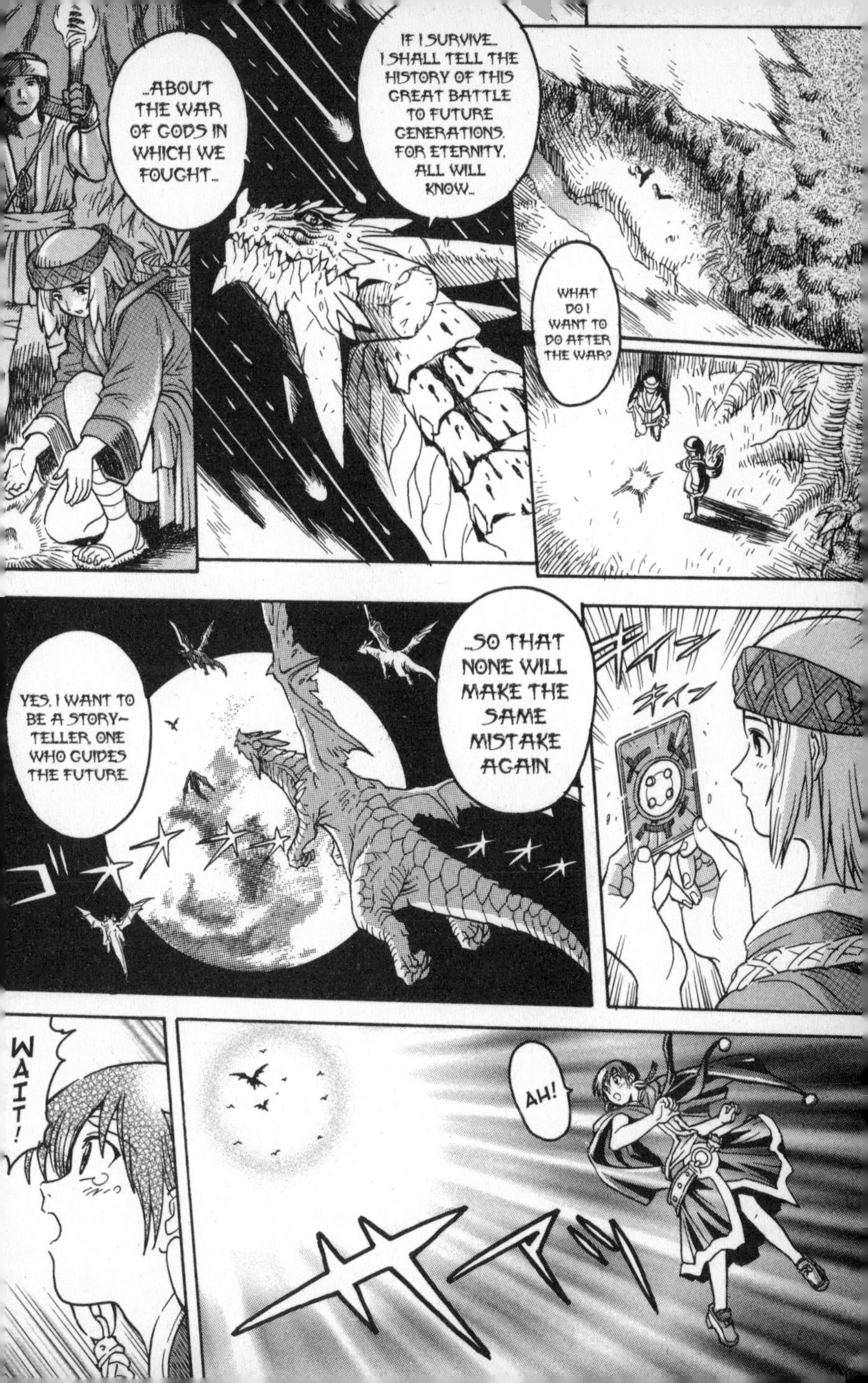
WHAT DO I WANT TO DO AFTER THE WAR?
IF I SURVIVE... I SHALL TELL THE HISTORY OF THIS GREAT BATTLE TO FUTURE GENERATIONS. FOR ETERNITY, ALL WILL KNOW...
...ABOUT THE WAR OF GODS IN WHICH WE FOUGHT...
...SO THAT NONE WILL MAKE THE SAME MISTAKE AGAIN.
YES, I WANT TO BE A STORY-TELLER, ONE WHO GUIDES THE FUTURE
AH!
WAIT!

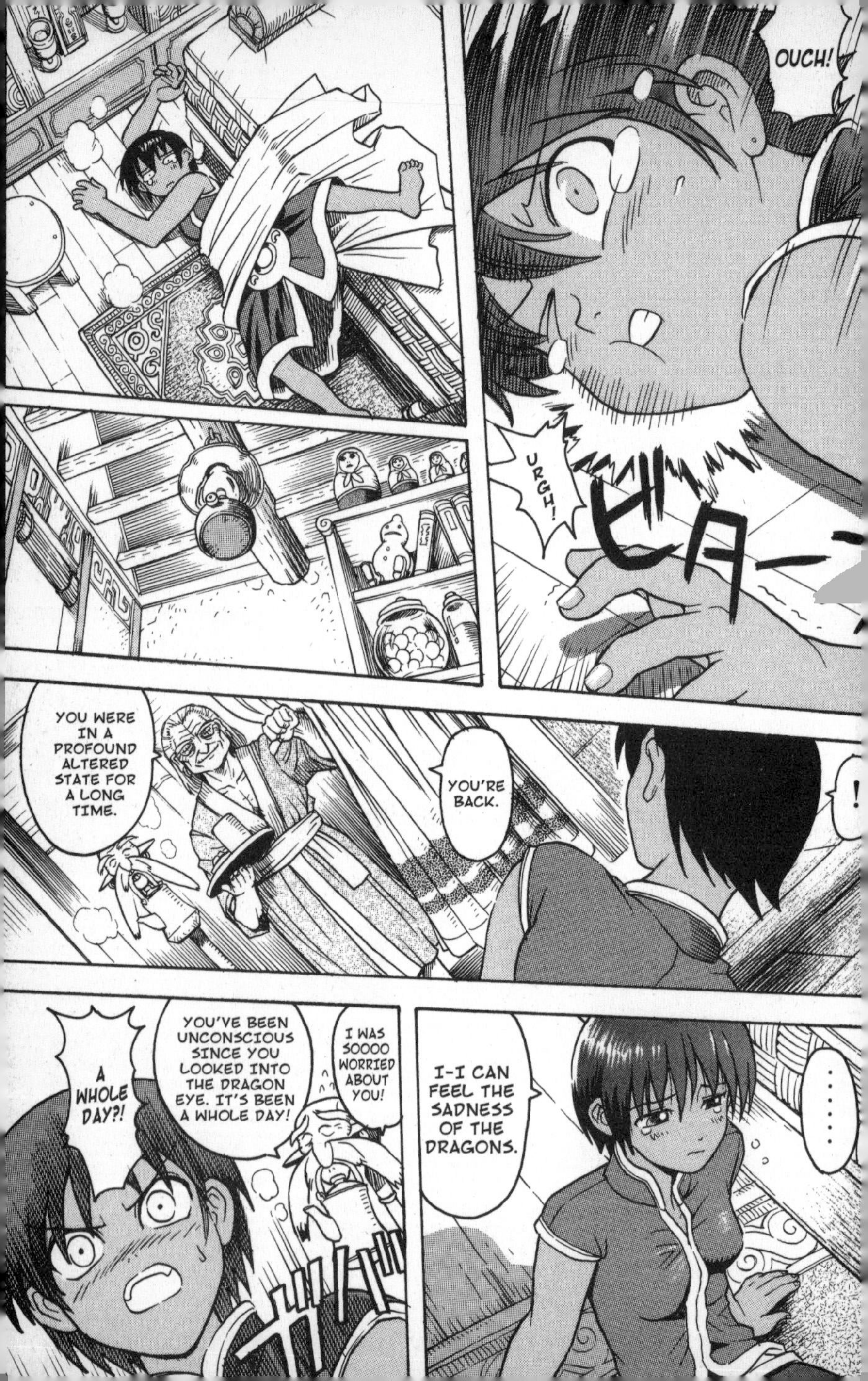
OUCH!
URGH!
!
YOU'RE BACK.
YOU WERE IN A PROFOUND ALTERED STATE FOR A LONG TIME.
......
I-I CAN FEEL THE SADNESS OF THE DRAGONS.
I WAS SOOOO WORRIED ABOUT YOU!
YOU'VE BEEN UNCONSCIOUS SINCE YOU LOOKED INTO THE DRAGON EYE. IT'S BEEN A WHOLE DAY!
A WHOLE DAY?!

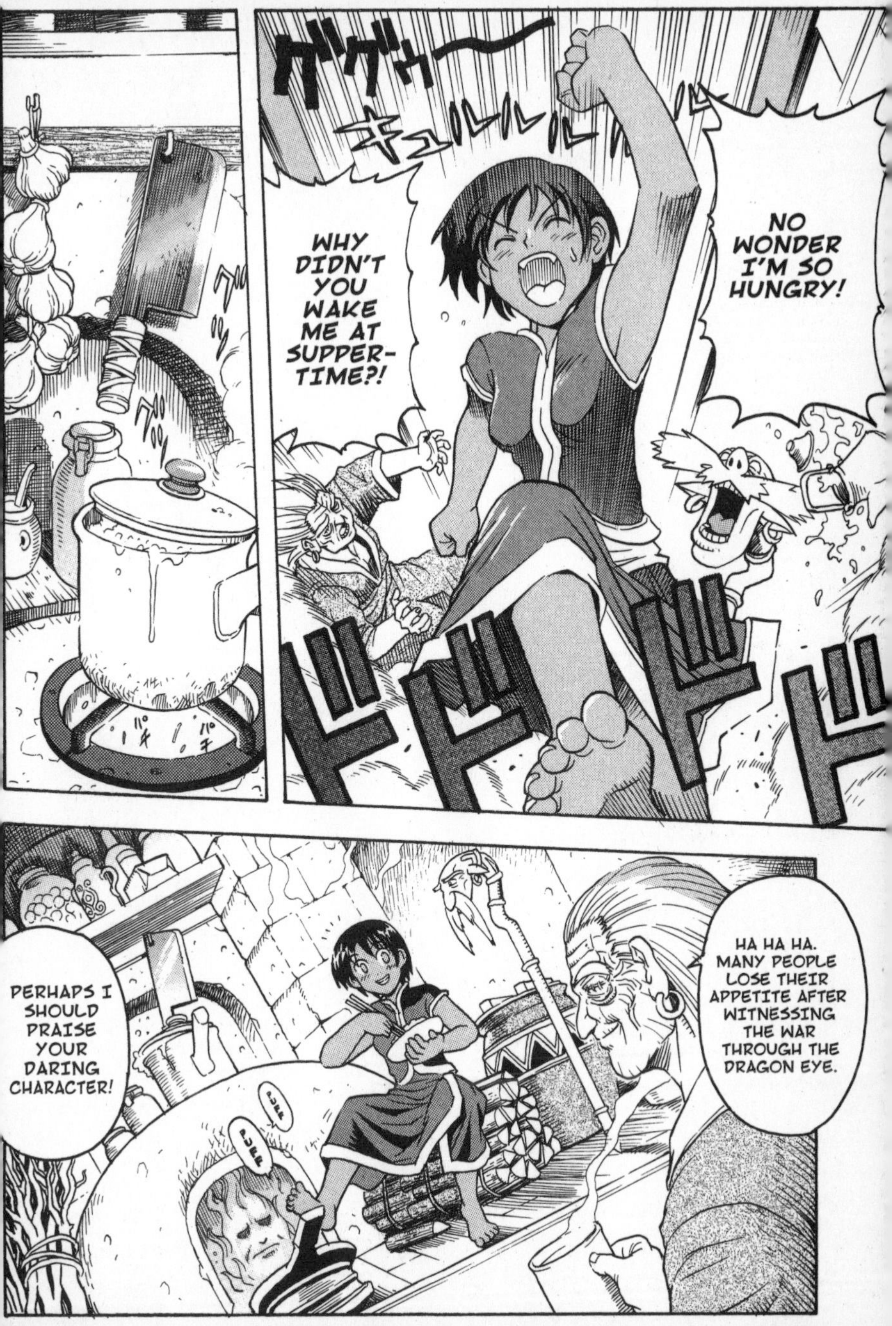
NO WONDER I'M SO HUNGRY!
WHY DIDN'T YOU WAKE ME AT SUPPER-TIME?!
HA HA HA. MANY PEOPLE LOSE THEIR APPETITE AFTER WITNESSING THE WAR THROUGH THE DRAGON EYE.
PERHAPS I SHOULD PRAISE YOUR DARING CHARACTER!

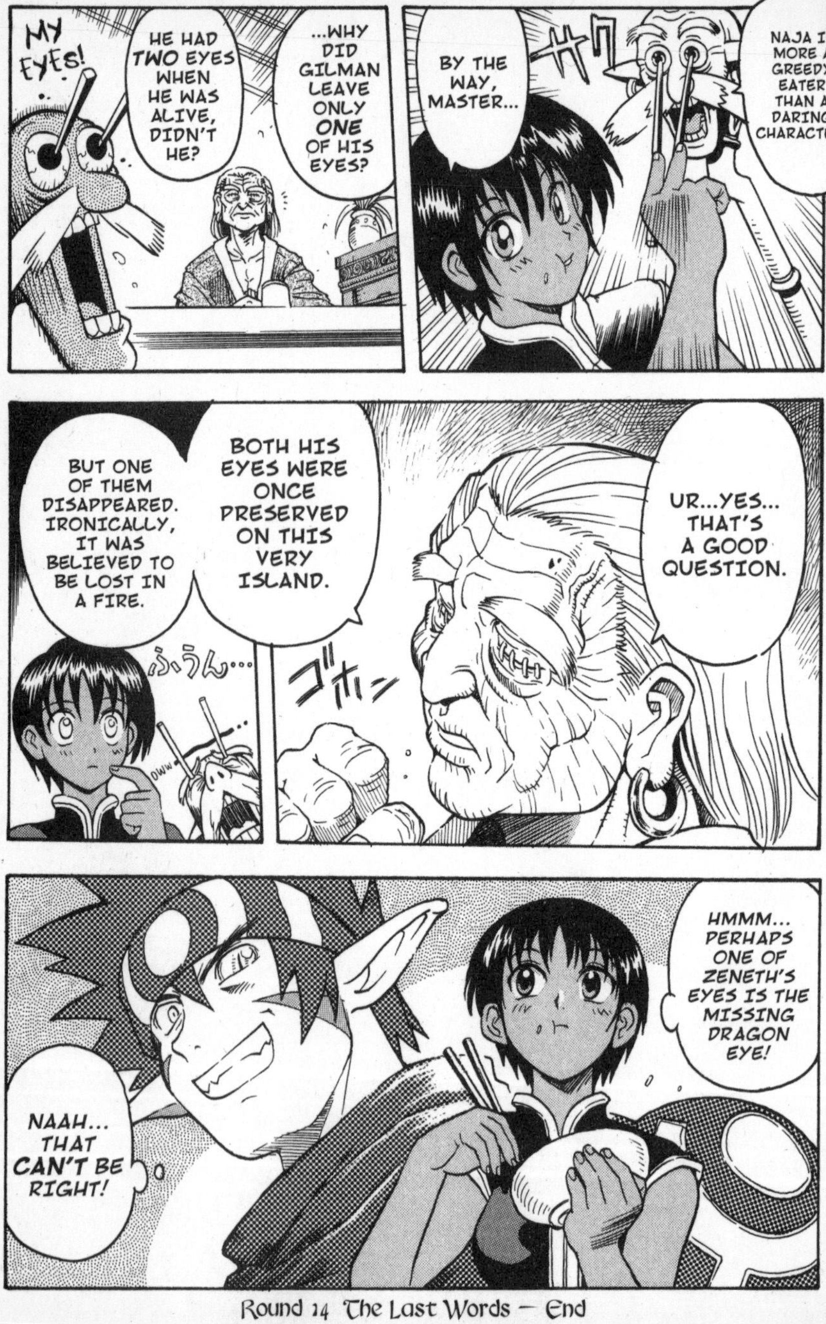
NAJA IS MORE A GREEDY EATER THAN A DARING CHARACTER
BY THE WAY, MASTER...
ザク
...WHY DID GILMAN LEAVE ONLY ONE OF HIS EYES?
HE HAD TWO EYES WHEN HE WAS ALIVE, DIDN'T HE?
MY EYES!
UR...YES... THAT'S A GOOD QUESTION.
ゴホン
BOTH HIS EYES WERE ONCE PRESERVED ON THIS VERY ISLAND.
BUT ONE OF THEM DISAPPEARED. IRONICALLY, IT WAS BELIEVED TO BE LOST IN A FIRE.
ふうん…
OWW
HMMM... PERHAPS ONE OF ZENETH'S EYES IS THE MISSING DRAGON EYE!
NAAH... THAT CAN'T BE RIGHT!

Round 14 The Last Words — End

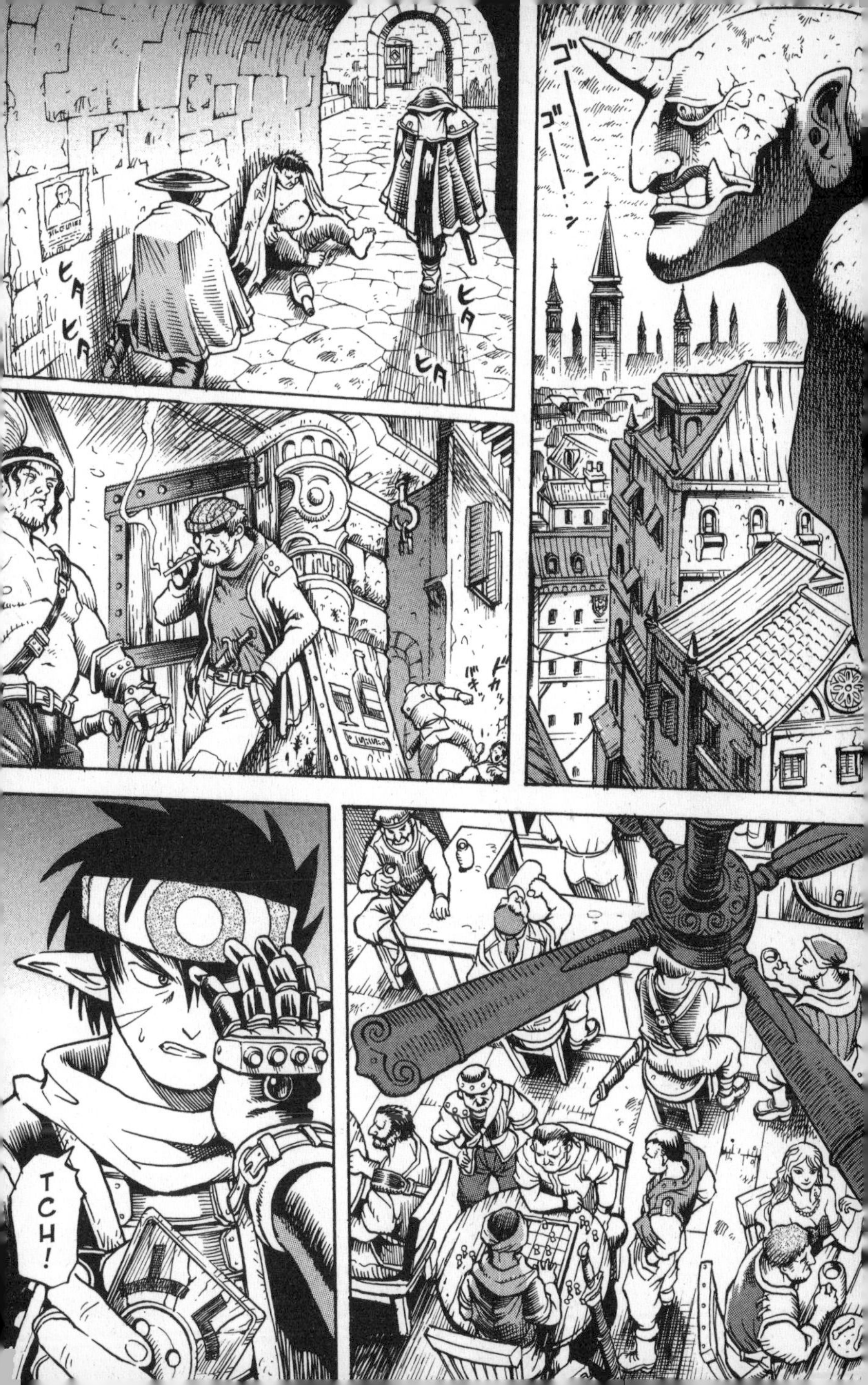
ゴーン
ゴーン
ヒタ
ヒタ
ヒタ
ヒタ
ドカッ
バキッ
TCH!

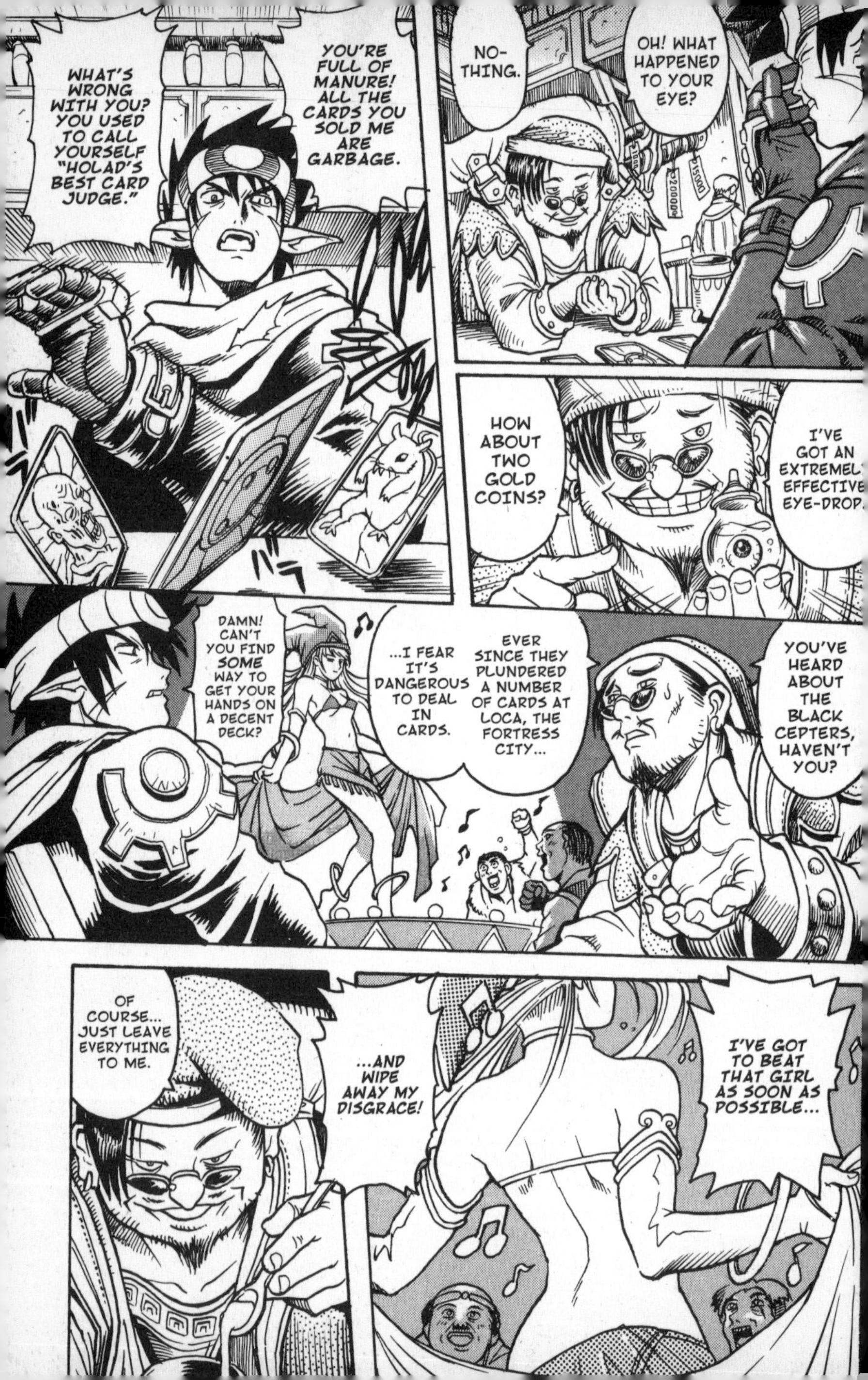
OH! WHAT HAPPENED TO YOUR EYE?
NO-THING.
I'VE GOT AN EXTREMEL EFFECTIVE EYE-DROP.
HOW ABOUT TWO GOLD COINS?
YOU'RE FULL OF MANURE! ALL THE CARDS YOU SOLD ME ARE GARBAGE.
WHAT'S WRONG WITH YOU? YOU USED TO CALL YOURSELF "HOLAD'S BEST CARD JUDGE."
YOU'VE HEARD ABOUT THE BLACK CEPTERS, HAVEN'T YOU?
EVER SINCE THEY PLUNDERED A NUMBER OF CARDS AT LOCA, THE FORTRESS CITY...
...I FEAR IT'S DANGEROUS TO DEAL IN CARDS.
DAMN! CAN'T YOU FIND **SOME** WAY TO GET YOUR HANDS ON A DECENT DECK?
I'VE GOT TO BEAT THAT GIRL AS SOON AS POSSIBLE...
...AND WIPE AWAY MY DISGRACE!
OF COURSE... JUST LEAVE EVERYTHING TO ME.

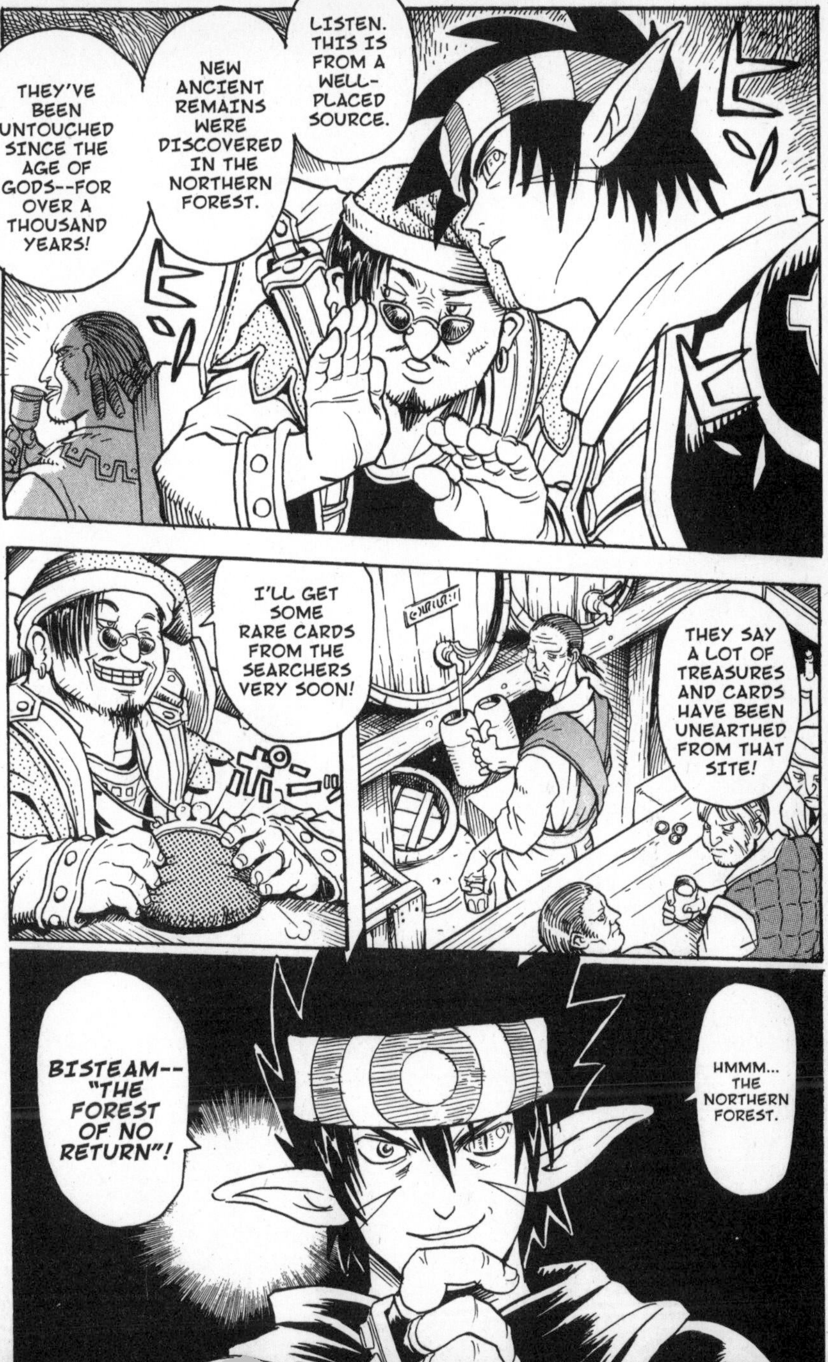

LISTEN. THIS IS FROM A WELL-PLACED SOURCE.
NEW ANCIENT REMAINS WERE DISCOVERED IN THE NORTHERN FOREST.
THEY'VE BEEN UNTOUCHED SINCE THE AGE OF GODS--FOR OVER A THOUSAND YEARS!
THEY SAY A LOT OF TREASURES AND CARDS HAVE BEEN UNEARTHED FROM THAT SITE!
I'LL GET SOME RARE CARDS FROM THE SEARCHERS VERY SOON!
ポーンッ
HMMM... THE NORTHERN FOREST.
BISTEAM--"THE FOREST OF NO RETURN"!

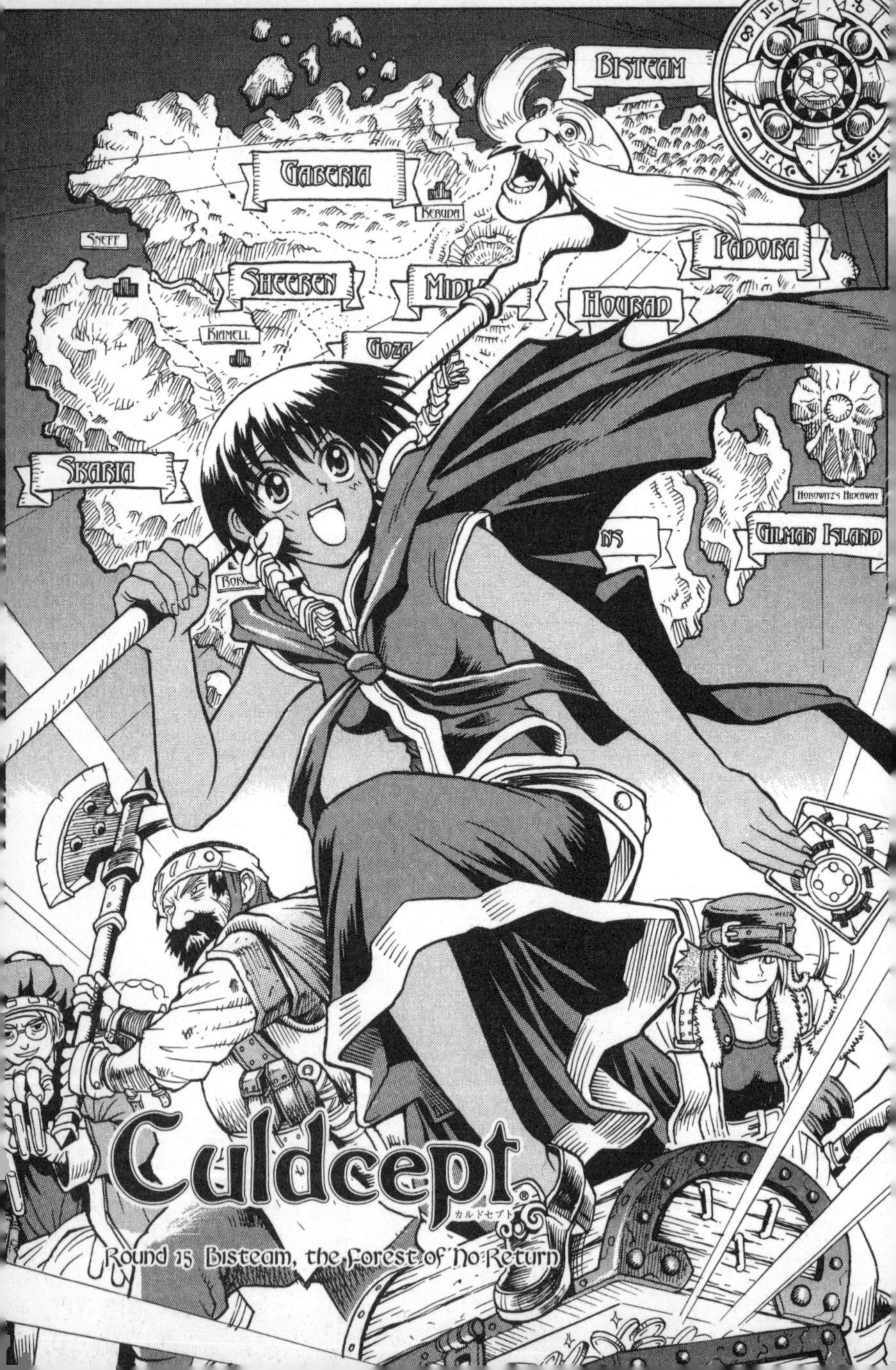
BISTEAM
GABERIA
KEBUDA
SNEFF
SHEEREN
PADORA
HOURAD
KIAMELL
GOZA
SKARIA
HOROWITZ'S HIDEAWAY
GILMAN ISLAND
Culdcept®
カルドセプト
Round 15 Bisteam, the Forest of No Return

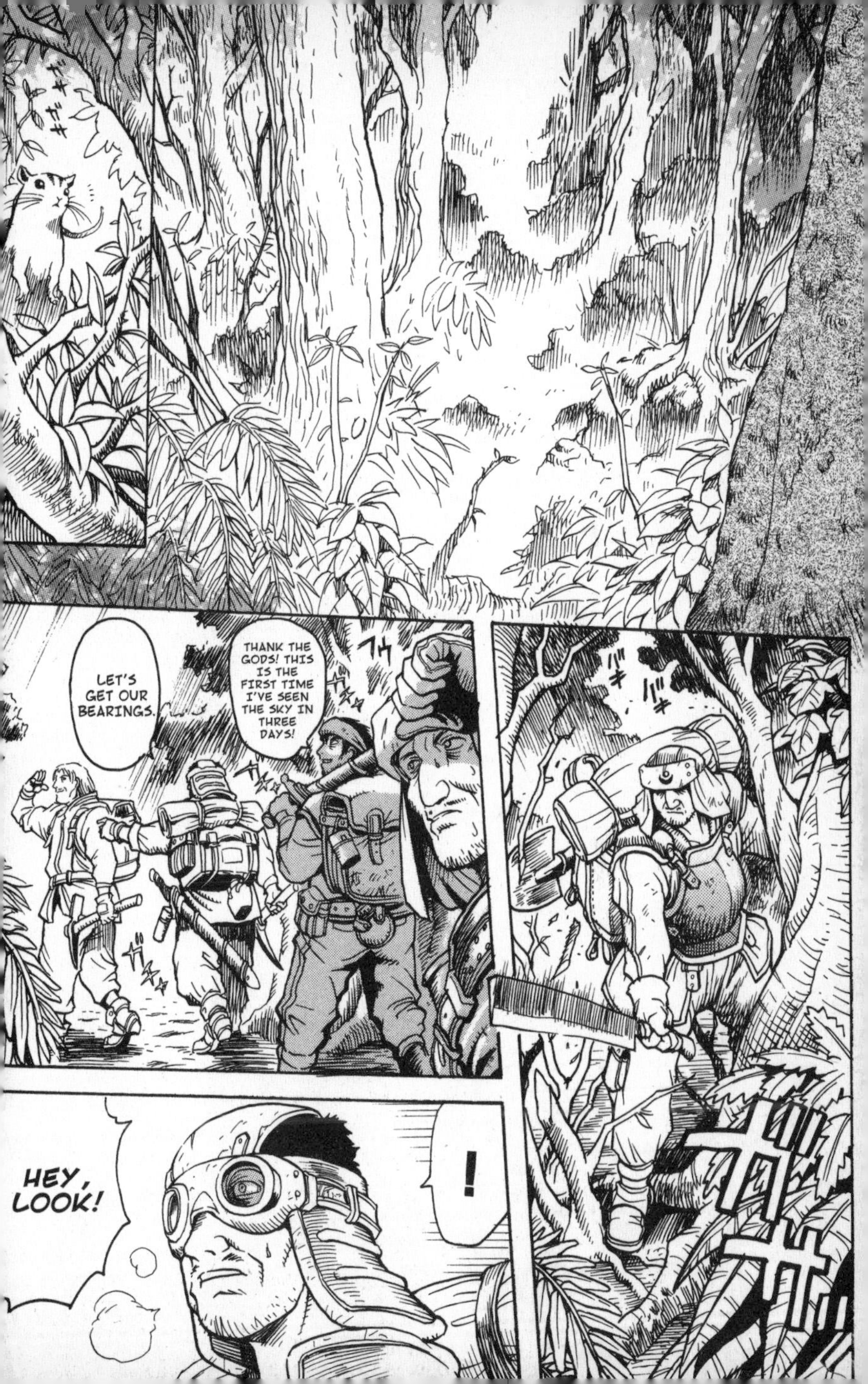
THANK THE GODS! THIS IS THE FIRST TIME I'VE SEEN THE SKY IN THREE DAYS!
LET'S GET OUR BEARINGS.
!
HEY, LOOK!

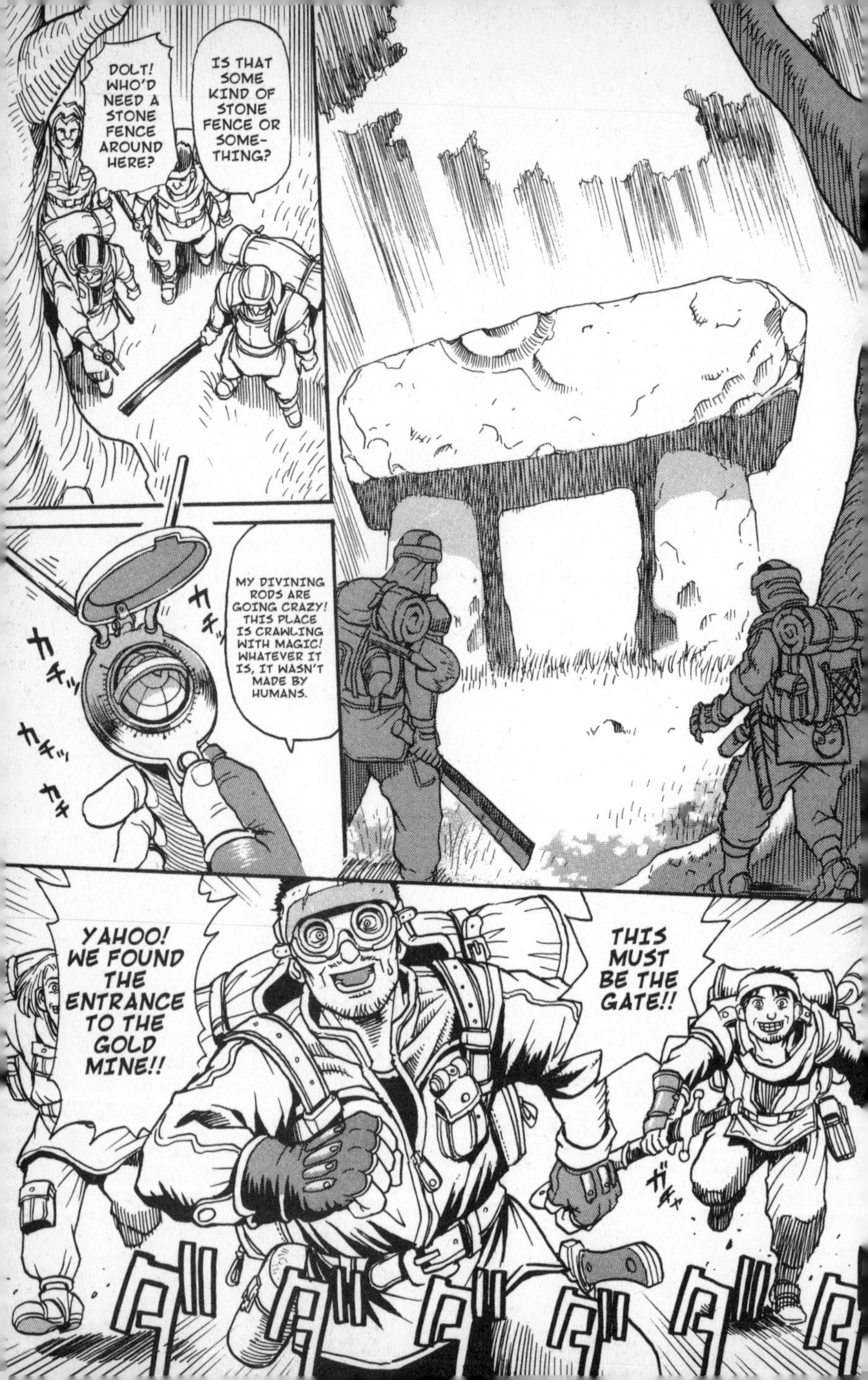
IS THAT SOME KIND OF STONE FENCE OR SOME-THING?
DOLT! WHO'D NEED A STONE FENCE AROUND HERE?
MY DIVINING RODS ARE GOING CRAZY! THIS PLACE IS CRAWLING WITH MAGIC! WHATEVER IT IS, IT WASN'T MADE BY HUMANS.
カチッ
カチッ
カチッ
カチ
THIS MUST BE THE GATE!!
YAHOO! WE FOUND THE ENTRANCE TO THE GOLD MINE!!
ガチャ

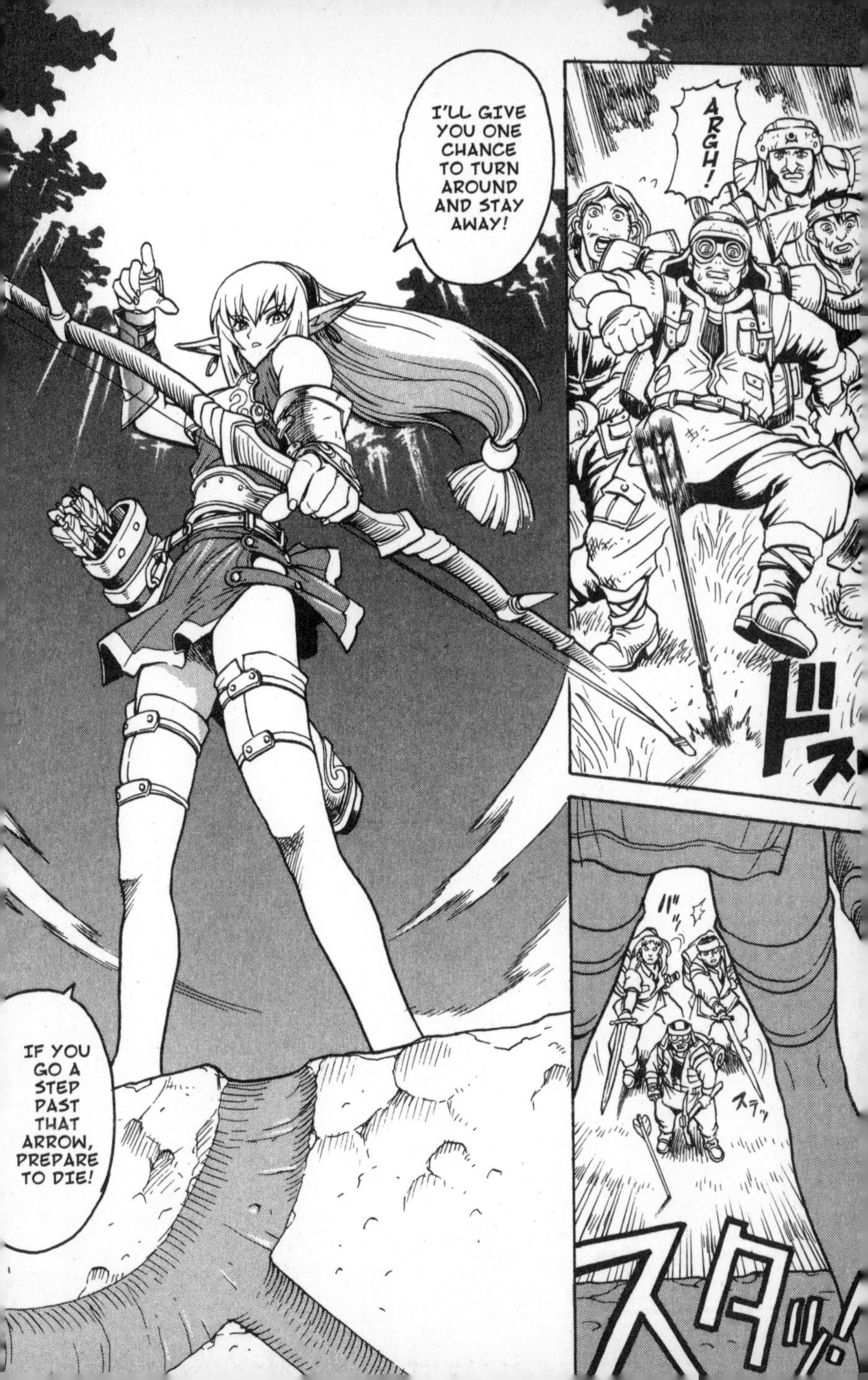
ARGH!
ドス
スタッ!
I'LL GIVE YOU ONE CHANCE TO TURN AROUND AND STAY AWAY!
IF YOU GO A STEP PAST THAT ARROW, PREPARE TO DIE!

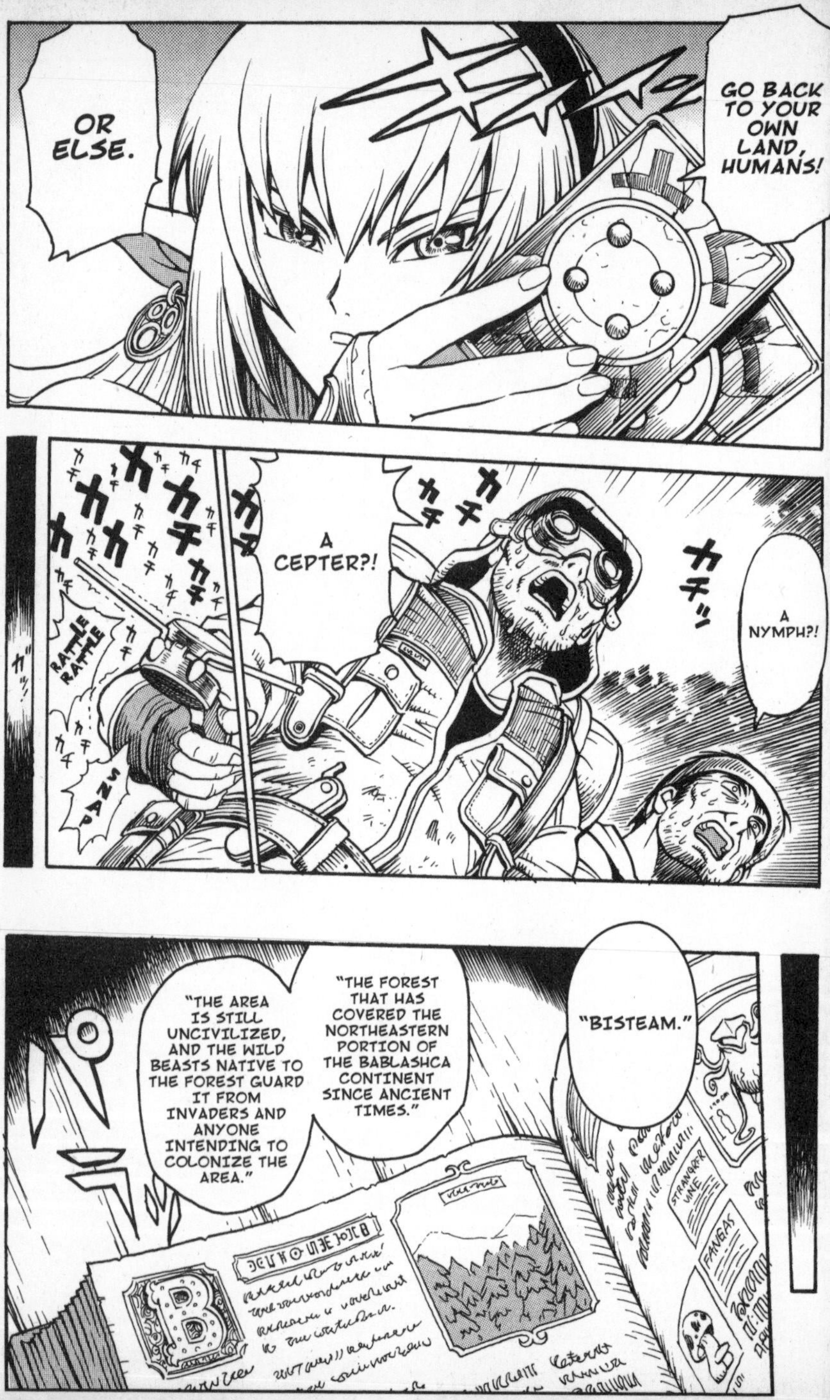
GO BACK TO YOUR OWN LAND, HUMANS!
OR ELSE.
A NYMPH?!
A CEPTER?!
RATTLE RATTLE
SNAP
"BISTEAM."
"THE FOREST THAT HAS COVERED THE NORTHEASTERN PORTION OF THE BABLASHCA CONTINENT SINCE ANCIENT TIMES."
"THE AREA IS STILL UNCIVILIZED, AND THE WILD BEASTS NATIVE TO THE FOREST GUARD IT FROM INVADERS AND ANYONE INTENDING TO COLONIZE THE AREA."
STRANGER VINE
FANGAS

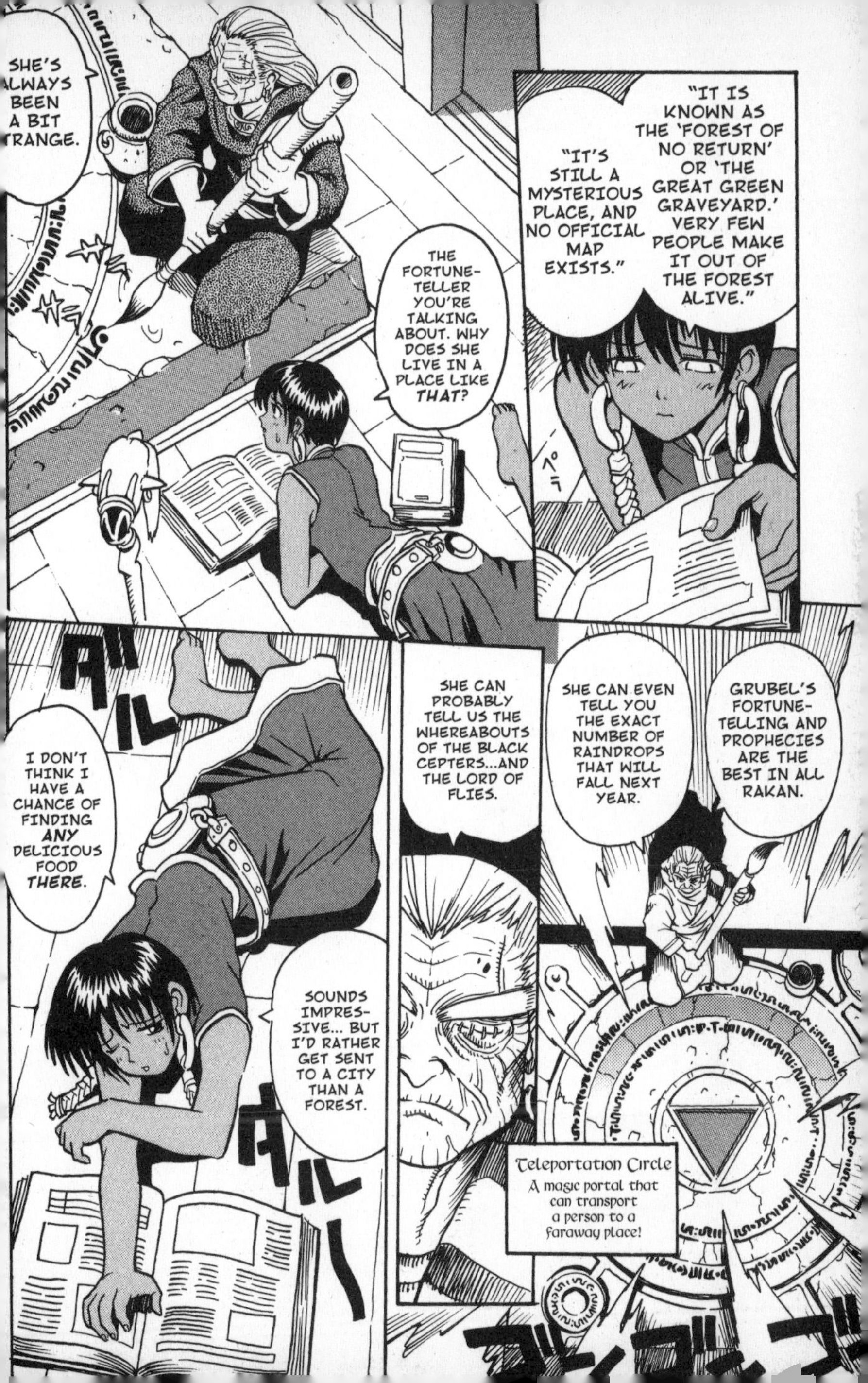
"IT IS KNOWN AS THE 'FOREST OF NO RETURN' OR 'THE GREAT GREEN GRAVEYARD.' VERY FEW PEOPLE MAKE IT OUT OF THE FOREST ALIVE."
"IT'S STILL A MYSTERIOUS PLACE, AND NO OFFICIAL MAP EXISTS."
THE FORTUNE-TELLER YOU'RE TALKING ABOUT. WHY DOES SHE LIVE IN A PLACE LIKE *THAT*?
SHE'S ALWAYS BEEN A BIT STRANGE.
GRUBEL'S FORTUNE-TELLING AND PROPHECIES ARE THE BEST IN ALL RAKAN.
SHE CAN EVEN TELL YOU THE EXACT NUMBER OF RAINDROPS THAT WILL FALL NEXT YEAR.
Teleportation Circle
A magic portal that can transport a person to a faraway place!
SHE CAN PROBABLY TELL US THE WHEREABOUTS OF THE BLACK CEPTERS...AND THE LORD OF FLIES.
SOUNDS IMPRESSIVE... BUT I'D RATHER GET SENT TO A CITY THAN A FOREST.
I DON'T THINK I HAVE A CHANCE OF FINDING *ANY* DELICIOUS FOOD *THERE*.

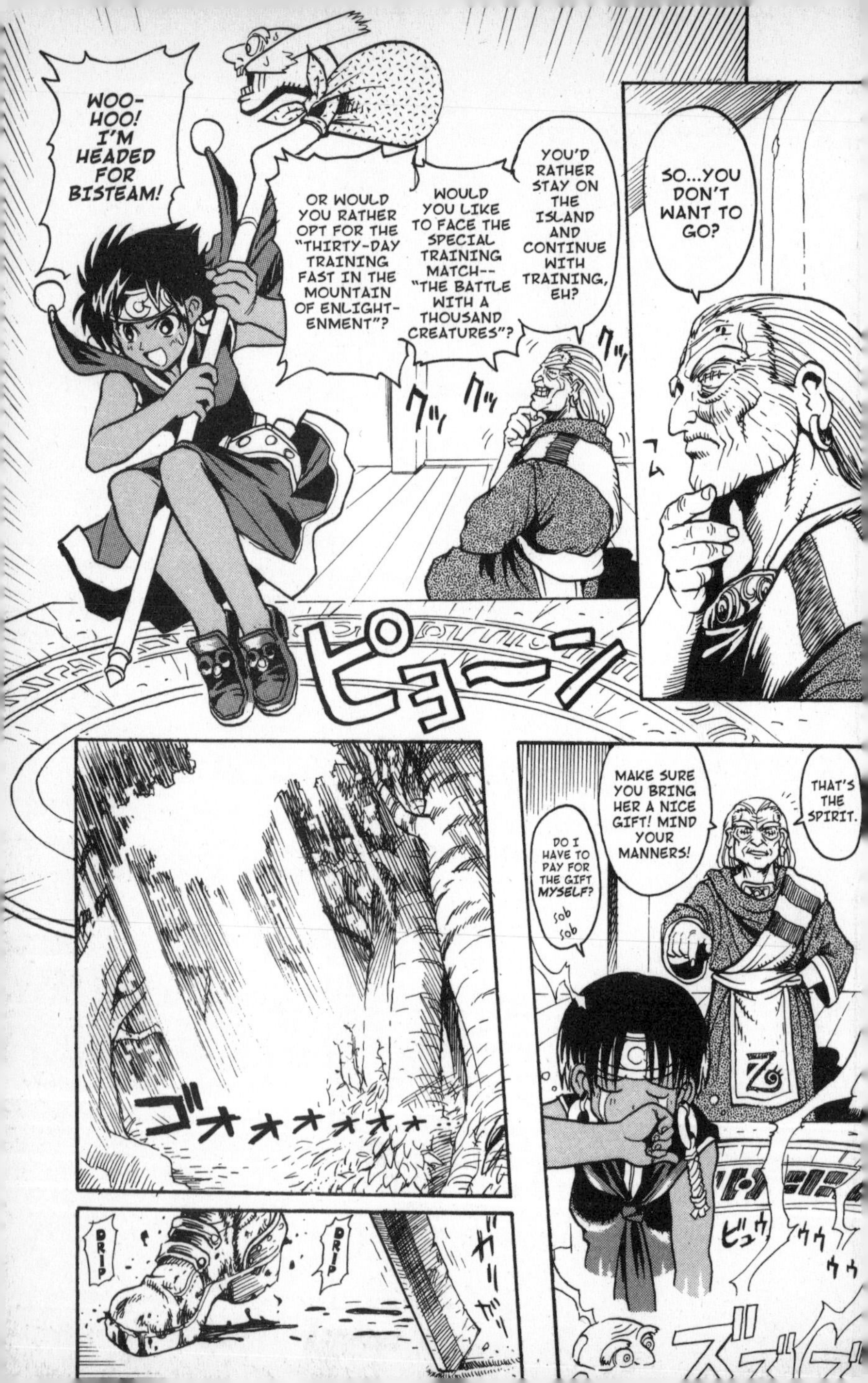
SO...YOU DON'T WANT TO GO?
フム
YOU'D RATHER STAY ON THE ISLAND AND CONTINUE WITH TRAINING, EH?
WOULD YOU LIKE TO FACE THE SPECIAL TRAINING MATCH-- "THE BATTLE WITH A THOUSAND CREATURES"?
OR WOULD YOU RATHER OPT FOR THE "THIRTY-DAY TRAINING FAST IN THE MOUNTAIN OF ENLIGHT-ENMENT"?
グッ
グッ
グッ
WOO-HOO! I'M HEADED FOR BISTEAM!
ピョ〜ン
THAT'S THE SPIRIT.
MAKE SURE YOU BRING HER A NICE GIFT! MIND YOUR MANNERS!
DO I HAVE TO PAY FOR THE GIFT MYSELF?
sob sob
ビュウウウウ
ゴオォォォォォォ
DRIP
DRIP
ガリガリ

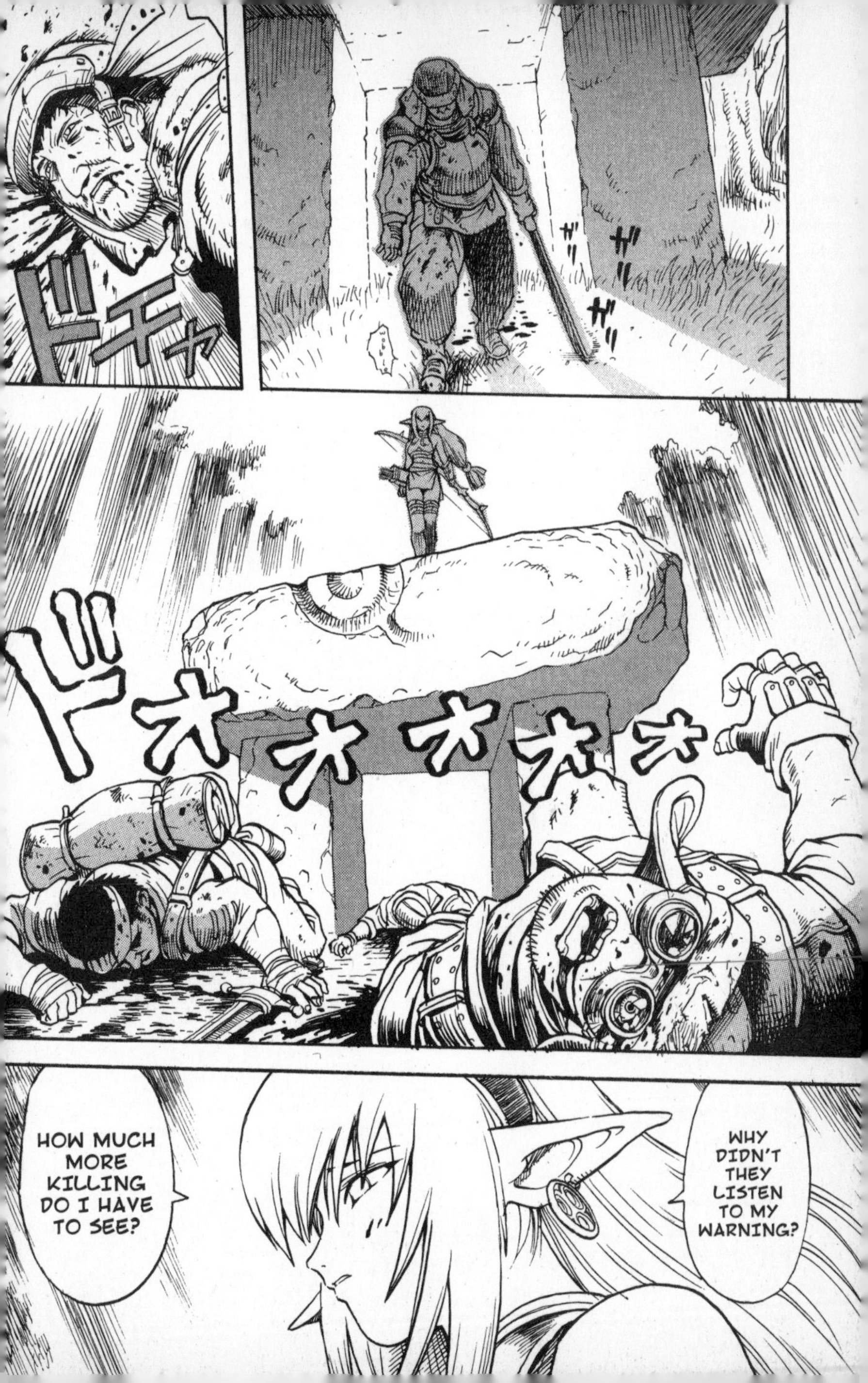
ザ
ザ
ザ
ドチャ
ドオオオオオ
WHY DIDN'T THEY LISTEN TO MY WARNING?
HOW MUCH MORE KILLING DO I HAVE TO SEE?

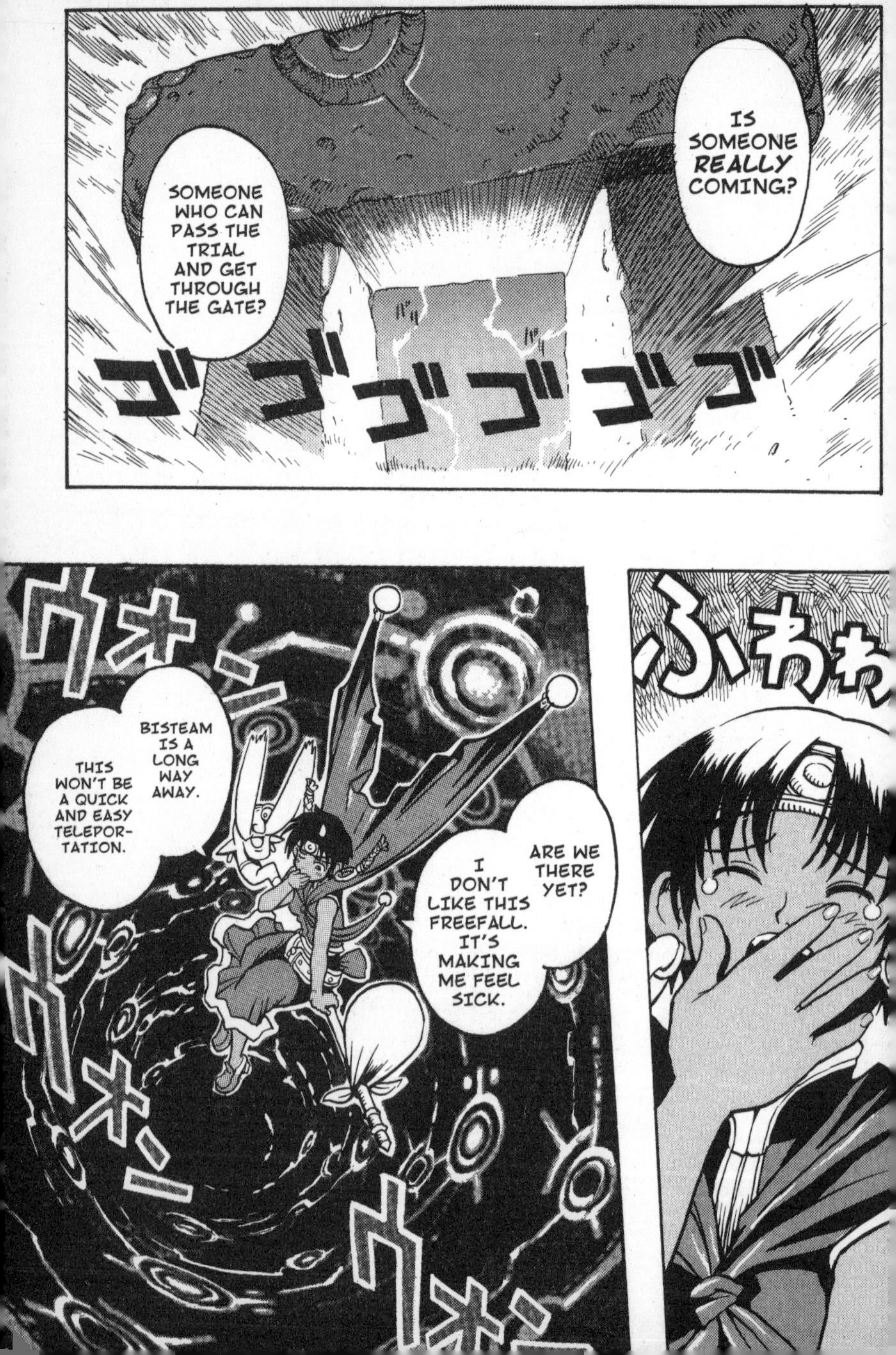
IS SOMEONE REALLY COMING?
SOMEONE WHO CAN PASS THE TRIAL AND GET THROUGH THE GATE?
ゴゴゴゴゴゴ
ふぉぉ
ARE WE THERE YET?
I DON'T LIKE THIS FREEFALL. IT'S MAKING ME FEEL SICK.
BISTEAM IS A LONG WAY AWAY.
THIS WON'T BE A QUICK AND EASY TELEPORTATION.
ウォーン
ウォーン
ウォ

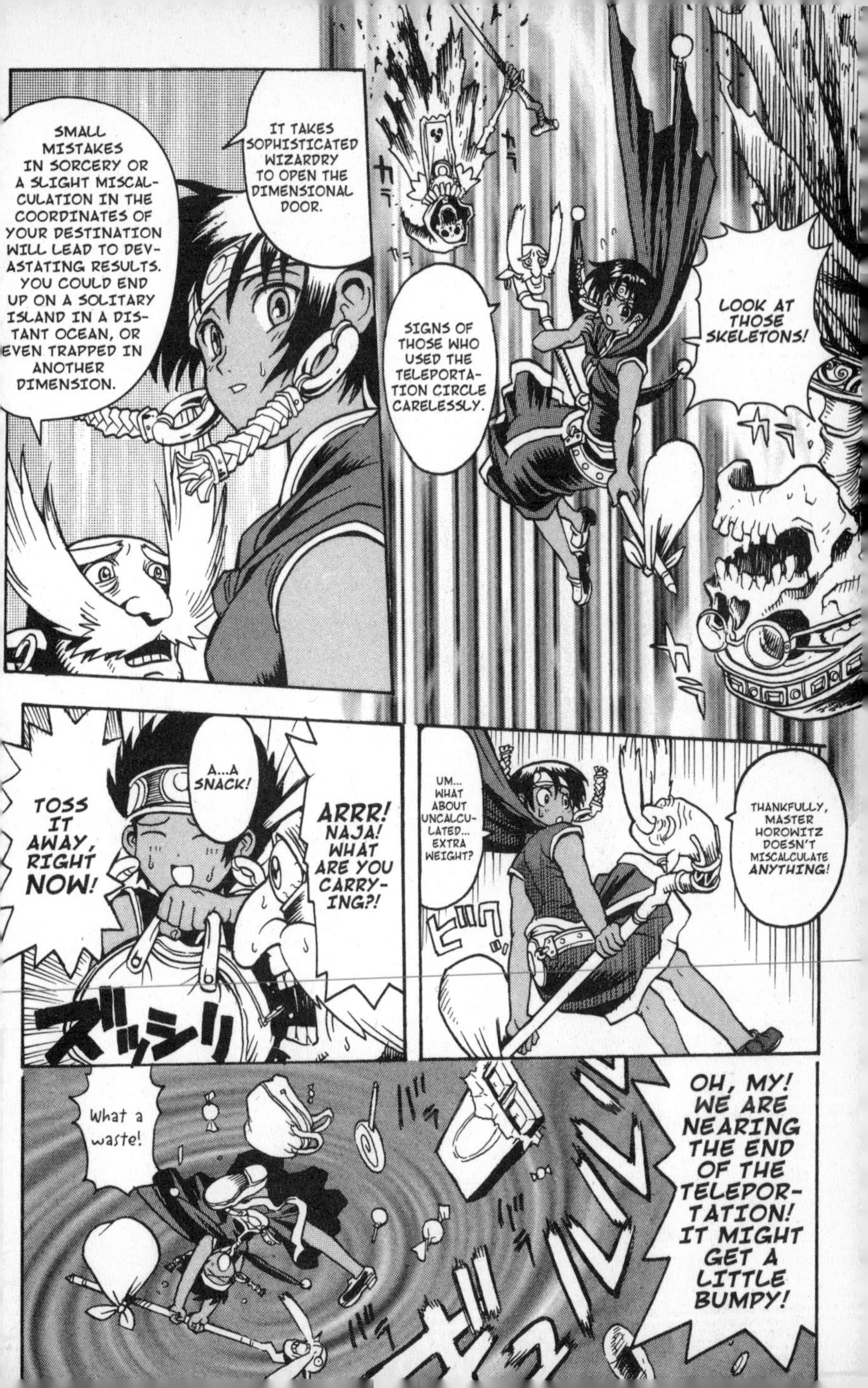
LOOK AT THOSE SKELETONS!
SIGNS OF THOSE WHO USED THE TELEPORTATION CIRCLE CARELESSLY.
IT TAKES SOPHISTICATED WIZARDRY TO OPEN THE DIMENSIONAL DOOR.
SMALL MISTAKES IN SORCERY OR A SLIGHT MISCALCULATION IN THE COORDINATES OF YOUR DESTINATION WILL LEAD TO DEVASTATING RESULTS. YOU COULD END UP ON A SOLITARY ISLAND IN A DISTANT OCEAN, OR EVEN TRAPPED IN ANOTHER DIMENSION.
THANKFULLY, MASTER HOROWITZ DOESN'T MISCALCULATE ANYTHING!
UM... WHAT ABOUT UNCALCULATED... EXTRA WEIGHT?
ARRR! NAJA! WHAT ARE YOU CARRYING?!
A...A SNACK!
TOSS IT AWAY, RIGHT NOW!
OH, MY! WE ARE NEARING THE END OF THE TELEPORTATION! IT MIGHT GET A LITTLE BUMPY!
What a waste!

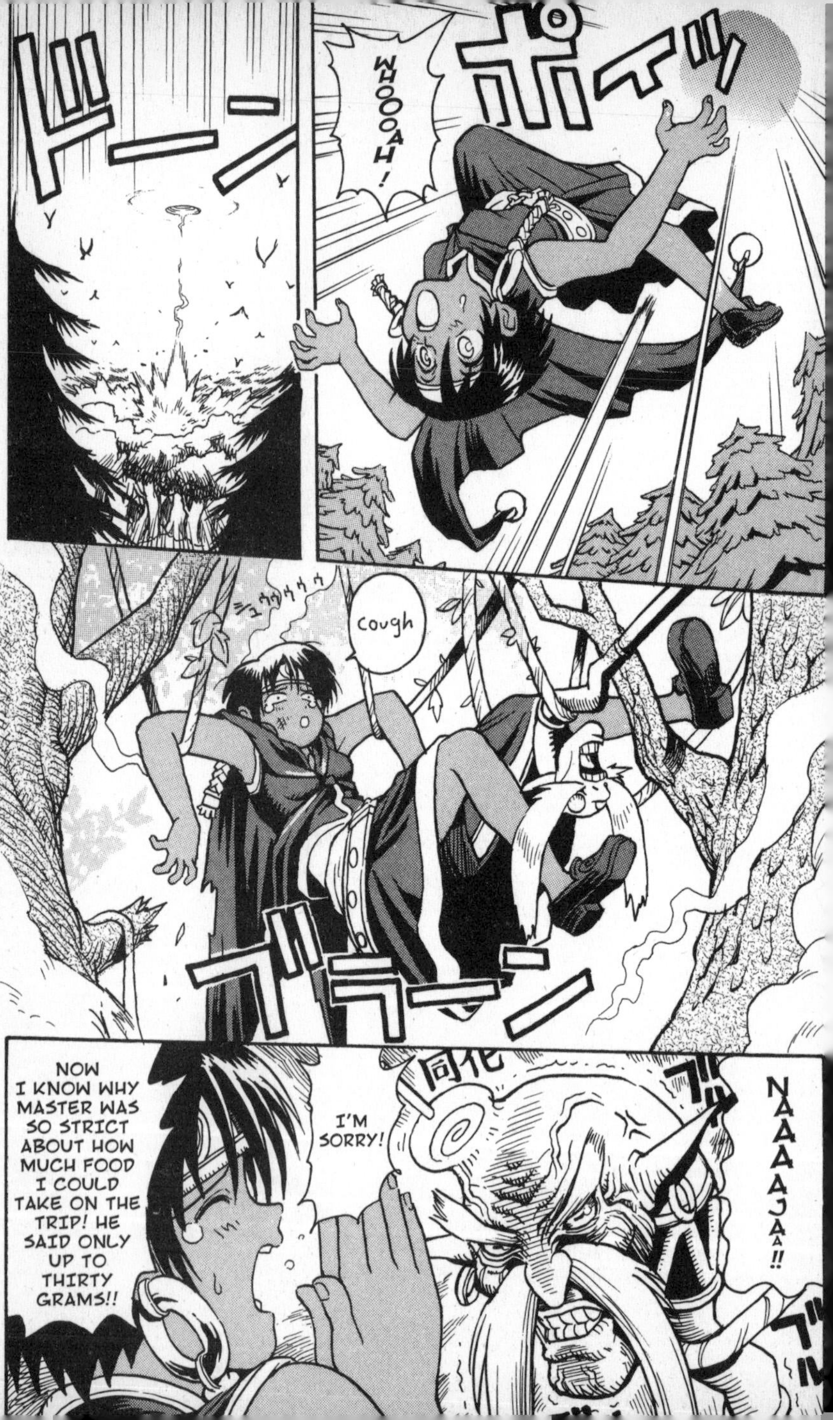

WHOOOAH!
ポイッ
ドーーン
cough
シュウウウウウ
ブラーン
NAAAAJA!!
同化
I'M SORRY!
NOW I KNOW WHY MASTER WAS SO STRICT ABOUT HOW MUCH FOOD I COULD TAKE ON THE TRIP! HE SAID ONLY UP TO THIRTY GRAMS!!

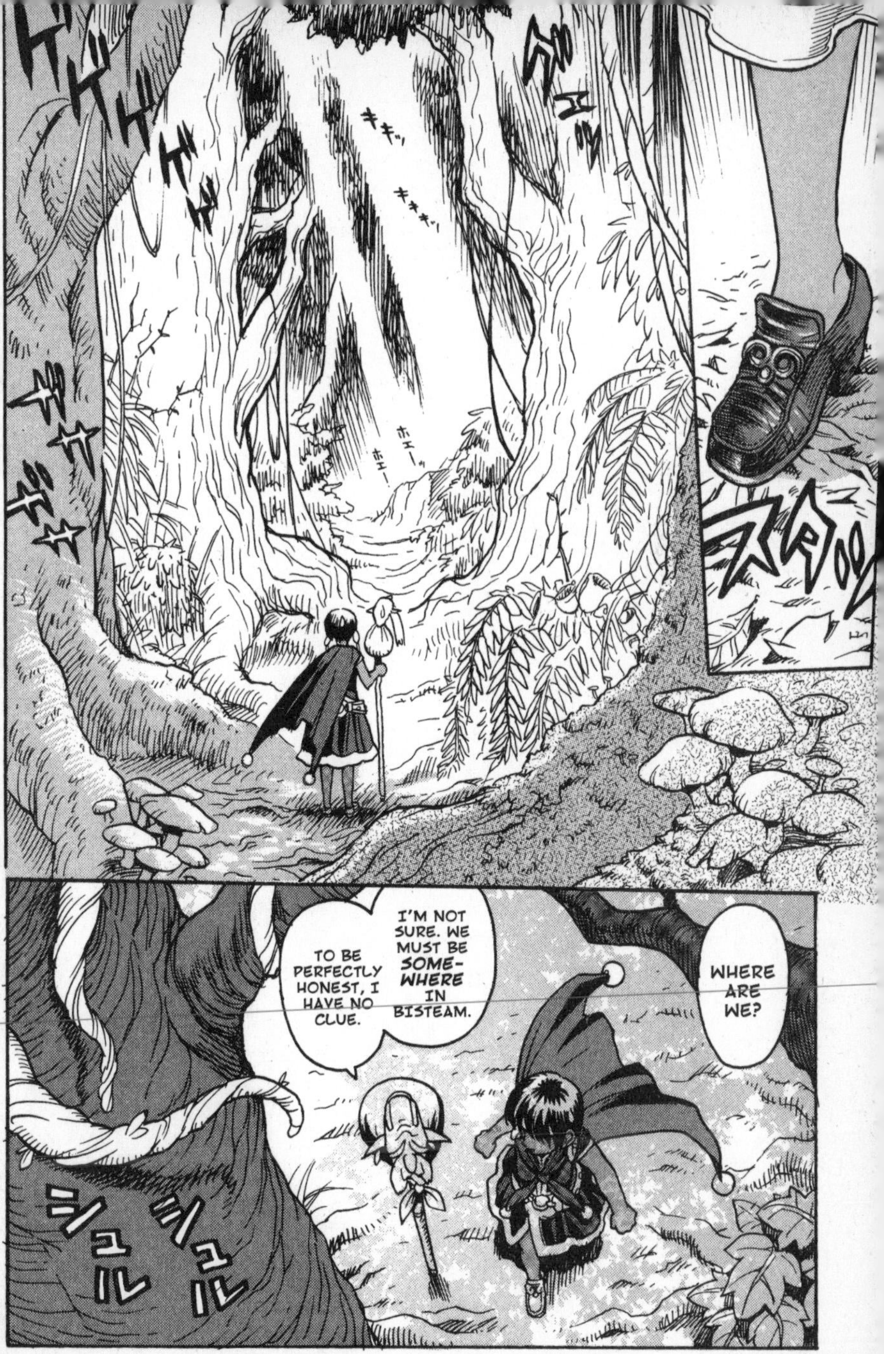
WHERE ARE WE?
I'M NOT SURE. WE MUST BE SOME-WHERE IN BISTEAM.
TO BE PERFECTLY HONEST, I HAVE NO CLUE.
シュル シュル

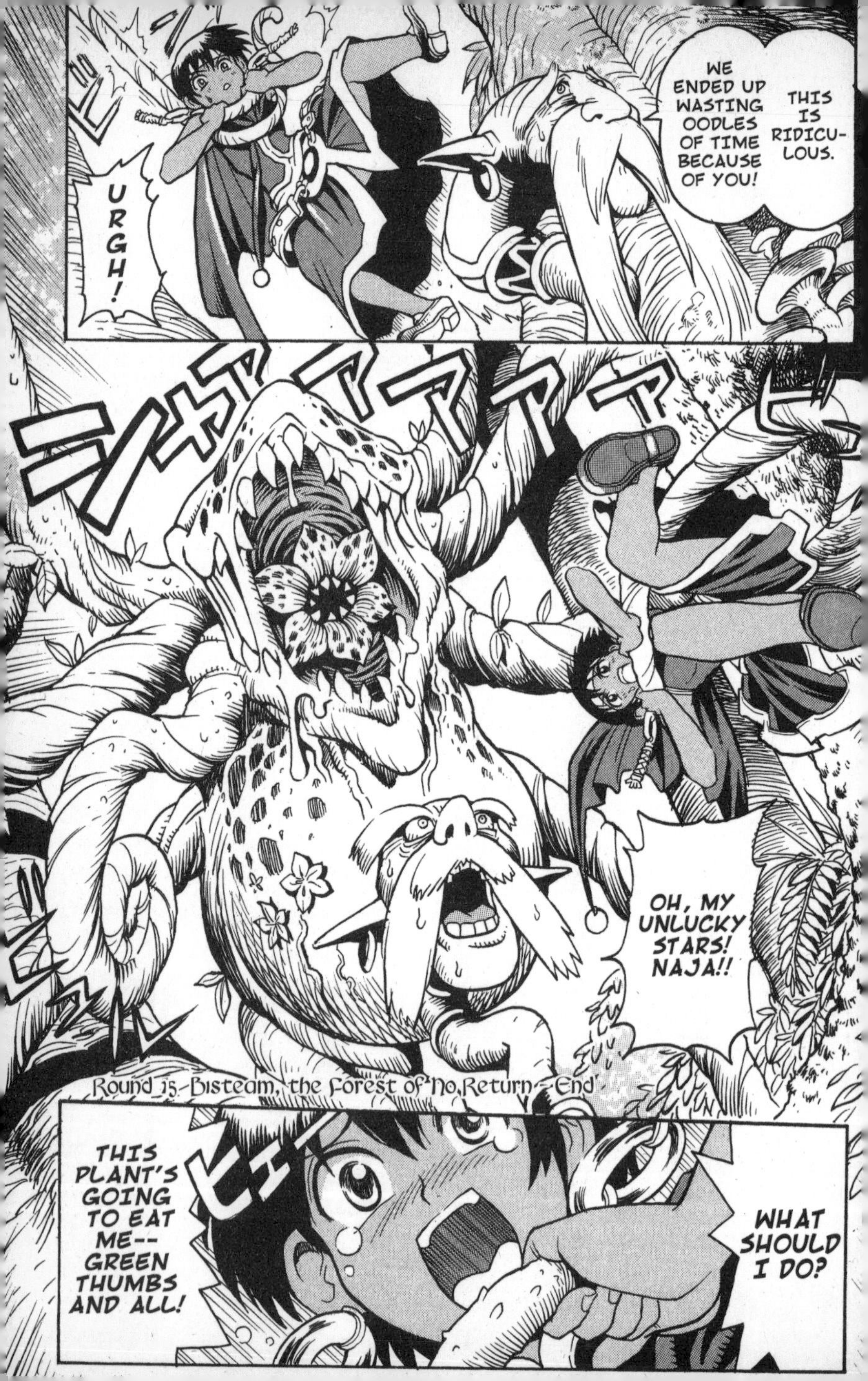
THIS IS RIDICULOUS.
WE ENDED UP WASTING OODLES OF TIME BECAUSE OF YOU!
URGH!
OH, MY UNLUCKY STARS! NAJA!!
Round 15: Bisteam, the Forest of No Return—End
WHAT SHOULD I DO?
THIS PLANT'S GOING TO EAT ME--GREEN THUMBS AND ALL!

CREATURES IN THE FOREST OF BISTEAM

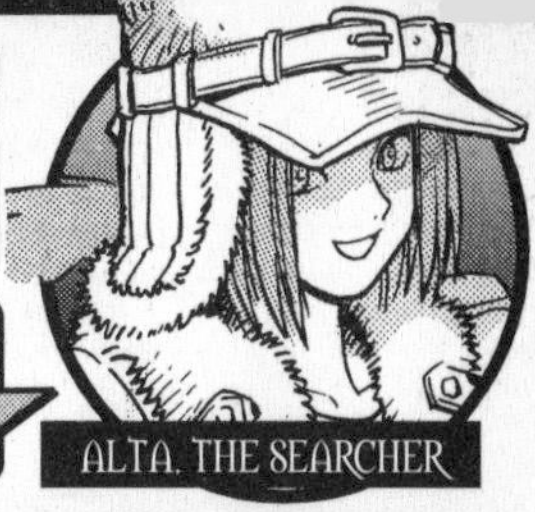
ALTA, THE SEARCHER

SEARCHERS GO ALL OVER THE WORLD LOOKING FOR TREASURES! THEY COME ACROSS INTERESTING REMAINS AND CREATURES. BUT, IN BISTEAM--THE FOREST OF NO RETURN--THERE ARE A LOT OF STRANGE CREATURES YOU'LL ENCOUNTER NOWHERE ELSE!

MANTRAP [EARTH]

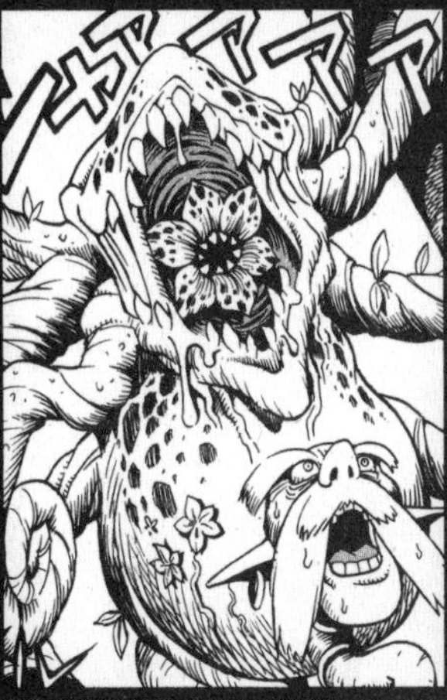

Attack Points	40
Defense Points	40
Summon Cost	70
Summon Condition	None
Special Abilites	Amazing defensive capabilities.

MANTRAP, OBVIOUSLY, IS A PLANT MONSTER. ACCORDING TO JOAQUIN, IT'S AN EXTINCT SPECIES, BUT THERE APPEAR TO BE SOME SURVIVING ONES IN BISTEAM. I WONDER IF THE ONE NAJARAN ATE WAS THE LAST SURVIVING SPECIES.

WOODFOLK [EARTH]

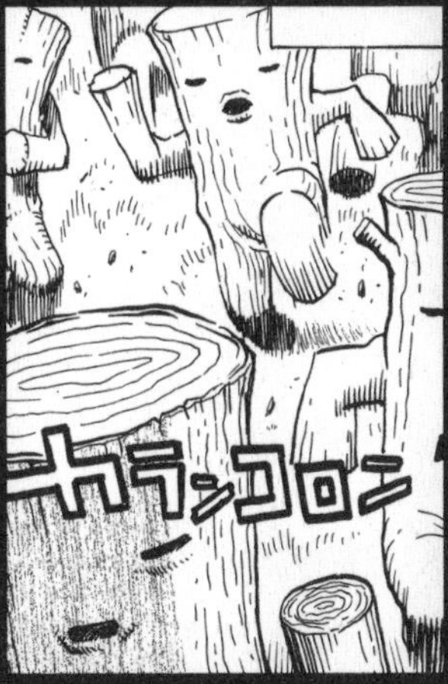
カランコロン

Attack Points	30
Defense Points	30
Summon Cost	70
Summon Condition	None
Special Abilites	Incredibly protective.

YOU CAN ALWAYS FIND WOODFOLK DEEP IN RICH FORESTS. THEY ARE GENTLE CREATURES THAT PROTECT THE TREES, BUT WILL ATTACK ANYONE TRYING TO DESTROY THEIR FOREST HOMELAND, MARCHING INTO BATTLE LIKE A WOODEN CAVALRY.

GARGOYLE [EARTH]

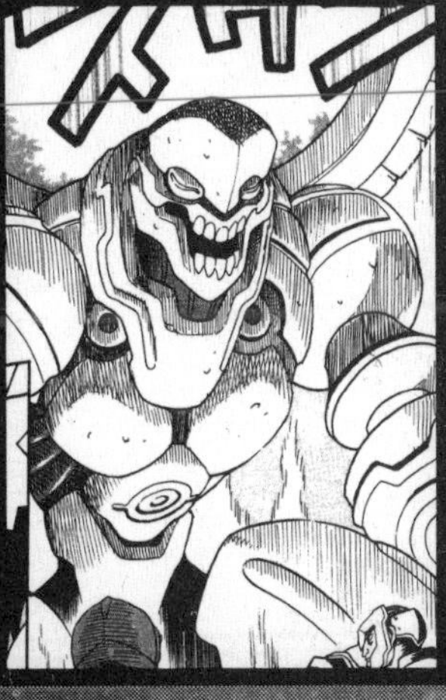

Attack Points	30(50)
Defense Points	50
Summon Cost	100
Summon Condition	None
Special Abilites	Preemptive strikes.

A STONE CREATURE THAT PROTECTS THE GATE OF BISTEAM FROM INVADERS. OLD REMAINS ARE USUALLY PROTECTED BY TRAPS OR CREATURES, OF WHICH THE GARGOYLE IS AMONG THE MOST POWERFUL.

NAJARAN [EATING CREATURE]

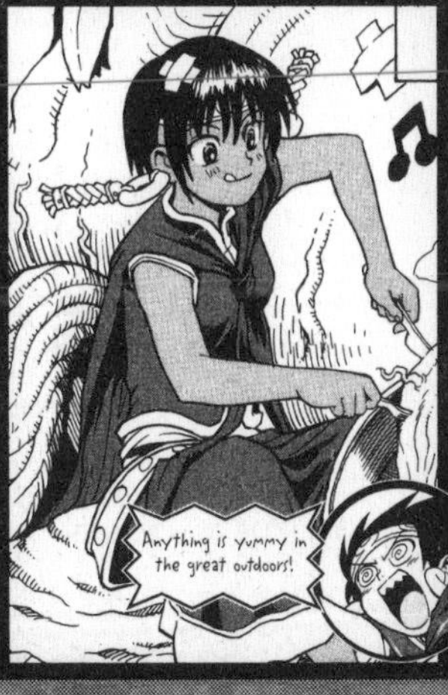
Anything is yummy in the great outdoors!

Attack Points	?
Defense Points	?
Summon Cost	Grocery Cost
Summon Condition	Food
Special Abilites	She is a Cepter.

SHE IS WORKING HER WAY UP THE BISTEAM FOOD CHAIN. A HUMAN CREATURE WHO WILL EAT ANYTHING.

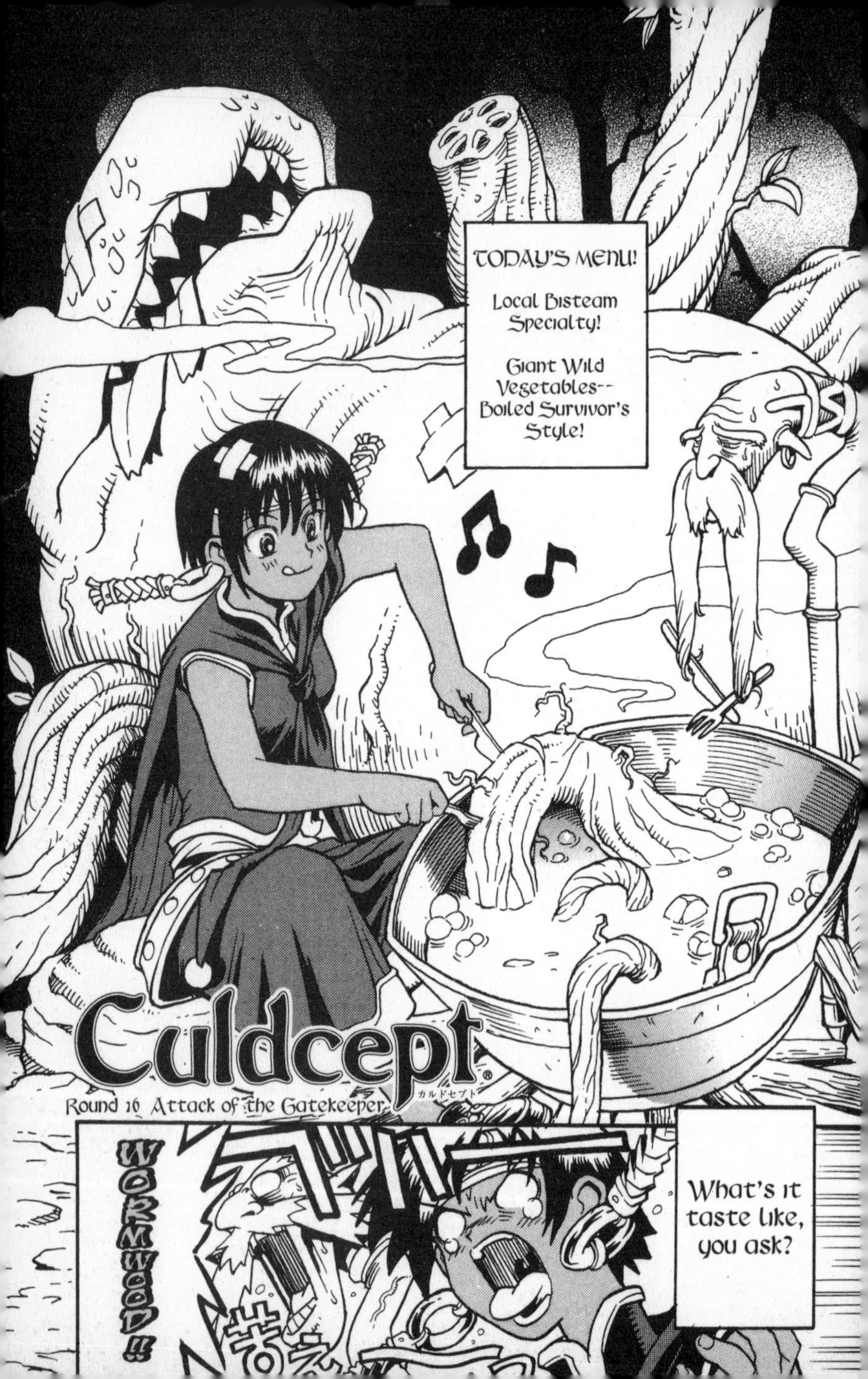
TODAY'S MENU!
Local Bisteam Specialty!
Giant Wild Vegetables--Boiled Survivor's Style!
Culdcept®
カルドセプト
Round 16 Attack of the Gatekeeper
What's it taste like, you ask?
WORMWOOD!!

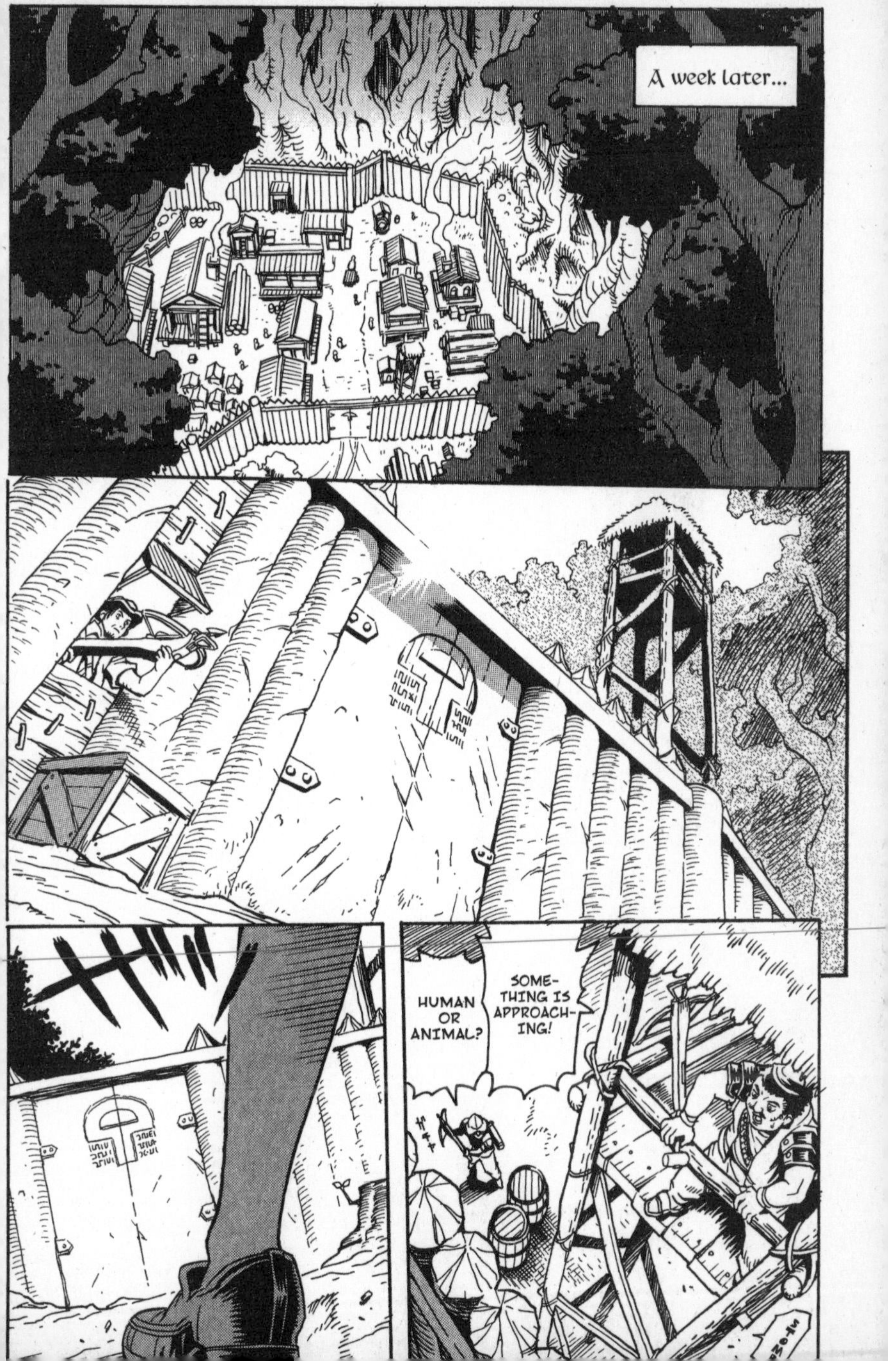
A week later...
SOME-THING IS APPROACH-ING!
HUMAN OR ANIMAL?

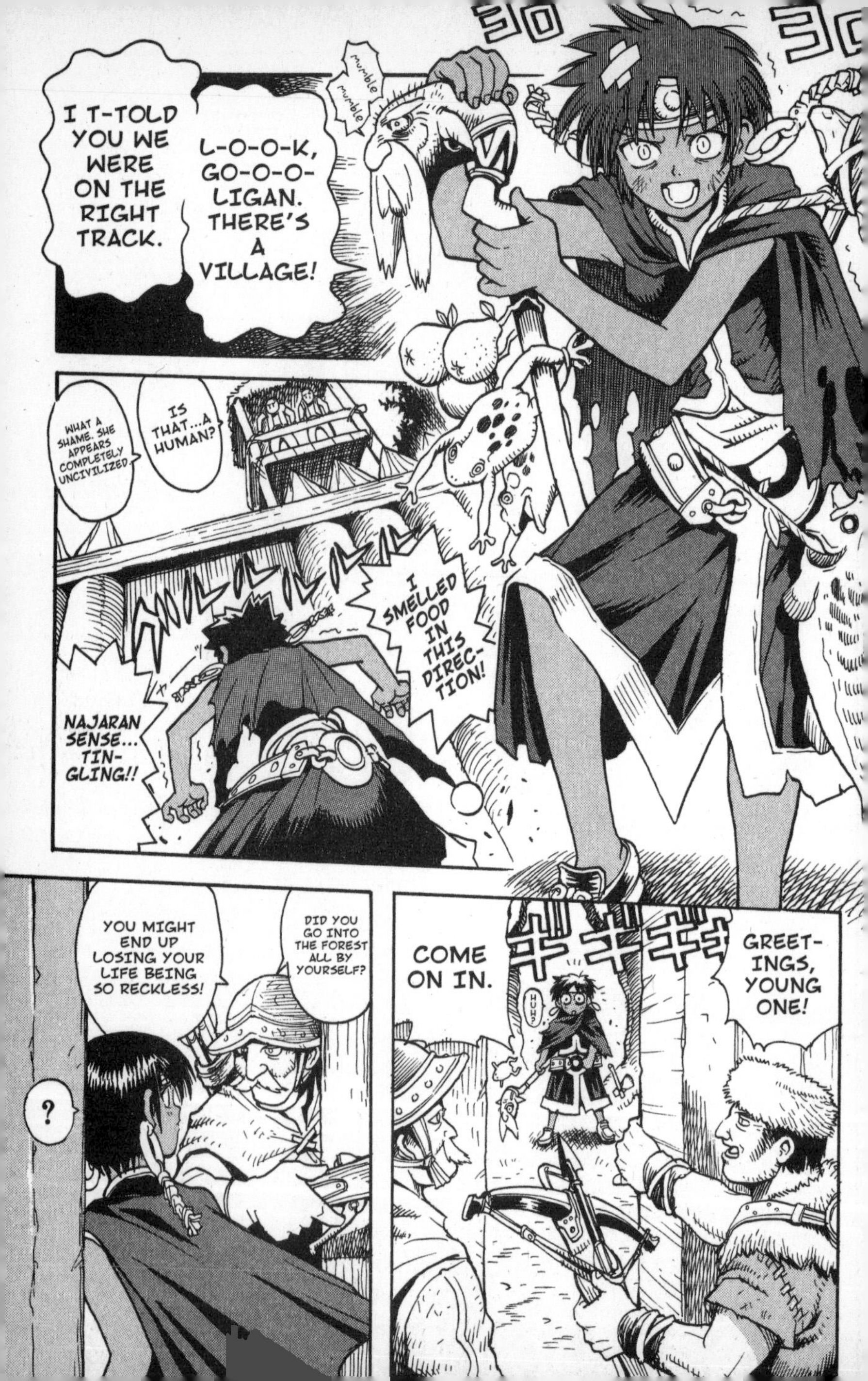
mumble mumble
L-O-O-K, GO-O-O-LIGAN. THERE'S A VILLAGE!
I T-TOLD YOU WE WERE ON THE RIGHT TRACK.
IS THAT...A HUMAN?
WHAT A SHAME. SHE APPEARS COMPLETELY UNCIVILIZED.
I SMELLED FOOD IN THIS DIRECTION!
NAJARAN SENSE... TINGLING!!
GREETINGS, YOUNG ONE!
HUH?
COME ON IN.
DID YOU GO INTO THE FOREST ALL BY YOURSELF?
YOU MIGHT END UP LOSING YOUR LIFE BEING SO RECKLESS!
?

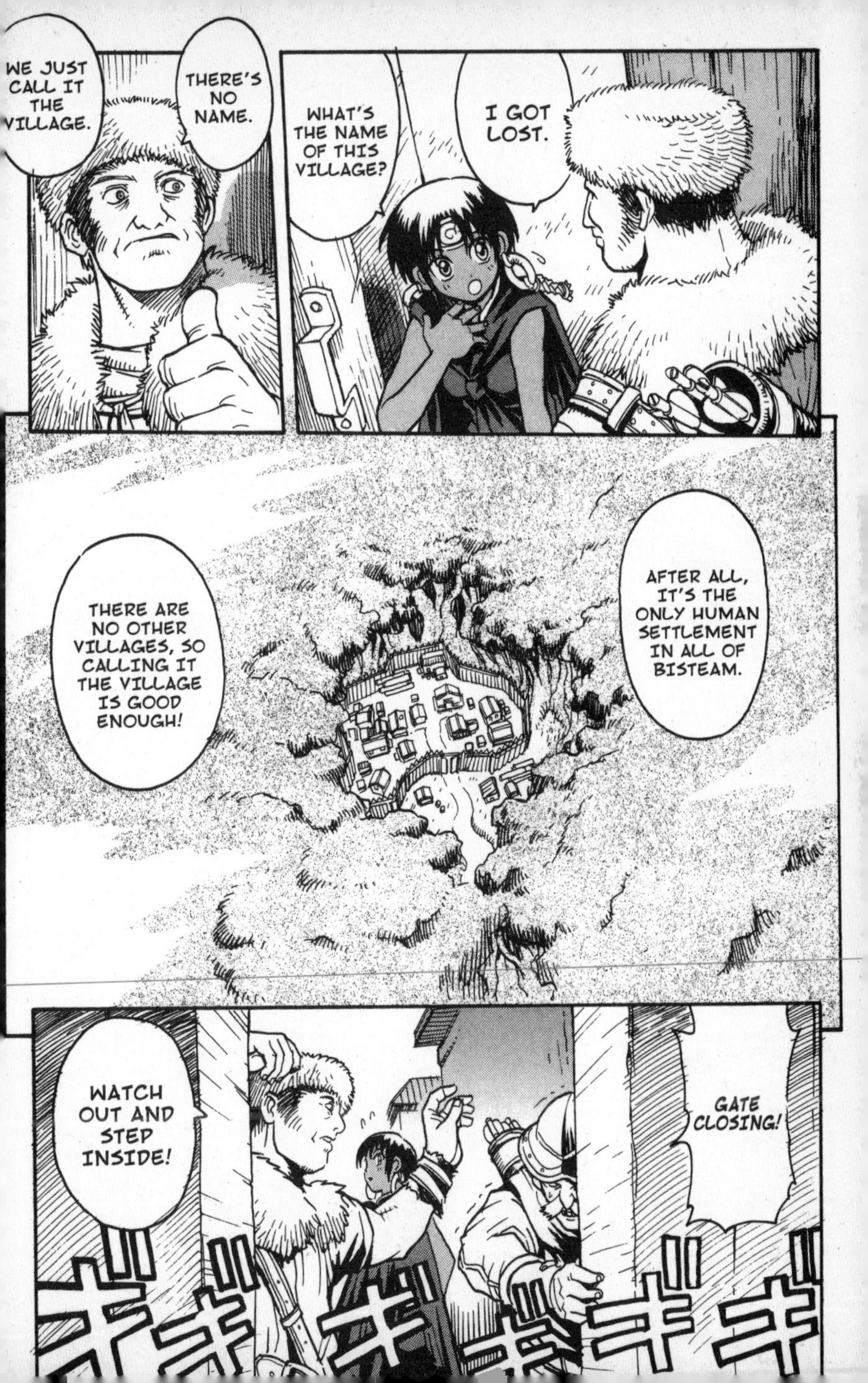
I GOT LOST.
WHAT'S THE NAME OF THIS VILLAGE?
THERE'S NO NAME.
WE JUST CALL IT THE VILLAGE.
AFTER ALL, IT'S THE ONLY HUMAN SETTLEMENT IN ALL OF BISTEAM.
THERE ARE NO OTHER VILLAGES, SO CALLING IT THE VILLAGE IS GOOD ENOUGH!
GATE CLOSING!
WATCH OUT AND STEP INSIDE!
ギギギギギギ

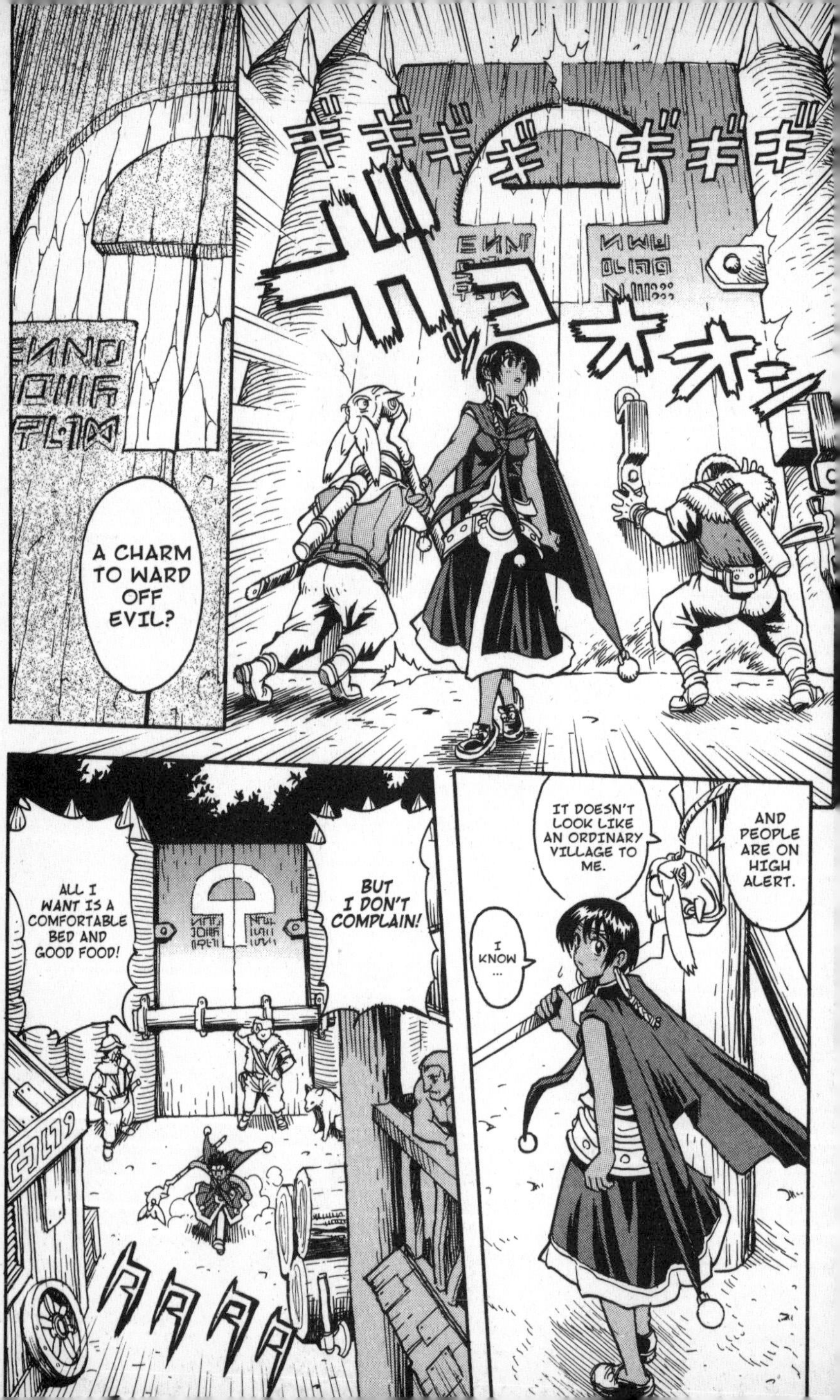
ギギギ ギギギ
ガコオオン
A CHARM TO WARD OFF EVIL?
IT DOESN'T LOOK LIKE AN ORDINARY VILLAGE TO ME.
AND PEOPLE ARE ON HIGH ALERT.
I KNOW ...
BUT I DON'T COMPLAIN!
ALL I WANT IS A COMFORTABLE BED AND GOOD FOOD!

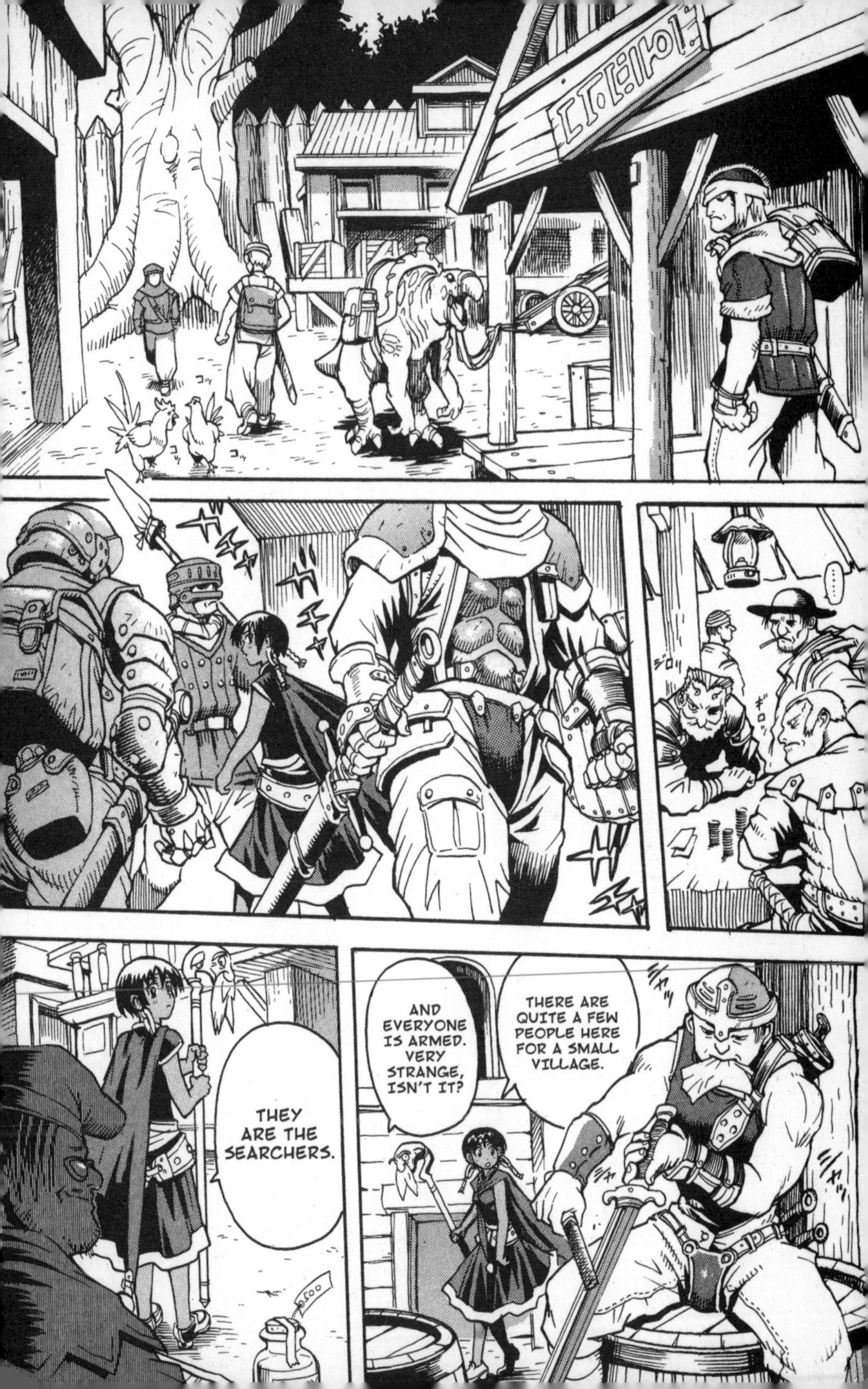
THERE ARE QUITE A FEW PEOPLE HERE FOR A SMALL VILLAGE.
AND EVERYONE IS ARMED. VERY STRANGE, ISN'T IT?
THEY ARE THE SEARCHERS.

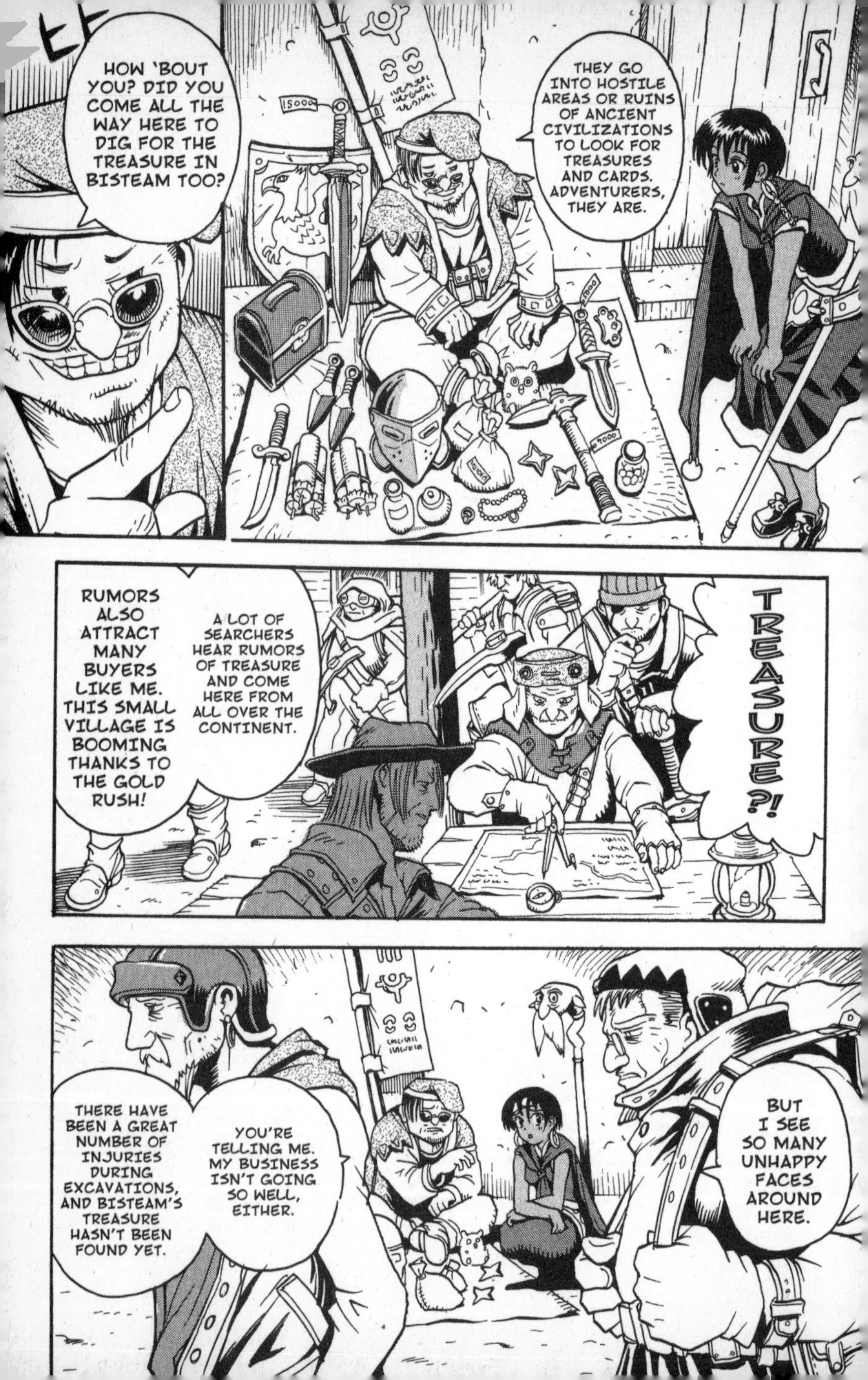
THEY GO INTO HOSTILE AREAS OR RUINS OF ANCIENT CIVILIZATIONS TO LOOK FOR TREASURES AND CARDS. ADVENTURERS, THEY ARE.
HOW 'BOUT YOU? DID YOU COME ALL THE WAY HERE TO DIG FOR THE TREASURE IN BISTEAM TOO?
TREASURE?!
A LOT OF SEARCHERS HEAR RUMORS OF TREASURE AND COME HERE FROM ALL OVER THE CONTINENT.
RUMORS ALSO ATTRACT MANY BUYERS LIKE ME. THIS SMALL VILLAGE IS BOOMING THANKS TO THE GOLD RUSH!
BUT I SEE SO MANY UNHAPPY FACES AROUND HERE.
YOU'RE TELLING ME. MY BUSINESS ISN'T GOING SO WELL, EITHER.
THERE HAVE BEEN A GREAT NUMBER OF INJURIES DURING EXCAVATIONS, AND BISTEAM'S TREASURE HASN'T BEEN FOUND YET.

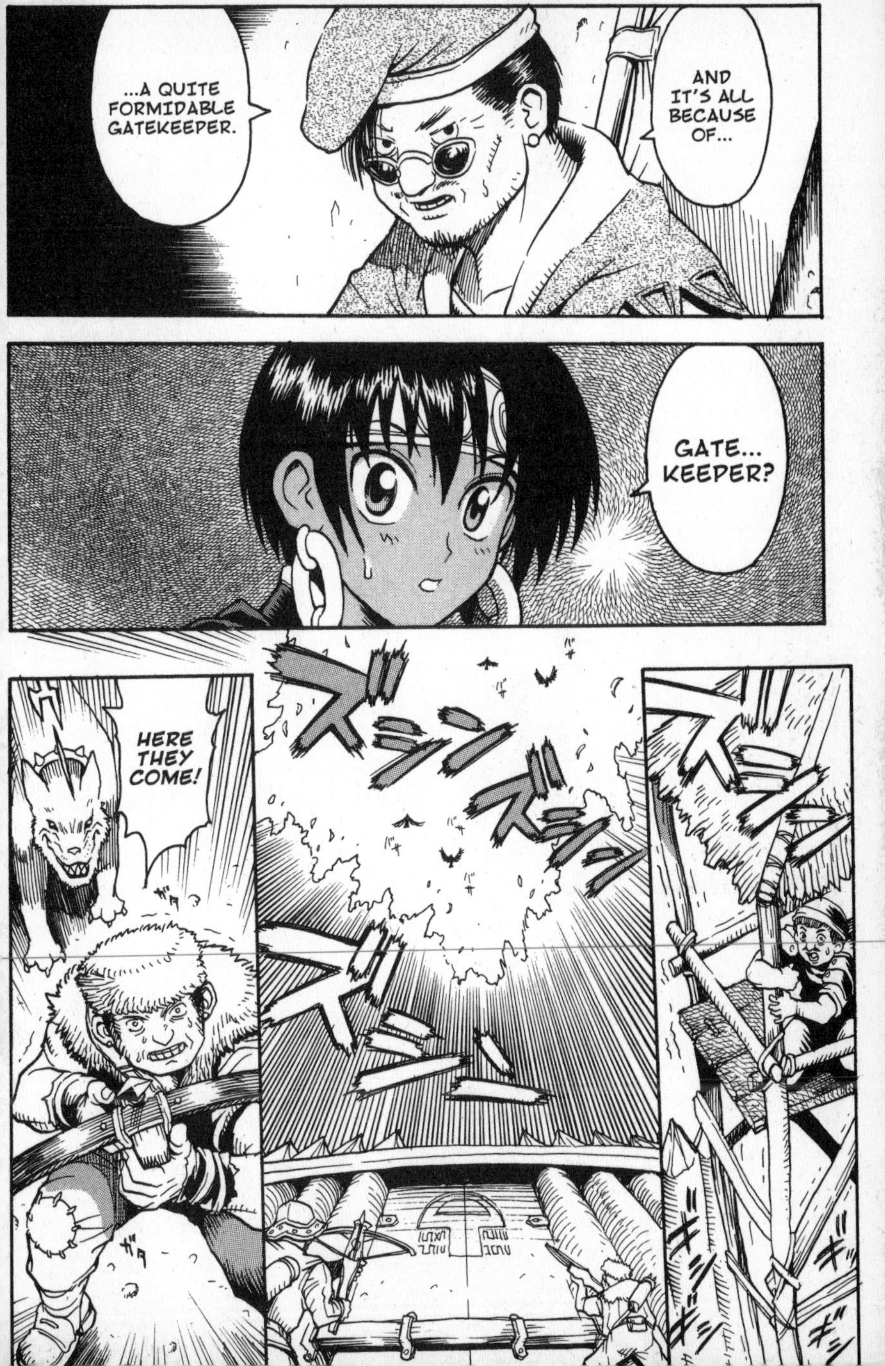
AND IT'S ALL BECAUSE OF...
...A QUITE FORMIDABLE GATEKEEPER.
GATE... KEEPER?
HERE THEY COME!

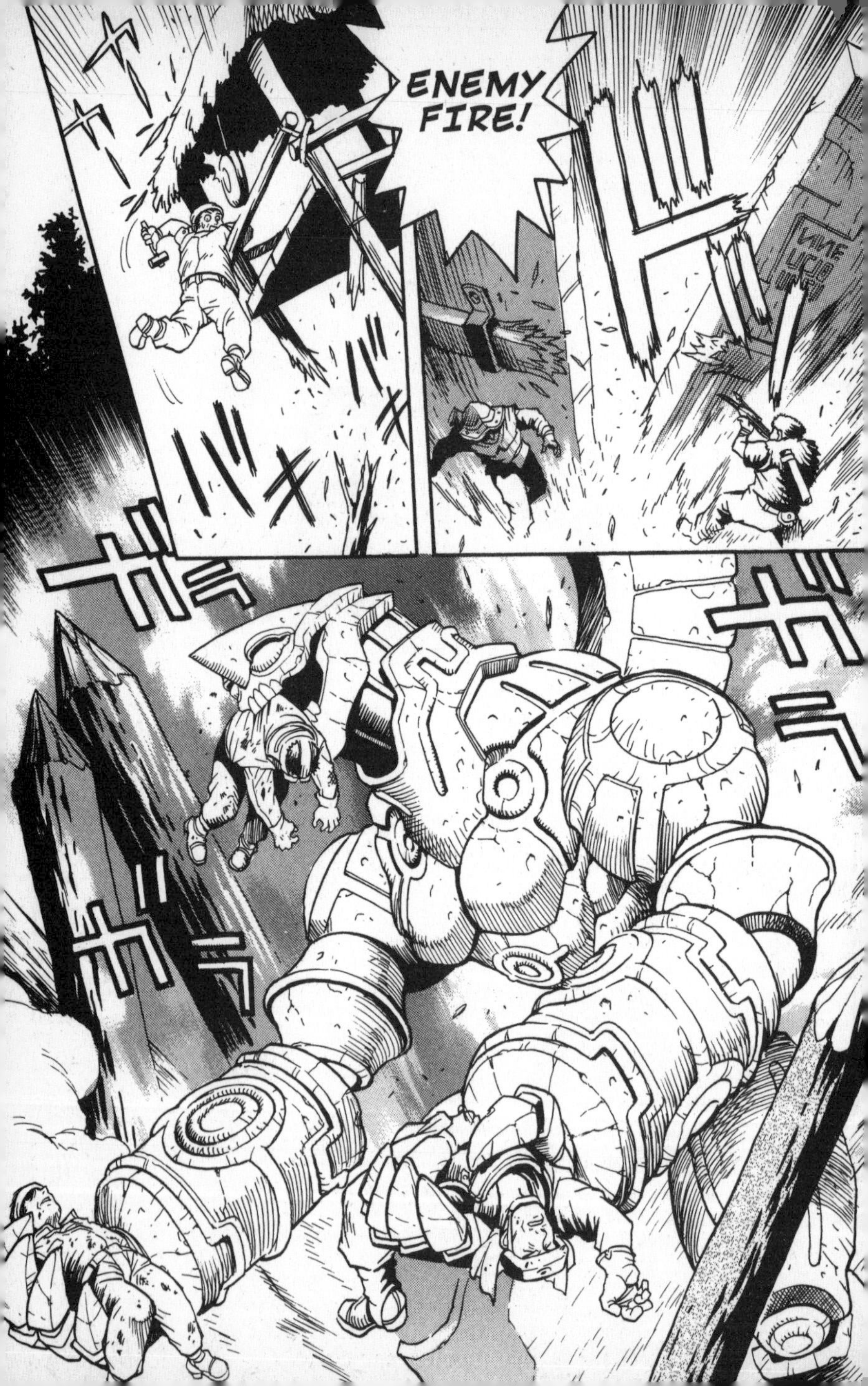
ENEMY FIRE!

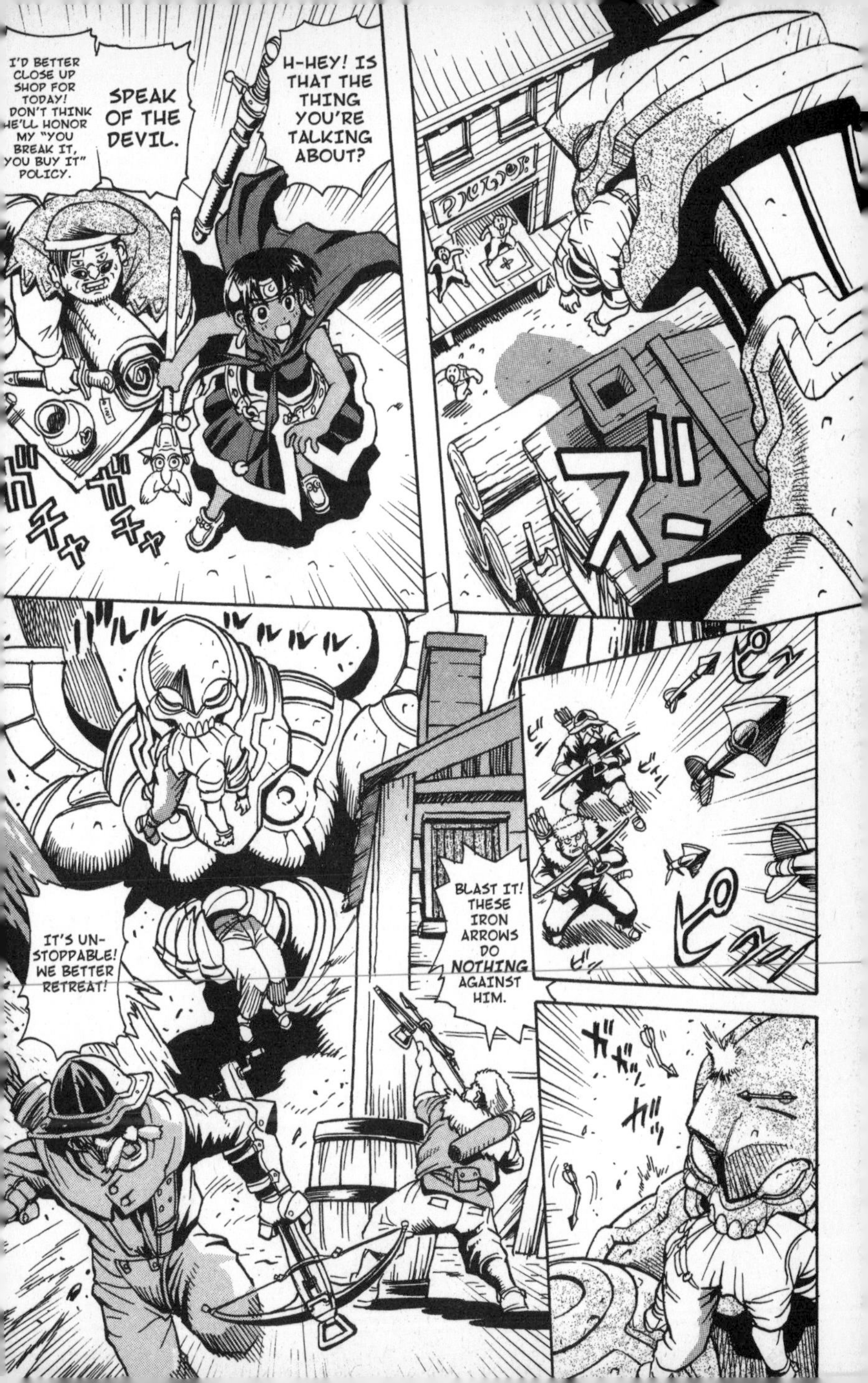
H-HEY! IS THAT THE THING YOU'RE TALKING ABOUT?
SPEAK OF THE DEVIL.
I'D BETTER CLOSE UP SHOP FOR TODAY! DON'T THINK HE'LL HONOR MY "YOU BREAK IT, YOU BUY IT" POLICY.
BLAST IT! THESE IRON ARROWS DO NOTHING AGAINST HIM.
IT'S UN-STOPPABLE! WE BETTER RETREAT!

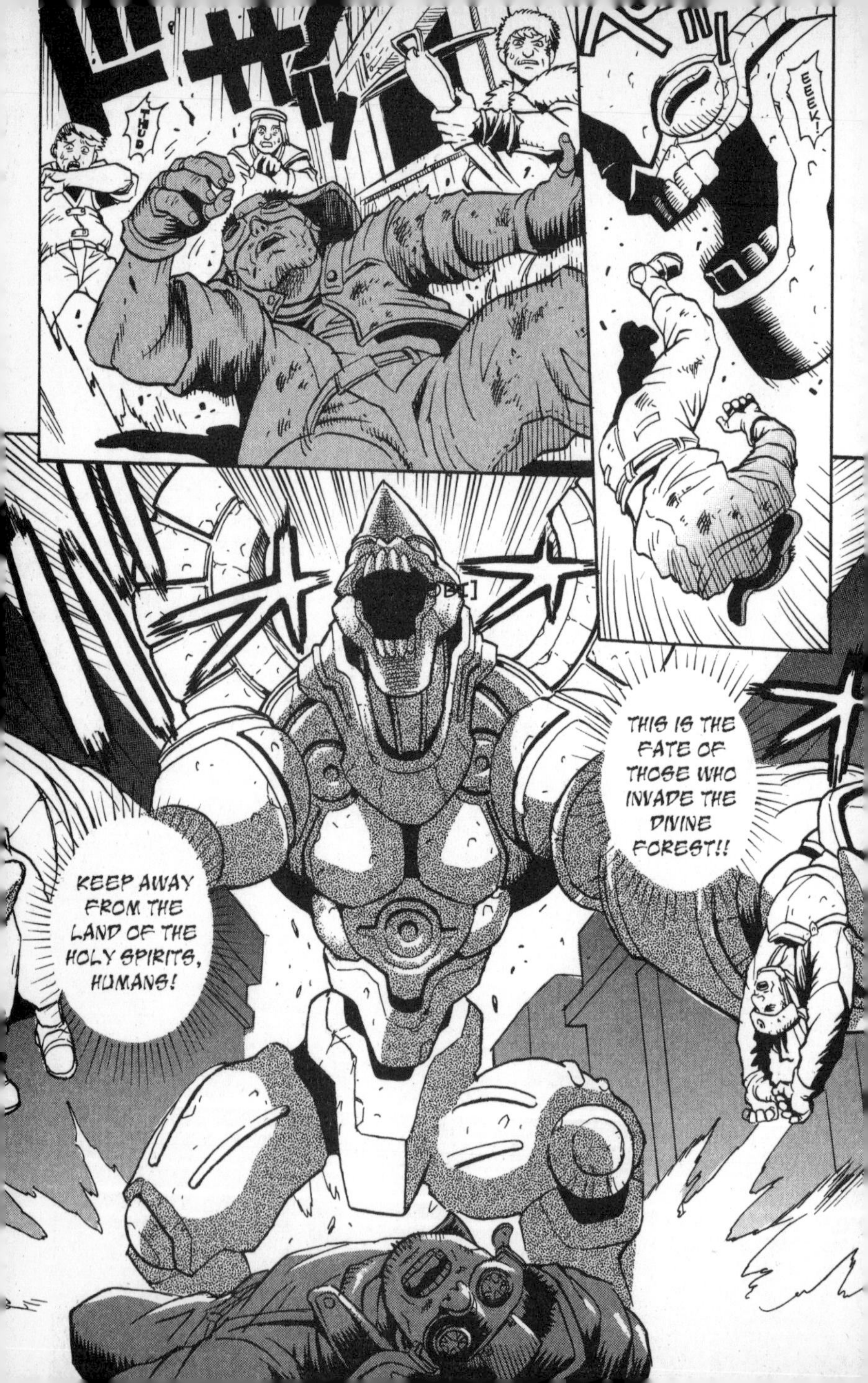
EEEK!
THUD
THIS IS THE FATE OF THOSE WHO INVADE THE DIVINE FOREST!!
KEEP AWAY FROM THE LAND OF THE HOLY SPIRITS, HUMANS!

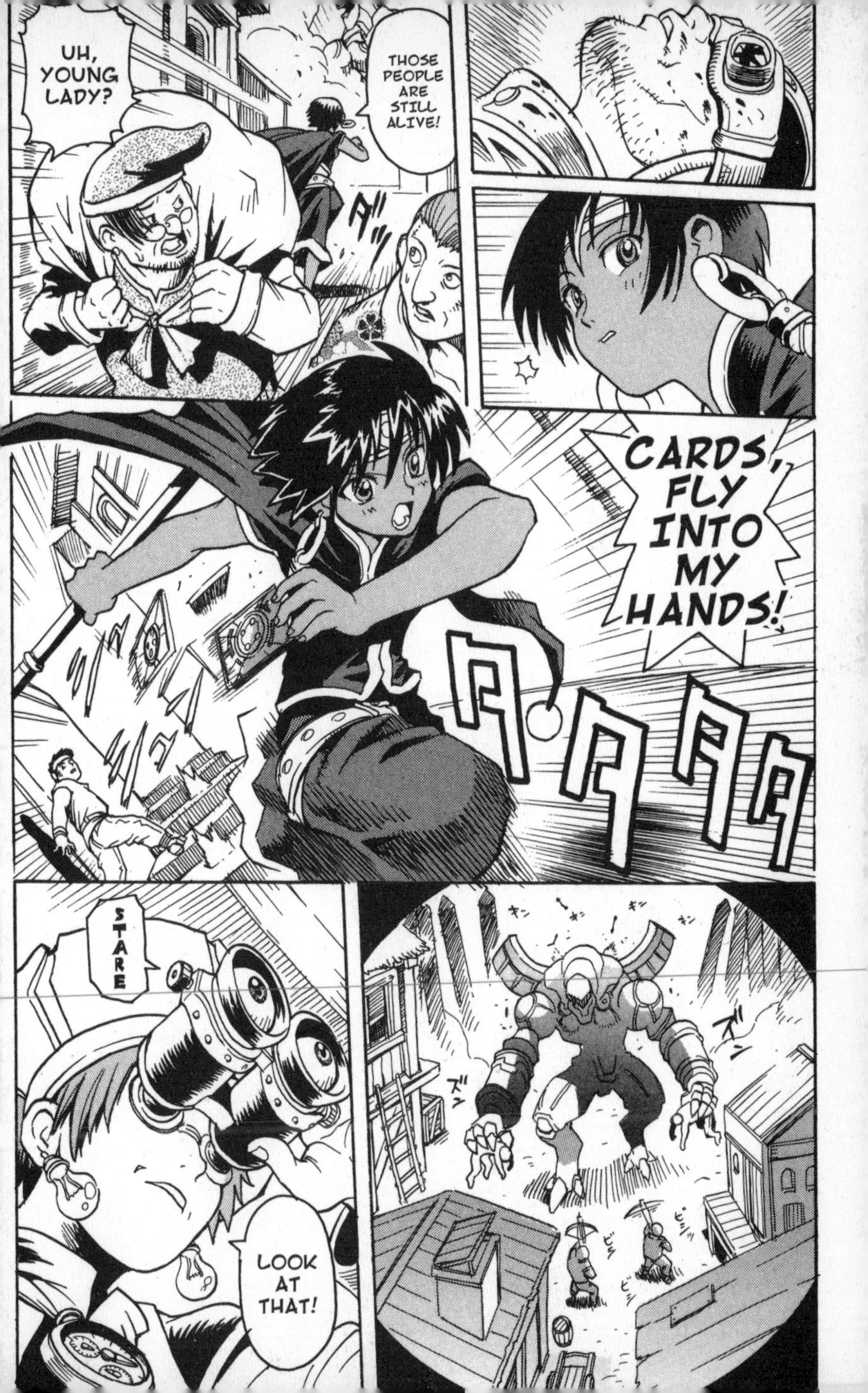
THOSE PEOPLE ARE STILL ALIVE!
UH, YOUNG LADY?
CARDS, FLY INTO MY HANDS!
STARE
LOOK AT THAT!

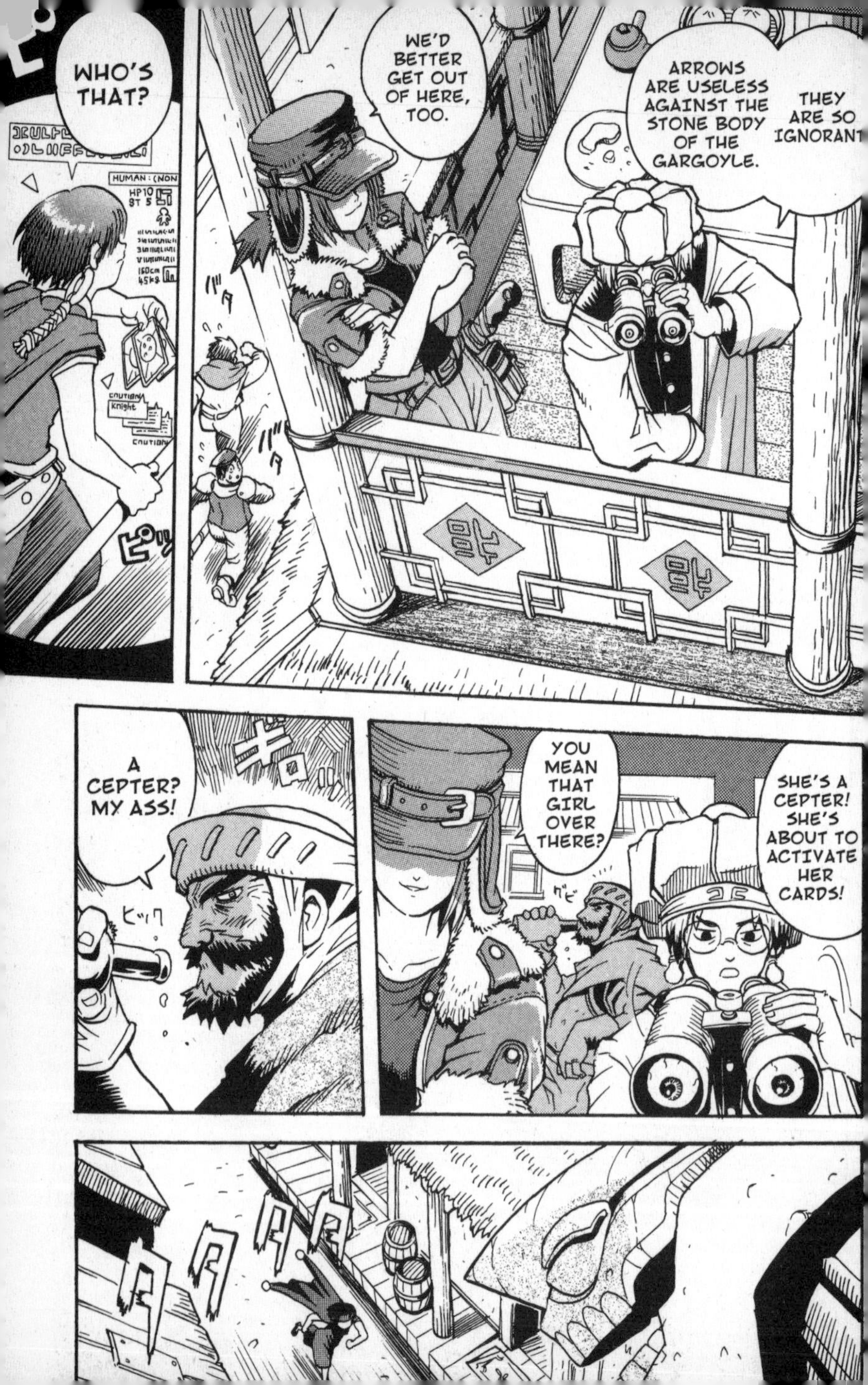
THEY ARE SO IGNORANT
ARROWS ARE USELESS AGAINST THE STONE BODY OF THE GARGOYLE.
WE'D BETTER GET OUT OF HERE, TOO.
WHO'S THAT?
HUMAN : (NON
HP10
ST 5
160cm
45kg
knight
SHE'S A CEPTER! SHE'S ABOUT TO ACTIVATE HER CARDS!
YOU MEAN THAT GIRL OVER THERE?
A CEPTER? MY ASS!

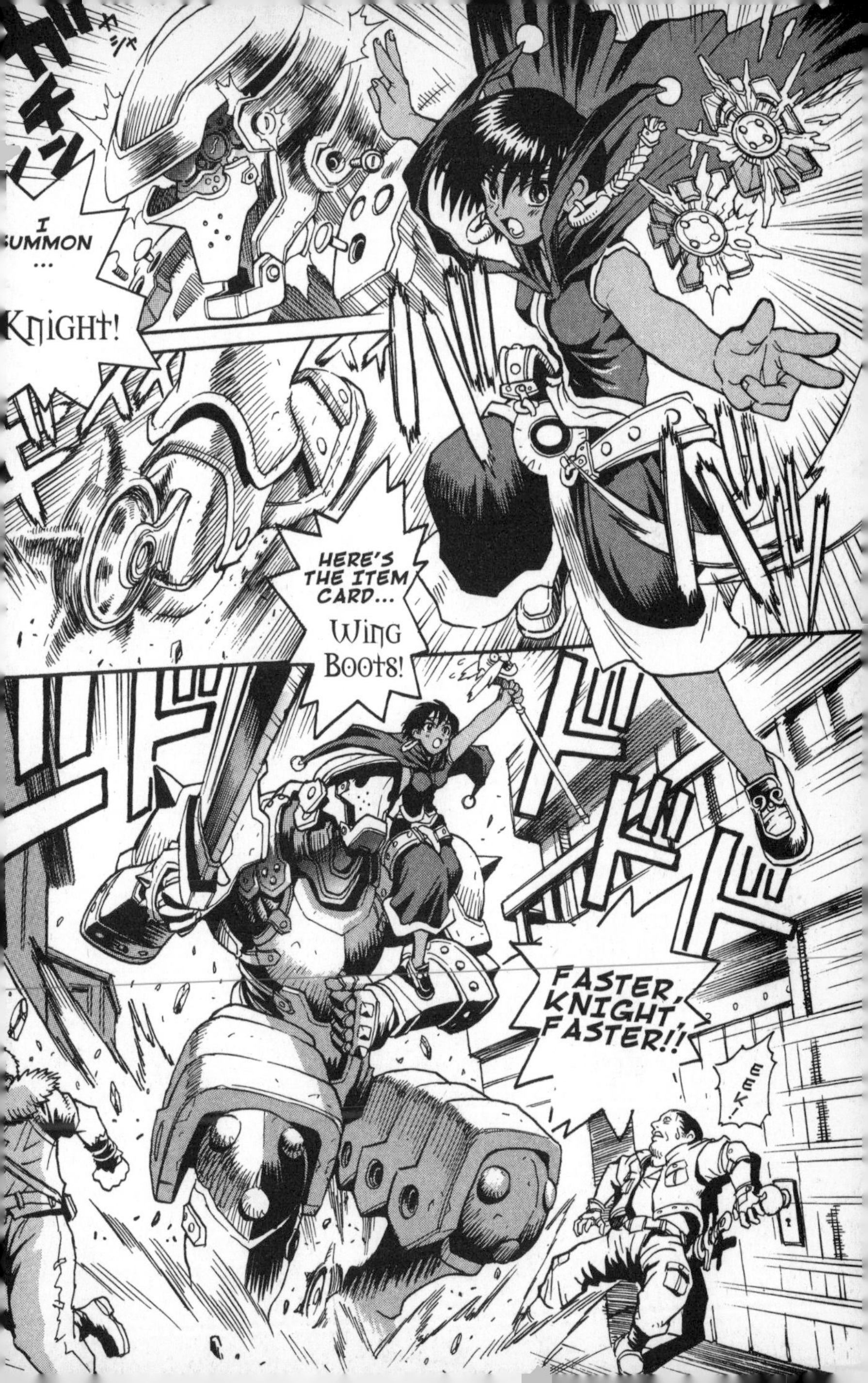
I SUMMON ...
KNIGHT!
HERE'S THE ITEM CARD...
WING BOOTS!
FASTER, KNIGHT FASTER!!
EEK!

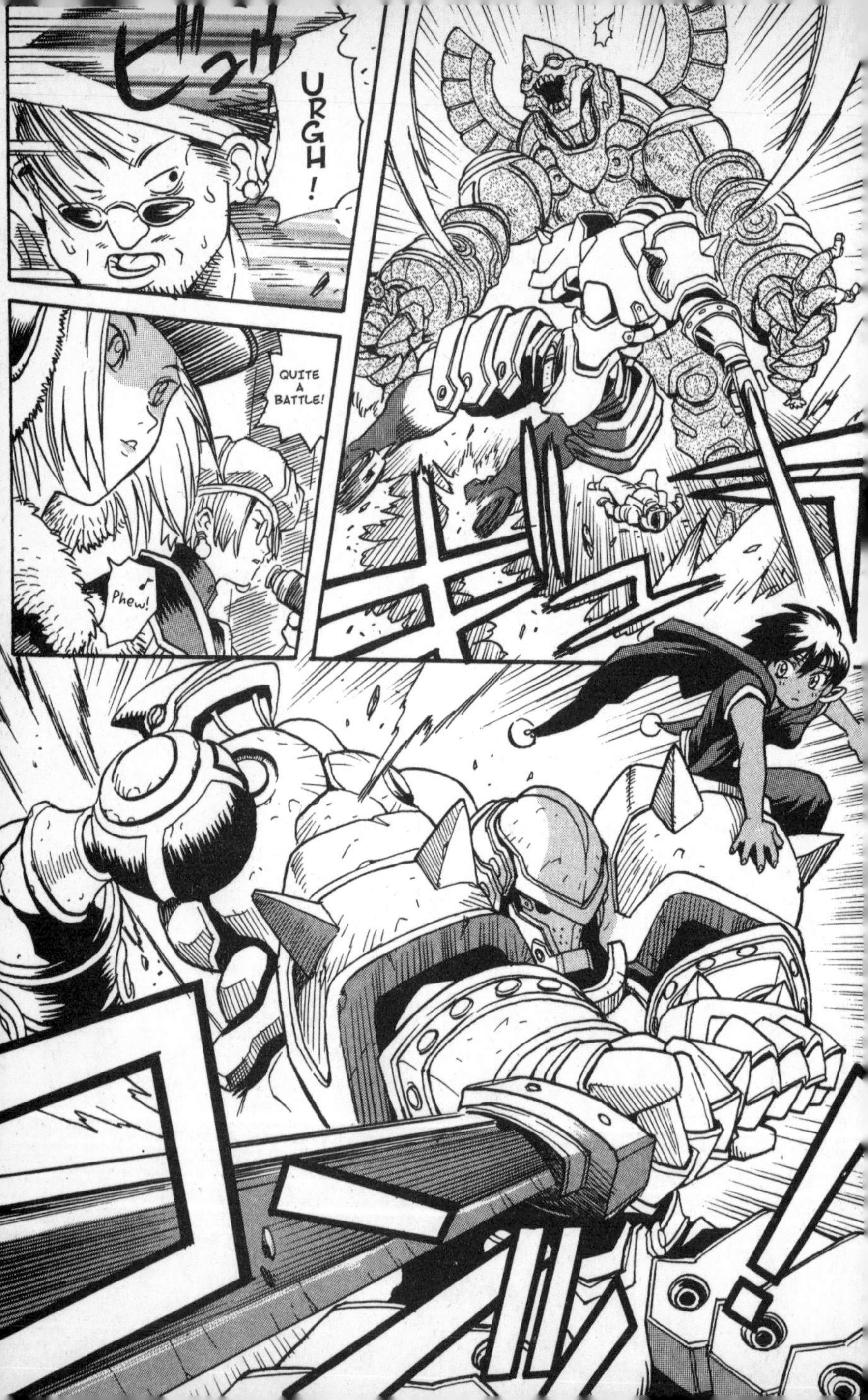
ビュッ
URGH!
QUITE A BATTLE!
Phew!

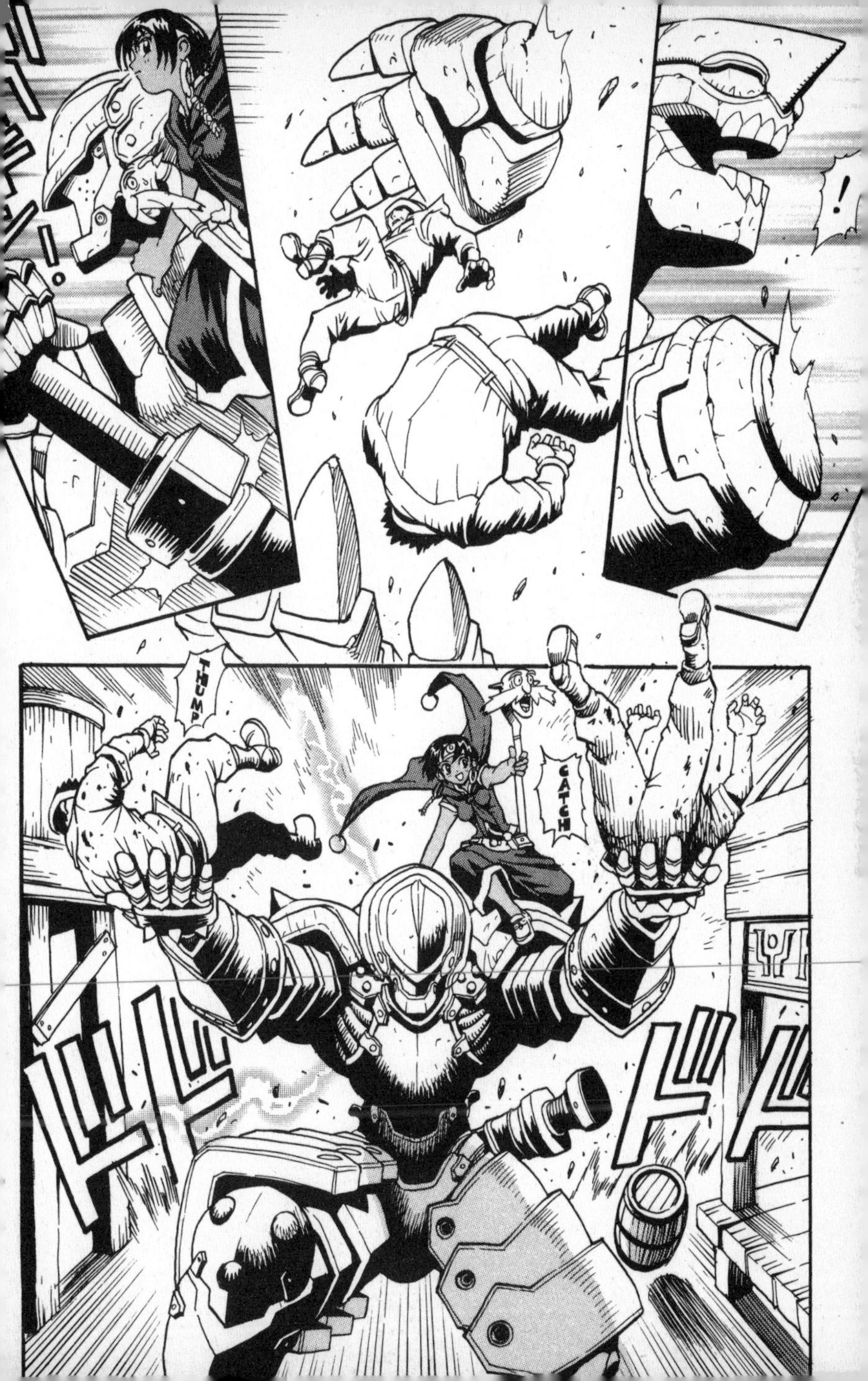
!
CATCH
THUMP

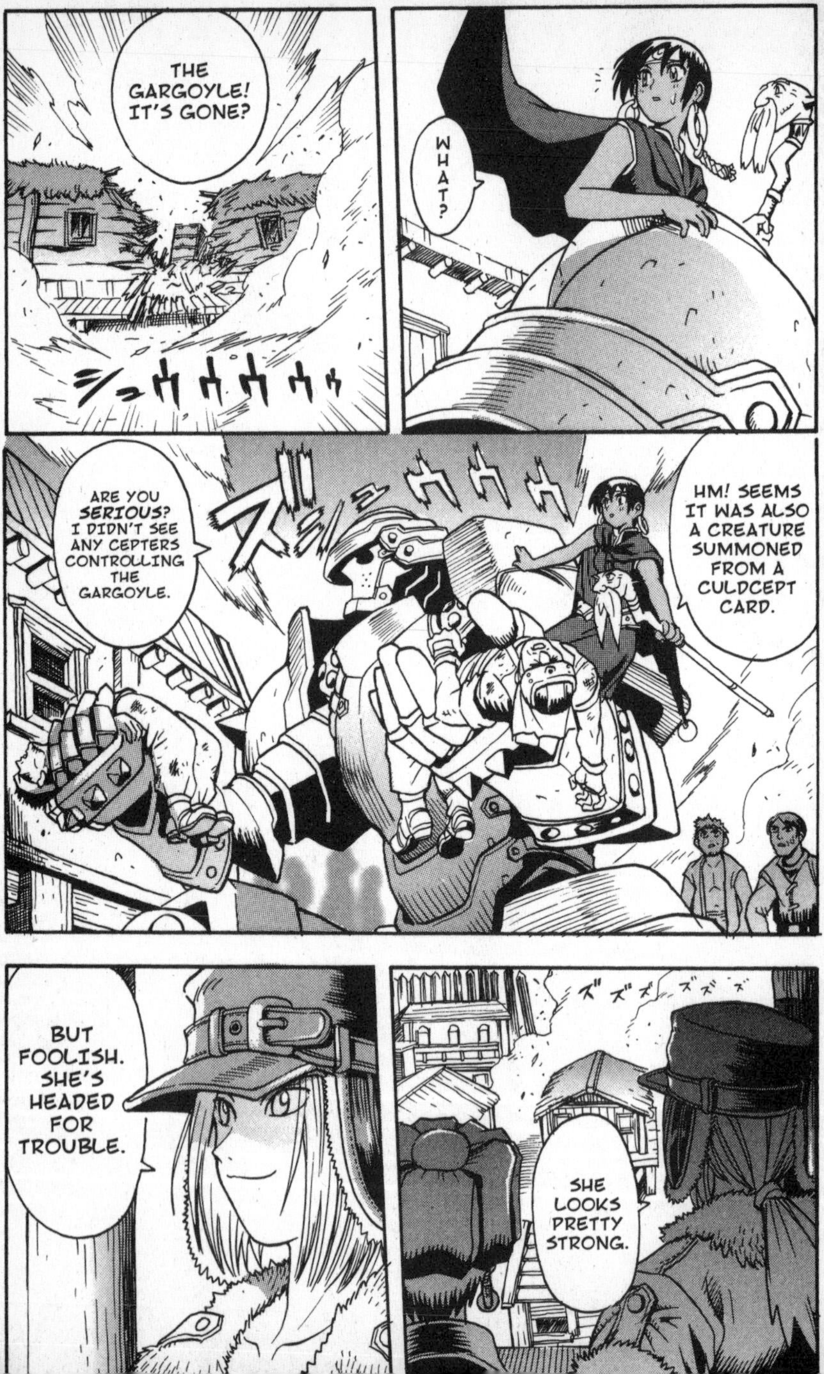
WHAT?
THE GARGOYLE! IT'S GONE?
HM! SEEMS IT WAS ALSO A CREATURE SUMMONED FROM A CULDCEPT CARD.
ARE YOU SERIOUS? I DIDN'T SEE ANY CEPTERS CONTROLLING THE GARGOYLE.
SHE LOOKS PRETTY STRONG.
BUT FOOLISH. SHE'S HEADED FOR TROUBLE.

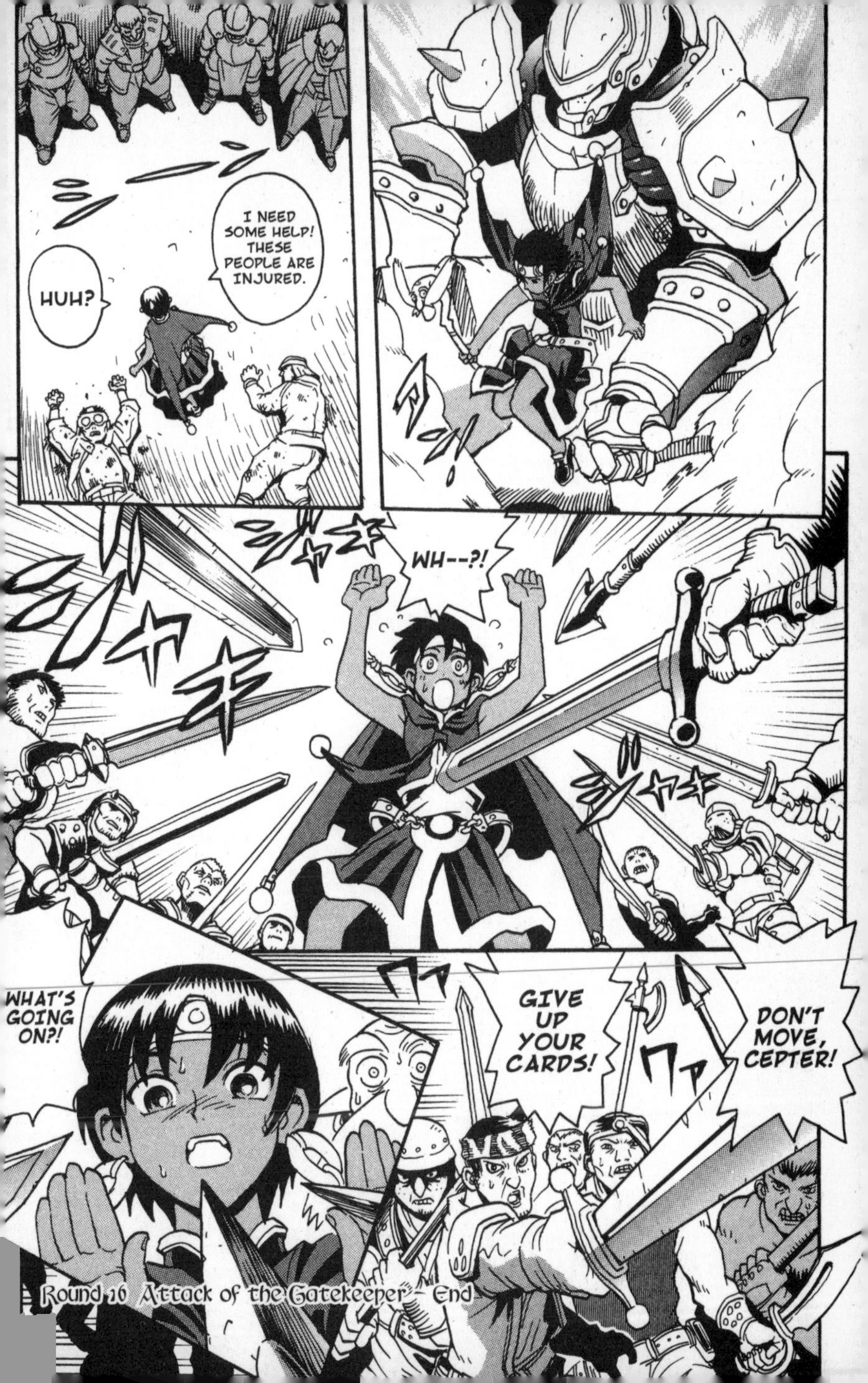
I NEED SOME HELP! THESE PEOPLE ARE INJURED.
HUH?
WH--?!
DON'T MOVE, CEPTER!
GIVE UP YOUR CARDS!
WHAT'S GOING ON?!
Round 16 Attack of the Gatekeeper - End

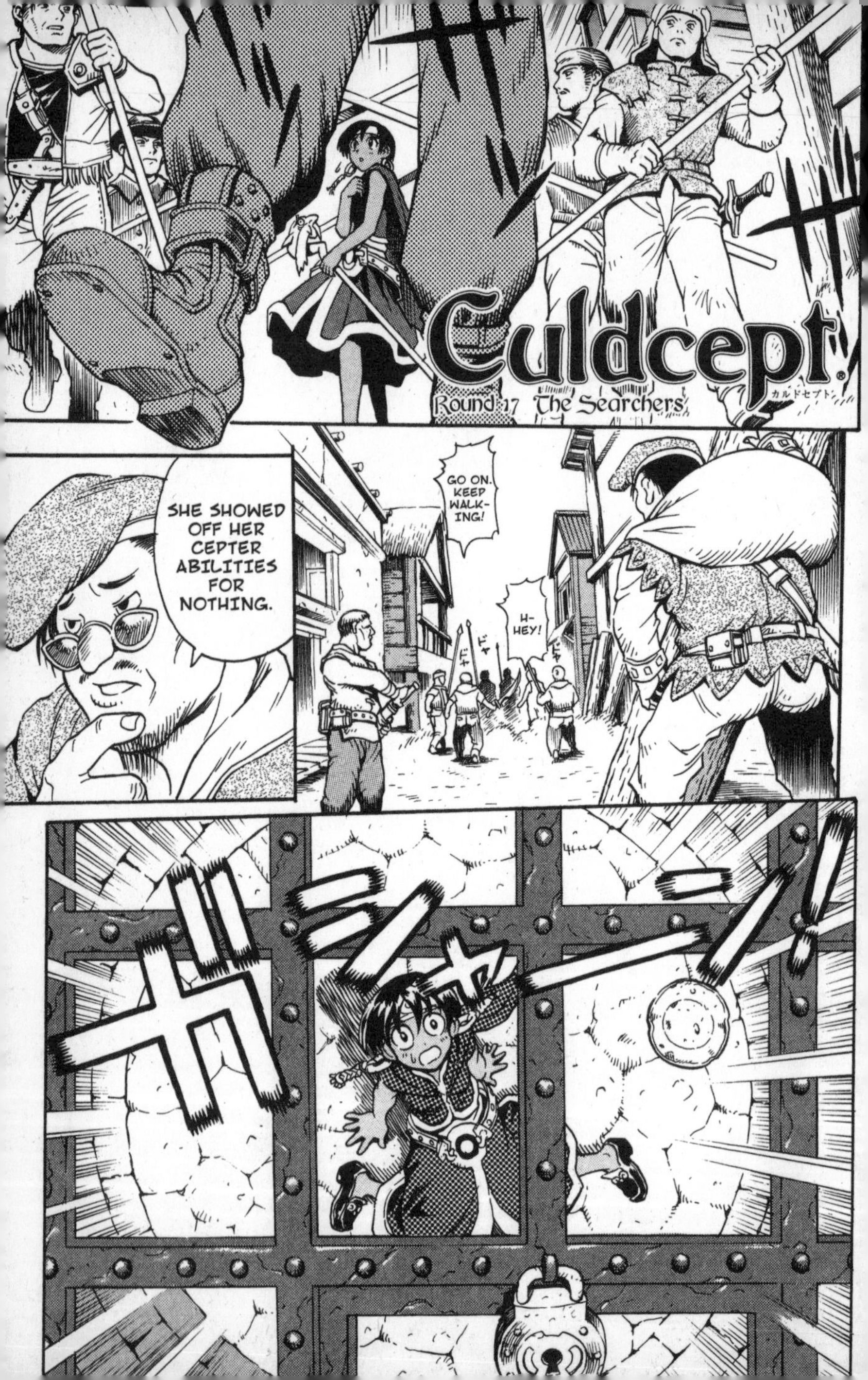
Culdcept
カルドセプト
Round 17 The Searchers
GO ON. KEEP WALKING!
H-HEY!
SHE SHOWED OFF HER CEPTER ABILITIES FOR NOTHING.
ガシャーン!

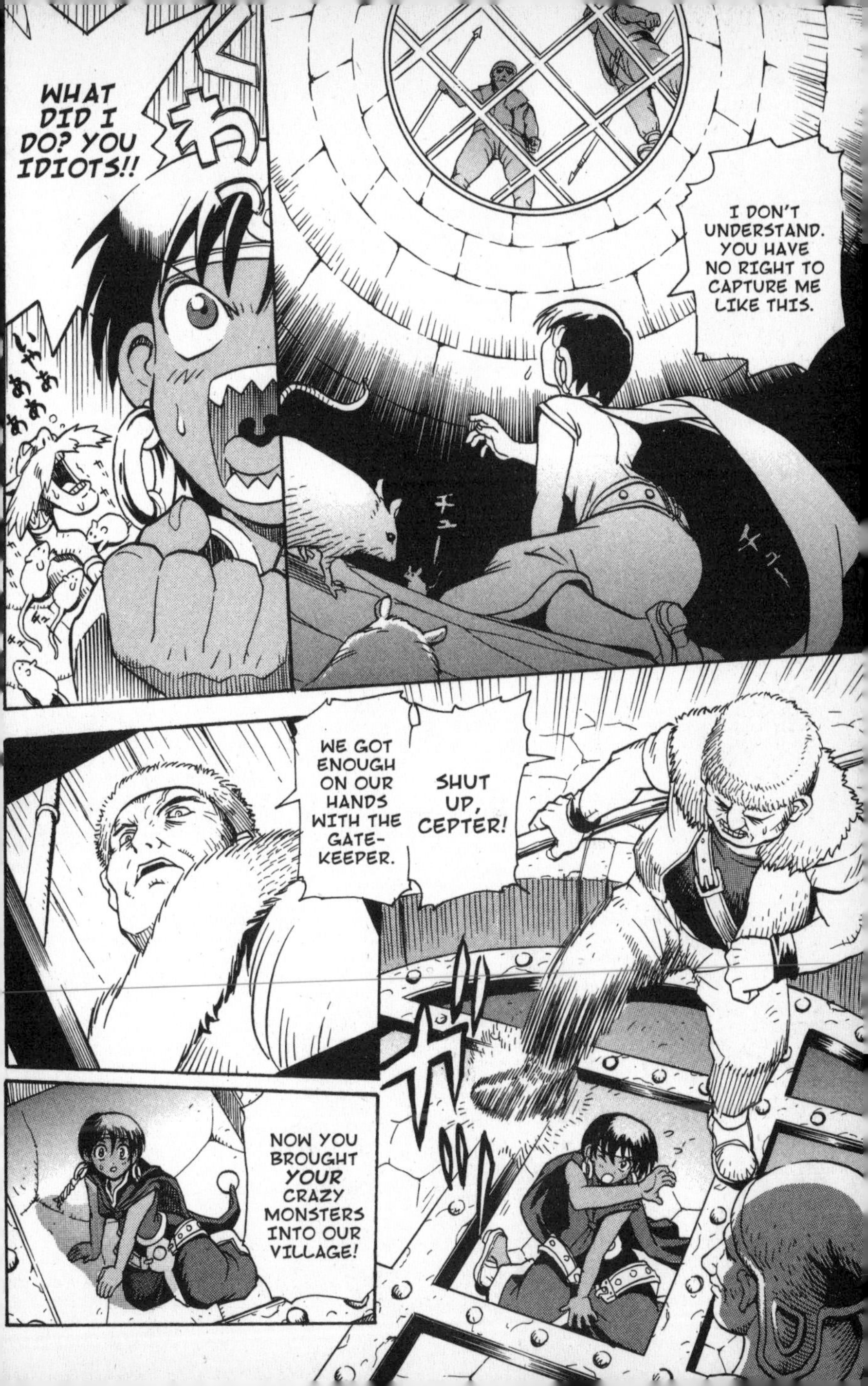
I DON'T UNDERSTAND. YOU HAVE NO RIGHT TO CAPTURE ME LIKE THIS.
チュー
WHAT DID I DO? YOU IDIOTS!!
いやあああ
SHUT UP, CEPTER!
WE GOT ENOUGH ON OUR HANDS WITH THE GATE-KEEPER.
NOW YOU BROUGHT *YOUR* CRAZY MONSTERS INTO OUR VILLAGE!

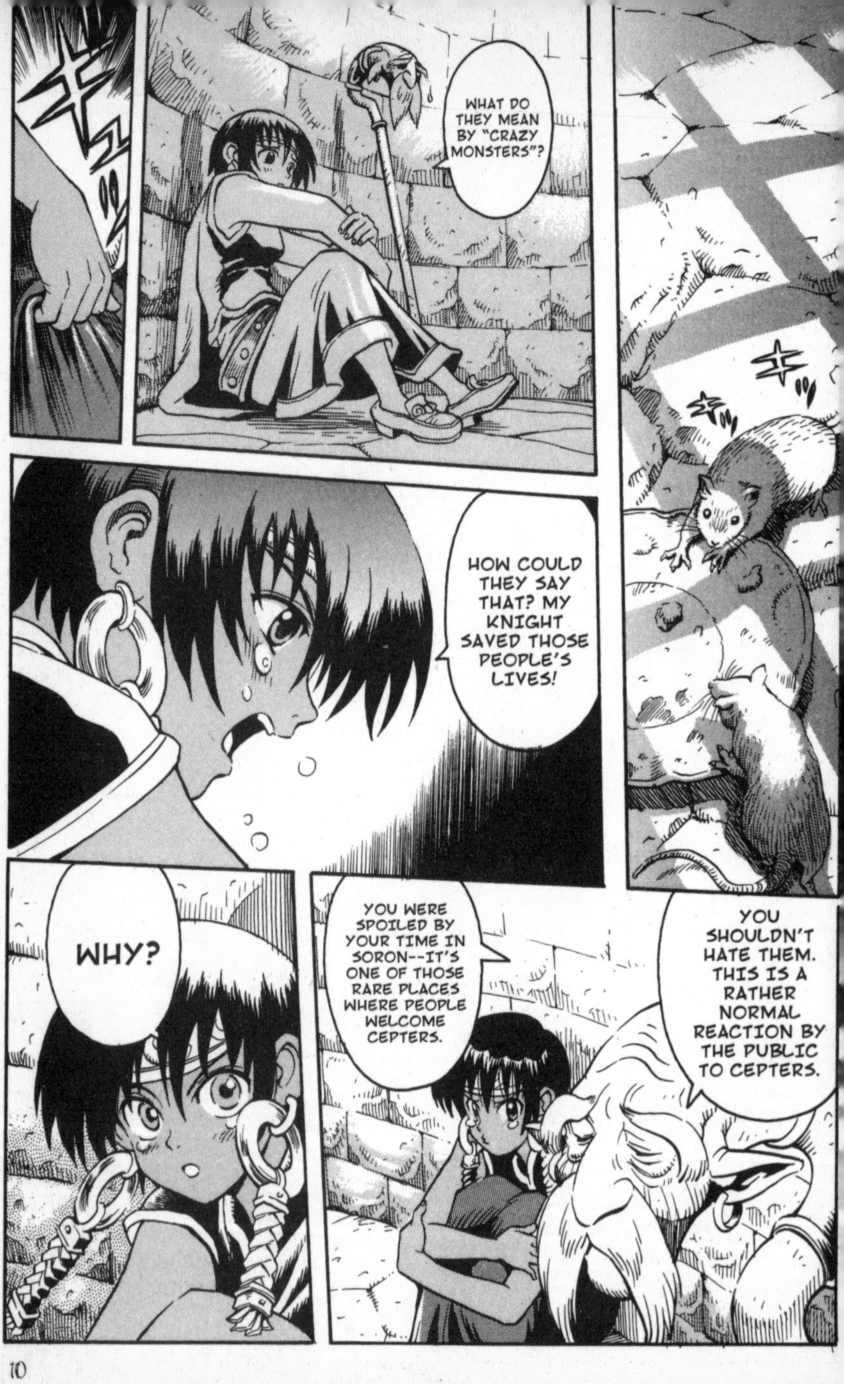
WHAT DO THEY MEAN BY "CRAZY MONSTERS"?
HOW COULD THEY SAY THAT? MY KNIGHT SAVED THOSE PEOPLE'S LIVES!
YOU SHOULDN'T HATE THEM. THIS IS A RATHER NORMAL REACTION BY THE PUBLIC TO CEPTERS.
YOU WERE SPOILED BY YOUR TIME IN SORON--IT'S ONE OF THOSE RARE PLACES WHERE PEOPLE WELCOME CEPTERS.
WHY?

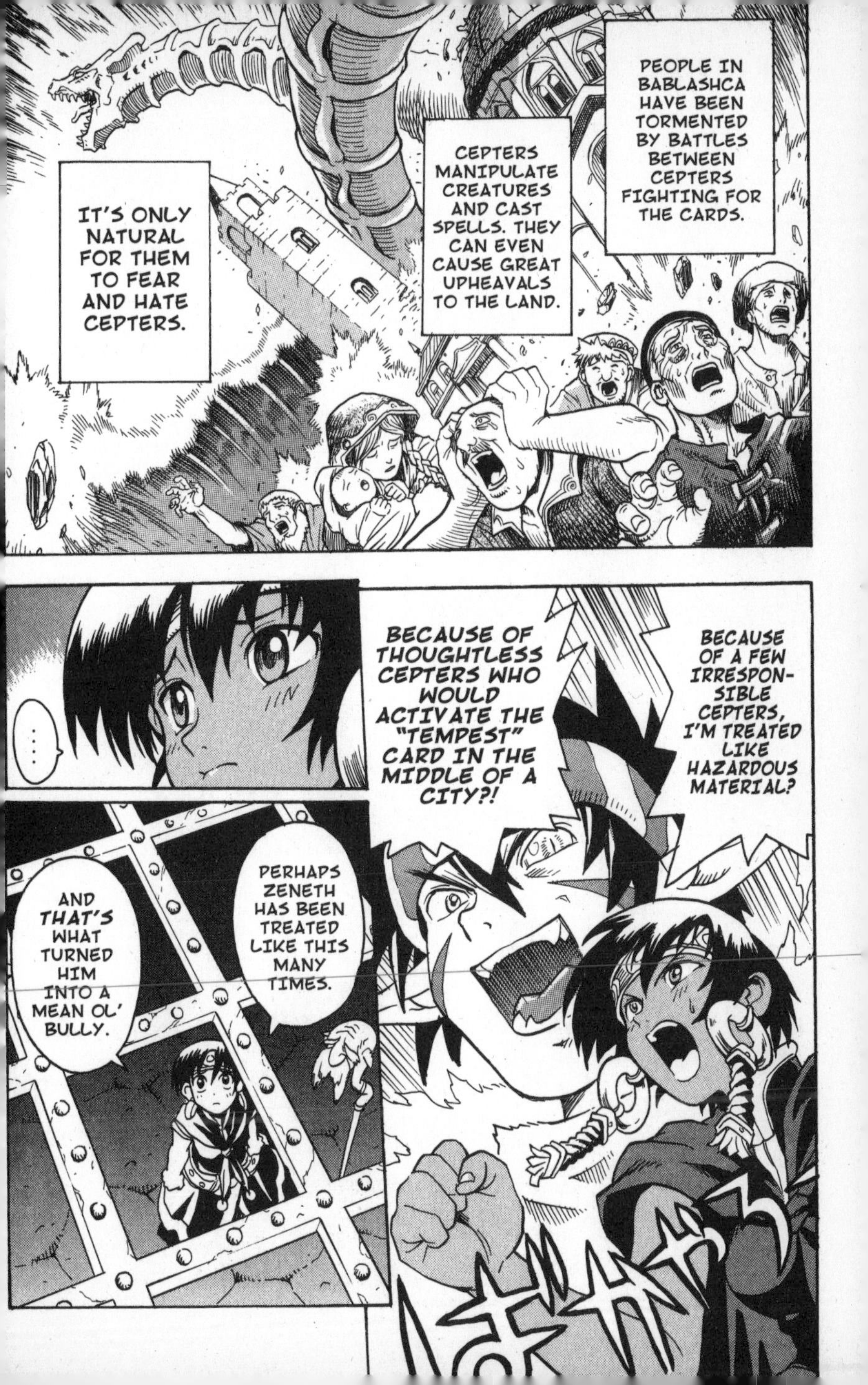
PEOPLE IN BABLASHCA HAVE BEEN TORMENTED BY BATTLES BETWEEN CEPTERS FIGHTING FOR THE CARDS.
CEPTERS MANIPULATE CREATURES AND CAST SPELLS. THEY CAN EVEN CAUSE GREAT UPHEAVALS TO THE LAND.
IT'S ONLY NATURAL FOR THEM TO FEAR AND HATE CEPTERS.
BECAUSE OF A FEW IRRESPON-SIBLE CEPTERS, I'M TREATED LIKE HAZARDOUS MATERIAL?
BECAUSE OF THOUGHTLESS CEPTERS WHO WOULD ACTIVATE THE "TEMPEST" CARD IN THE MIDDLE OF A CITY?!
....
PERHAPS ZENETH HAS BEEN TREATED LIKE THIS MANY TIMES.
AND THAT'S WHAT TURNED HIM INTO A MEAN OL' BULLY.

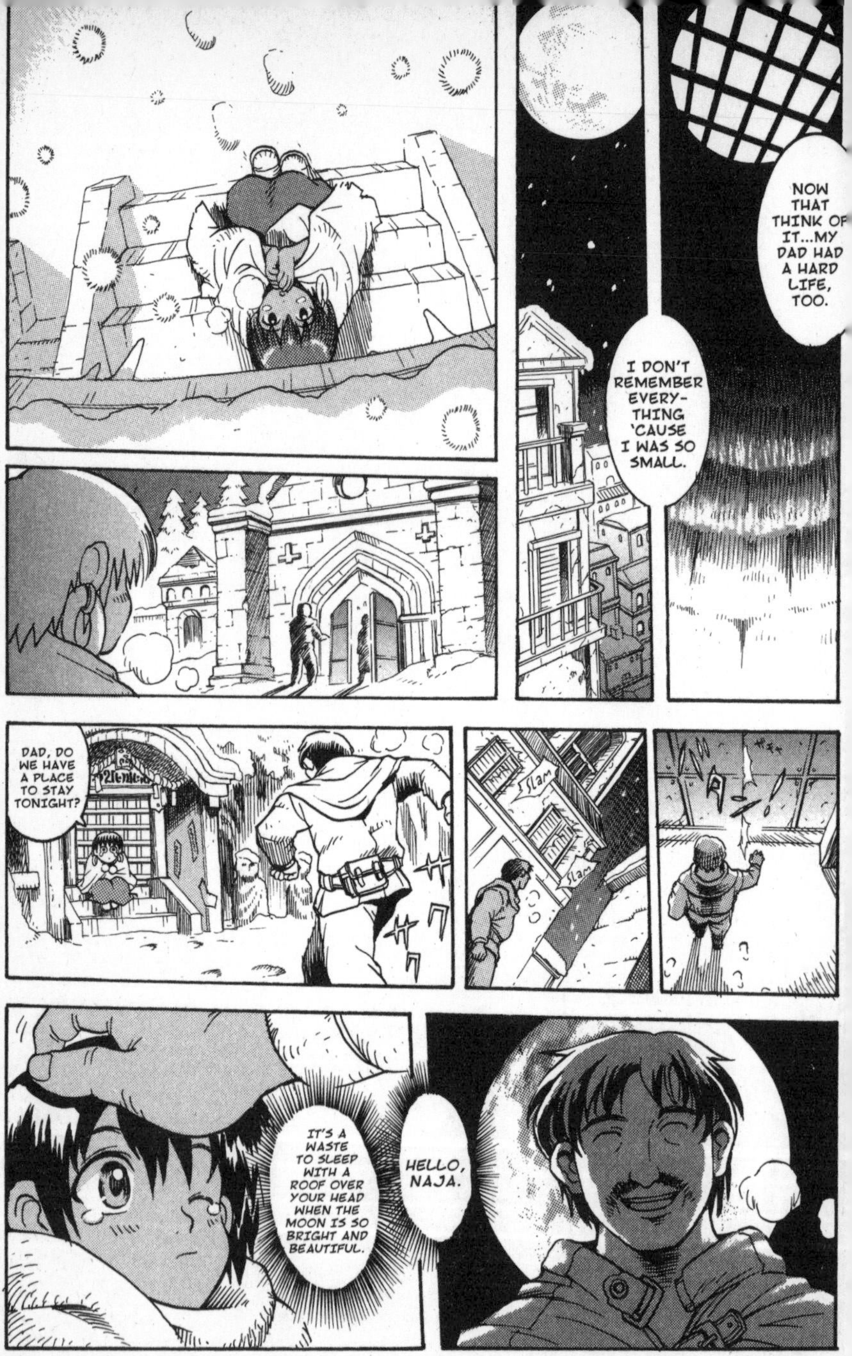
NOW THAT THINK OF IT...MY DAD HAD A HARD LIFE, TOO.
I DON'T REMEMBER EVERYTHING 'CAUSE I WAS SO SMALL.
Slam
Slam
DAD, DO WE HAVE A PLACE TO STAY TONIGHT?
HELLO, NAJA.
IT'S A WASTE TO SLEEP WITH A ROOF OVER YOUR HEAD WHEN THE MOON IS SO BRIGHT AND BEAUTIFUL.

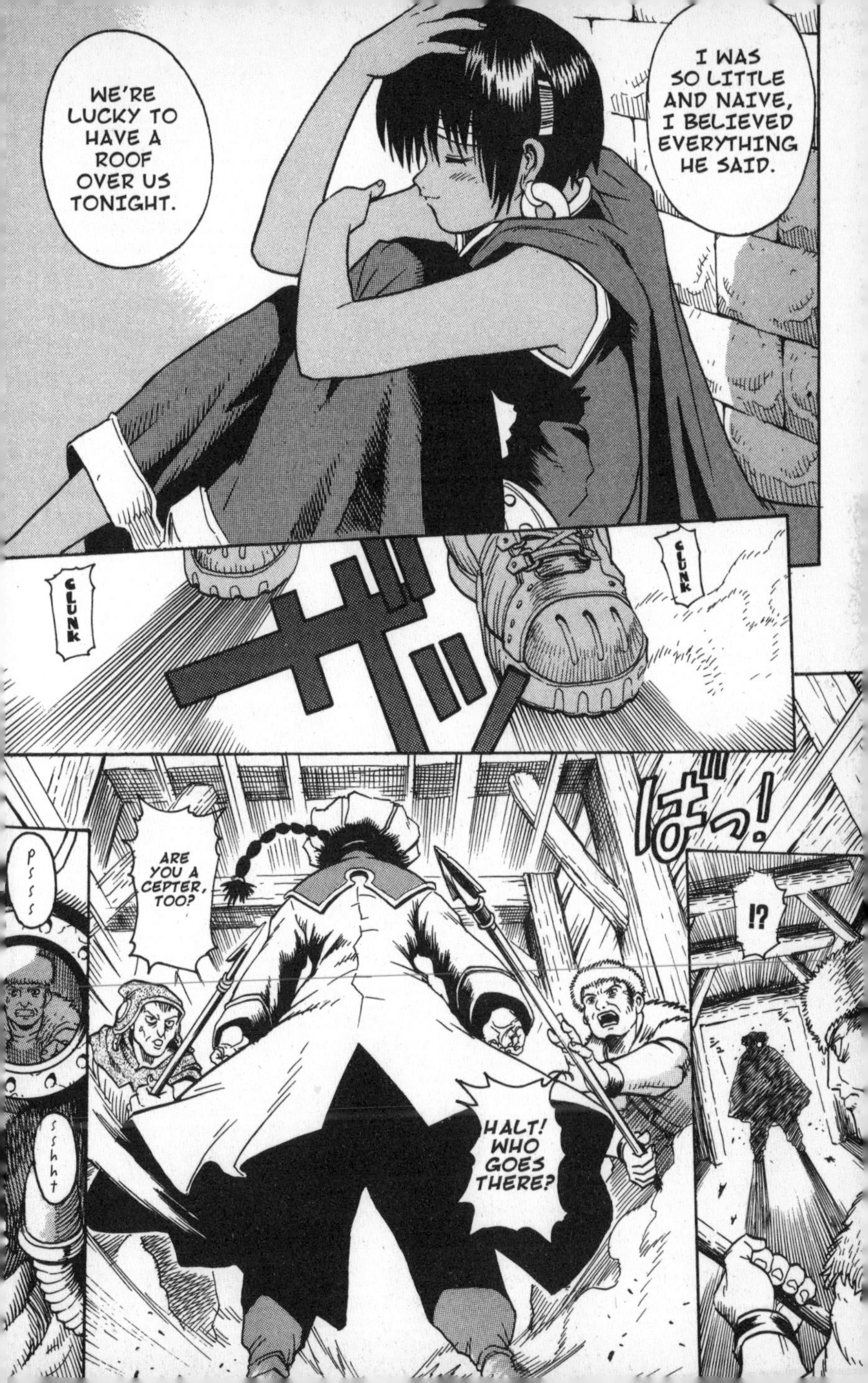
I WAS SO LITTLE AND NAIVE, I BELIEVED EVERYTHING HE SAID.
WE'RE LUCKY TO HAVE A ROOF OVER US TONIGHT.
GLUNK
ギッ
GLUNK
ぱっ!
!?
ARE YOU A CEPTER, TOO?
HALT! WHO GOES THERE?
Psss
sshht

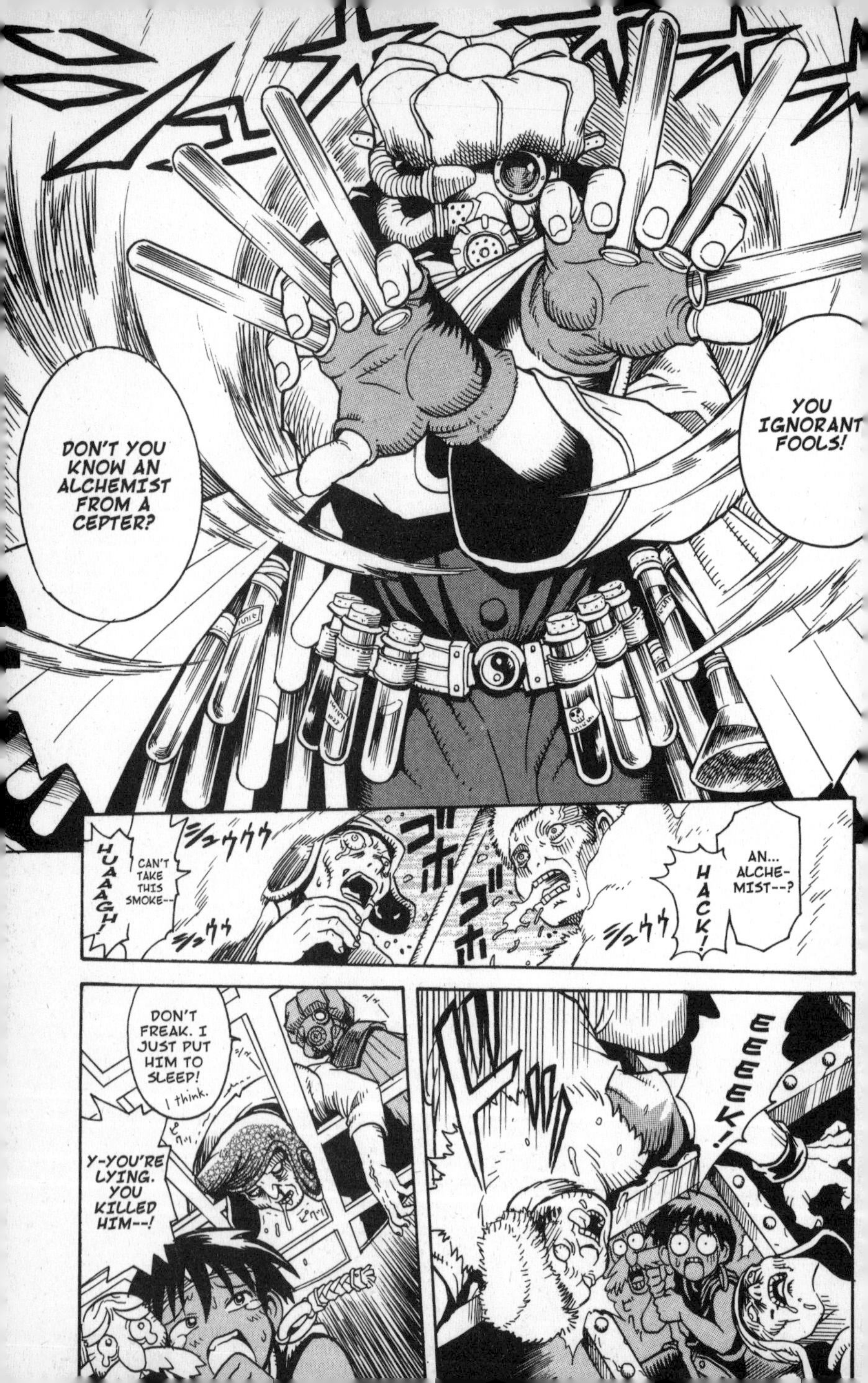
YOU IGNORANT FOOLS!
DON'T YOU KNOW AN ALCHEMIST FROM A CEPTER?
AN... ALCHE-MIST--?
HACK!
CAN'T TAKE THIS SMOKE--
HUAAAGH!
EEEEEK!
DON'T FREAK. I JUST PUT HIM TO SLEEP!
I think.
Y-YOU'RE LYING. YOU KILLED HIM--!

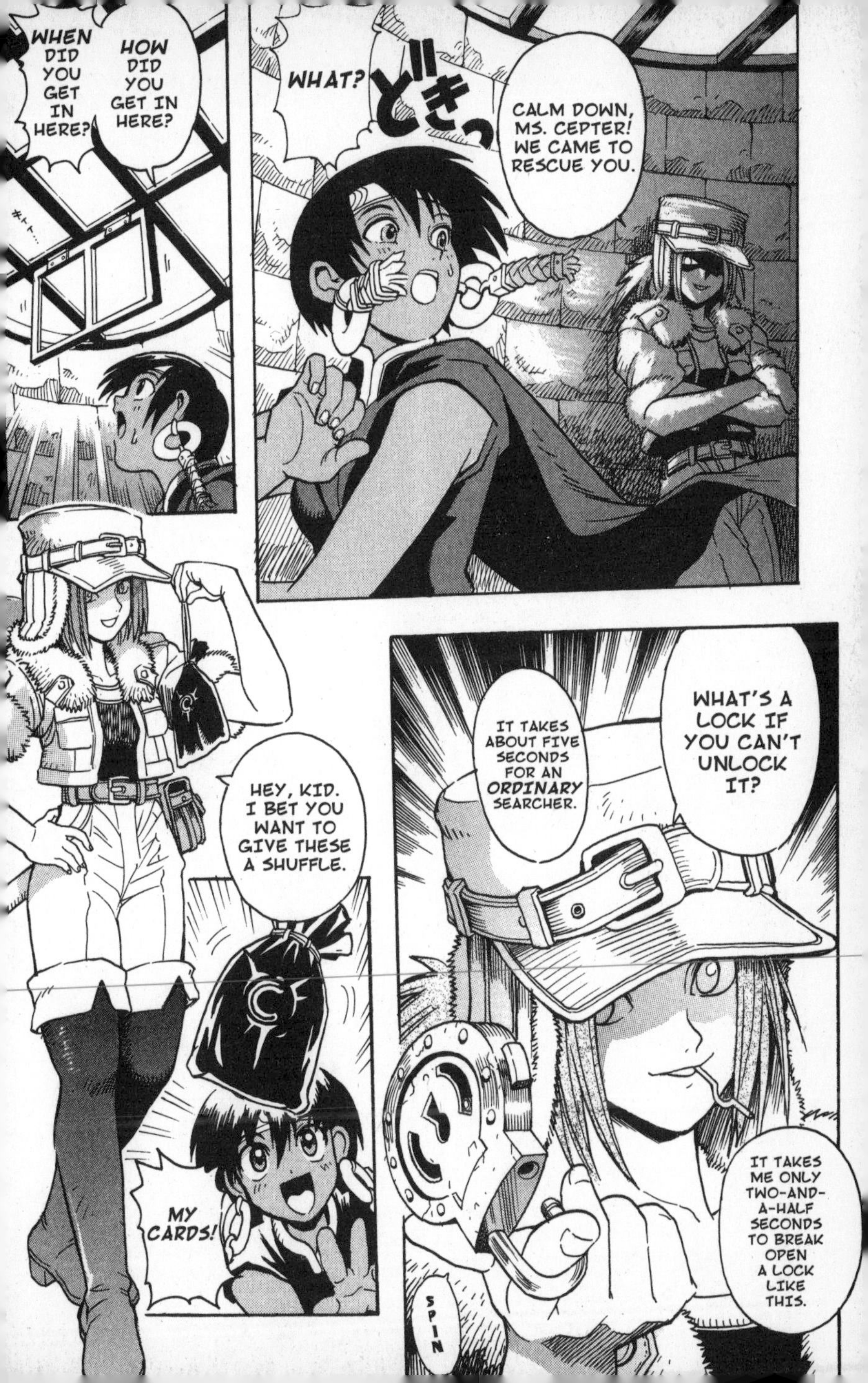
CALM DOWN, MS. CEPTER! WE CAME TO RESCUE YOU.
どきっ
WHAT?
HOW DID YOU GET IN HERE?
WHEN DID YOU GET IN HERE?
WHAT'S A LOCK IF YOU CAN'T UNLOCK IT?
IT TAKES ABOUT FIVE SECONDS FOR AN ORDINARY SEARCHER.
IT TAKES ME ONLY TWO-AND-A-HALF SECONDS TO BREAK OPEN A LOCK LIKE THIS.
SPIN
HEY, KID. I BET YOU WANT TO GIVE THESE A SHUFFLE.
MY CARDS!

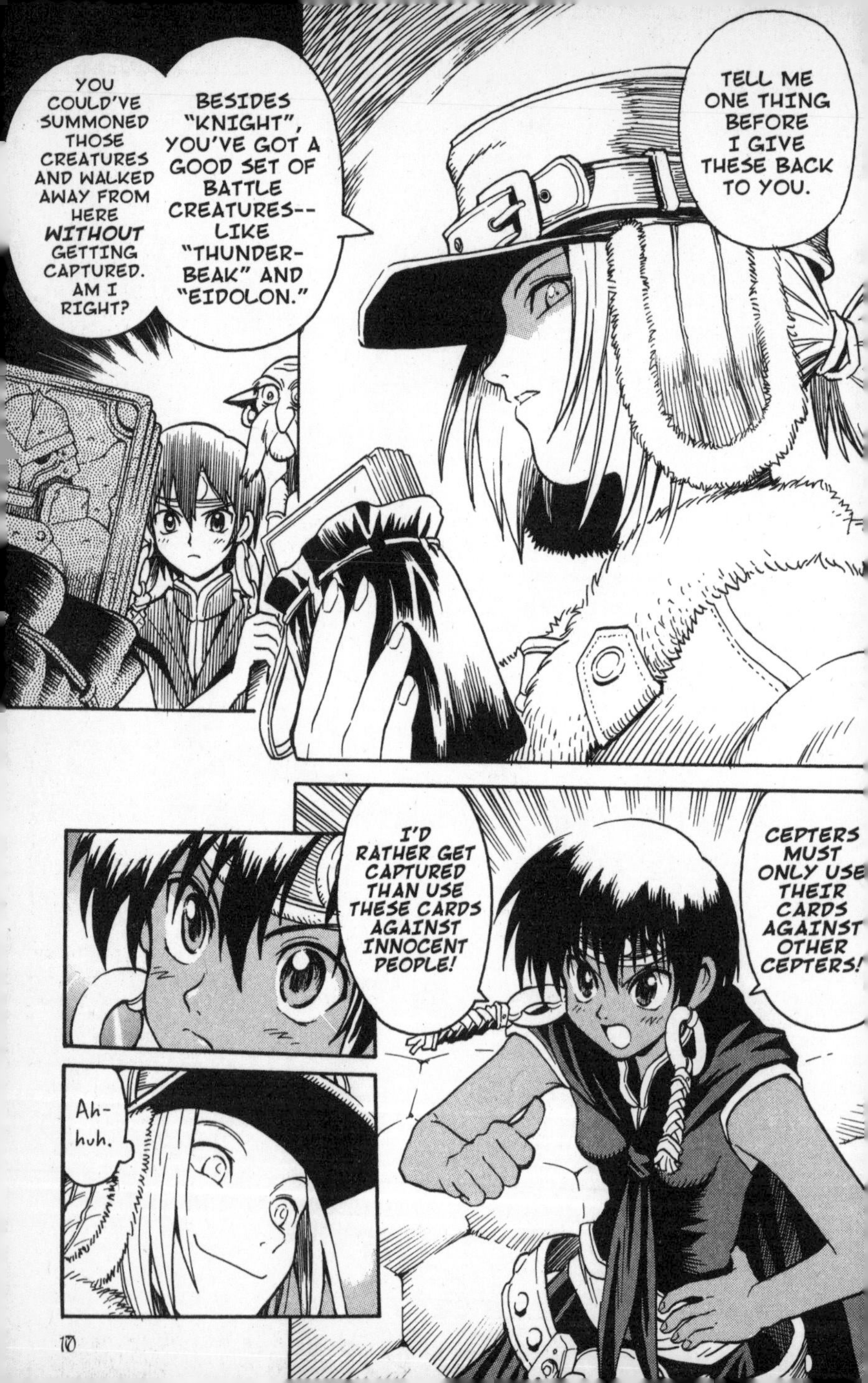
TELL ME ONE THING BEFORE I GIVE THESE BACK TO YOU.
BESIDES "KNIGHT", YOU'VE GOT A GOOD SET OF BATTLE CREATURES--LIKE "THUNDER-BEAK" AND "EIDOLON."
YOU COULD'VE SUMMONED THOSE CREATURES AND WALKED AWAY FROM HERE *WITHOUT* GETTING CAPTURED. AM I RIGHT?
CEPTERS MUST ONLY USE THEIR CARDS AGAINST OTHER CEPTERS!
I'D RATHER GET CAPTURED THAN USE THESE CARDS AGAINST INNOCENT PEOPLE!
Ah-huh.

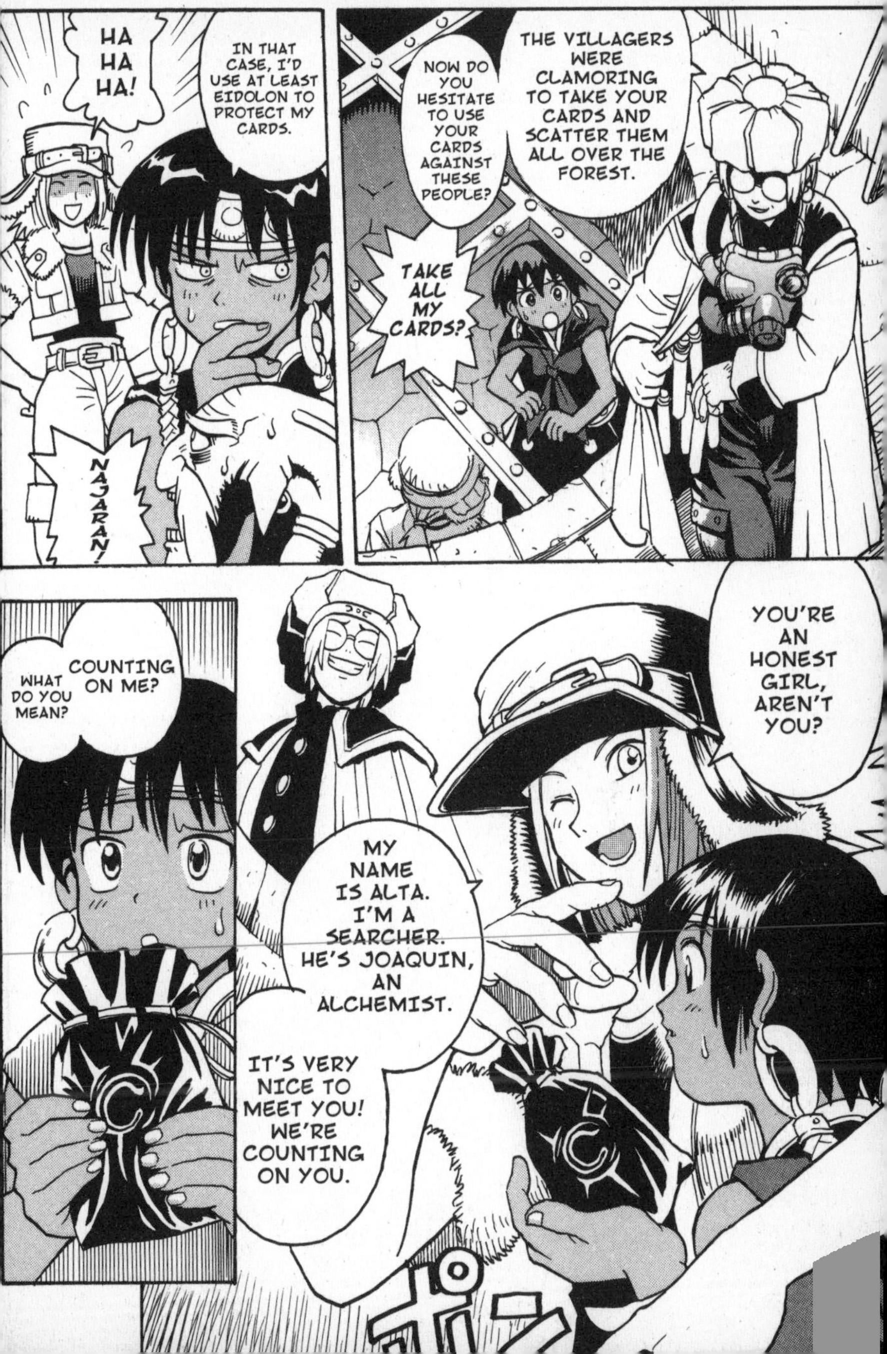
THE VILLAGERS WERE CLAMORING TO TAKE YOUR CARDS AND SCATTER THEM ALL OVER THE FOREST.
NOW DO YOU HESITATE TO USE YOUR CARDS AGAINST THESE PEOPLE?
TAKE ALL MY CARDS?
IN THAT CASE, I'D USE AT LEAST EIDOLON TO PROTECT MY CARDS.
HA HA HA!
NAJARAN!
YOU'RE AN HONEST GIRL, AREN'T YOU?
MY NAME IS ALTA. I'M A SEARCHER. HE'S JOAQUIN, AN ALCHEMIST.
IT'S VERY NICE TO MEET YOU! WE'RE COUNTING ON YOU.
COUNTING ON ME?
WHAT DO YOU MEAN?

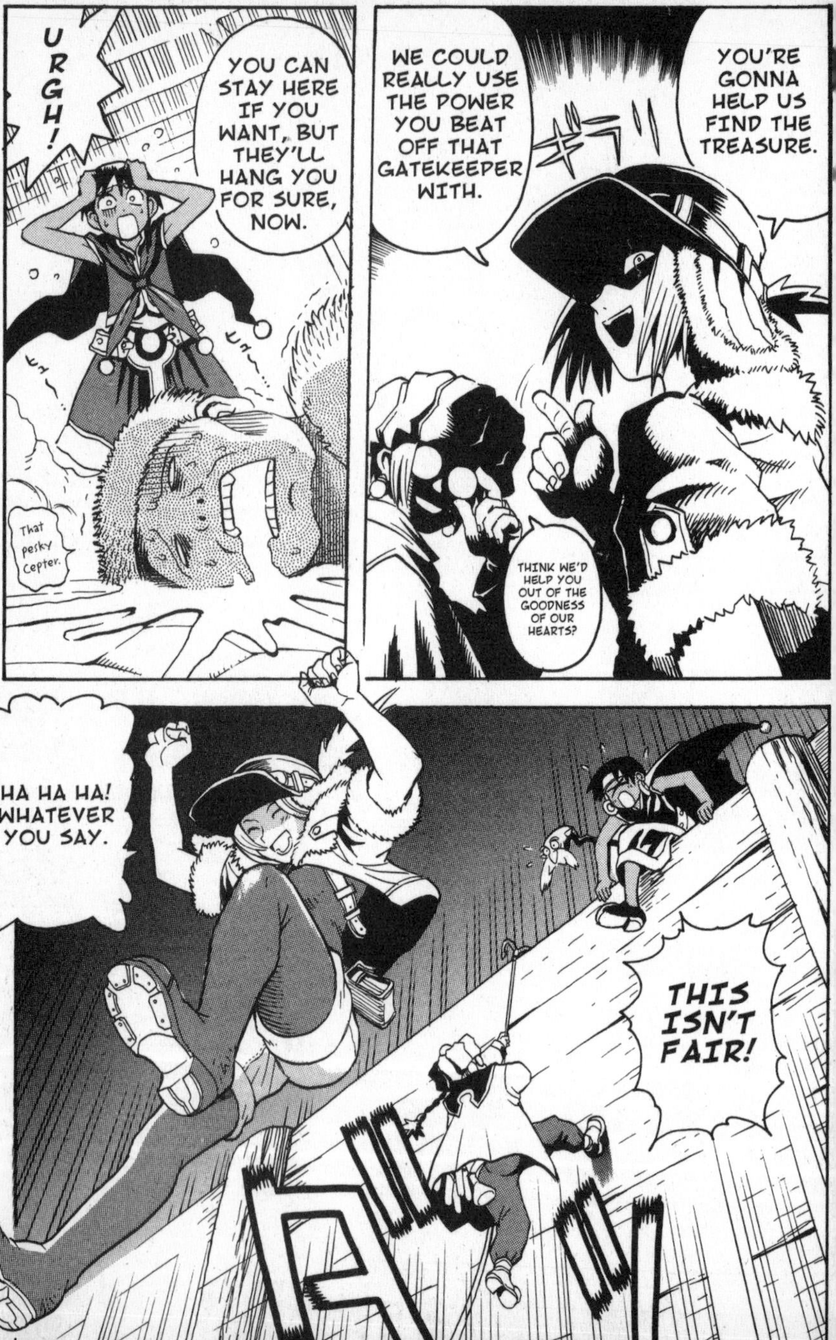
YOU'RE GONNA HELP US FIND THE TREASURE.
WE COULD REALLY USE THE POWER YOU BEAT OFF THAT GATEKEEPER WITH.
THINK WE'D HELP YOU OUT OF THE GOODNESS OF OUR HEARTS?
YOU CAN STAY HERE IF YOU WANT, BUT THEY'LL HANG YOU FOR SURE, NOW.
URGH!
That pesky Cepter.
THIS ISN'T FAIR!
HA HA HA! WHATEVER YOU SAY.

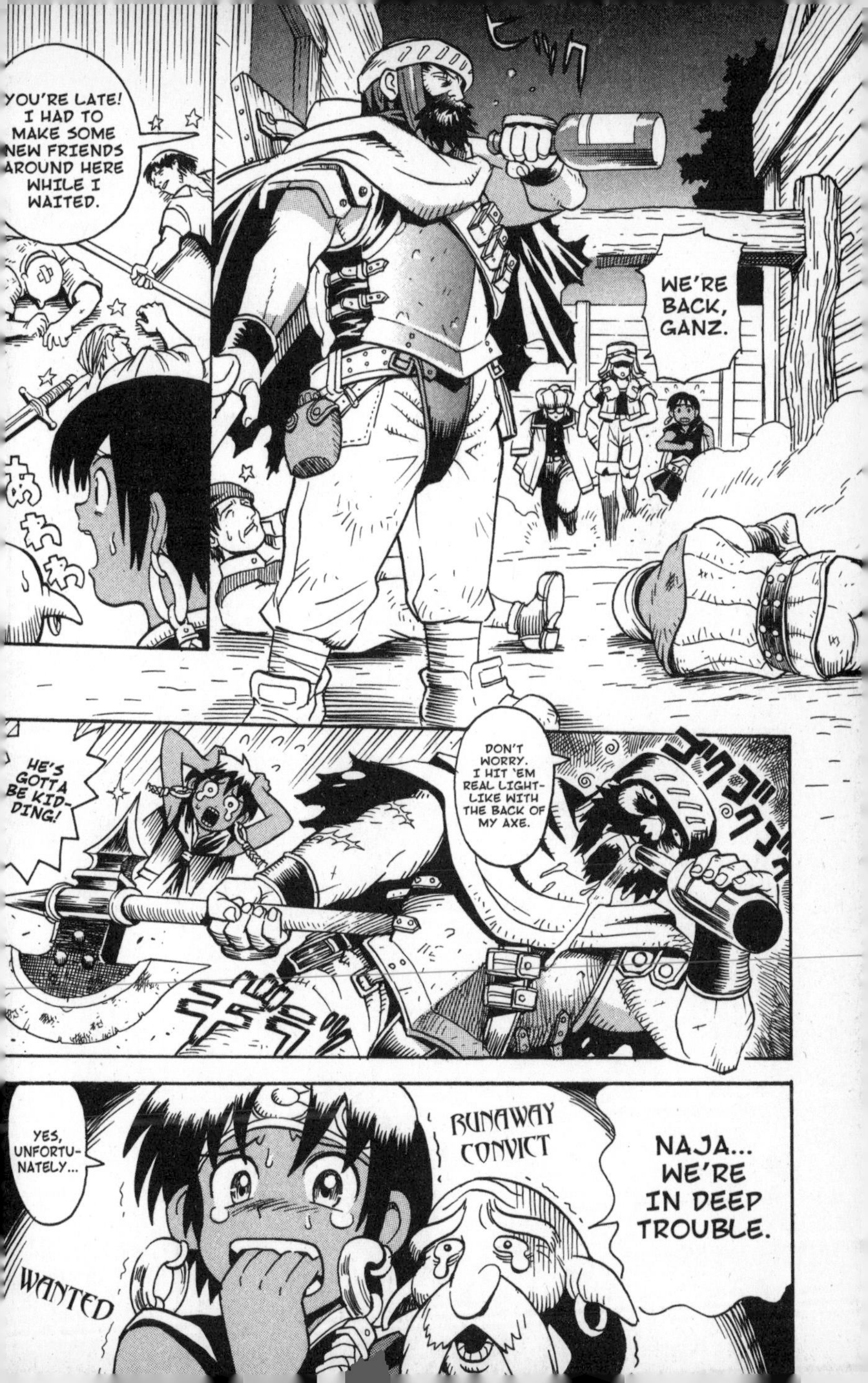
ヒック
WE'RE BACK, GANZ.
YOU'RE LATE! I HAD TO MAKE SOME NEW FRIENDS AROUND HERE WHILE I WAITED.
あわわ
DON'T WORRY. I HIT 'EM REAL LIGHT-LIKE WITH THE BACK OF MY AXE.
HE'S GOTTA BE KID-DING!
NAJA... WE'RE IN DEEP TROUBLE.
RUNAWAY CONVICT
YES, UNFORTU-NATELY...
WANTED

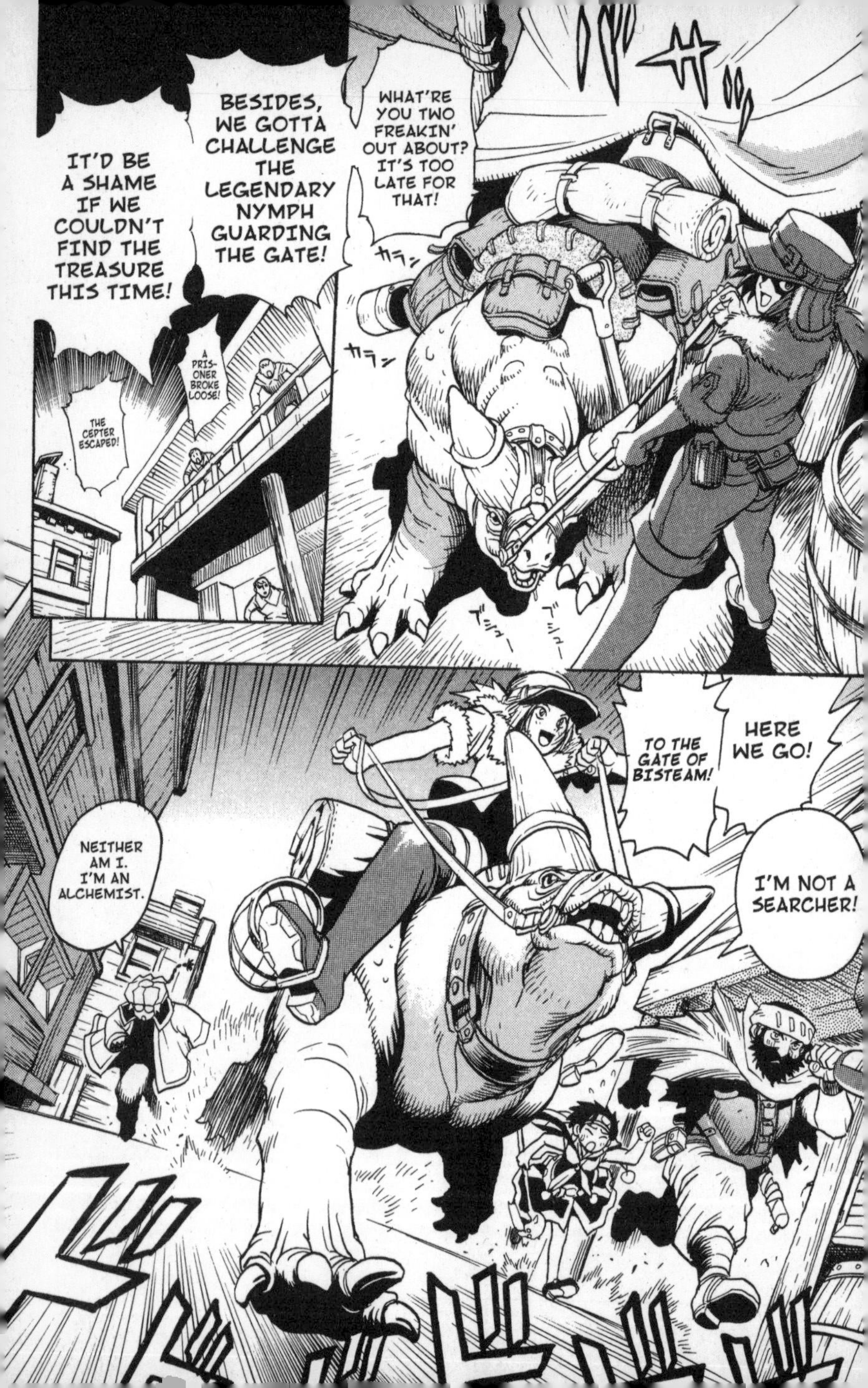
WHAT'RE YOU TWO FREAKIN' OUT ABOUT? IT'S TOO LATE FOR THAT!
BESIDES, WE GOTTA CHALLENGE THE LEGENDARY NYMPH GUARDING THE GATE!
IT'D BE A SHAME IF WE COULDN'T FIND THE TREASURE THIS TIME!
A PRIS-ONER BROKE LOOSE!
THE CEPTER ESCAPED!
HERE WE GO!
TO THE GATE OF BISTEAM!
I'M NOT A SEARCHER!
NEITHER AM I. I'M AN ALCHEMIST.

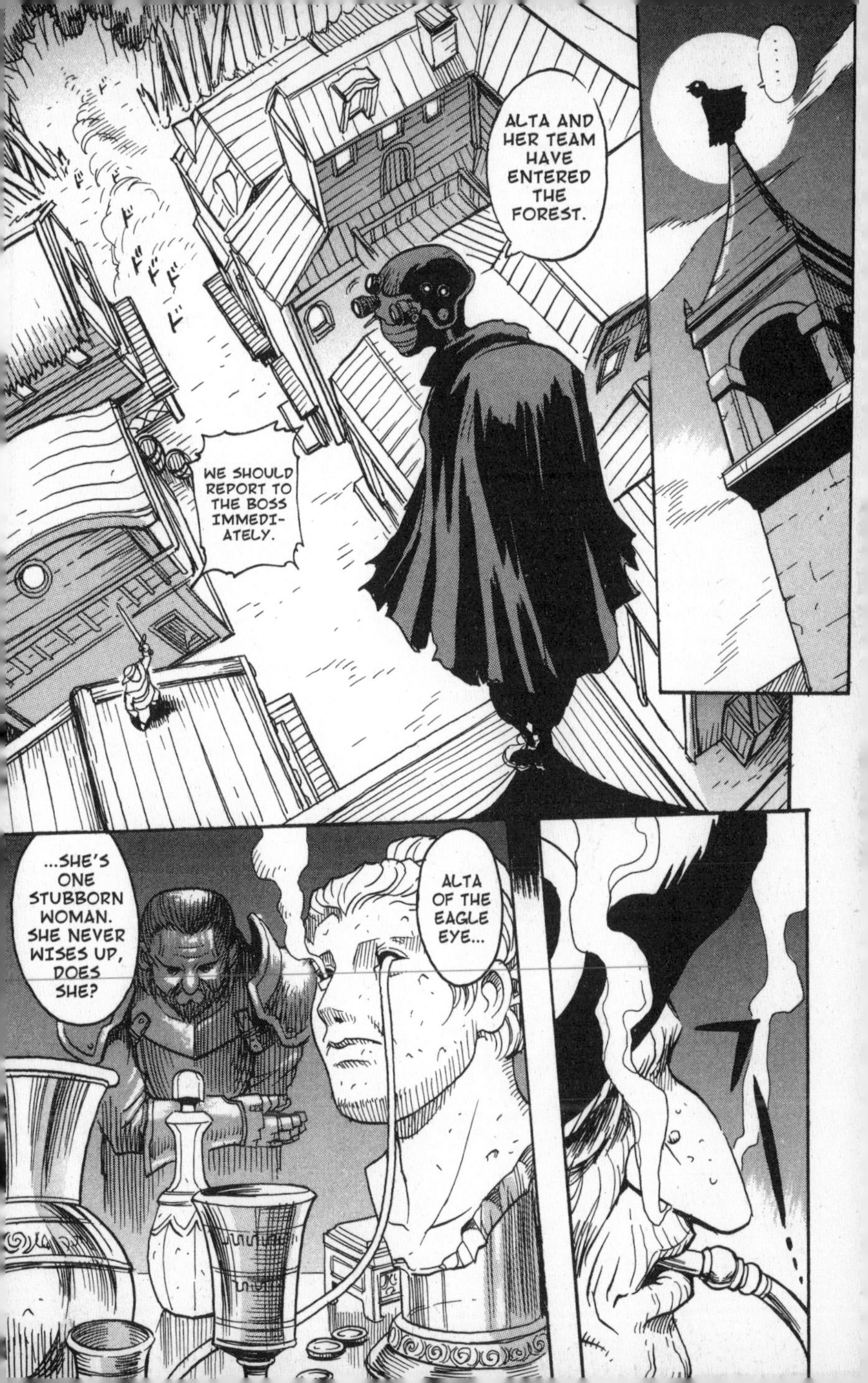
...
ALTA AND HER TEAM HAVE ENTERED THE FOREST.
WE SHOULD REPORT TO THE BOSS IMMEDIATELY.
ALTA OF THE EAGLE EYE...
...SHE'S ONE STUBBORN WOMAN. SHE NEVER WISES UP, DOES SHE?

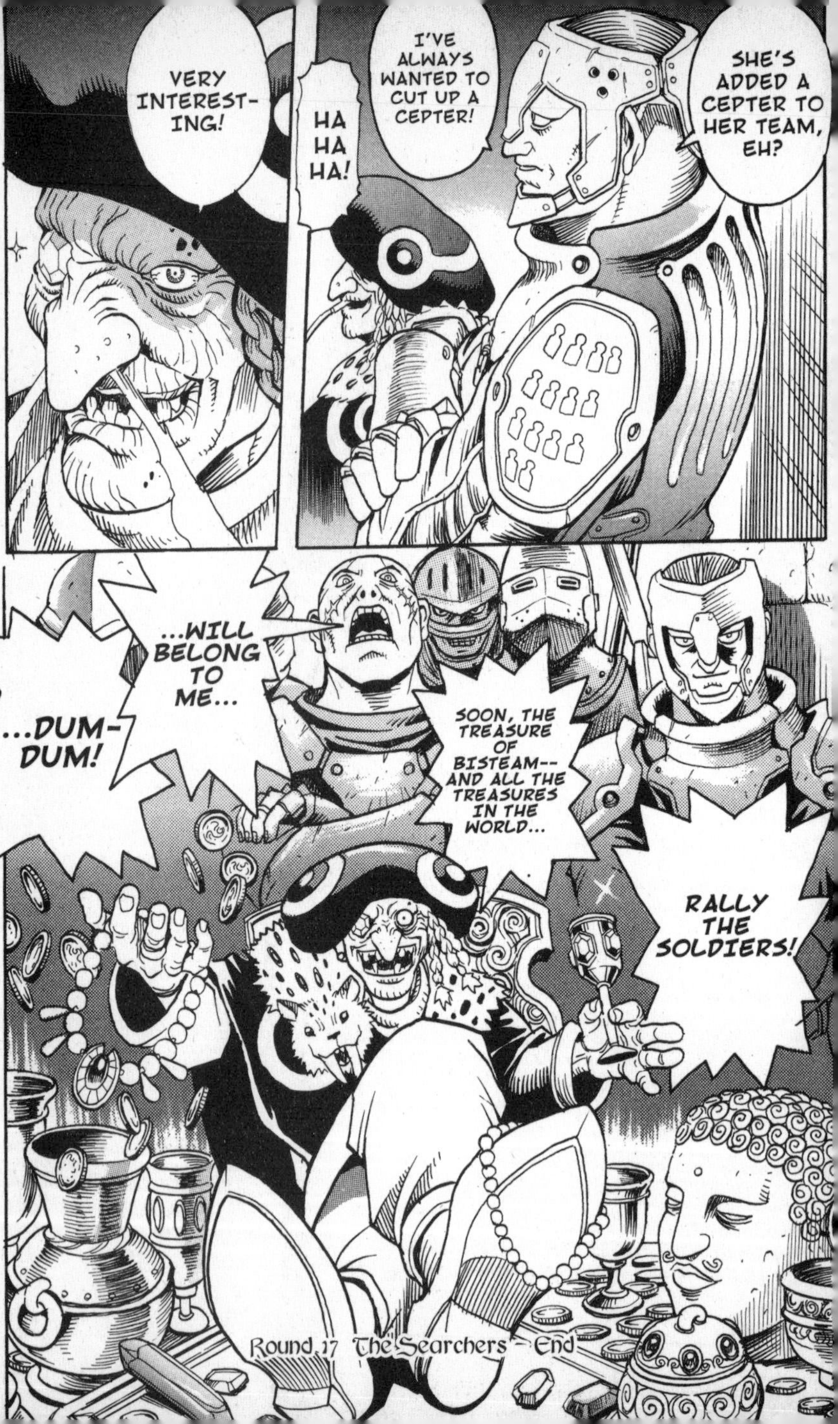
SHE'S ADDED A CEPTER TO HER TEAM, EH?
I'VE ALWAYS WANTED TO CUT UP A CEPTER!
HA HA HA!
VERY INTEREST-ING!
SOON, THE TREASURE OF BISTEAM-- AND ALL THE TREASURES IN THE WORLD...
...WILL BELONG TO ME...
...DUM-DUM!
RALLY THE SOLDIERS!
Round 17 The Searchers - End

Forest of Bisteam - Character Profiles

A Searcher is a hired gun. They work for merchants or the Cepter Guild, hunting for cards, items, and treasures. Searchers are all over the world—in mountains, at sea and on the Bablashca continent. Many of the cards that Cepters possess were found by Searchers.

THE SEARCHER
ALTA

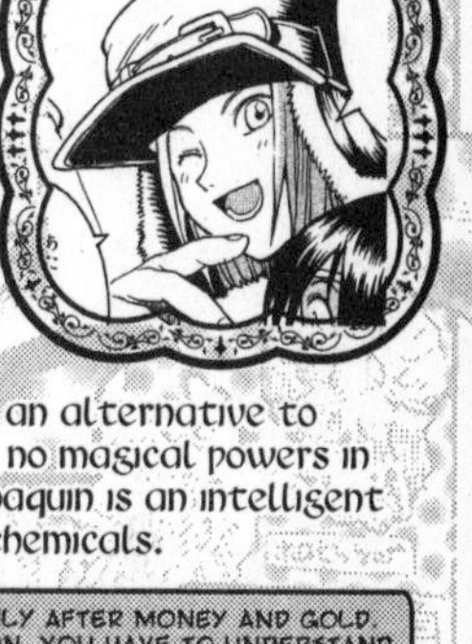

DON'T CALL ME A "LOOTER"! BEING A GOOD SEARCHER ISN'T EASY. YOU'VE GOT TO BE PRETTY SHARP AT LOCATING TREASURE. IT TAKES A LOT OF GUTS AND KNOWLEDGE. YOU'VE ALSO GOT TO BE QUICK ON YOUR FEET. IF YOU HAVE THESE QUALITIES, YOUR CHANCE OF DIGGING UP TREASURE AT AN EXCAVATION SITE IS GOOD. THE SEARCHER IS INVOLVED IN THE NOBLE PROFESSION OF FINDING TREASURES WHICH WERE LOST BY THEIR OWNERS AND RECYCLING THEM INTO THE WORLD. YOU KNOW WHAT I MEAN? HUH? SITES PROTECTED BY GUARDS AREN'T EXACTLY REMAINS? YOU STILL THINK SEARCHERS ARE THIEVES? WELL, DON'T ARGUE WITH ME!

SELF-PROCLAIMED GENIUS
JOAQUIN

He is an alchemist who uses modern science as an alternative to spells and witchcraft. People in Rakan, having no magical powers in general, depend on the power of alchemists. Joaquin is an intelligent young man who loves books and enjoys mixing chemicals.

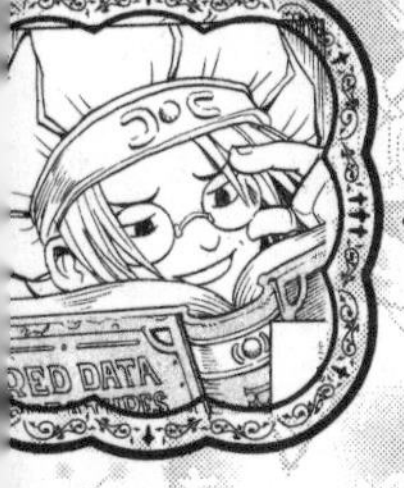
RED DATA

SOME SAY ALCHEMY IS PHONY, AND ALCHEMISTS ARE ONLY AFTER MONEY AND GOLD. THEY'RE ABSOLUTELY WRONG. TO CREATE GOLD FROM IRON, YOU HAVE TO UNDERSTAND THE FUNDAMENTAL NATURE OF MATTER. WHY ARE NO DOGS BORN FROM CHICKENS? HOW SHOULD YOU ALTER THE BIOLOGY OF A CHICKEN SO THAT IT WILL GIVE BIRTH TO A DOG? ALCHEMY ANSWERS QUESTIONS REGARDING THE FUNDAMENTAL NATURE OF THE UNIVERSE AND ALL MATTER. OF COURSE, ALCHEMY INVOLVES SOME UNPLEASANT TOOLS, SUCH AS EXPLOSIVES AND POISONOUS GASES. THESE ARE MERELY TOOLS, AFTER ALL. THEY SAY THE NYMPHS OF BISTEAM POSSESS TREASURES. I'M VERY INTERESTED IN THEIR WITCHCRAFT TO REFINE METAL! I HEAR THEY MAKE THE METAL MOLECULES BIND TIGHTER WITH EACH OTHER. ANOTHER THEORY IS THAT THEY CREATE UNBREAKABLE MATERIALS BY CREATING A SPECIAL MOLECULAR ARRANGEMENT--' SNIP '

HEY! DON'T CUT MY EXPLANATION SHORT! THERE ARE TWELVE MORE THEORIES ABOUT HOW THIS WITCHERY WORKS, AND--' SNIP '

RED-NOSED BODYGUARD
GANZ

Swords are powerful weapons on the Bablashca Continent where battles between Cepters take place. Swordsmen skilled enough can even confront creatures from a Cepter card with their swordplay. Ganz, one of the great sword-masters, doesn't even remember how good he is.

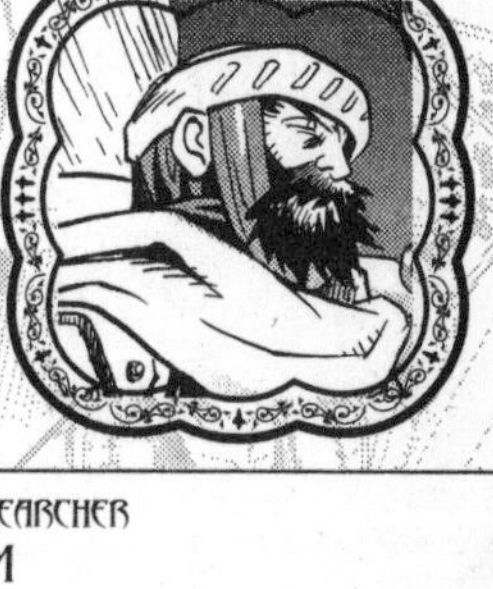

COME ON, YOUNG MAN. HAVE ANOTHER ROUND WITH ME! WHAT? THIS IS YOUR DRINK? OH, WELL, WHATEVER. IT'S MINE NOW. GULP, GULP. THIS IS GREAT. BOOZE MAKES ME FORGET ABOUT TRIVIAL THINGS--MY DEBTS, FACES OF THE MEN I'VE KILLED. BY THE WAY, WHO THE HECK ARE YOU AGAIN? OH, WELL, COME ON, KEEP UP WITH YOUR DRINKING!

THE FORMIDABLE SEARCHER
DUM-DUM

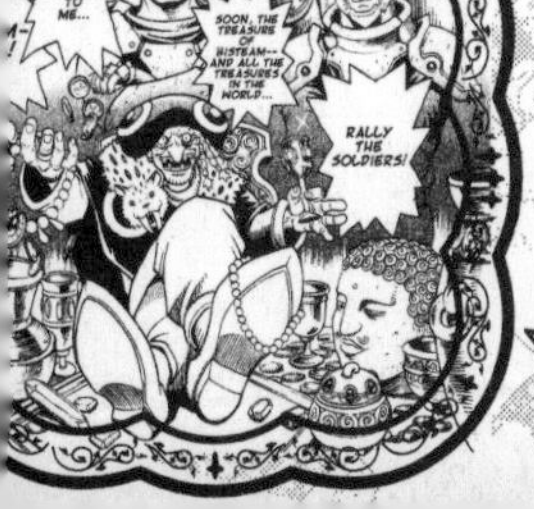
SOON, THE TREASURE OF BISTEAM--AND ALL THE TREASURES IN THE WORLD...
...WILL BELONG TO ME...
RALLY THE SOLDIERS!

There are a group of armed Searchers that fellow Searchers love to hate. They're more like a roving gang of looters. Dum-Dum's activities are kept secret, and his soldiers leave no witnesses alive.

"YOURS IS MINE!" "TREASURES FROM ANCIENT TIMES AND WITHOUT OWNERS ARE ALL MINE!" "I SHOOT WHATEVER MOVES BEFORE ME!" "ANYONE WHO RUNS AWAY FROM ME IS AN ENEMY! IF HE CAN'T RUN FAST ENOUGH, HE DESERVES DEATH!" "WE'RE THE GREATEST SEARCHERS IN ALL OF RAKAN!"
-DUM-DUM

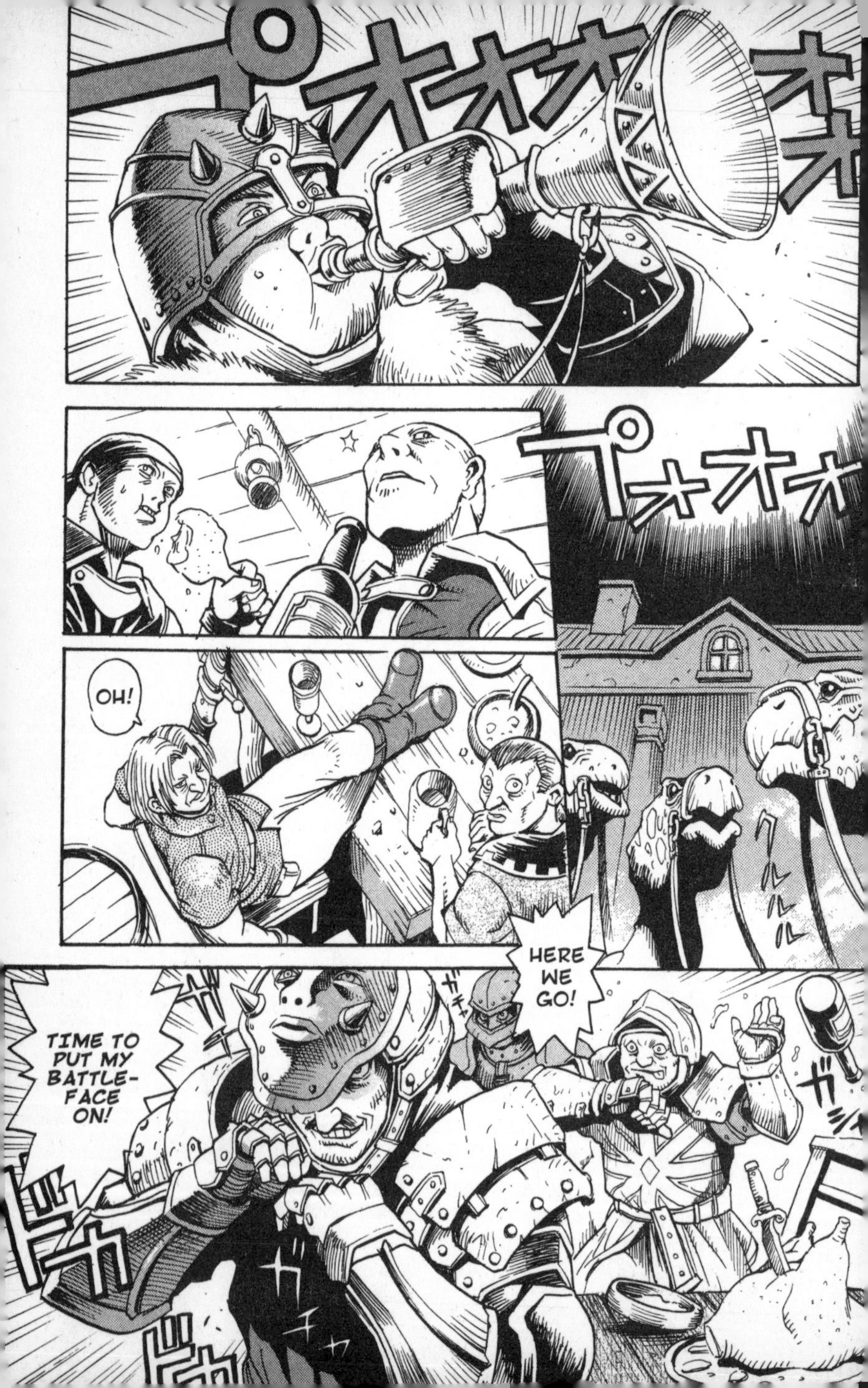

プオオオオオ
プォオオオ
クルルル
OH!
HERE WE GO!
ガシャ
TIME TO PUT MY BATTLE-FACE ON!

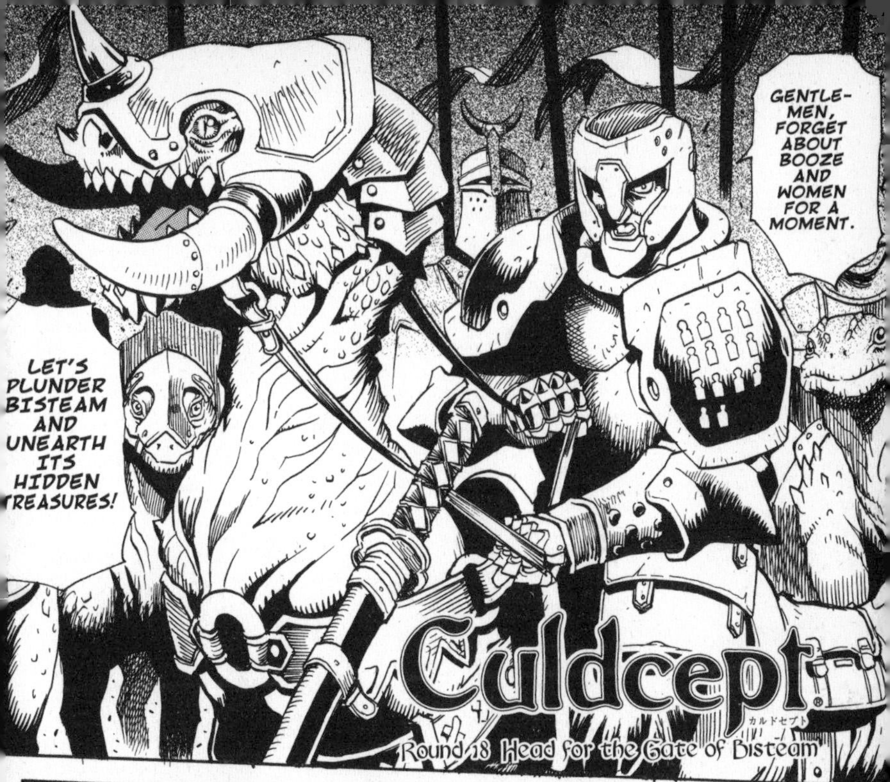
GENTLE-MEN, FORGET ABOUT BOOZE AND WOMEN FOR A MOMENT.
LET'S PLUNDER BISTEAM AND UNEARTH ITS HIDDEN TREASURES!
Culdcept®
カルドセプト
Round 18 Head for the Gate of Bisteam

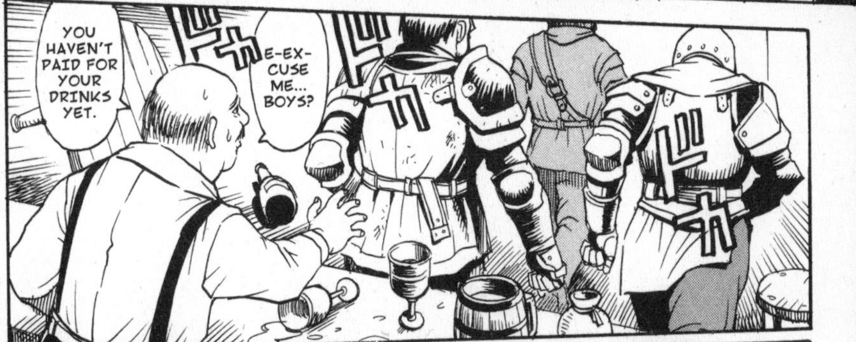
ドカ
E-EX-CUSE ME... BOYS?
YOU HAVEN'T PAID FOR YOUR DRINKS YET.
ドカ

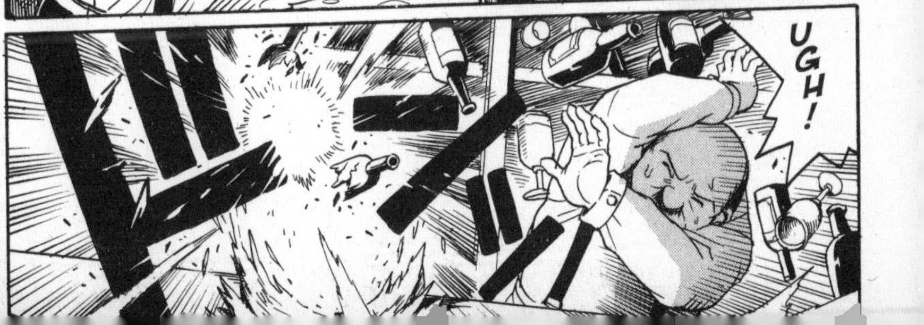
UGH!

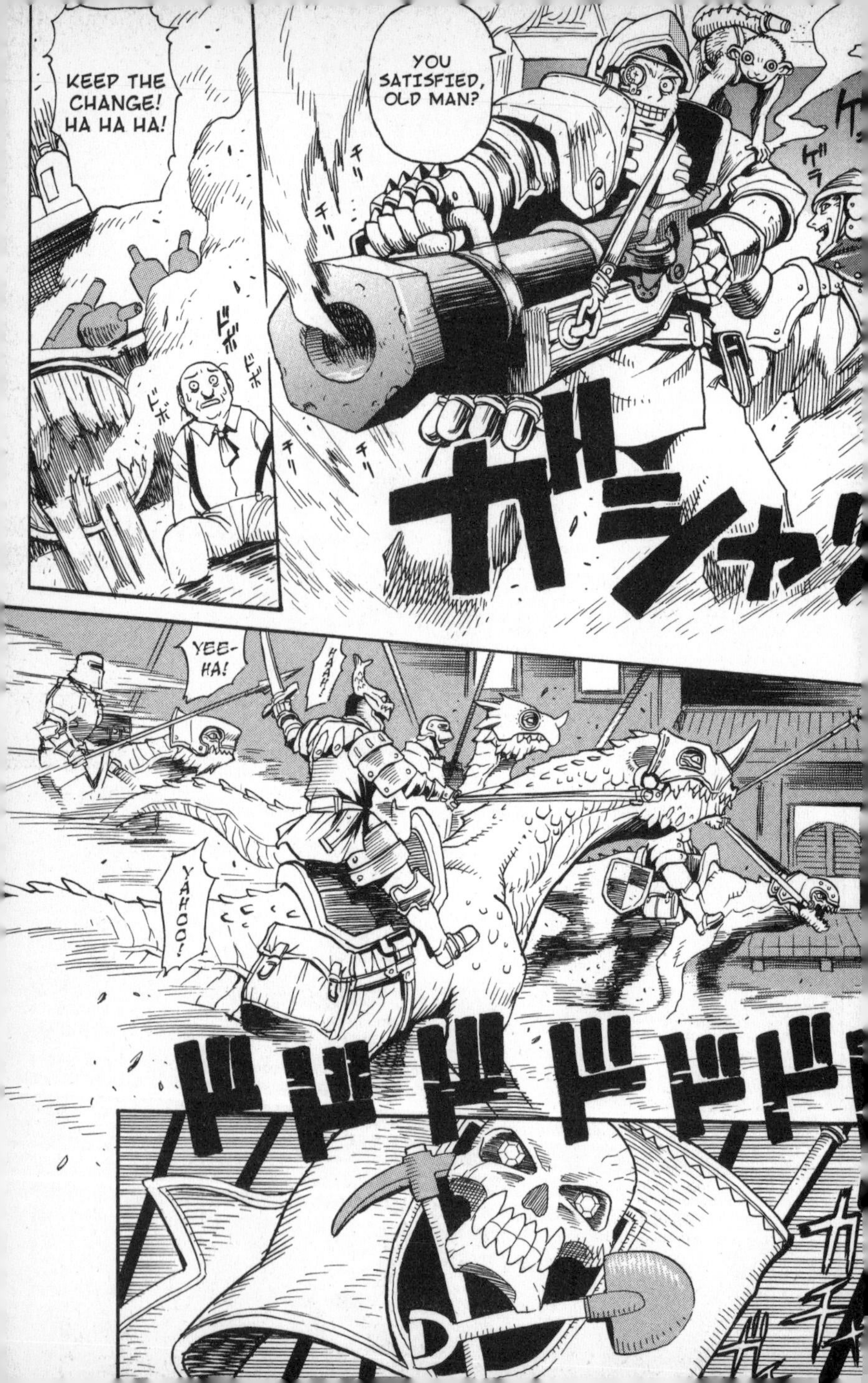
YOU SATISFIED, OLD MAN?
チリ
チリ
チリ
チリ
ゲラ
ゲラ
KEEP THE CHANGE! HA HA HA!
ドボ
ドボ
ドボ
HAAH!
YEE-HA!
YAHOO!

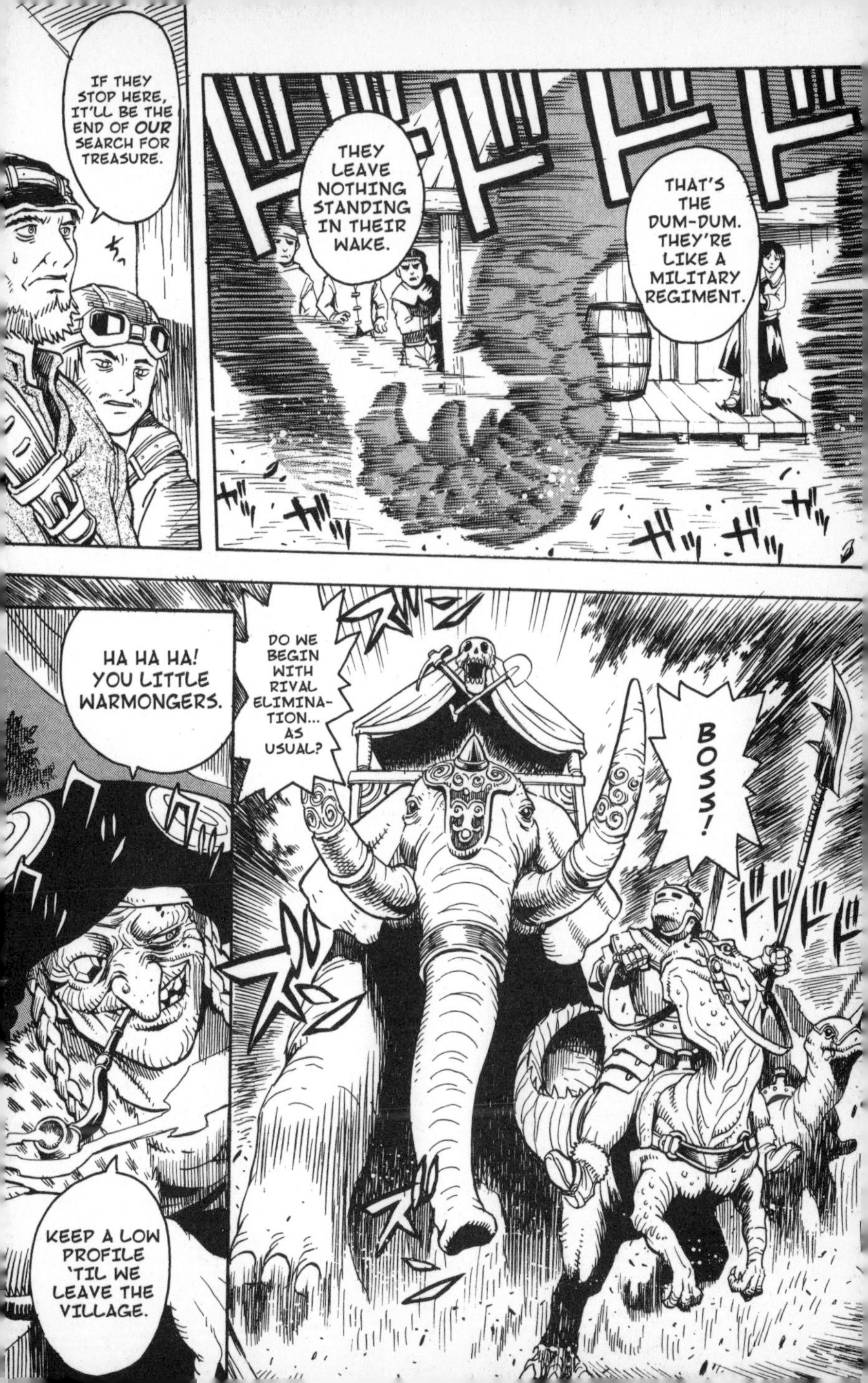
THAT'S THE DUM-DUM. THEY'RE LIKE A MILITARY REGIMENT.
THEY LEAVE NOTHING STANDING IN THEIR WAKE.
IF THEY STOP HERE, IT'LL BE THE END OF OUR SEARCH FOR TREASURE.
BOSS!
DO WE BEGIN WITH RIVAL ELIMINATION... AS USUAL?
HA HA HA! YOU LITTLE WARMONGERS.
KEEP A LOW PROFILE 'TIL WE LEAVE THE VILLAGE.

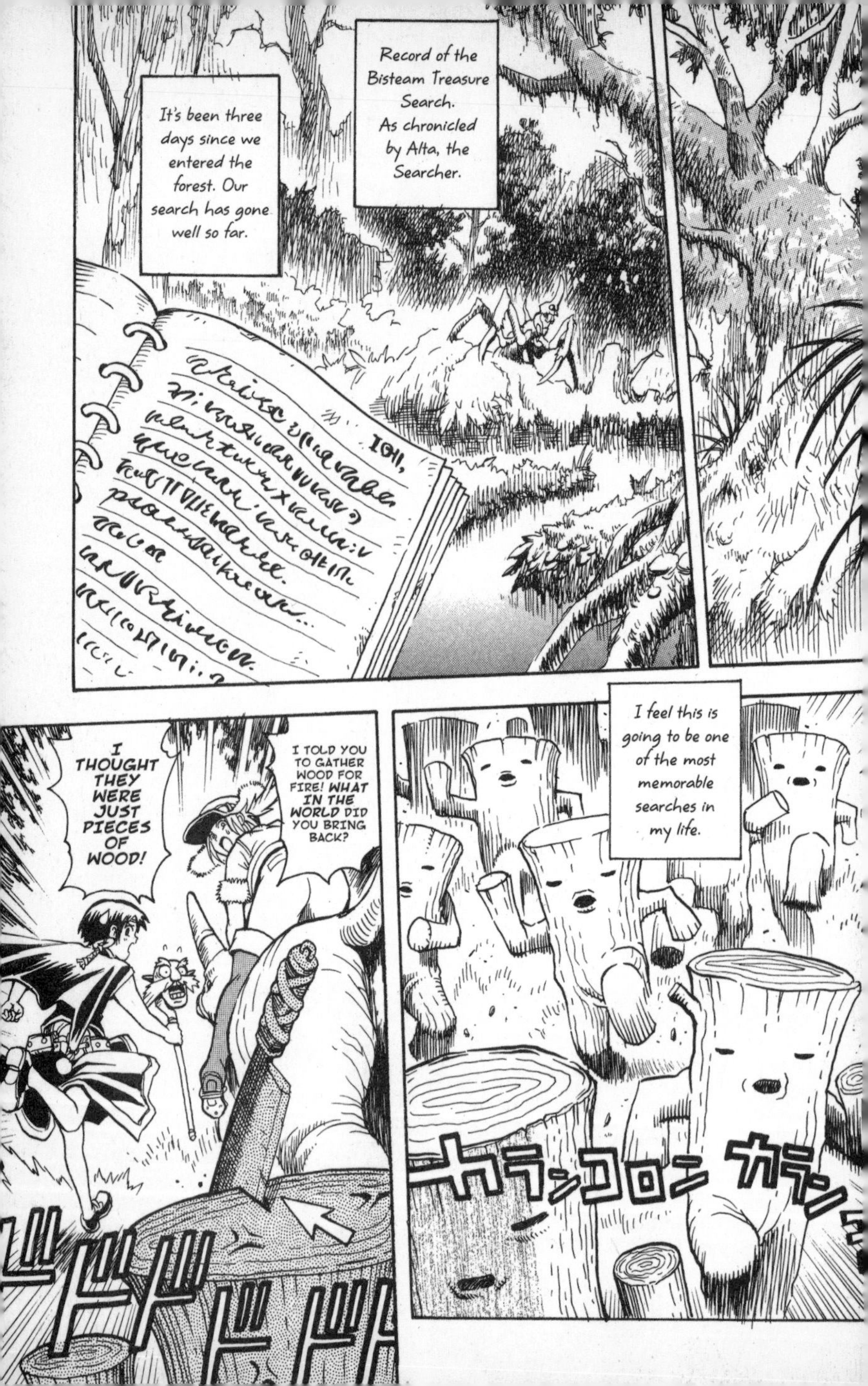
Record of the Bisteam Treasure Search. As chronicled by Alta, the Searcher.
It's been three days since we entered the forest. Our search has gone well so far.
I feel this is going to be one of the most memorable searches in my life.
カランコロン カラン
I TOLD YOU TO GATHER WOOD FOR FIRE! WHAT IN THE WORLD DID YOU BRING BACK?
I THOUGHT THEY WERE JUST PIECES OF WOOD!

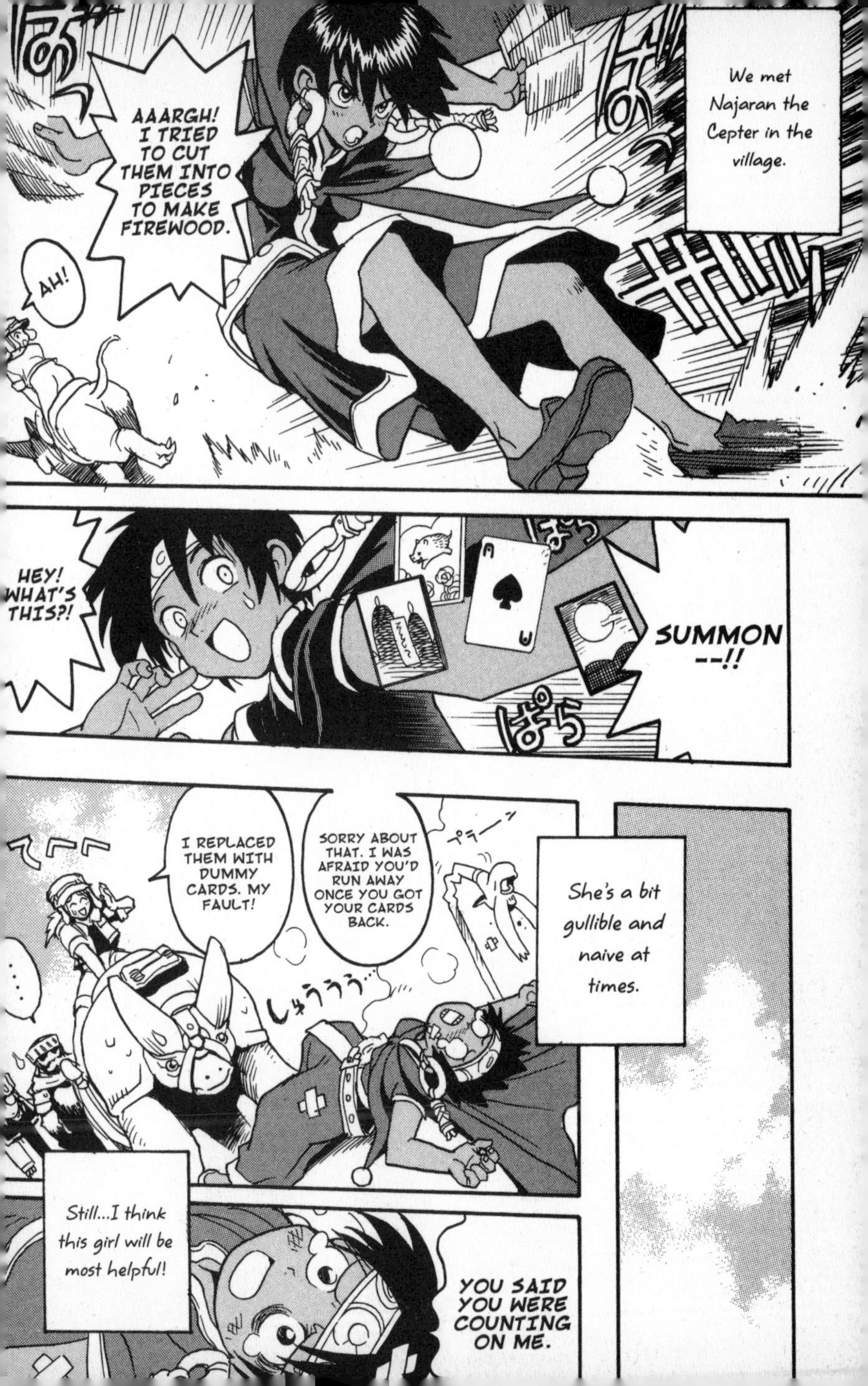
We met Najaran the Cepter in the village.
AAARGH! I TRIED TO CUT THEM INTO PIECES TO MAKE FIREWOOD.
AH!
SUMMON --!!
ぱら
ぱら
HEY! WHAT'S THIS?!
She's a bit gullible and naive at times.
SORRY ABOUT THAT. I WAS AFRAID YOU'D RUN AWAY ONCE YOU GOT YOUR CARDS BACK.
I REPLACED THEM WITH DUMMY CARDS. MY FAULT!
...
YOU SAID YOU WERE COUNTING ON ME.
Still...I think this girl will be most helpful!

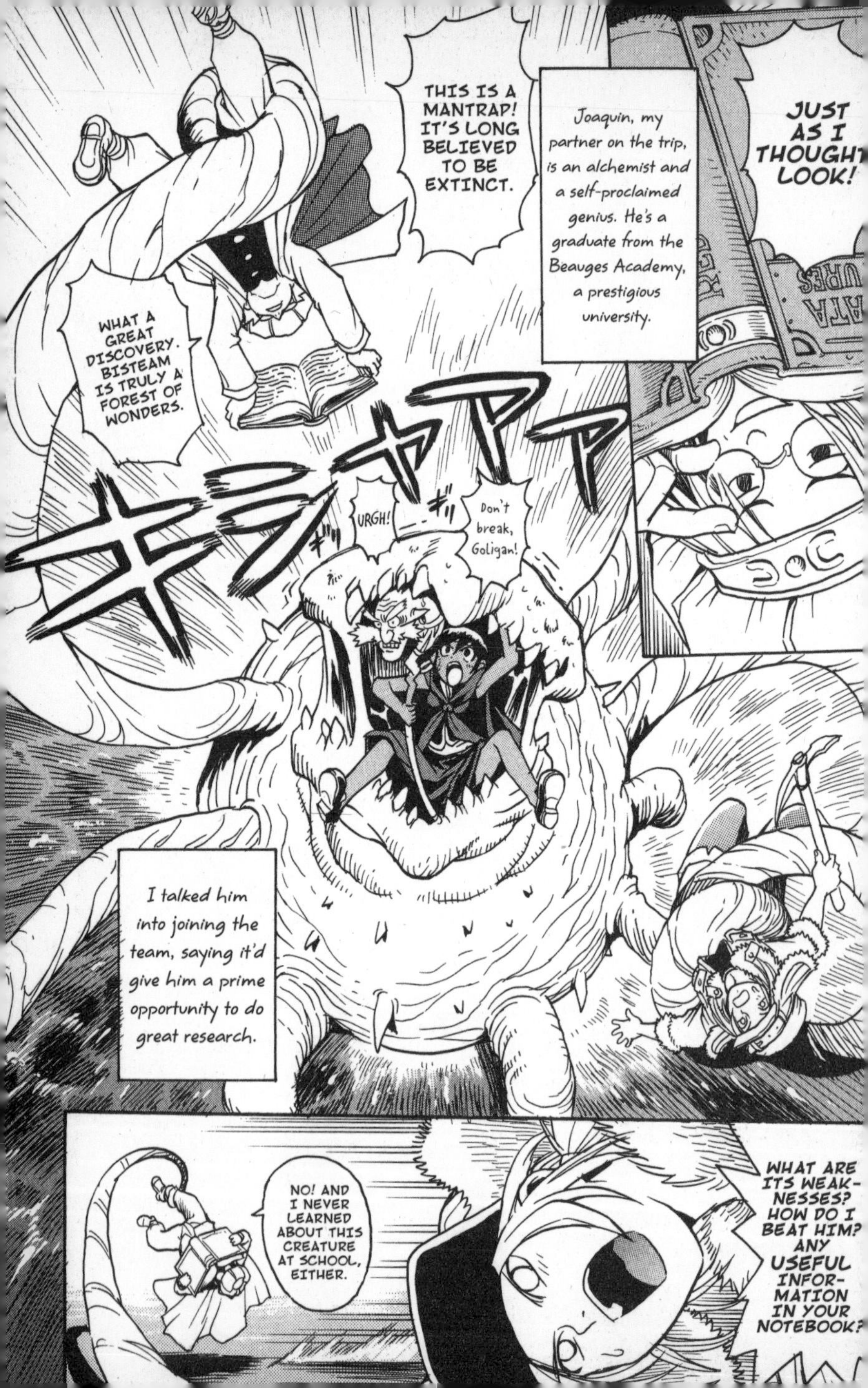
JUST AS I THOUGHT LOOK!
Joaquin, my partner on the trip, is an alchemist and a self-proclaimed genius. He's a graduate from the Beauges Academy, a prestigious university.
THIS IS A MANTRAP! IT'S LONG BELIEVED TO BE EXTINCT.
WHAT A GREAT DISCOVERY. BISTEAM IS TRULY A FOREST OF WONDERS.
Don't break, Goligan!
URGH!
I talked him into joining the team, saying it'd give him a prime opportunity to do great research.
WHAT ARE ITS WEAK-NESSES? HOW DO I BEAT HIM? ANY USEFUL INFOR-MATION IN YOUR NOTEBOOK?
NO! AND I NEVER LEARNED ABOUT THIS CREATURE AT SCHOOL, EITHER.

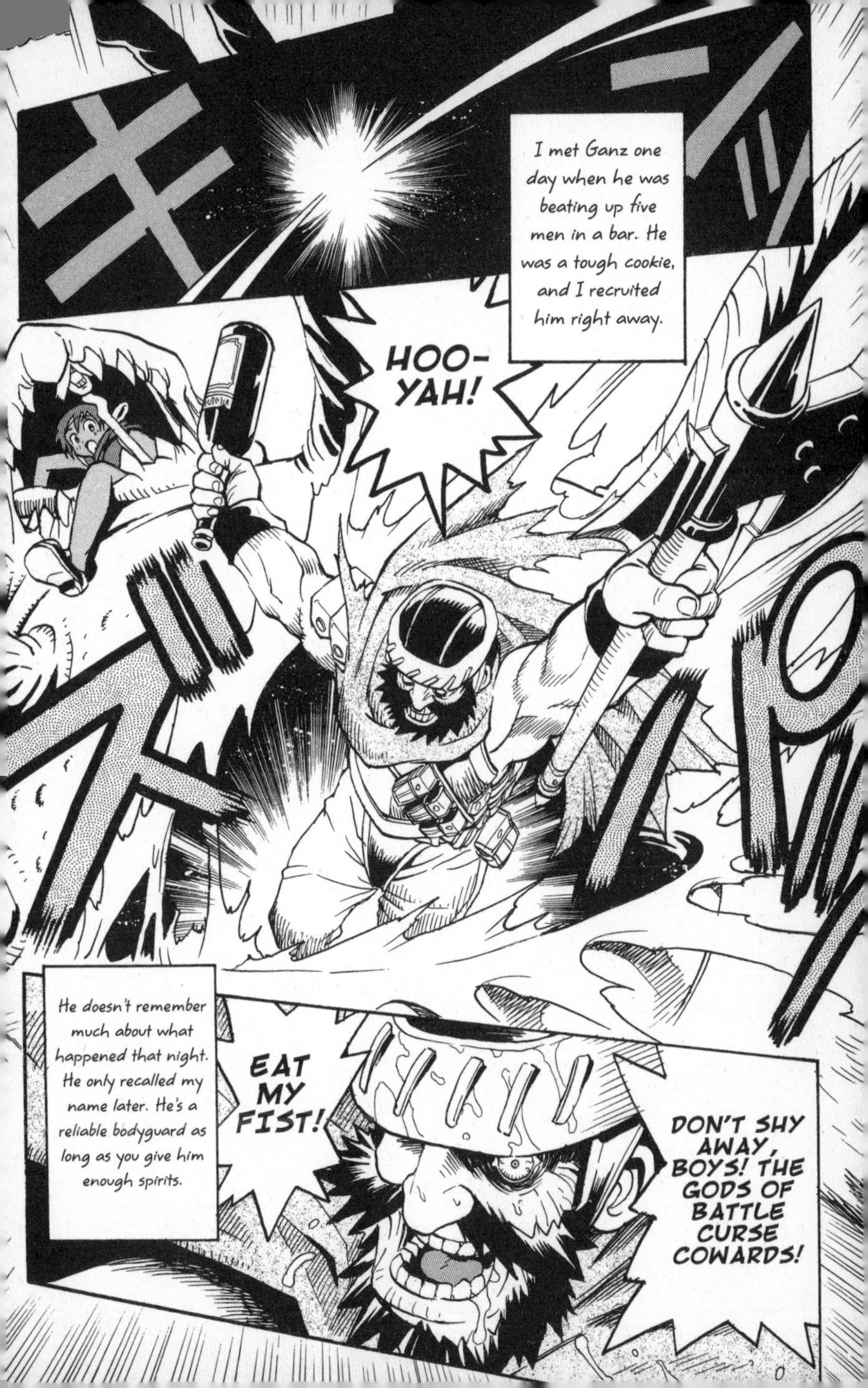
I met Ganz one day when he was beating up five men in a bar. He was a tough cookie, and I recruited him right away.
HOO-YAH!
DON'T SHY AWAY, BOYS! THE GODS OF BATTLE CURSE COWARDS!
EAT MY FIST!
He doesn't remember much about what happened that night. He only recalled my name later. He's a reliable bodyguard as long as you give him enough spirits.

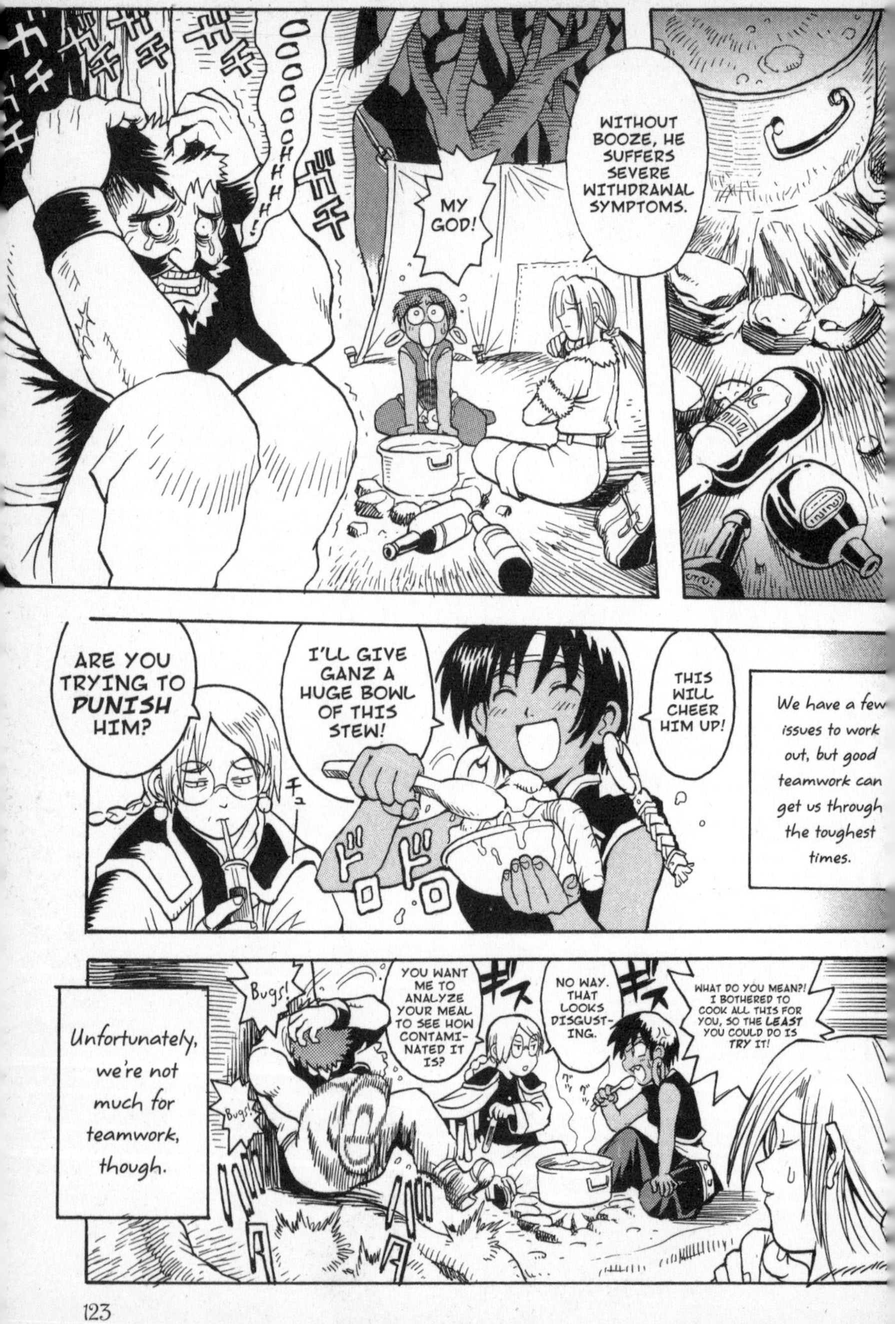
WITHOUT BOOZE, HE SUFFERS SEVERE WITHDRAWAL SYMPTOMS.
MY GOD!
OOOOOOHHHH!
We have a few issues to work out, but good teamwork can get us through the toughest times.
THIS WILL CHEER HIM UP!
I'LL GIVE GANZ A HUGE BOWL OF THIS STEW!
ARE YOU TRYING TO **PUNISH** HIM?
WHAT DO YOU MEAN?! I BOTHERED TO COOK ALL THIS FOR YOU, SO THE **LEAST** YOU COULD DO IS **TRY** IT!
NO WAY. THAT LOOKS DISGUSTING.
YOU WANT ME TO ANALYZE YOUR MEAL TO SEE HOW CONTAMINATED IT IS?
Bugs!
Bugs!
Unfortunately, we're not much for teamwork, though.

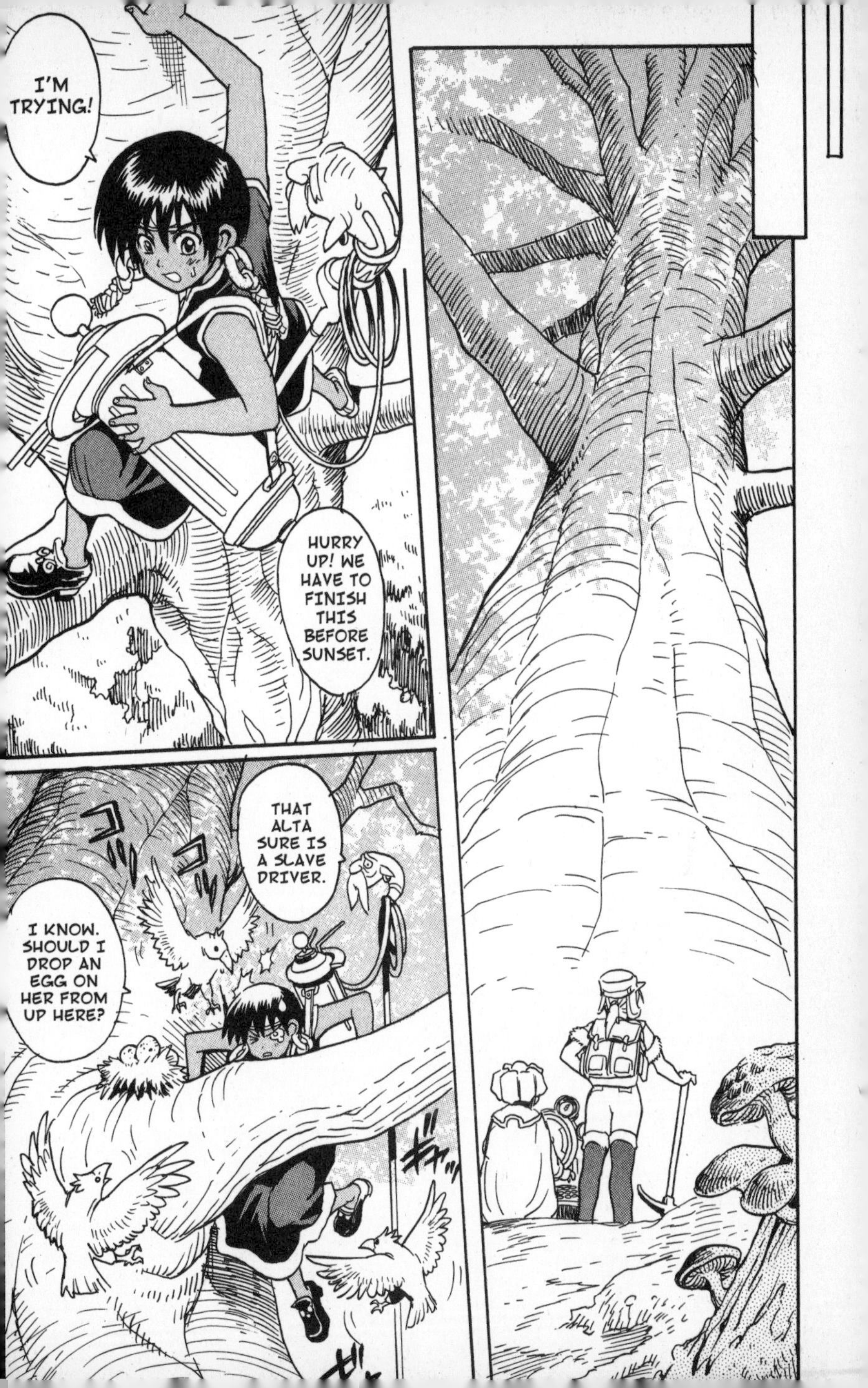
HURRY UP! WE HAVE TO FINISH THIS BEFORE SUNSET.
I'M TRYING!
THAT ALTA SURE IS A SLAVE DRIVER.
I KNOW. SHOULD I DROP AN EGG ON HER FROM UP HERE?

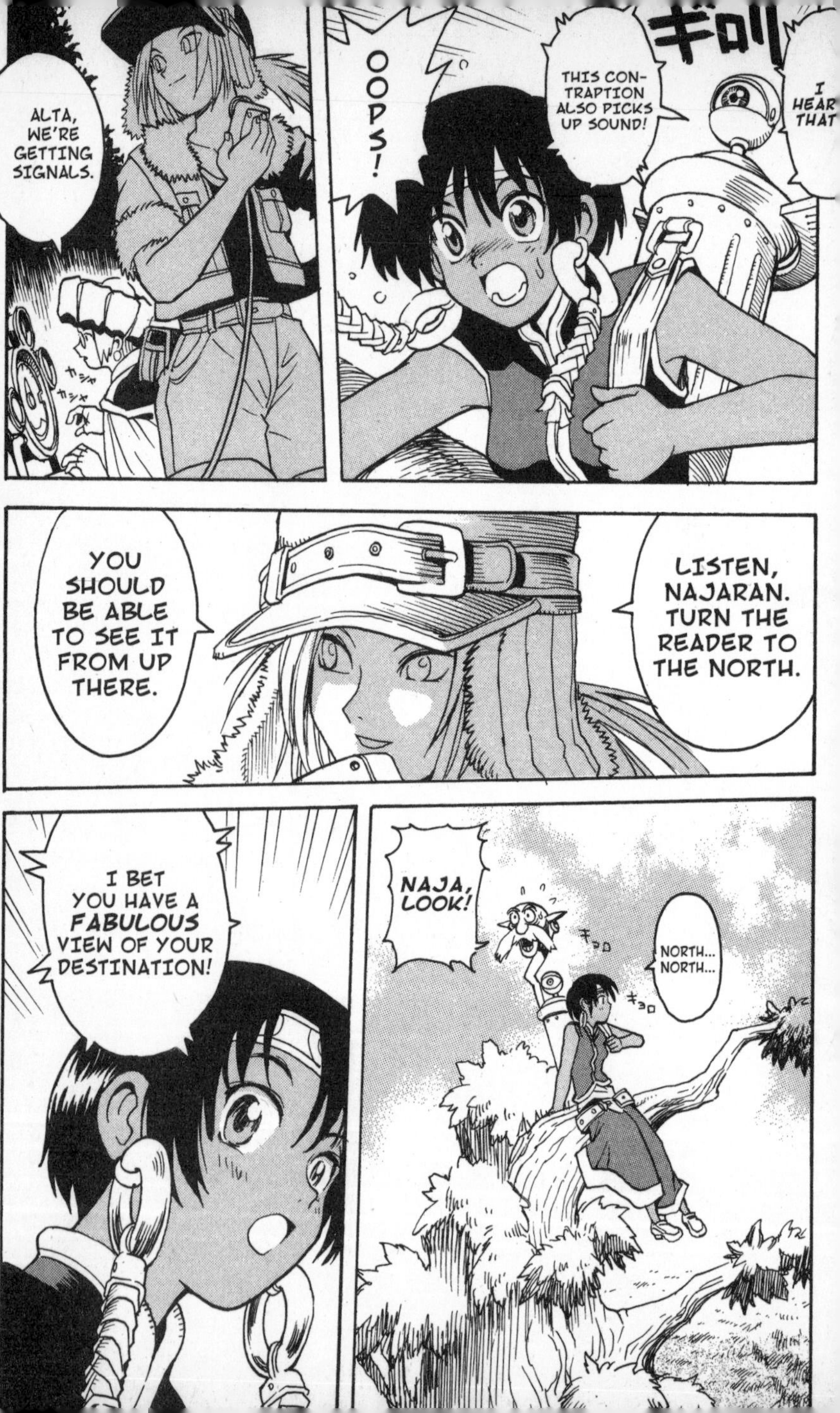
I HEAR THAT
ギロリ
THIS CON-TRAPTION ALSO PICKS UP SOUND!
OOPS!
ALTA, WE'RE GETTING SIGNALS.
LISTEN, NAJARAN. TURN THE READER TO THE NORTH.
YOU SHOULD BE ABLE TO SEE IT FROM UP THERE.
NORTH... NORTH...
NAJA, LOOK!
I BET YOU HAVE A FABULOUS VIEW OF YOUR DESTINATION!

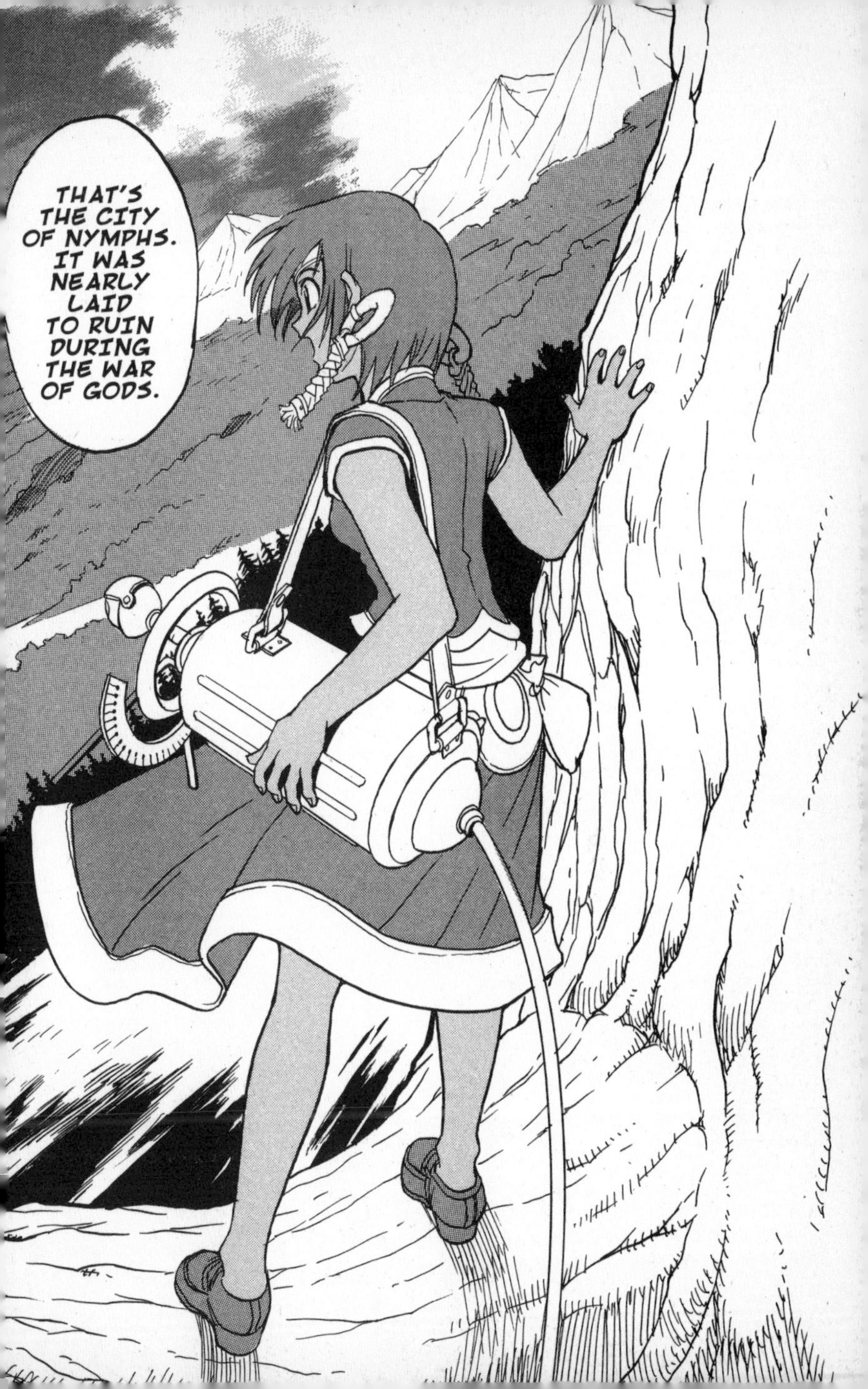
THAT'S THE CITY OF NYMPHS. IT WAS NEARLY LAID TO RUIN DURING THE WAR OF GODS.

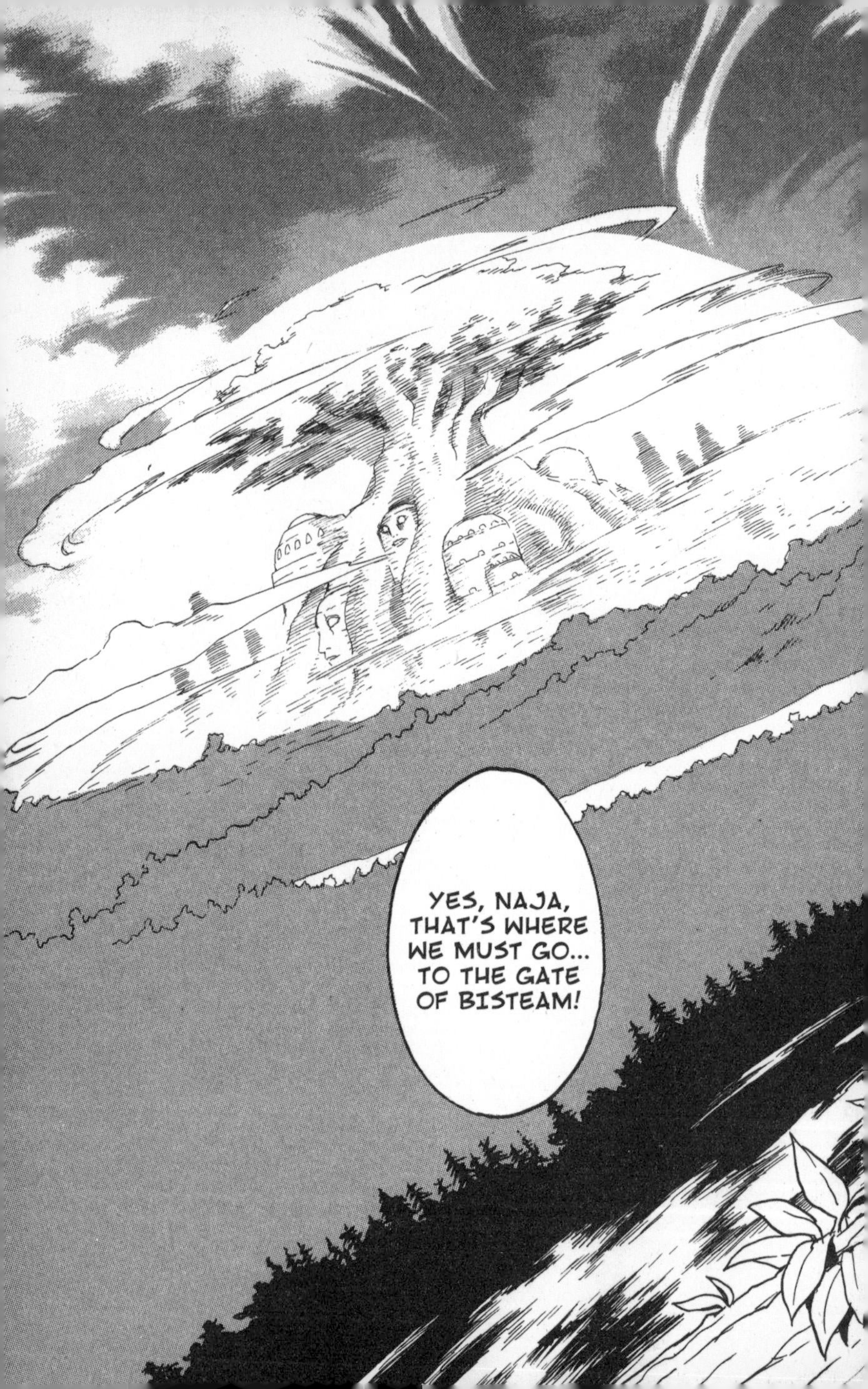
YES, NAJA, THAT'S WHERE WE MUST GO... TO THE GATE OF BISTEAM!

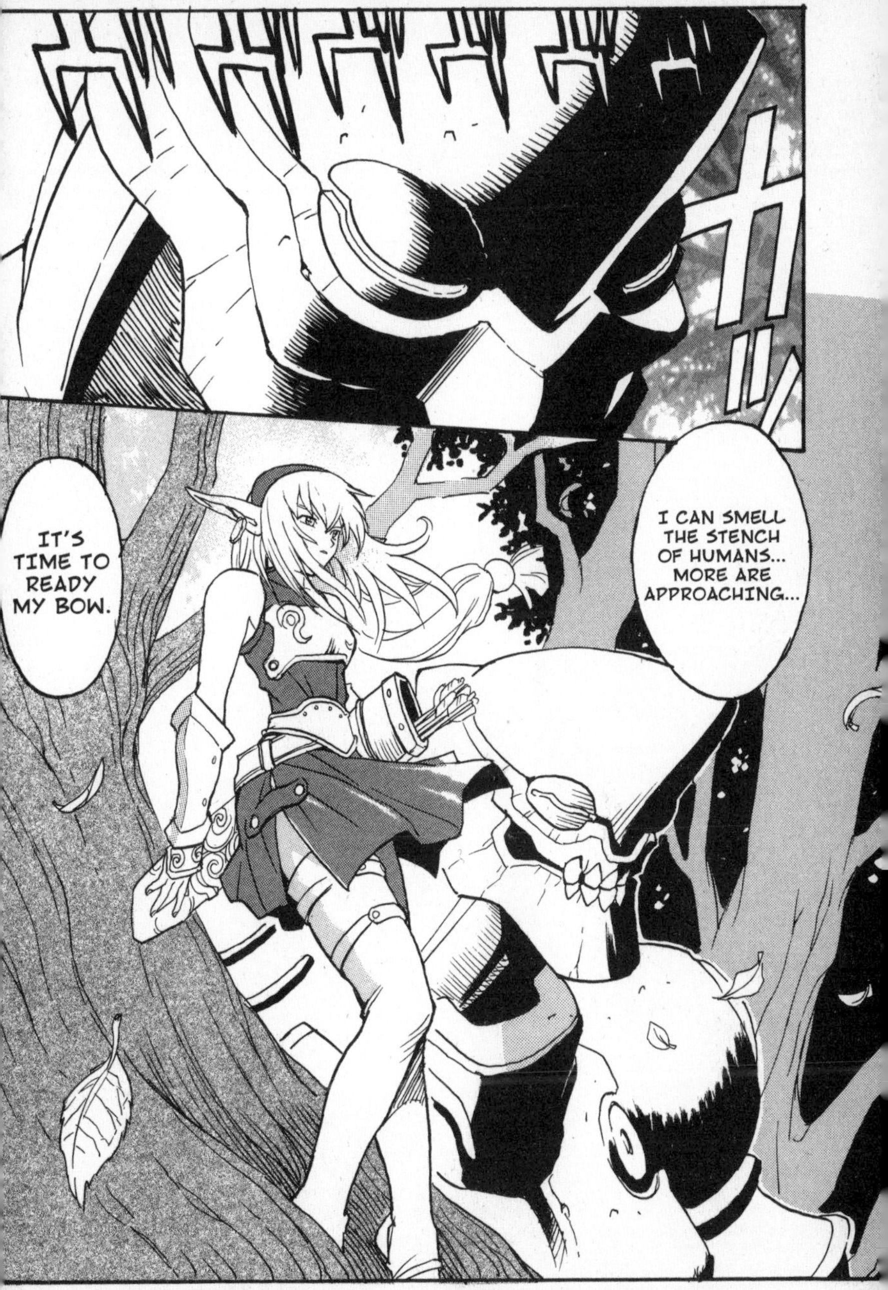
I CAN SMELL THE STENCH OF HUMANS... MORE ARE APPROACHING...
IT'S TIME TO READY MY BOW.

Round 18 Head for the Gate of Bisteam - End

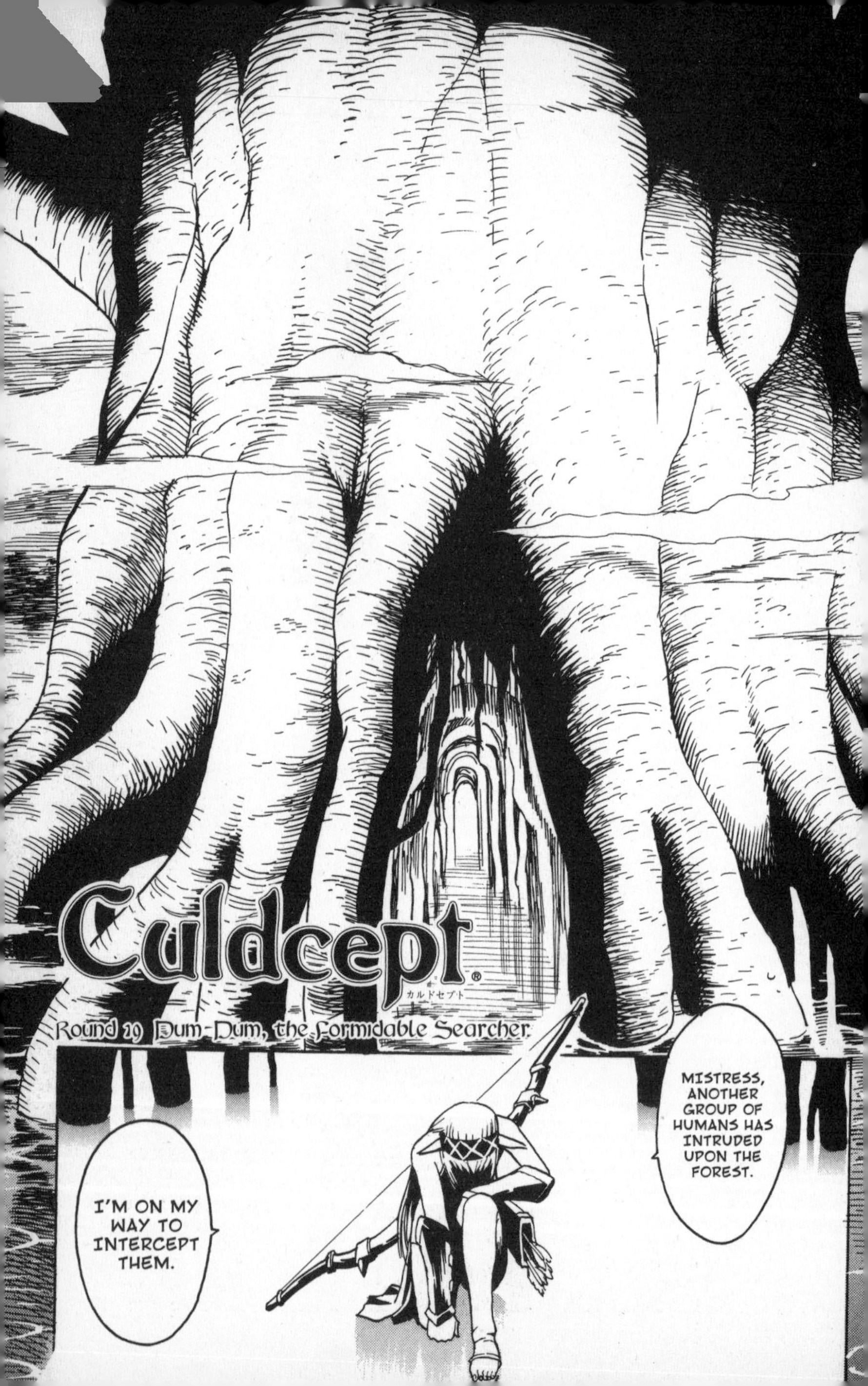
Culdcept®
カルドセプト
Round 19 Dum-Dum, the Formidable Searcher
MISTRESS, ANOTHER GROUP OF HUMANS HAS INTRUDED UPON THE FOREST.
I'M ON MY WAY TO INTERCEPT THEM.

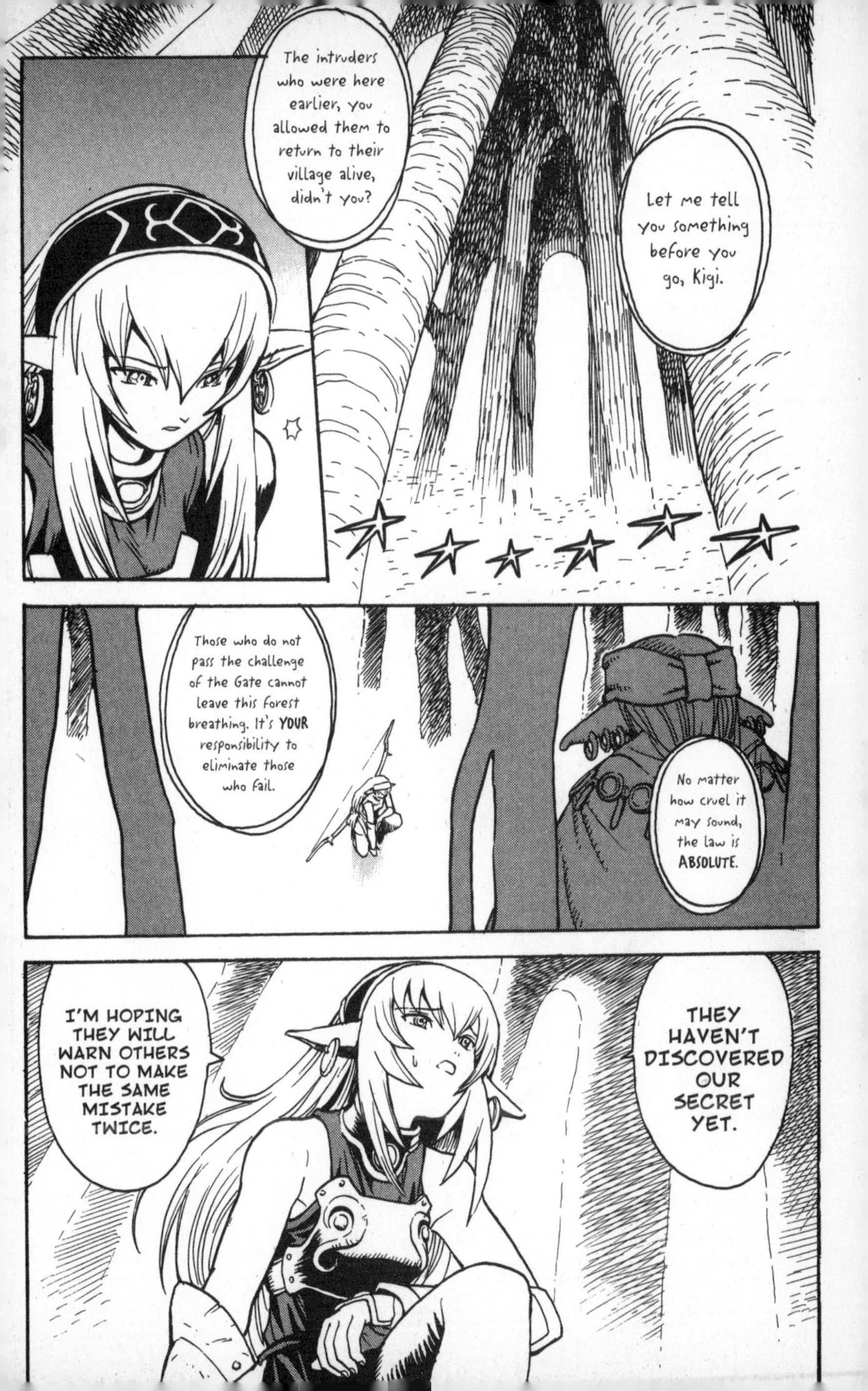
Let me tell you something before you go, Kigi.
The intruders who were here earlier, you allowed them to return to their village alive, didn't you?
Those who do not pass the challenge of the Gate cannot leave this forest breathing. It's YOUR responsibility to eliminate those who fail.
No matter how cruel it may sound, the law is ABSOLUTE.
THEY HAVEN'T DISCOVERED OUR SECRET YET.
I'M HOPING THEY WILL WARN OTHERS NOT TO MAKE THE SAME MISTAKE TWICE.

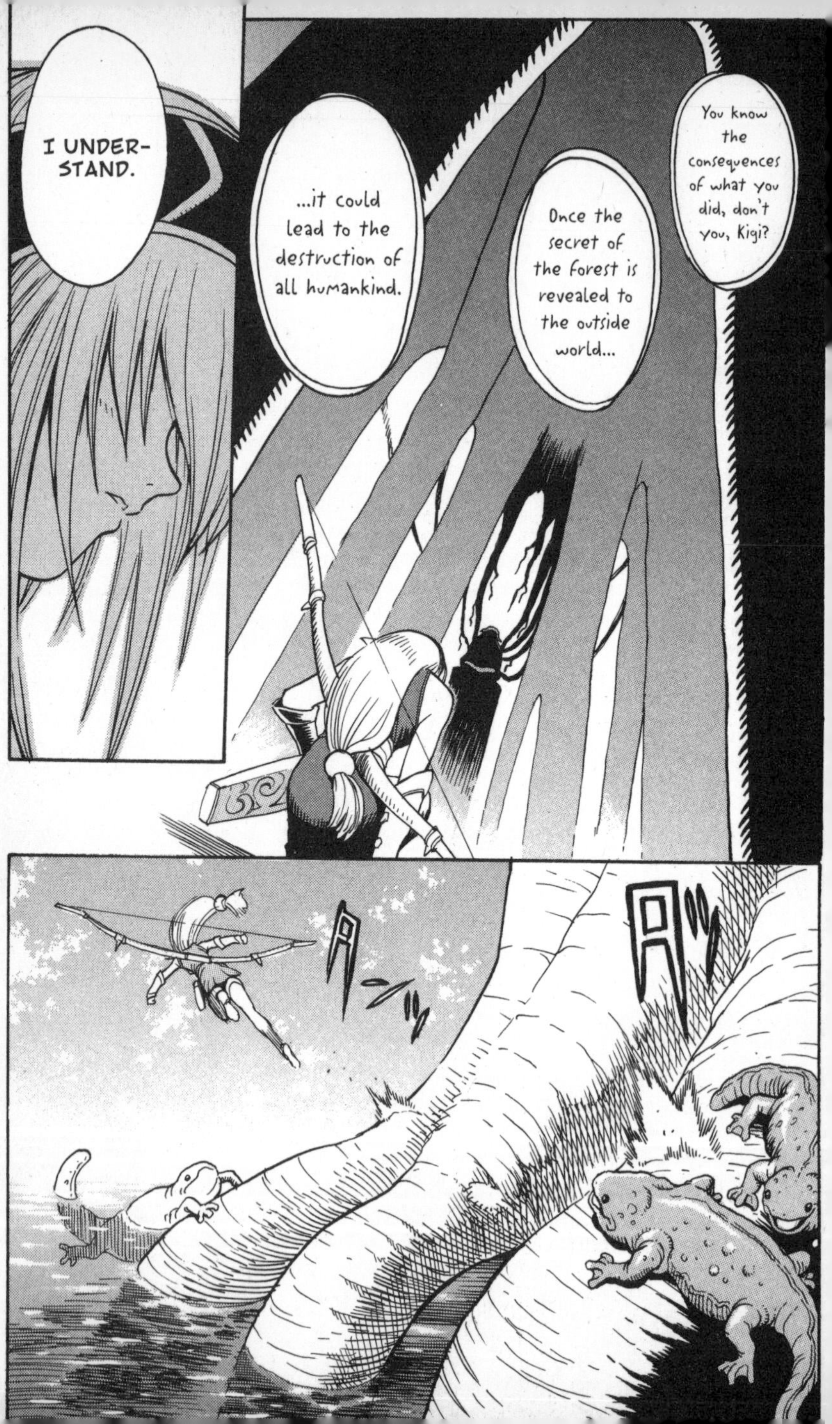
You know the consequences of what you did, don't you, Kigi?
Once the secret of the forest is revealed to the outside world...
...it could lead to the destruction of all humankind.
I UNDER-STAND.

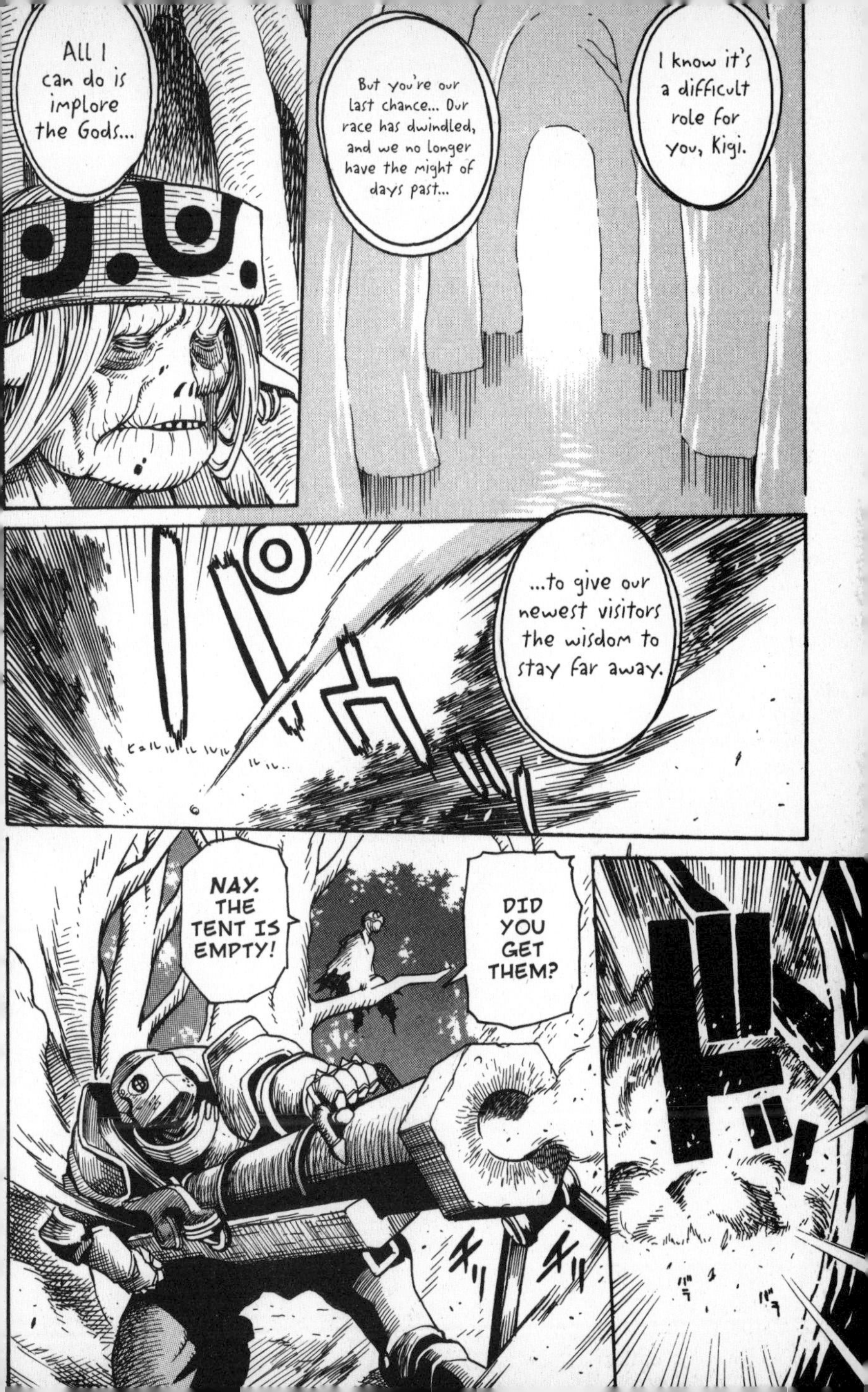

I know it's a difficult role for you, Kigi.
But you're our last chance... Our race has dwindled, and we no longer have the might of days past...
All I can do is implore the Gods...
...to give our newest visitors the wisdom to stay far away.
DID YOU GET THEM?
NAY. THE TENT IS EMPTY!

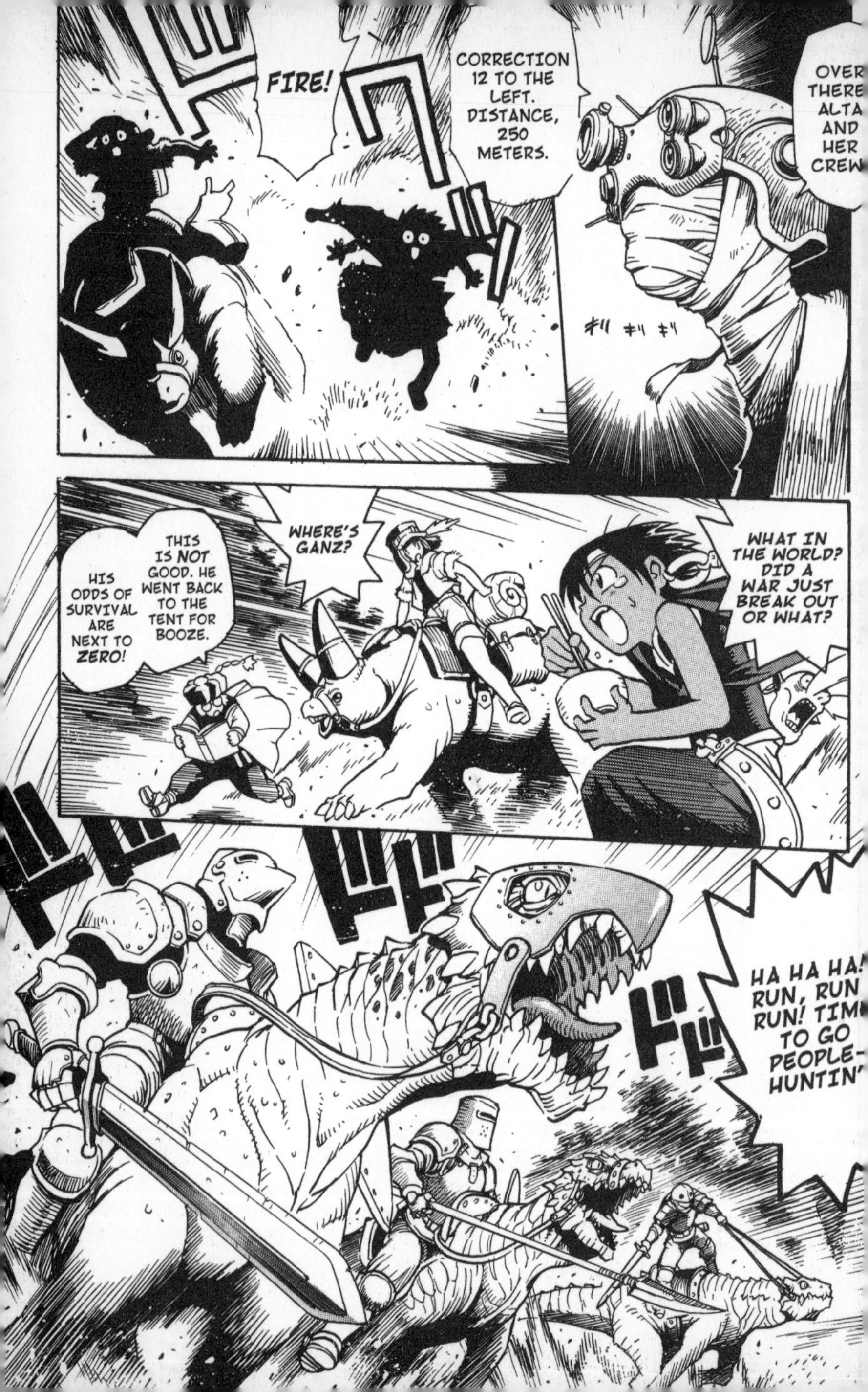
OVER THERE ALTA AND HER CREW
ギリ ギリ ギリ
CORRECTION 12 TO THE LEFT. DISTANCE, 250 METERS.
FIRE!
WHAT IN THE WORLD? DID A WAR JUST BREAK OUT OR WHAT?
WHERE'S GANZ?
THIS IS NOT GOOD. HE WENT BACK TO THE TENT FOR BOOZE.
HIS ODDS OF SURVIVAL ARE NEXT TO ZERO!
HA HA HA! RUN, RUN RUN! TIM TO GO PEOPLE-HUNTIN'

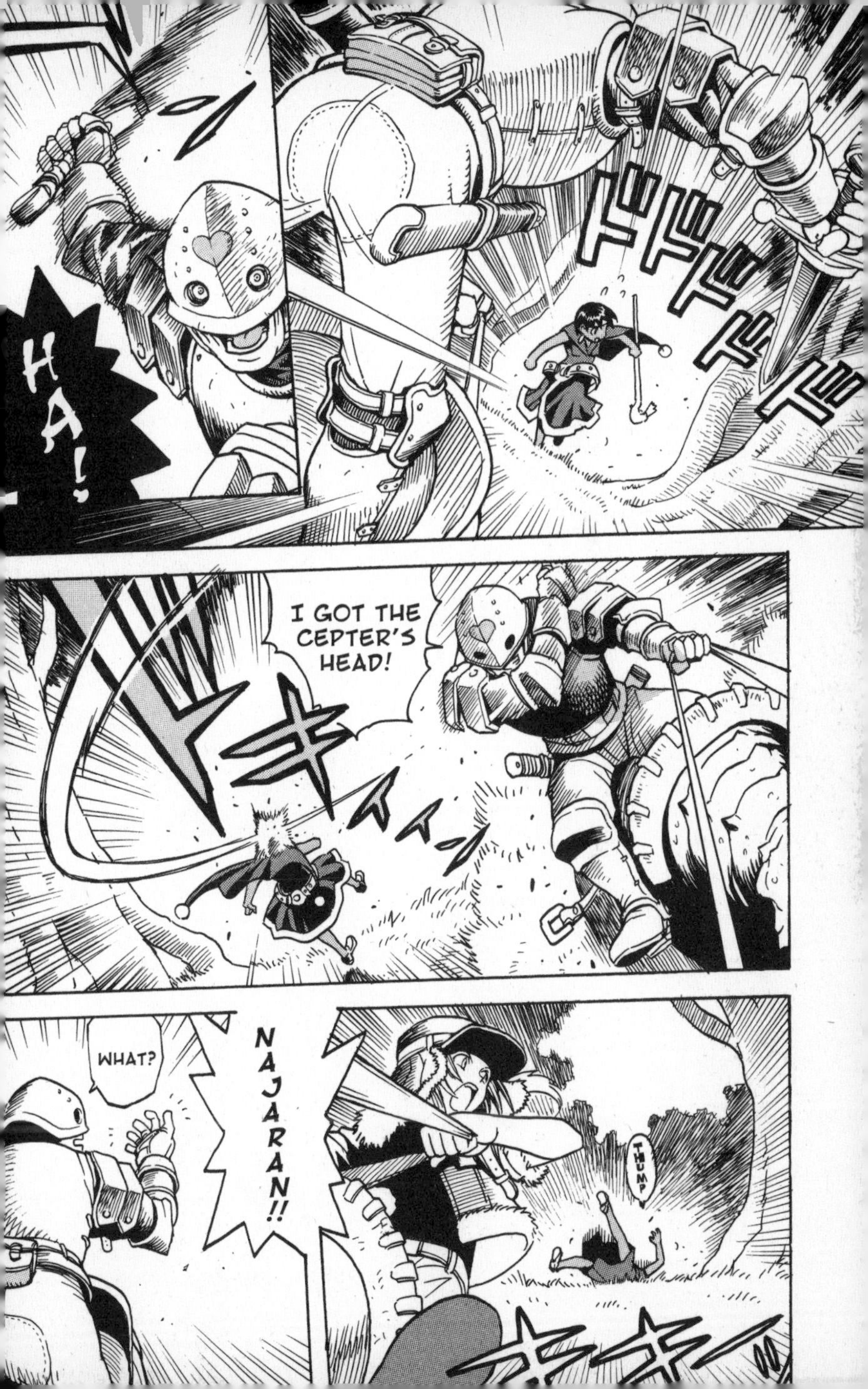
HA!
I GOT THE CEPTER'S HEAD!
NAJARAN!!
WHAT?
THUMP

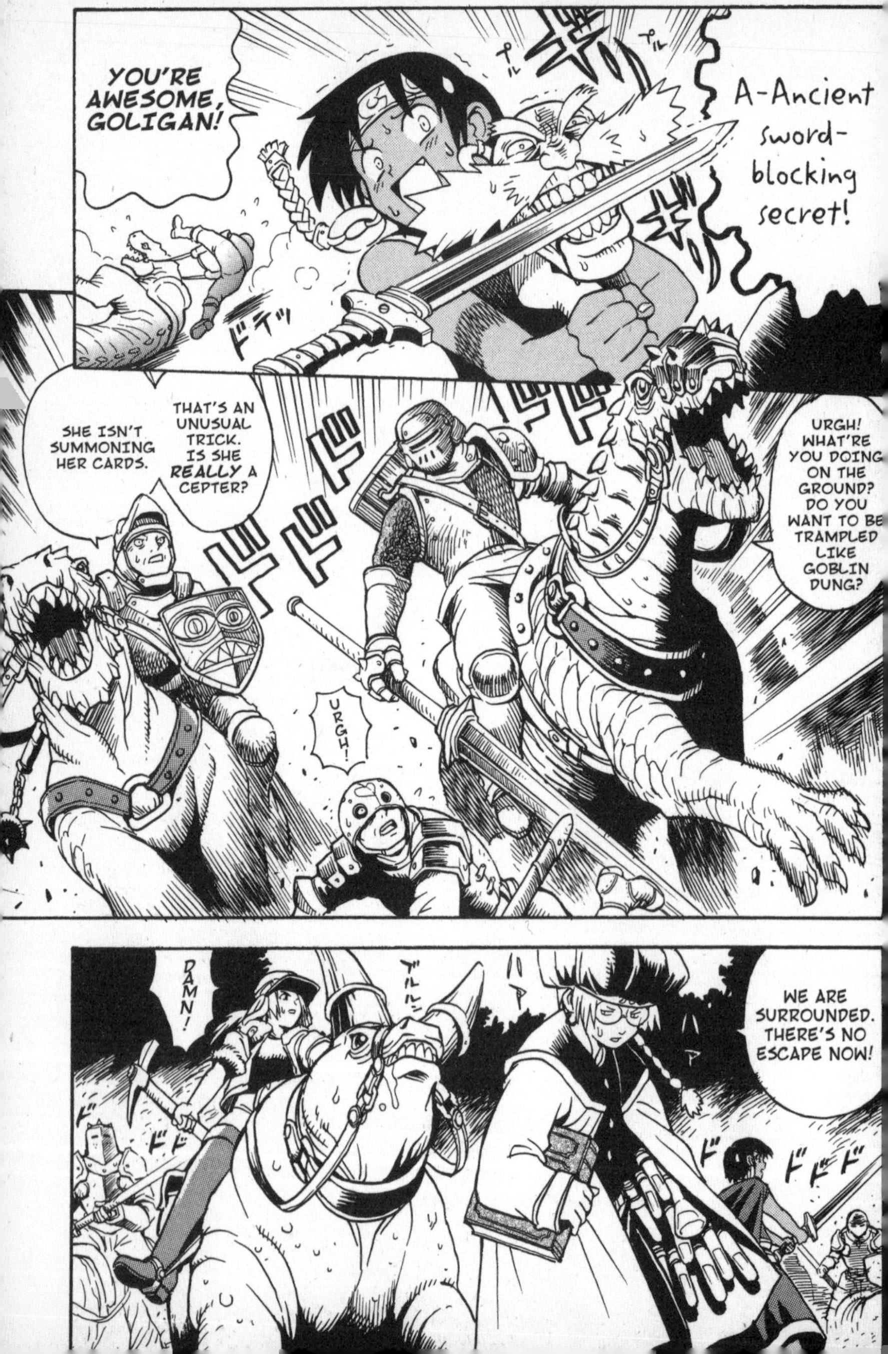
A-Ancient sword-blocking secret!
YOU'RE AWESOME, GOLIGAN!
ドテッ
URGH! WHAT'RE YOU DOING ON THE GROUND? DO YOU WANT TO BE TRAMPLED LIKE GOBLIN DUNG?
THAT'S AN UNUSUAL TRICK. IS SHE REALLY A CEPTER?
SHE ISN'T SUMMONING HER CARDS.
URGH!
WE ARE SURROUNDED. THERE'S NO ESCAPE NOW!
DAMN!

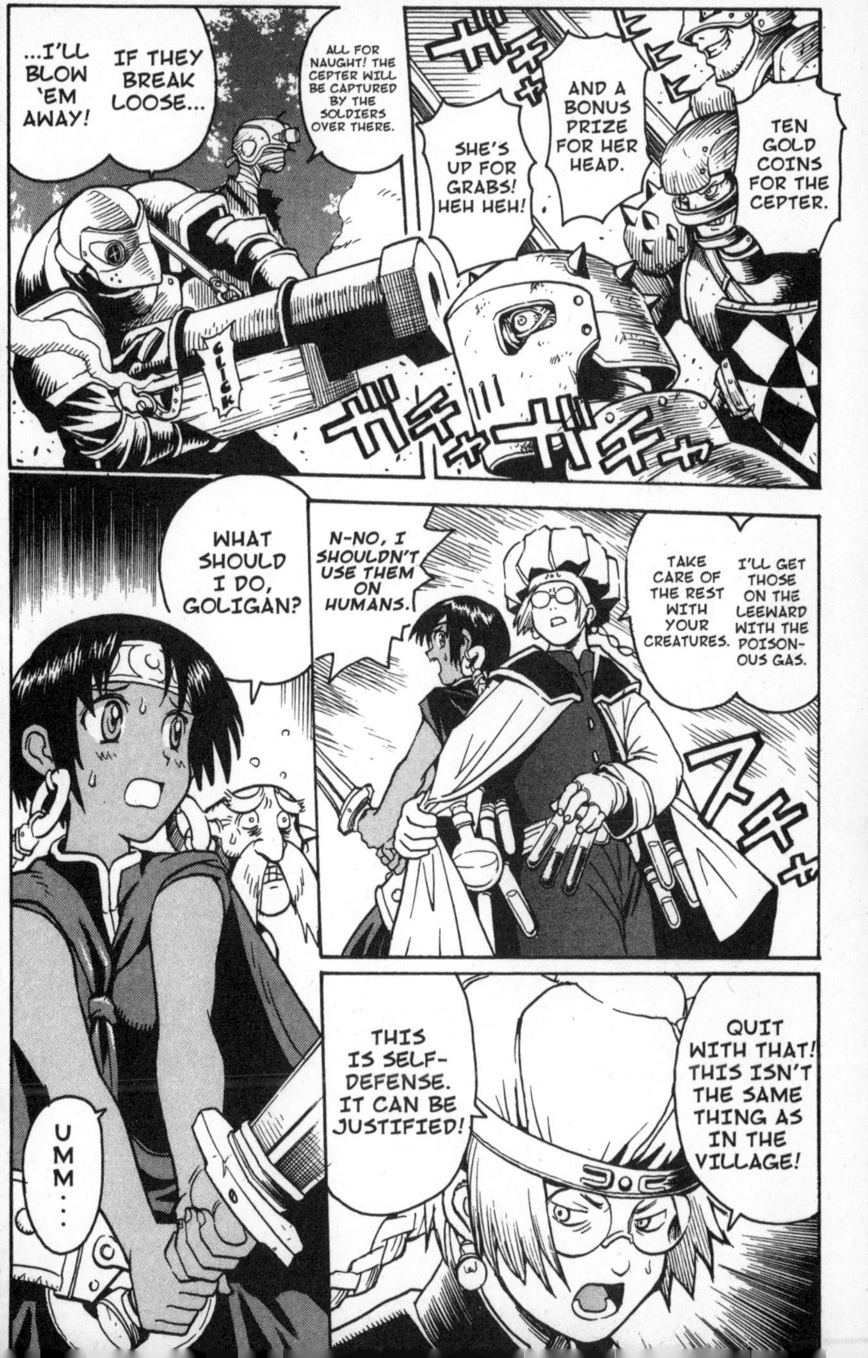
TEN GOLD COINS FOR THE CEPTER.
AND A BONUS PRIZE FOR HER HEAD.
SHE'S UP FOR GRABS! HEH HEH!
ALL FOR NAUGHT! THE CEPTER WILL BE CAPTURED BY THE SOLDIERS OVER THERE.
IF THEY BREAK LOOSE...
...I'LL BLOW 'EM AWAY!
CLICK
I'LL GET THOSE ON THE LEEWARD WITH THE POISONOUS GAS.
TAKE CARE OF THE REST WITH YOUR CREATURES.
N-NO, I SHOULDN'T USE THEM ON HUMANS.
QUIT WITH THAT! THIS ISN'T THE SAME THING AS IN THE VILLAGE!
THIS IS SELF-DEFENSE. IT CAN BE JUSTIFIED!
WHAT SHOULD I DO, GOLIGAN?
UMM...

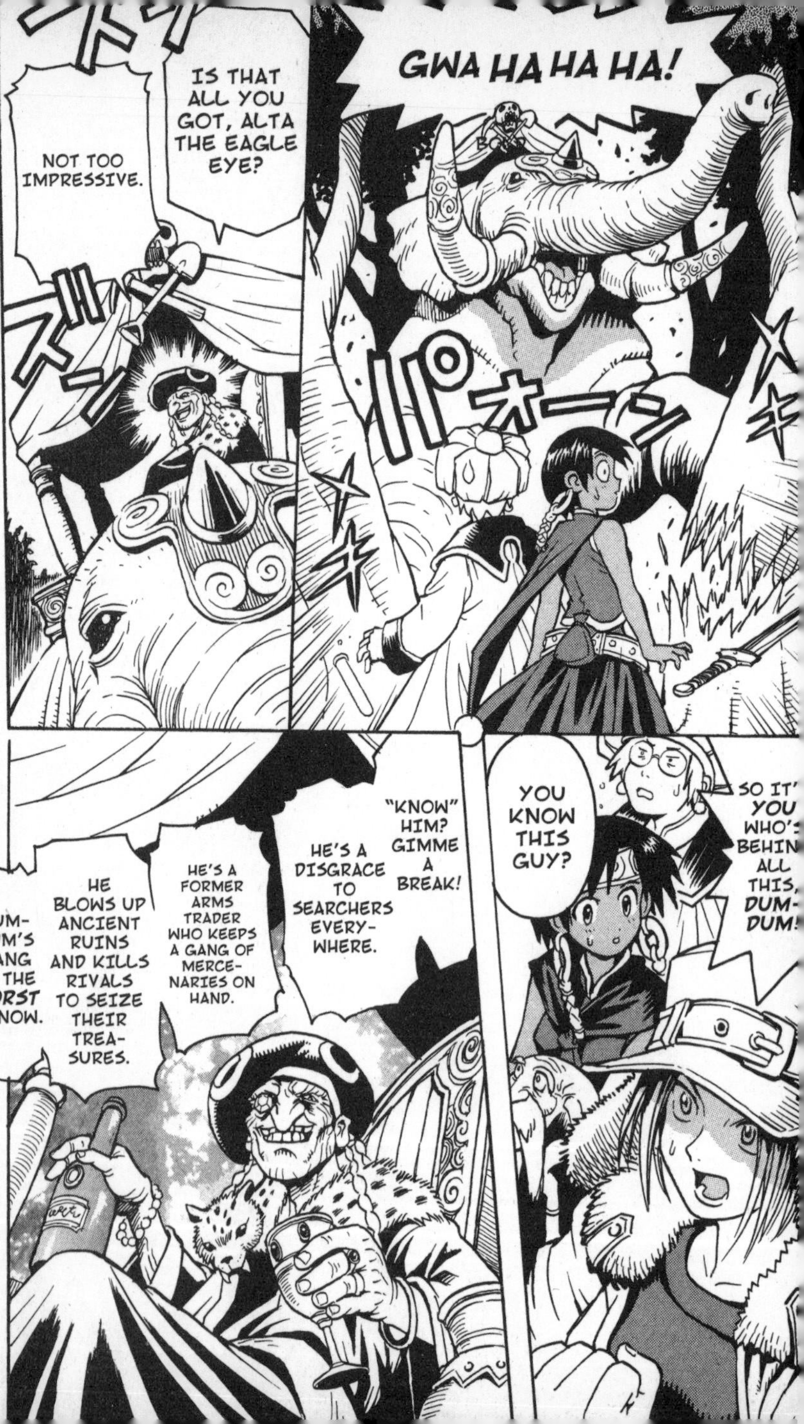
GWA HA HA HA!
IS THAT ALL YOU GOT, ALTA THE EAGLE EYE?
NOT TOO IMPRESSIVE.
SO IT' YOU WHO'S BEHIN ALL THIS, DUM-DUM!
YOU KNOW THIS GUY?
"KNOW" HIM? GIMME A BREAK!
HE'S A DISGRACE TO SEARCHERS EVERY-WHERE.
HE'S A FORMER ARMS TRADER WHO KEEPS A GANG OF MERCE-NARIES ON HAND.
HE BLOWS UP ANCIENT RUINS AND KILLS RIVALS TO SEIZE THEIR TREA-SURES.
DUM-DUM'S GANG IS THE WORST I KNOW.

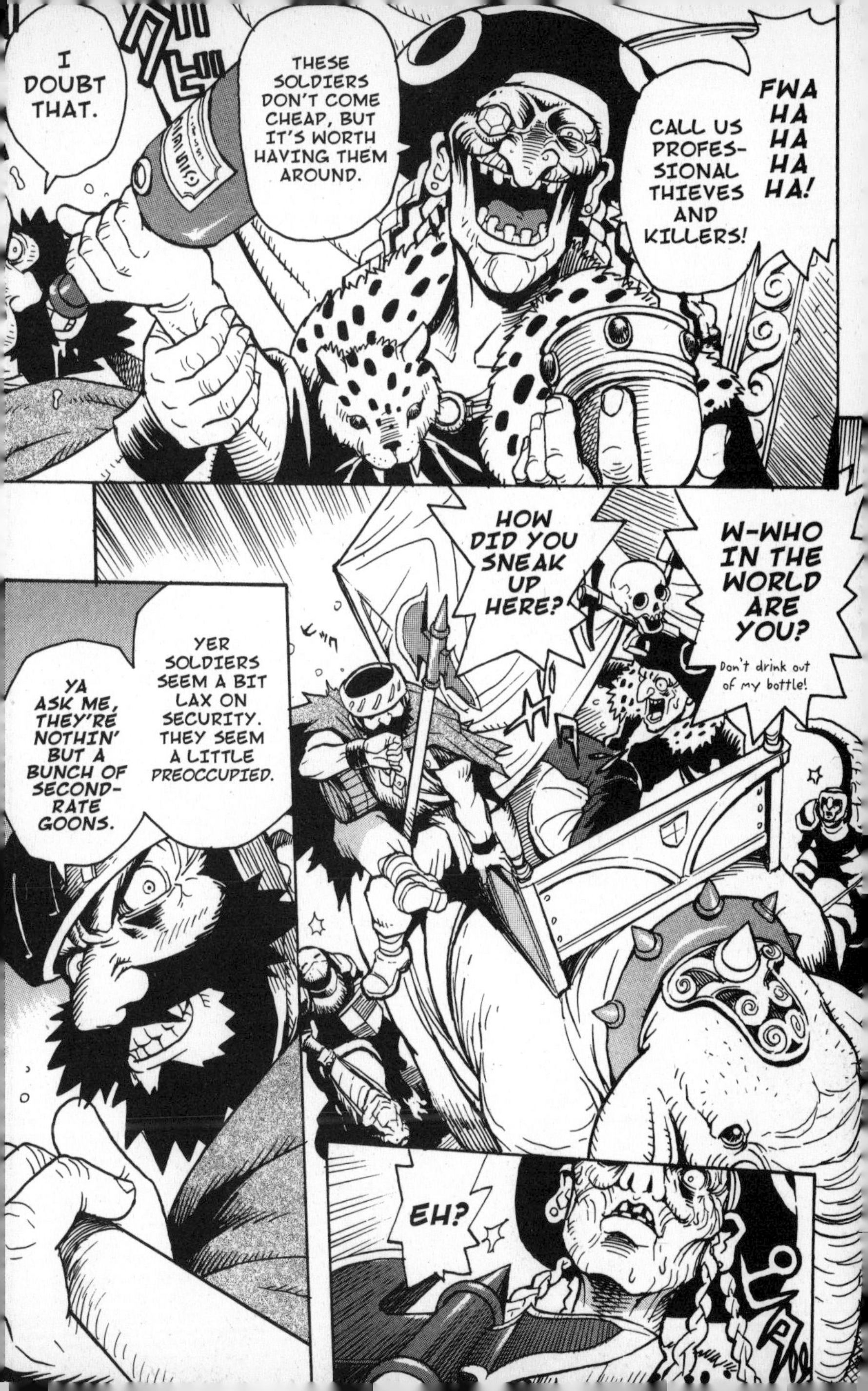
FWA HA HA HA HA!
CALL US PROFES-SIONAL THIEVES AND KILLERS!
THESE SOLDIERS DON'T COME CHEAP, BUT IT'S WORTH HAVING THEM AROUND.
I DOUBT THAT.
W-WHO IN THE WORLD ARE YOU?
Don't drink out of my bottle!
HOW DID YOU SNEAK UP HERE?
YER SOLDIERS SEEM A BIT LAX ON SECURITY. THEY SEEM A LITTLE PREOCCUPIED.
YA ASK ME, THEY'RE NOTHIN' BUT A BUNCH OF SECOND-RATE GOONS.
EH?

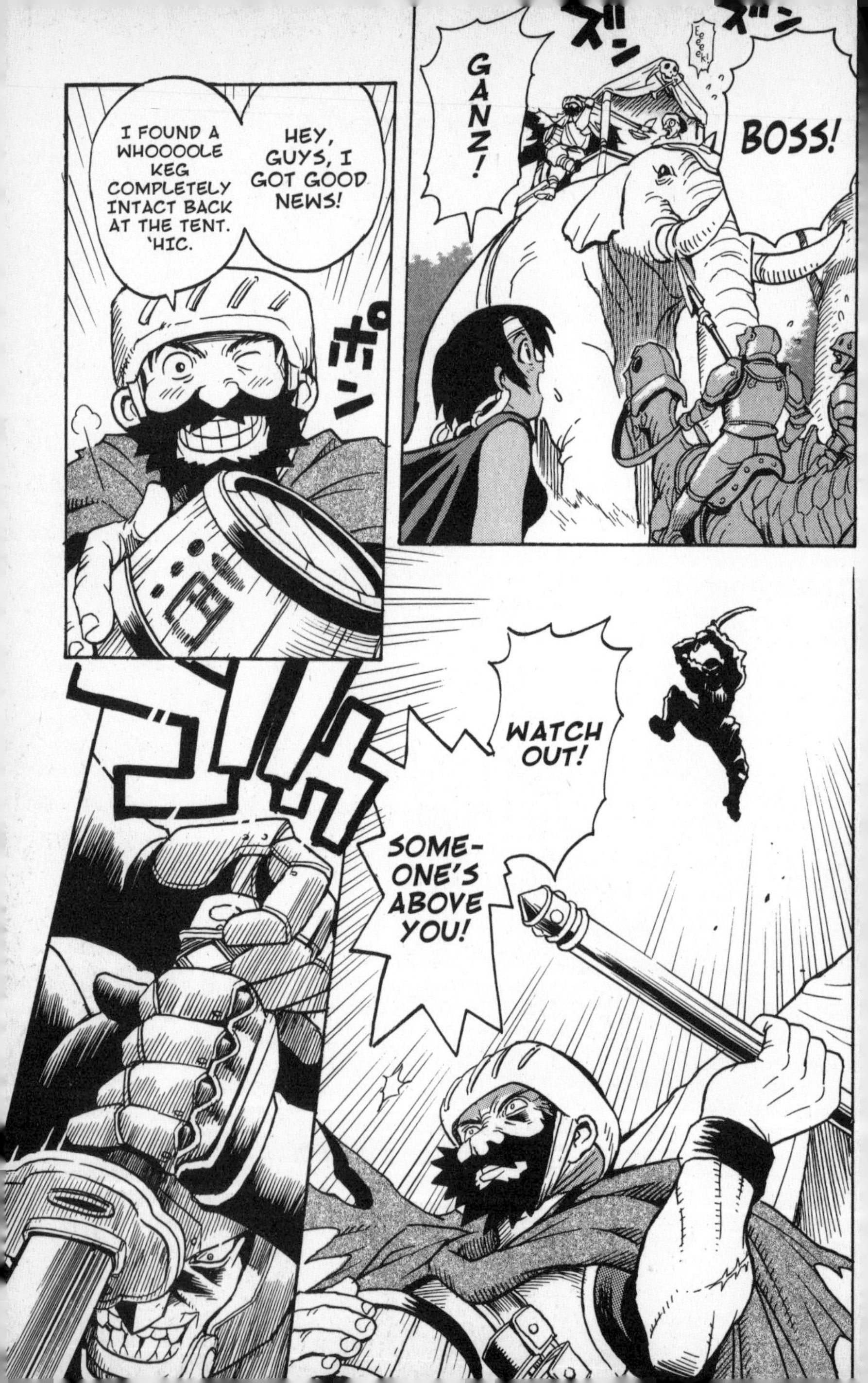
ズン
Eeeeek!
ズン
BOSS!
GANZ!
HEY, GUYS, I GOT GOOD NEWS!
I FOUND A WHOOOOLE KEG COMPLETELY INTACT BACK AT THE TENT. 'HIC.
ポン
WATCH OUT!
SOME-ONE'S ABOVE YOU!

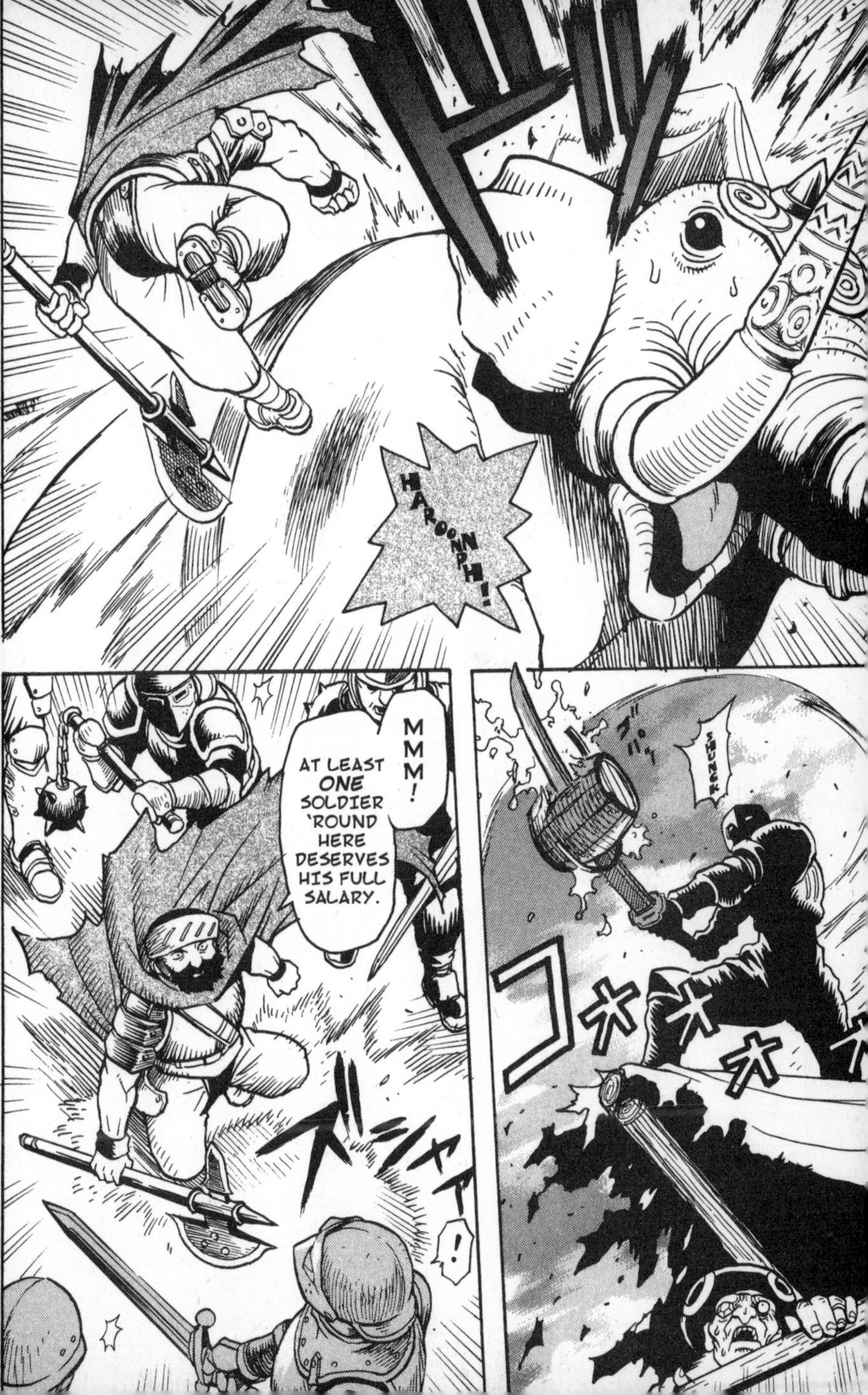
HAROOONPH!
SHUNCK
フォオオオ
MMM!
AT LEAST ONE SOLDIER 'ROUND HERE DESERVES HIS FULL SALARY.
ズシャア!

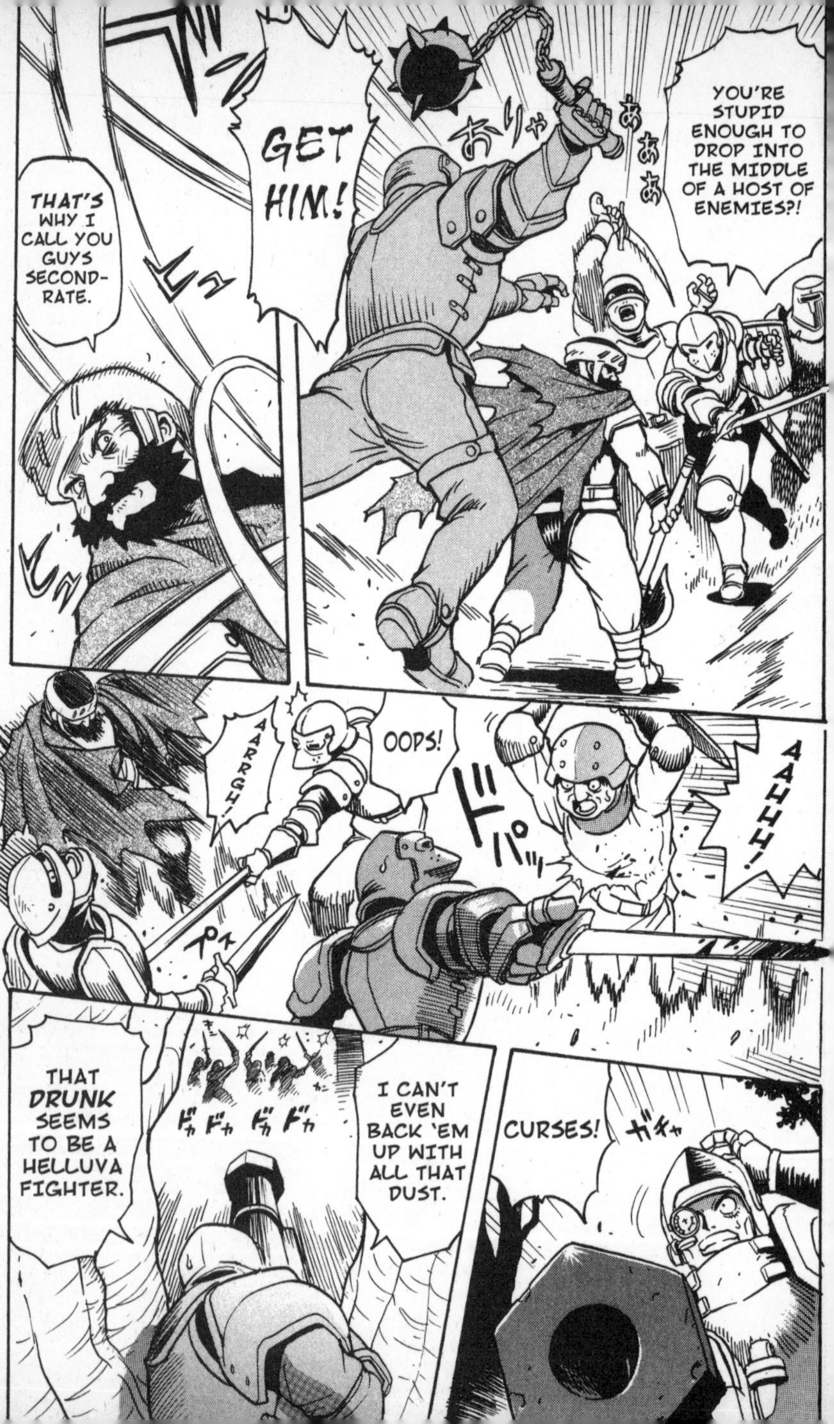
YOU'RE STUPID ENOUGH TO DROP INTO THE MIDDLE OF A HOST OF ENEMIES?!
おりゃあああ
GET HIM!
THAT'S WHY I CALL YOU GUYS SECOND-RATE.
AAHHH!
ドパッ
OOPS!
AARRGH!
ガチャ
CURSES!
I CAN'T EVEN BACK 'EM UP WITH ALL THAT DUST.
ドカドカ ドカドカ
THAT DRUNK SEEMS TO BE A HELLUVA FIGHTER.

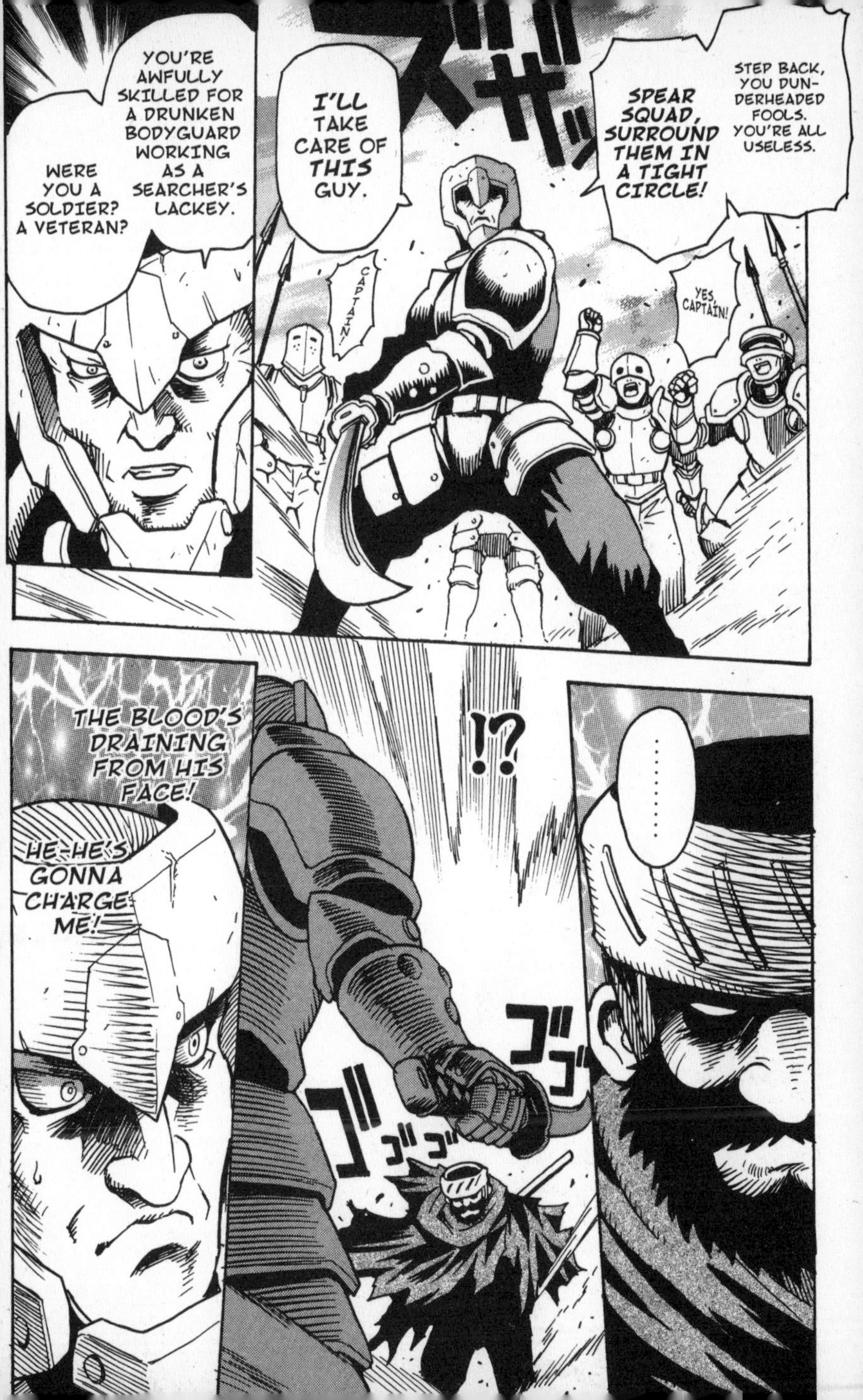
STEP BACK, YOU DUNDERHEADED FOOLS. YOU'RE ALL USELESS.
SPEAR SQUAD, SURROUND THEM IN A TIGHT CIRCLE!
YES, CAPTAIN!
I'LL TAKE CARE OF THIS GUY.
CAPTAIN!
YOU'RE AWFULLY SKILLED FOR A DRUNKEN BODYGUARD WORKING AS A SEARCHER'S LACKEY.
WERE YOU A SOLDIER? A VETERAN?
......
!?
THE BLOOD'S DRAINING FROM HIS FACE!
HE-HE'S GONNA CHARGE ME!

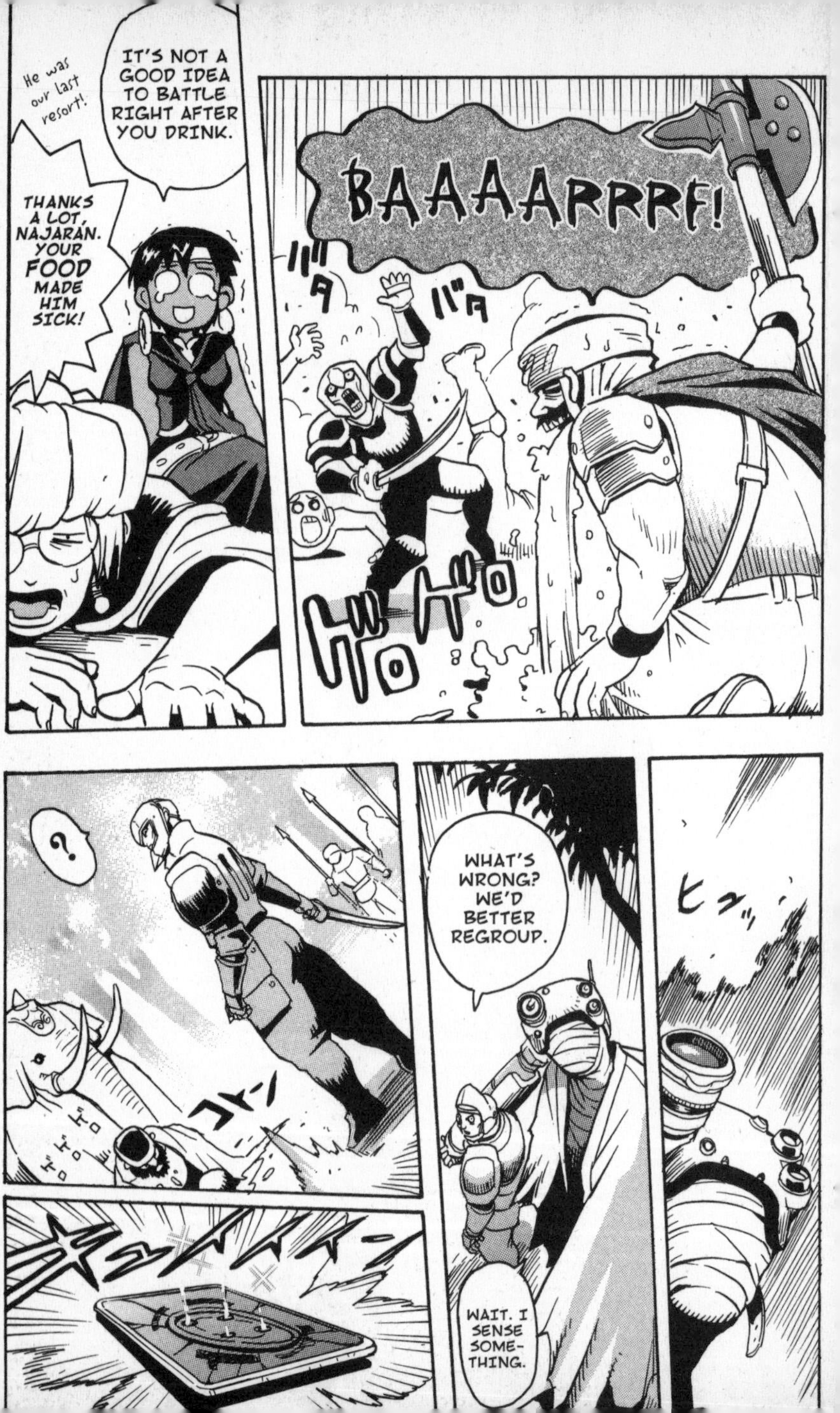
BAAAARRRF!
バタ
バタ
IT'S NOT A GOOD IDEA TO BATTLE RIGHT AFTER YOU DRINK.
He was our last resort!
THANKS A LOT, NAJARAN. YOUR FOOD MADE HIM SICK!
ヒュッ
WHAT'S WRONG? WE'D BETTER REGROUP.
WAIT. I SENSE SOMETHING.
?

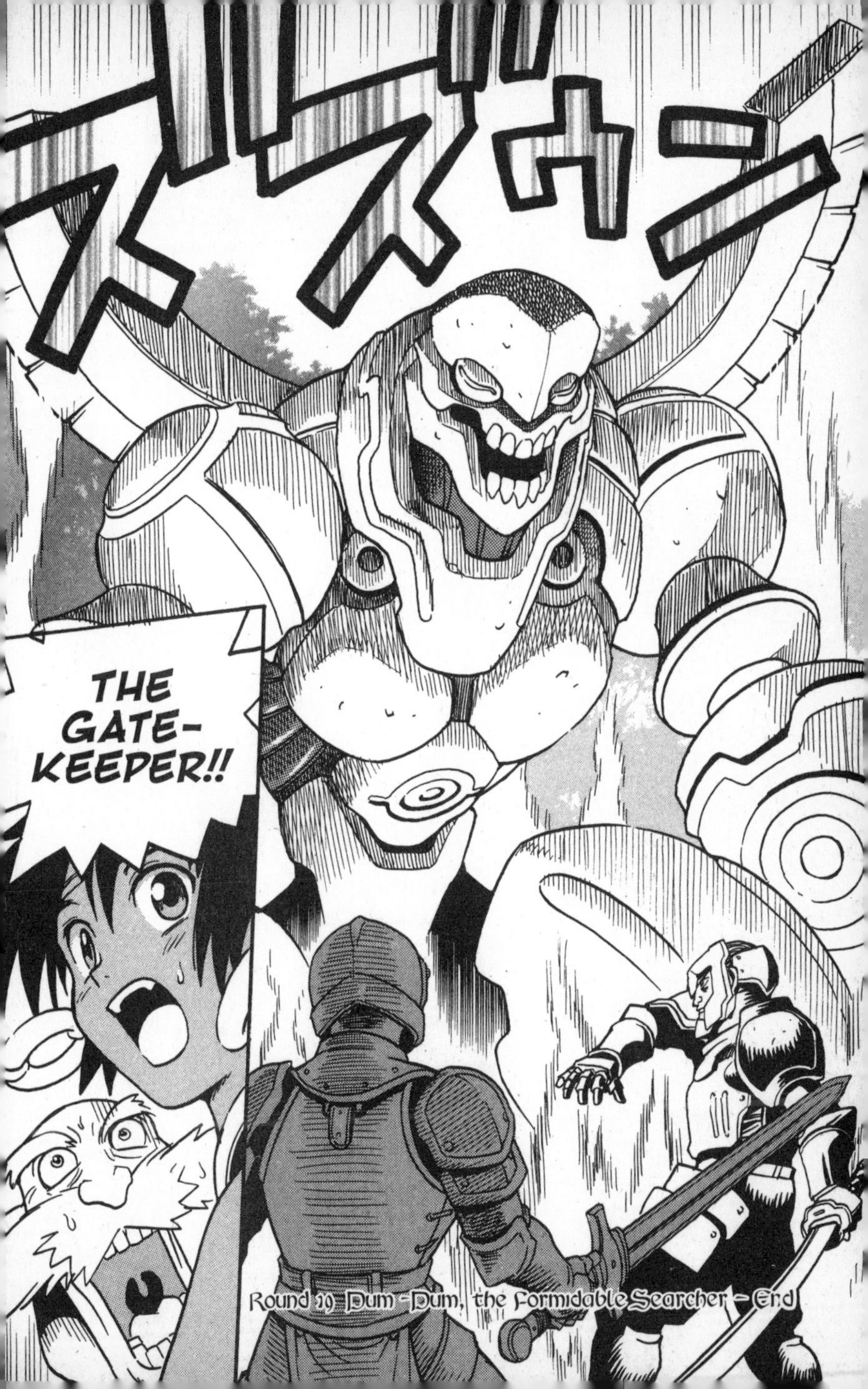
ズズゥン
THE GATE-KEEPER!!
Round 19: Dum-Dum, the Formidable Searcher - End

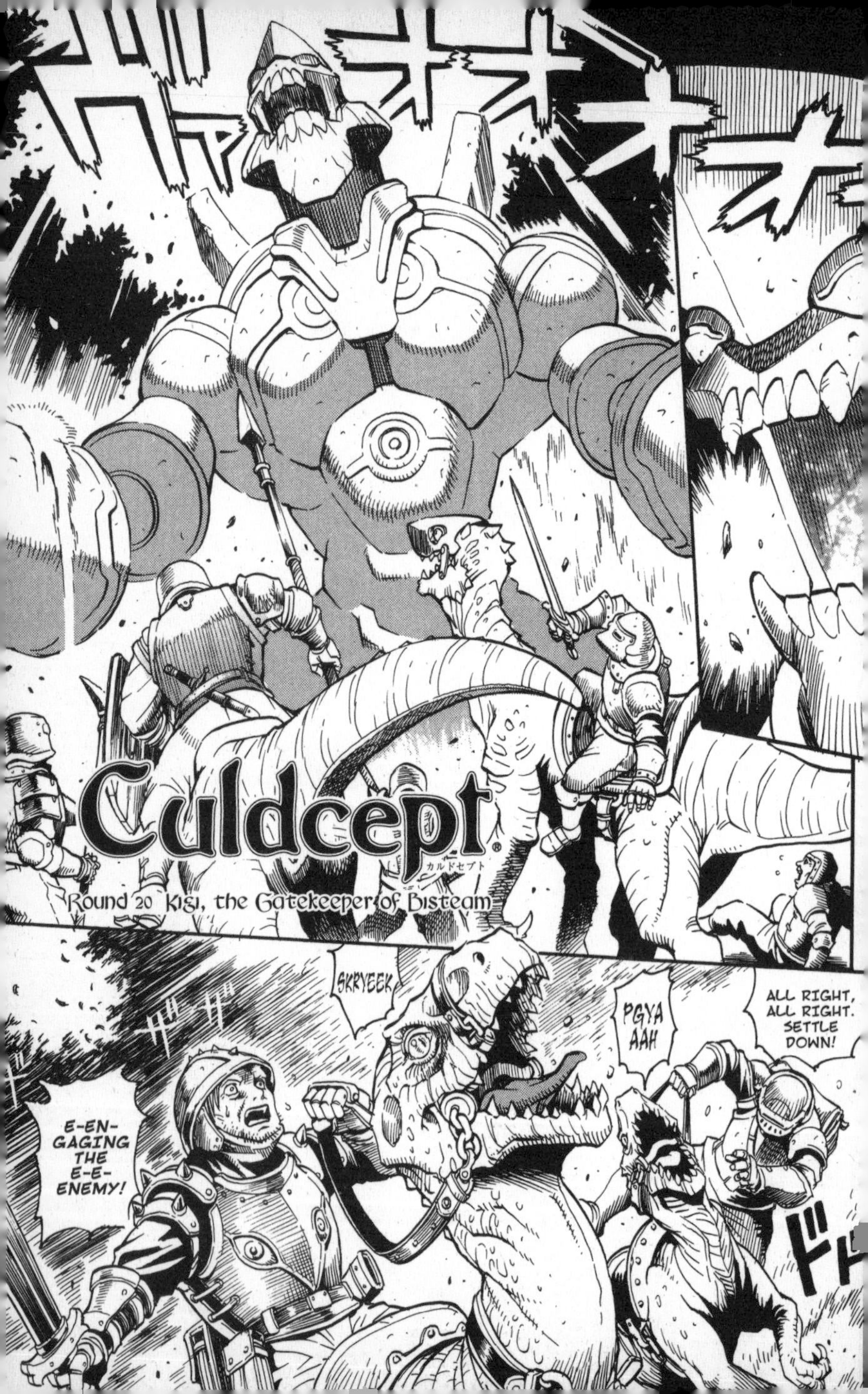
Culdcept
カルドセプト
Round 20 Kigi, the Gatekeeper of Bisteam
ALL RIGHT, ALL RIGHT. SETTLE DOWN!
PGYA AAH
SKRYEEK
E-EN-GAGING THE E-E-ENEMY!

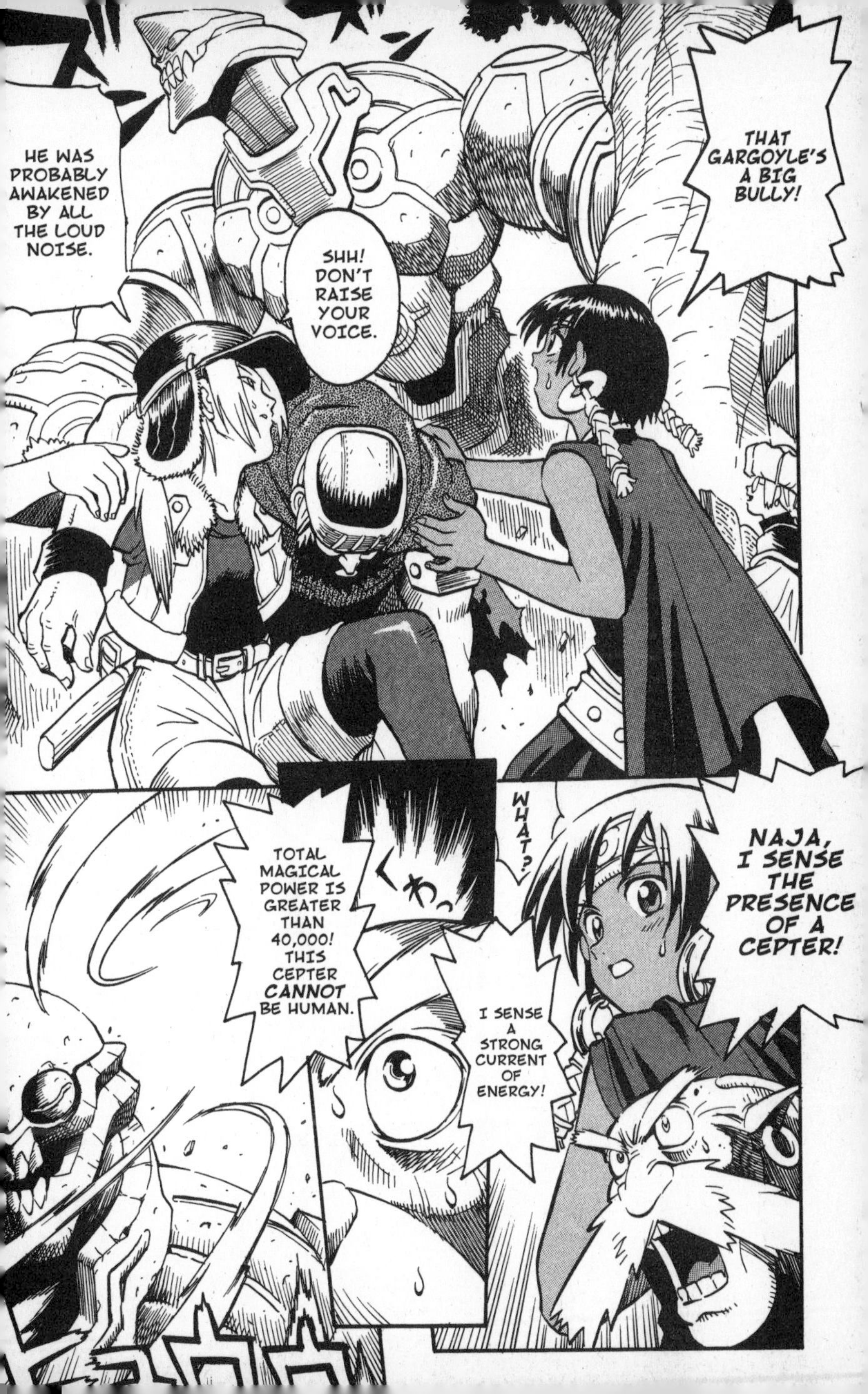
THAT GARGOYLE'S A BIG BULLY!
SHH! DON'T RAISE YOUR VOICE.
HE WAS PROBABLY AWAKENED BY ALL THE LOUD NOISE.
NAJA, I SENSE THE PRESENCE OF A CEPTER!
WHAT?
I SENSE A STRONG CURRENT OF ENERGY!
TOTAL MAGICAL POWER IS GREATER THAN 40,000! THIS CEPTER CANNOT BE HUMAN.

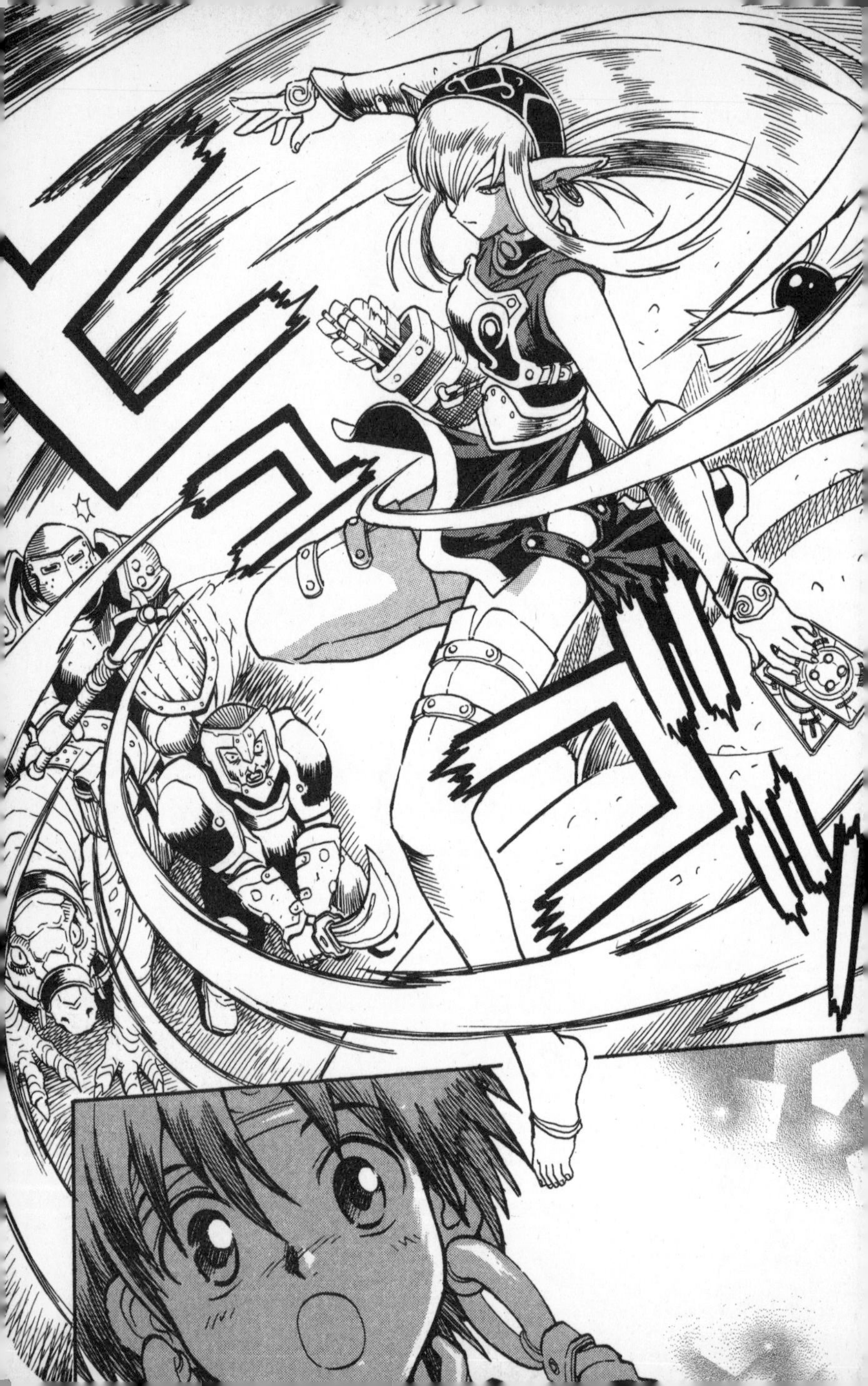

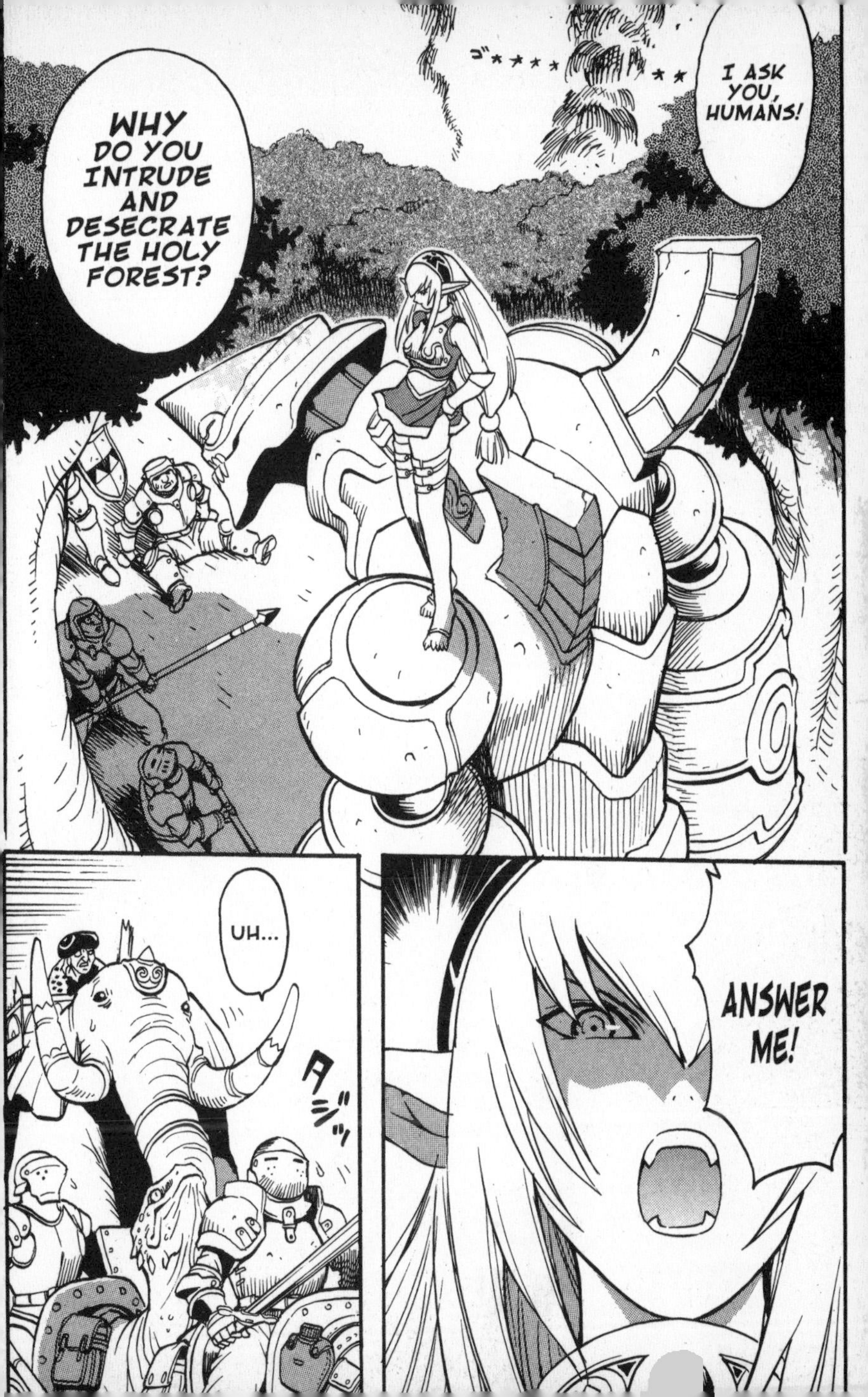
I ASK YOU, HUMANS!
WHY DO YOU INTRUDE AND DESECRATE THE HOLY FOREST?
ANSWER ME!
UH...

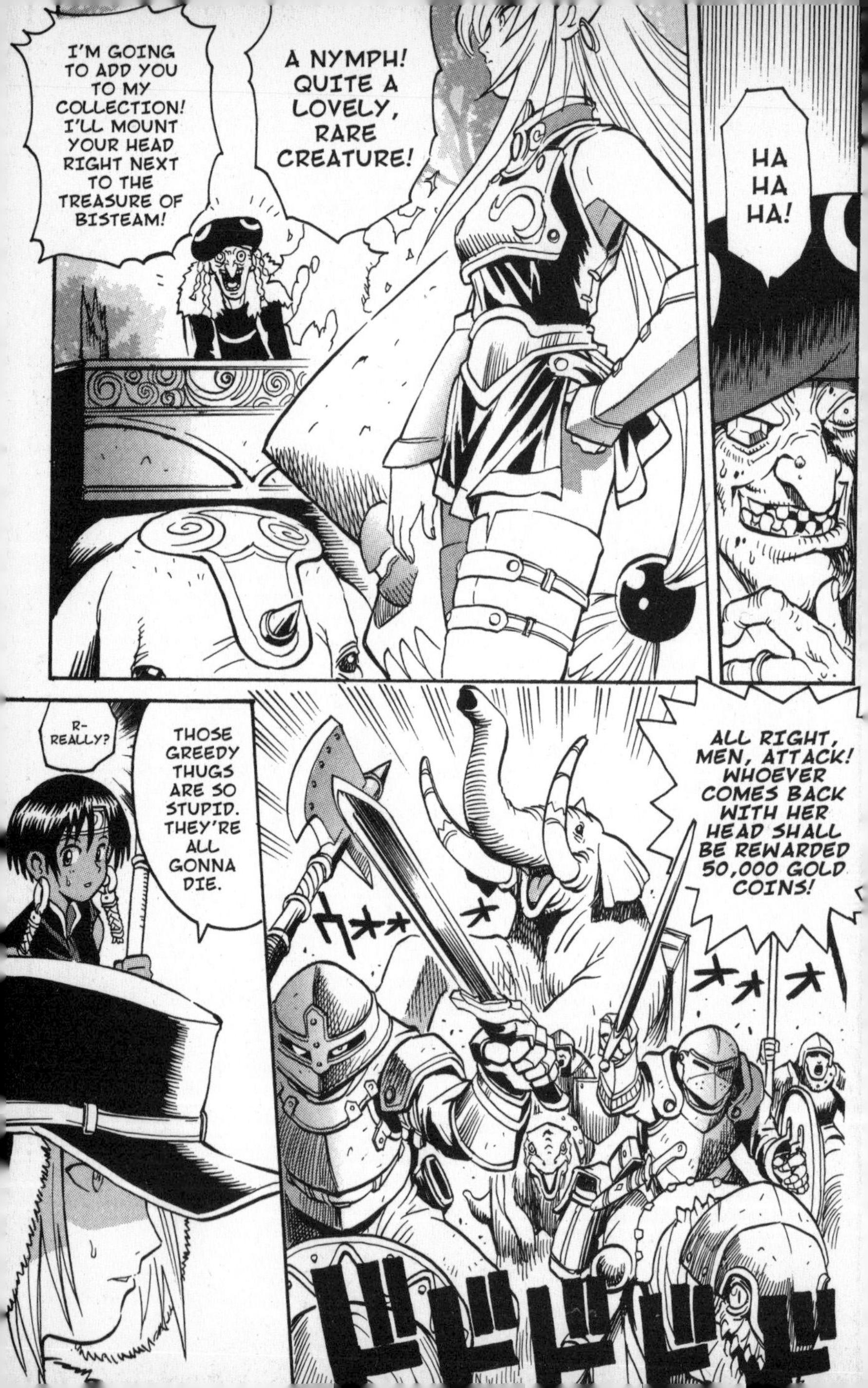
HA HA HA!
A NYMPH! QUITE A LOVELY, RARE CREATURE!
I'M GOING TO ADD YOU TO MY COLLECTION! I'LL MOUNT YOUR HEAD RIGHT NEXT TO THE TREASURE OF BISTEAM!
ALL RIGHT, MEN, ATTACK! WHOEVER COMES BACK WITH HER HEAD SHALL BE REWARDED 50,000 GOLD COINS!
THOSE GREEDY THUGS ARE SO STUPID. THEY'RE ALL GONNA DIE.
R-REALLY?

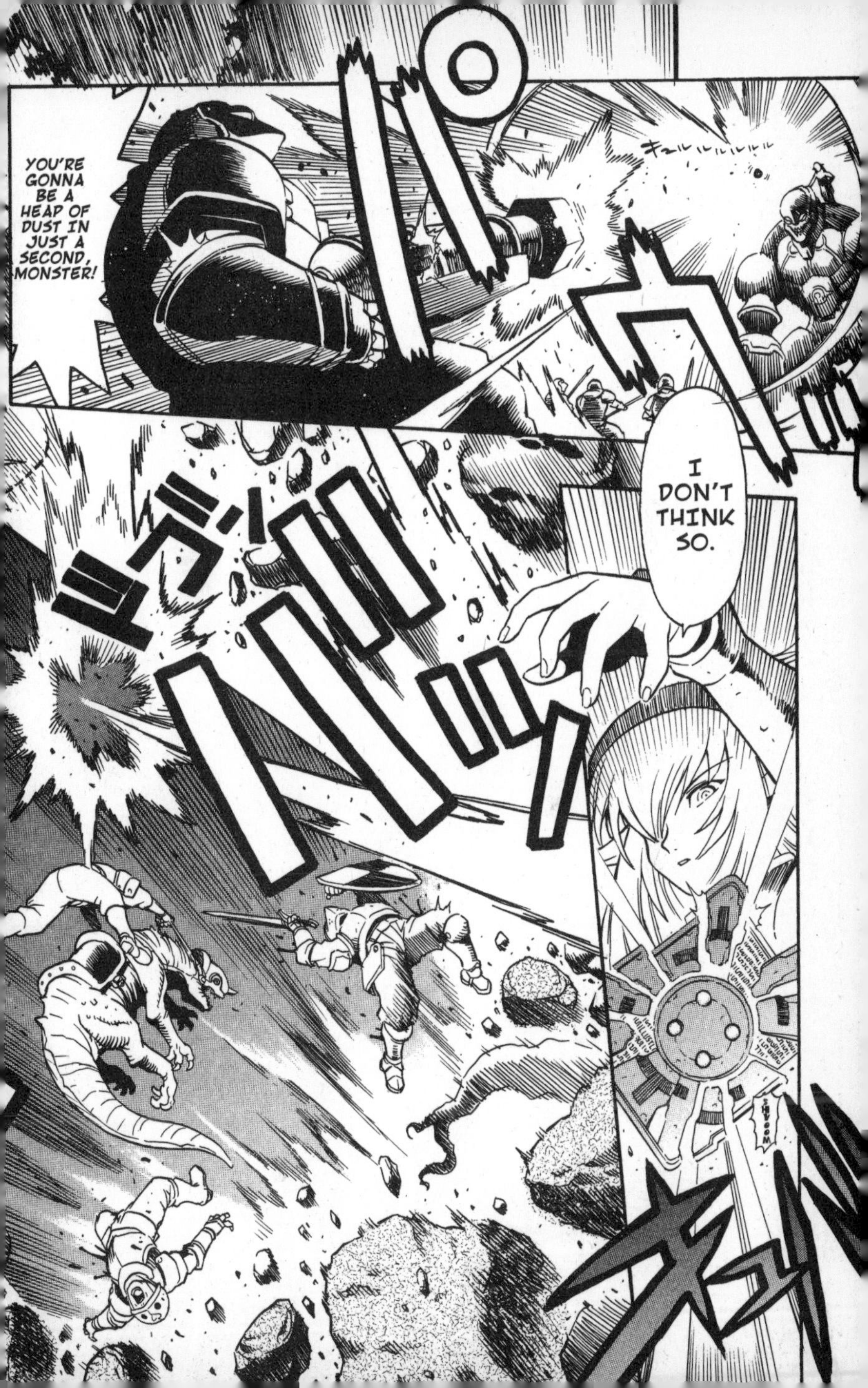
YOU'RE GONNA BE A HEAP OF DUST IN JUST A SECOND, MONSTER!
I DON'T THINK SO.
SHVOOM

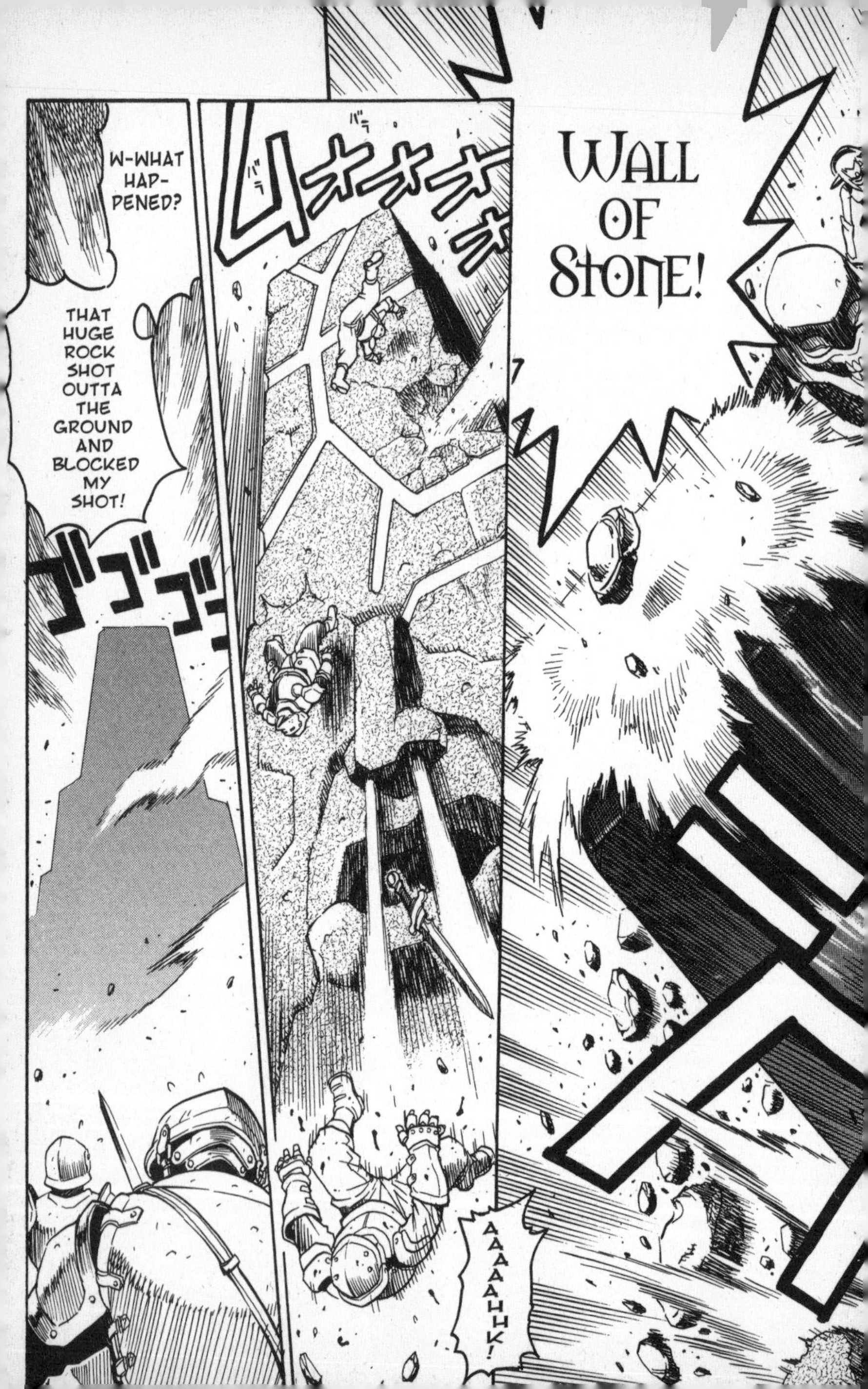
WALL OF STONE!
ムオオオオ
バラ
バラ
AAAAAHK!
W-WHAT HAPPENED?
THAT HUGE ROCK SHOT OUTTA THE GROUND AND BLOCKED MY SHOT!
ゴゴゴ

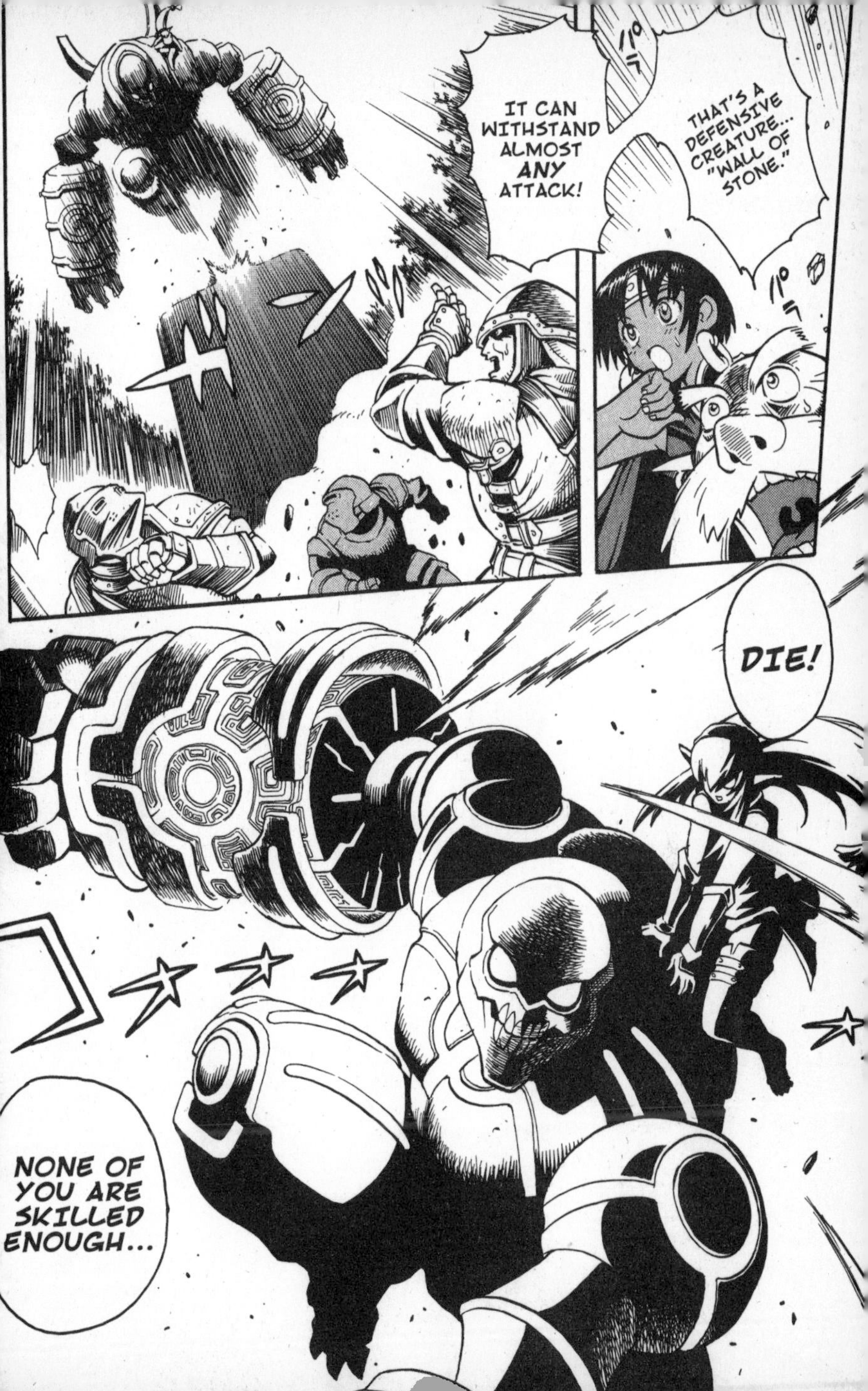
THAT'S A DEFENSIVE CREATURE... "WALL OF STONE."
IT CAN WITHSTAND ALMOST ANY ATTACK!
DIE!
NONE OF YOU ARE SKILLED ENOUGH...

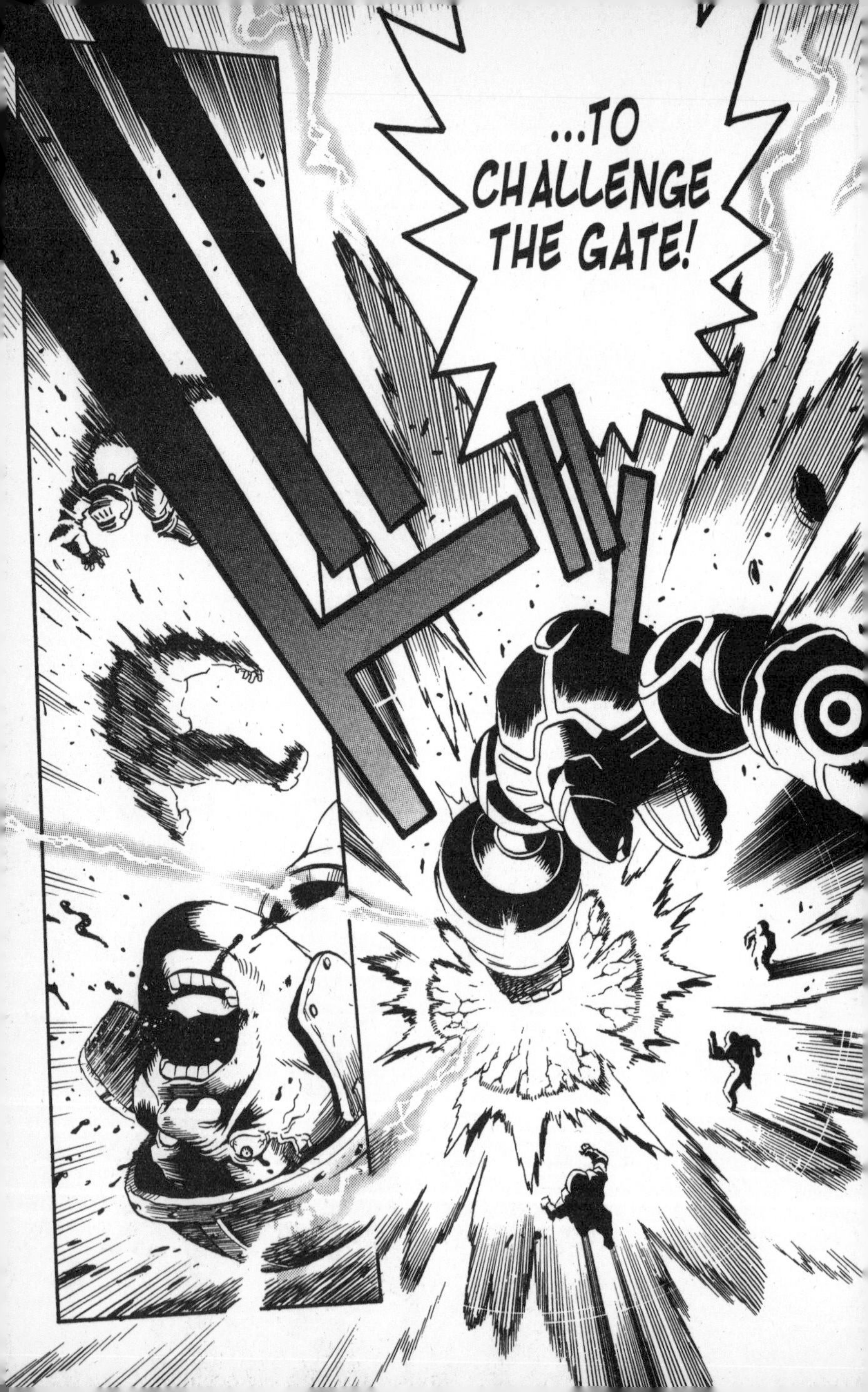
...TO CHALLENGE THE GATE!

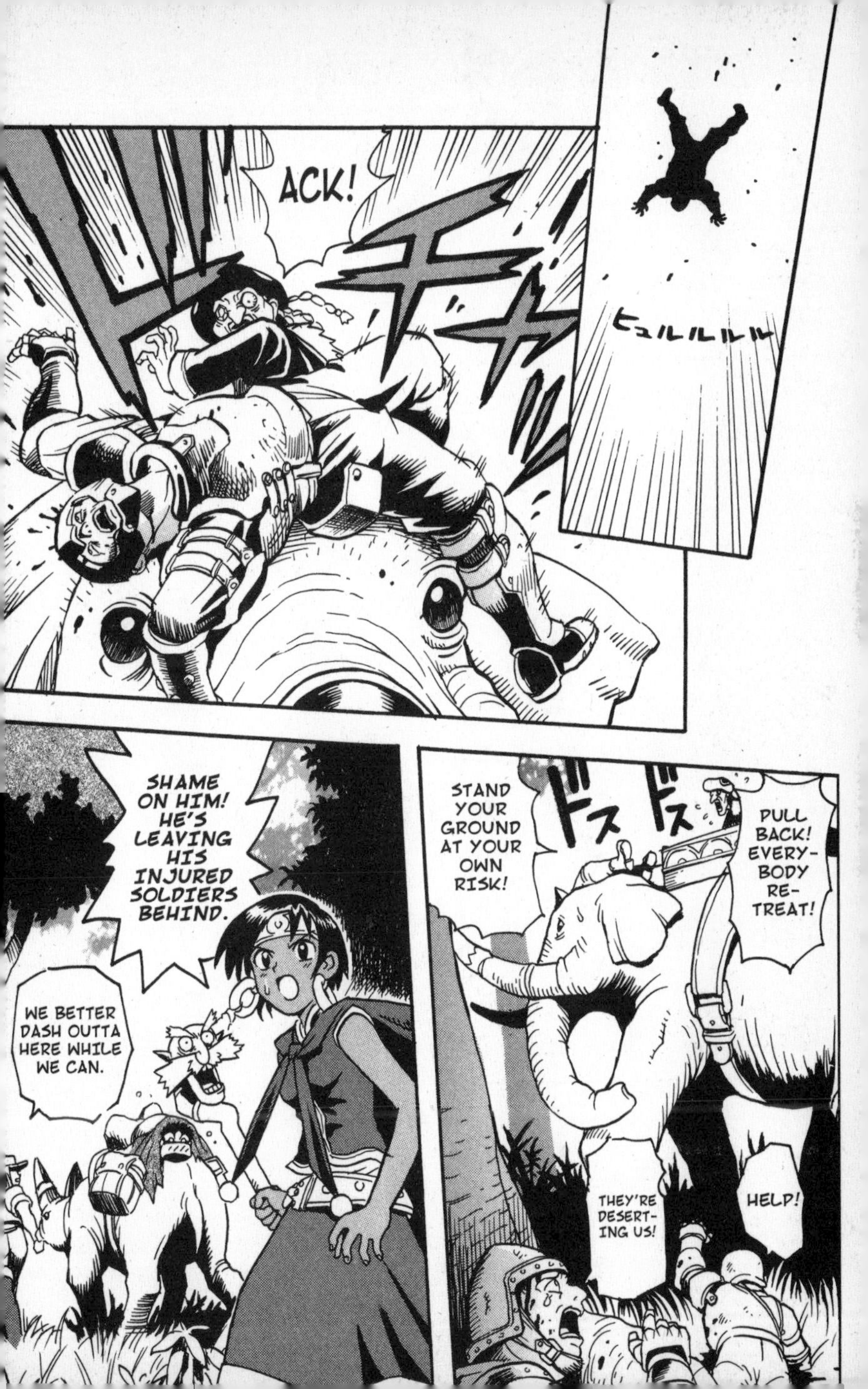
ヒュルルルル
ACK!
ドスドス
PULL BACK! EVERYBODY RETREAT!
STAND YOUR GROUND AT YOUR OWN RISK!
HELP!
THEY'RE DESERTING US!
SHAME ON HIM! HE'S LEAVING HIS INJURED SOLDIERS BEHIND.
WE BETTER DASH OUTTA HERE WHILE WE CAN.

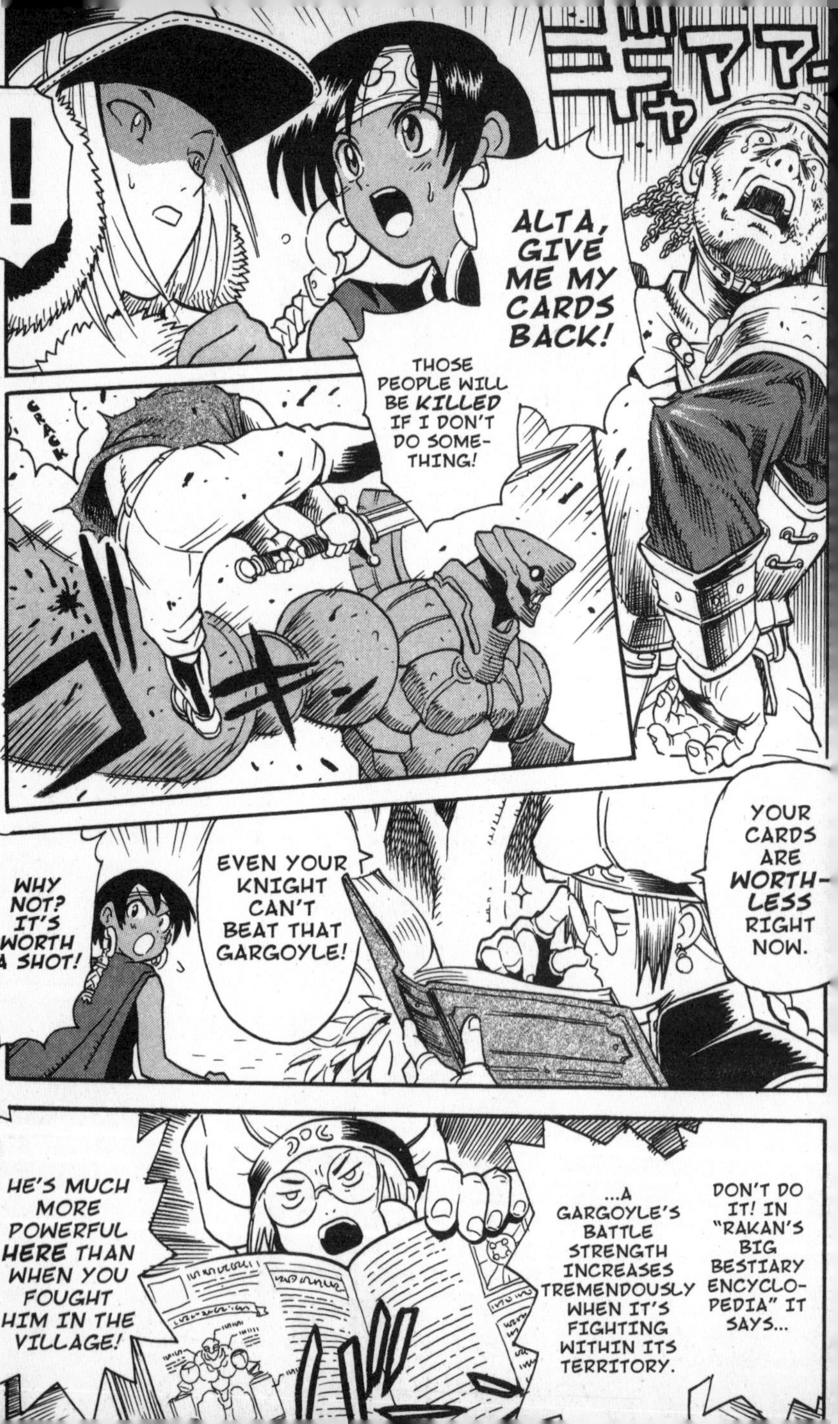
ギャアアー
ALTA, GIVE ME MY CARDS BACK!
!
THOSE PEOPLE WILL BE KILLED IF I DON'T DO SOME-THING!
CRACK
YOUR CARDS ARE WORTH-LESS RIGHT NOW.
EVEN YOUR KNIGHT CAN'T BEAT THAT GARGOYLE!
WHY NOT? IT'S WORTH A SHOT!
DON'T DO IT! IN "RAKAN'S BIG BESTIARY ENCYCLO-PEDIA" IT SAYS...
...A GARGOYLE'S BATTLE STRENGTH INCREASES TREMENDOUSLY WHEN IT'S FIGHTING WITHIN ITS TERRITORY.
HE'S MUCH MORE POWERFUL HERE THAN WHEN YOU FOUGHT HIM IN THE VILLAGE!

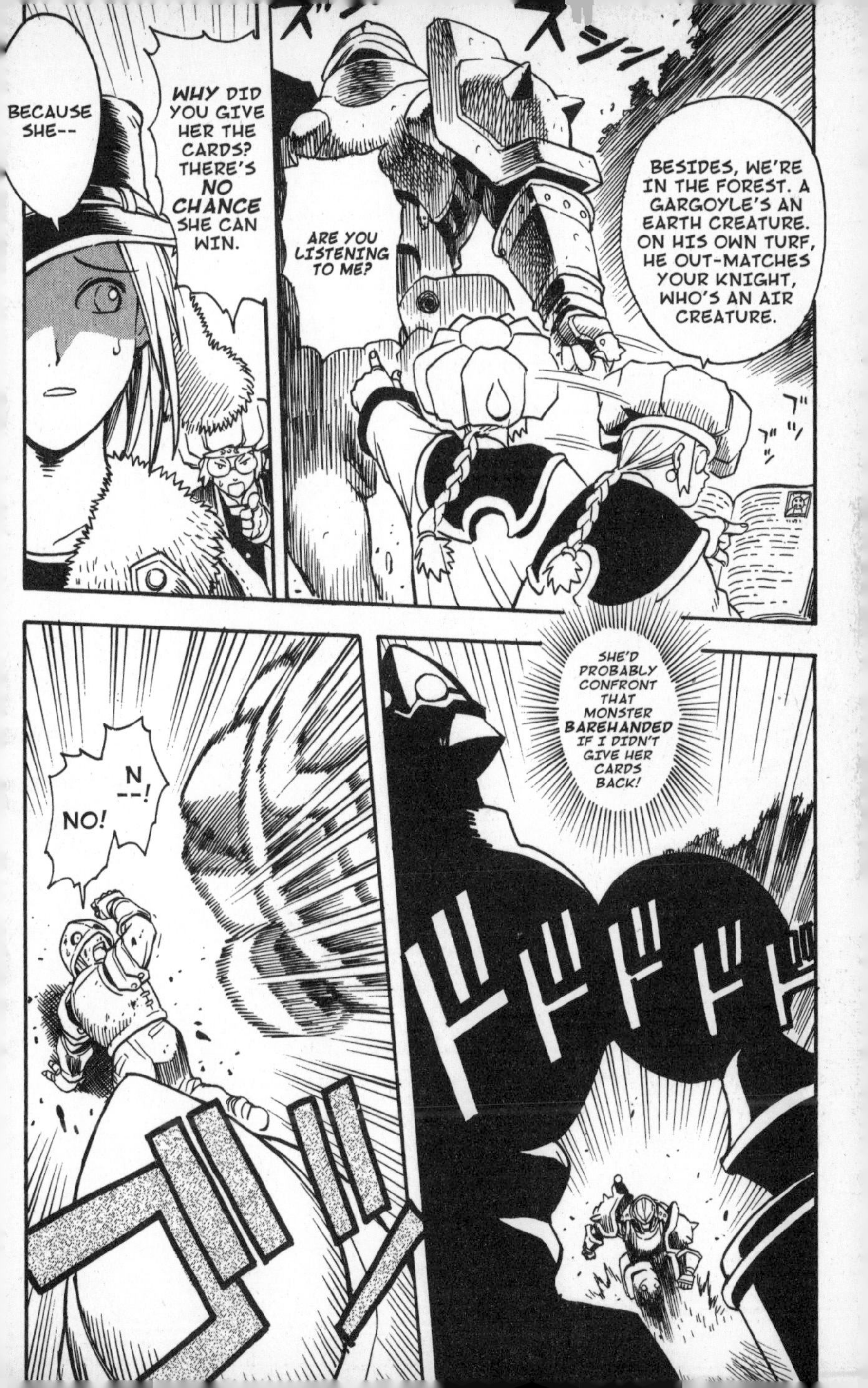

BESIDES, WE'RE IN THE FOREST. A GARGOYLE'S AN EARTH CREATURE. ON HIS OWN TURF, HE OUT-MATCHES YOUR KNIGHT, WHO'S AN AIR CREATURE.
ARE YOU LISTENING TO ME?
WHY DID YOU GIVE HER THE CARDS? THERE'S NO CHANCE SHE CAN WIN.
BECAUSE SHE--
SHE'D PROBABLY CONFRONT THAT MONSTER BAREHANDED IF I DIDN'T GIVE HER CARDS BACK!
ドドドドド
N--!
NO!

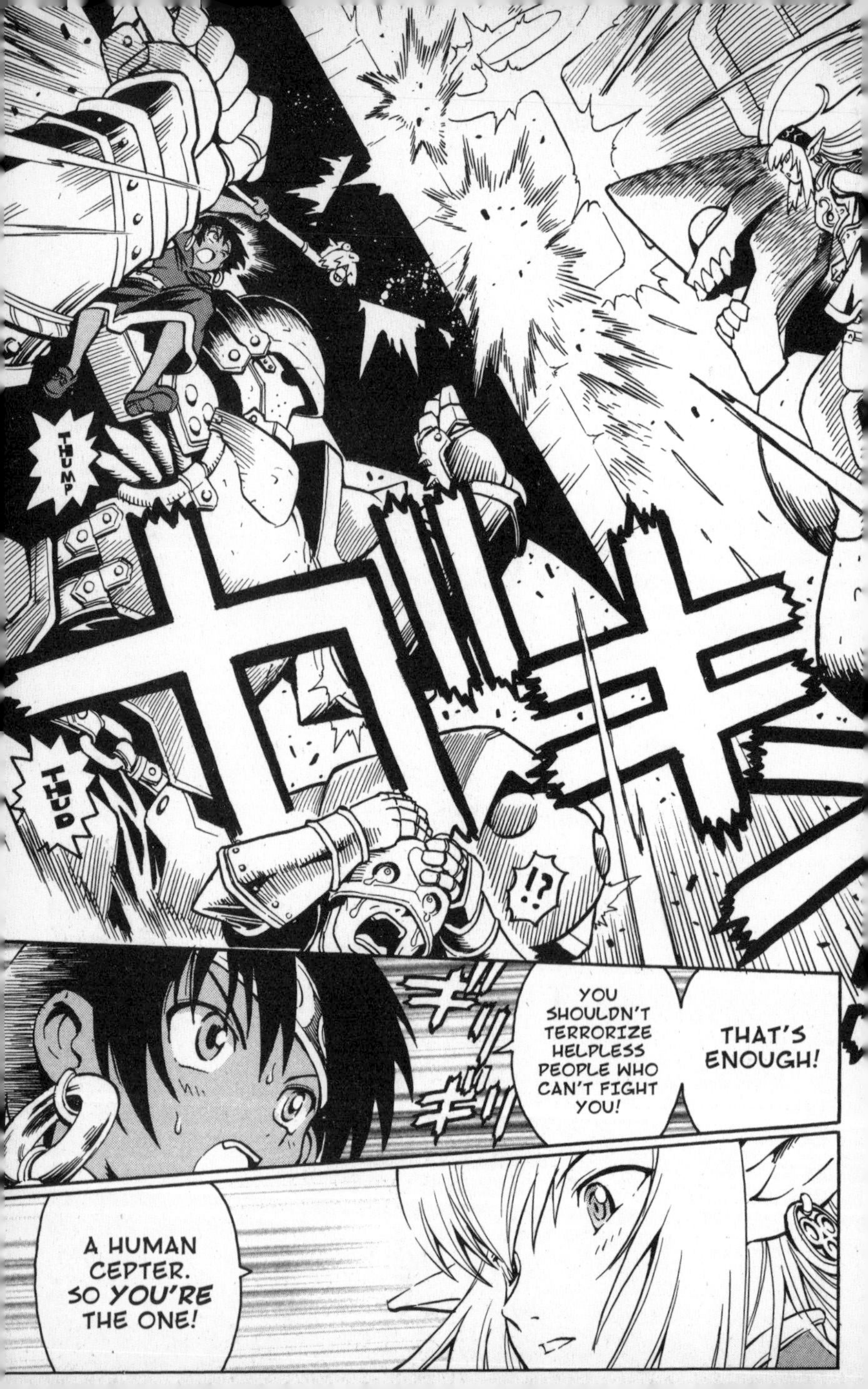
THUMP
THUD
!?
THAT'S ENOUGH!
YOU SHOULDN'T TERRORIZE HELPLESS PEOPLE WHO CAN'T FIGHT YOU!
A HUMAN CEPTER. SO *YOU'RE* THE ONE!

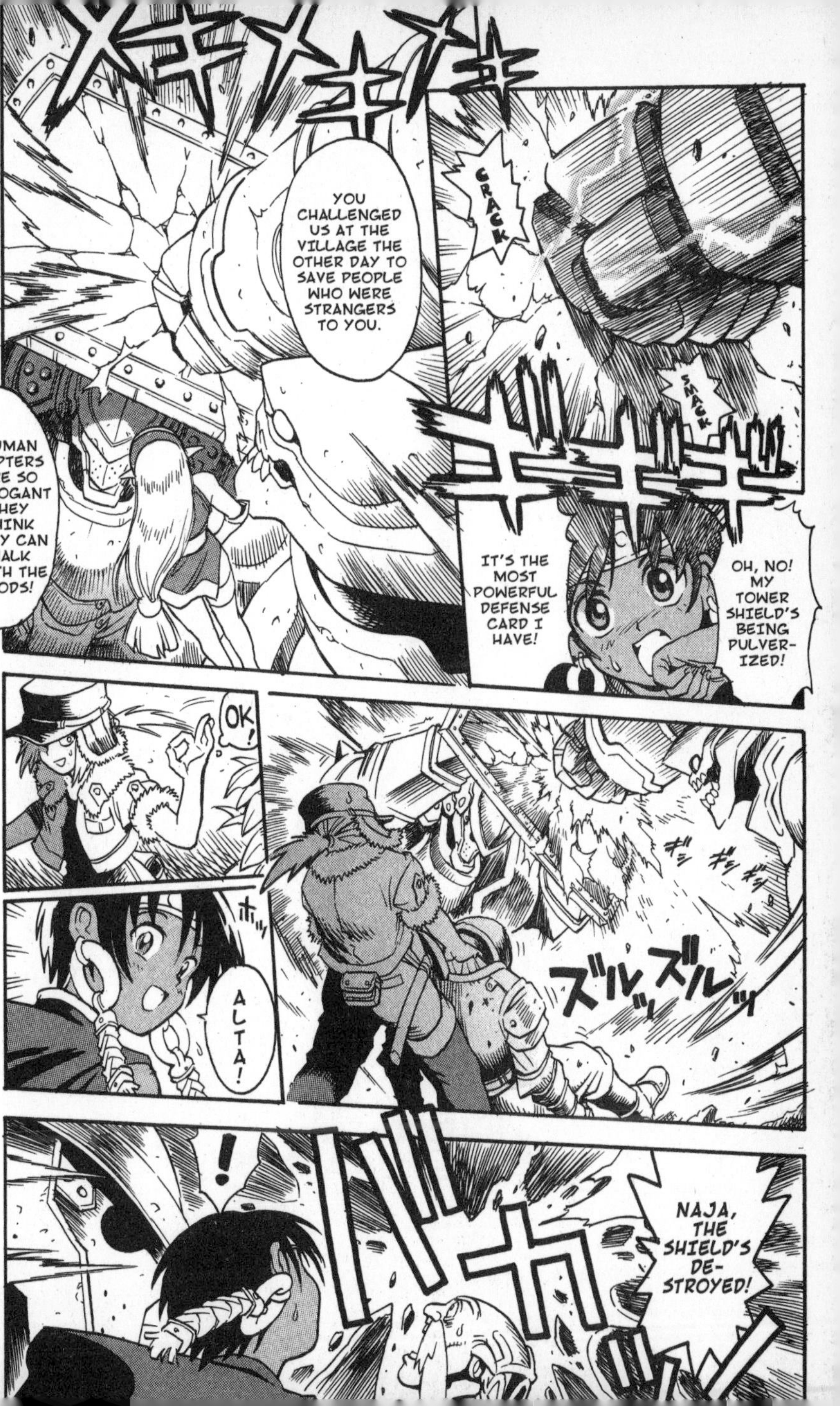
CRACK
SMACK
OH, NO! MY TOWER SHIELD'S BEING PULVER-IZED!
IT'S THE MOST POWERFUL DEFENSE CARD I HAVE!
YOU CHALLENGED US AT THE VILLAGE THE OTHER DAY TO SAVE PEOPLE WHO WERE STRANGERS TO YOU.
HUMAN CEPTERS ARE SO ARROGANT THEY THINK THEY CAN WALK WITH THE GODS!
OK!
ALTA!
NAJA, THE SHIELD'S DE-STROYED!
!

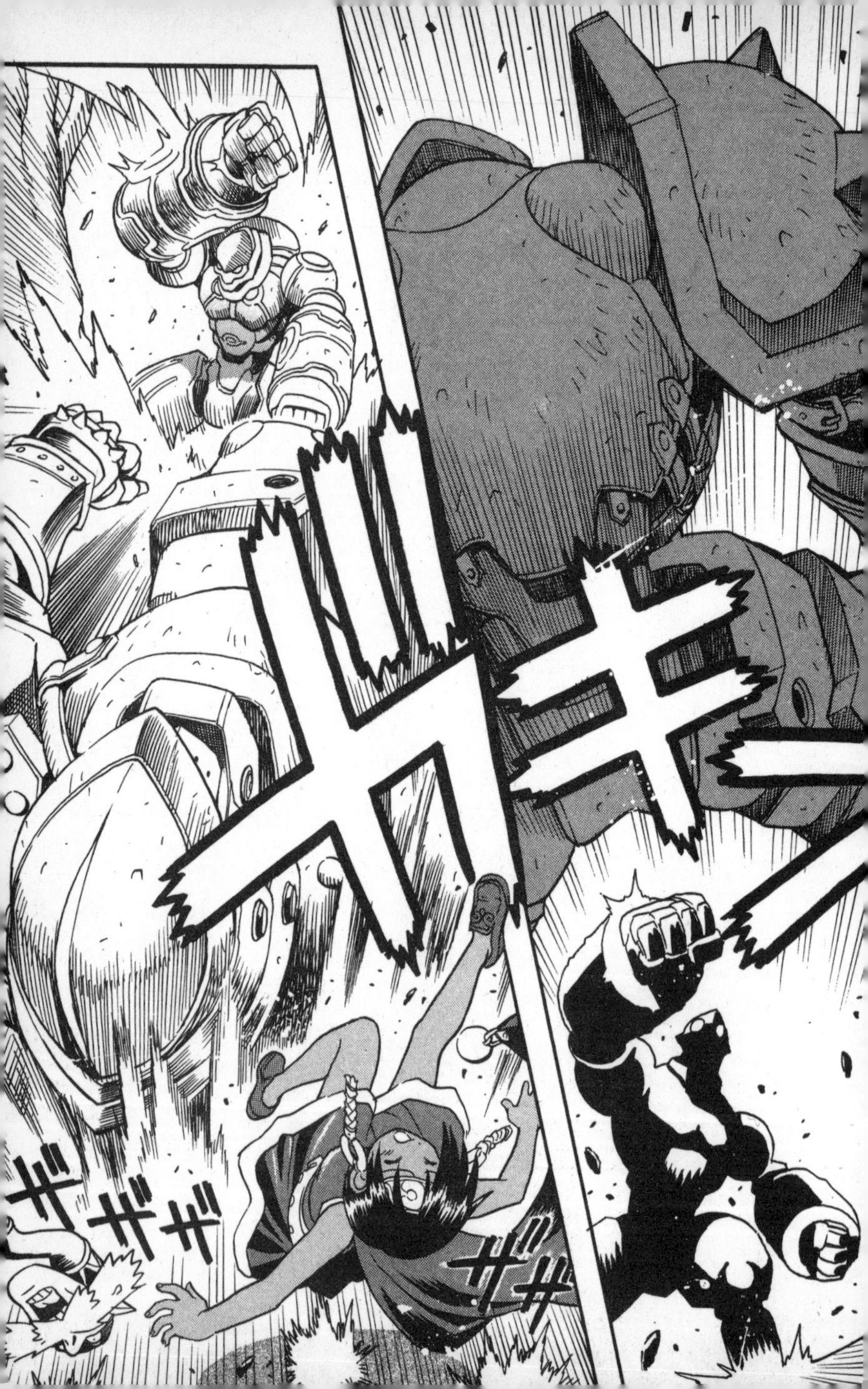
ガキン
ザザ
ザザザ

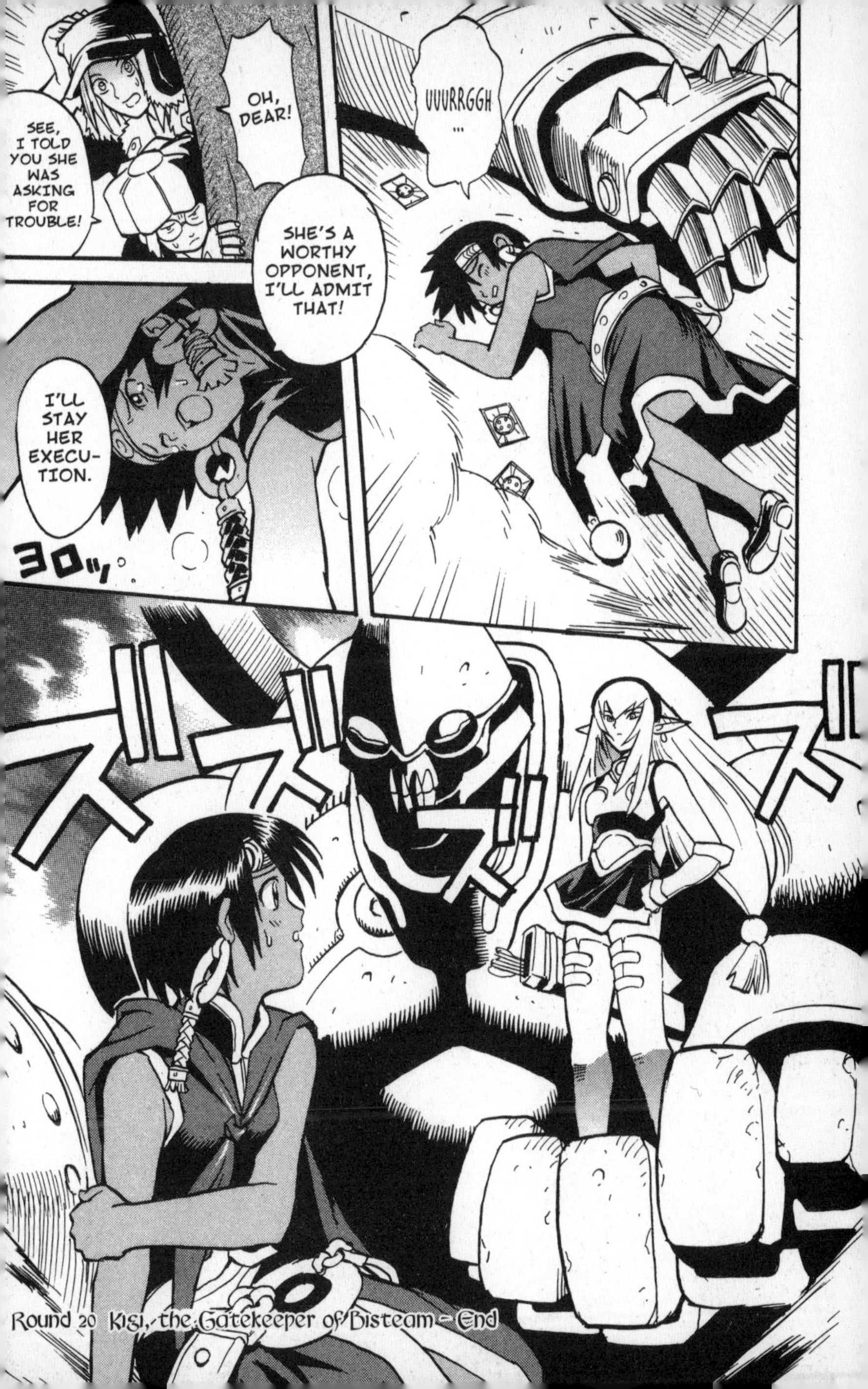
UUURRGGH ...
OH, DEAR!
SEE, I TOLD YOU SHE WAS ASKING FOR TROUBLE!
SHE'S A WORTHY OPPONENT, I'LL ADMIT THAT!
I'LL STAY HER EXECUTION.
ヨロッ
ズズズズ
Round 20 Kigi, the Gatekeeper of Bisteam - End

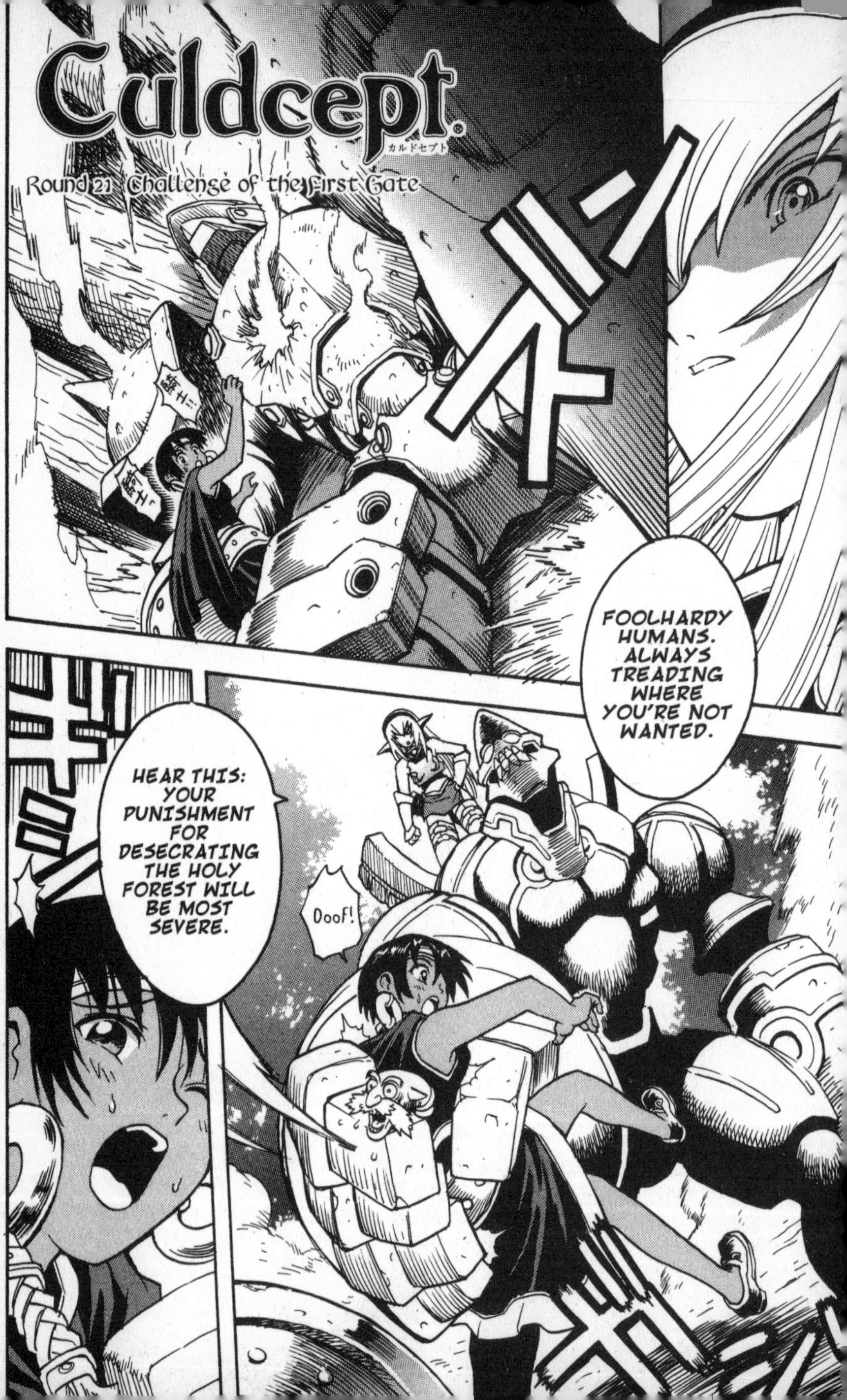
Culdcept
カルドセプト
Round 21: Challenge of the First Gate
FOOLHARDY HUMANS. ALWAYS TREADING WHERE YOU'RE NOT WANTED.
HEAR THIS: YOUR PUNISHMENT FOR DESECRATING THE HOLY FOREST WILL BE MOST SEVERE.
Doof!

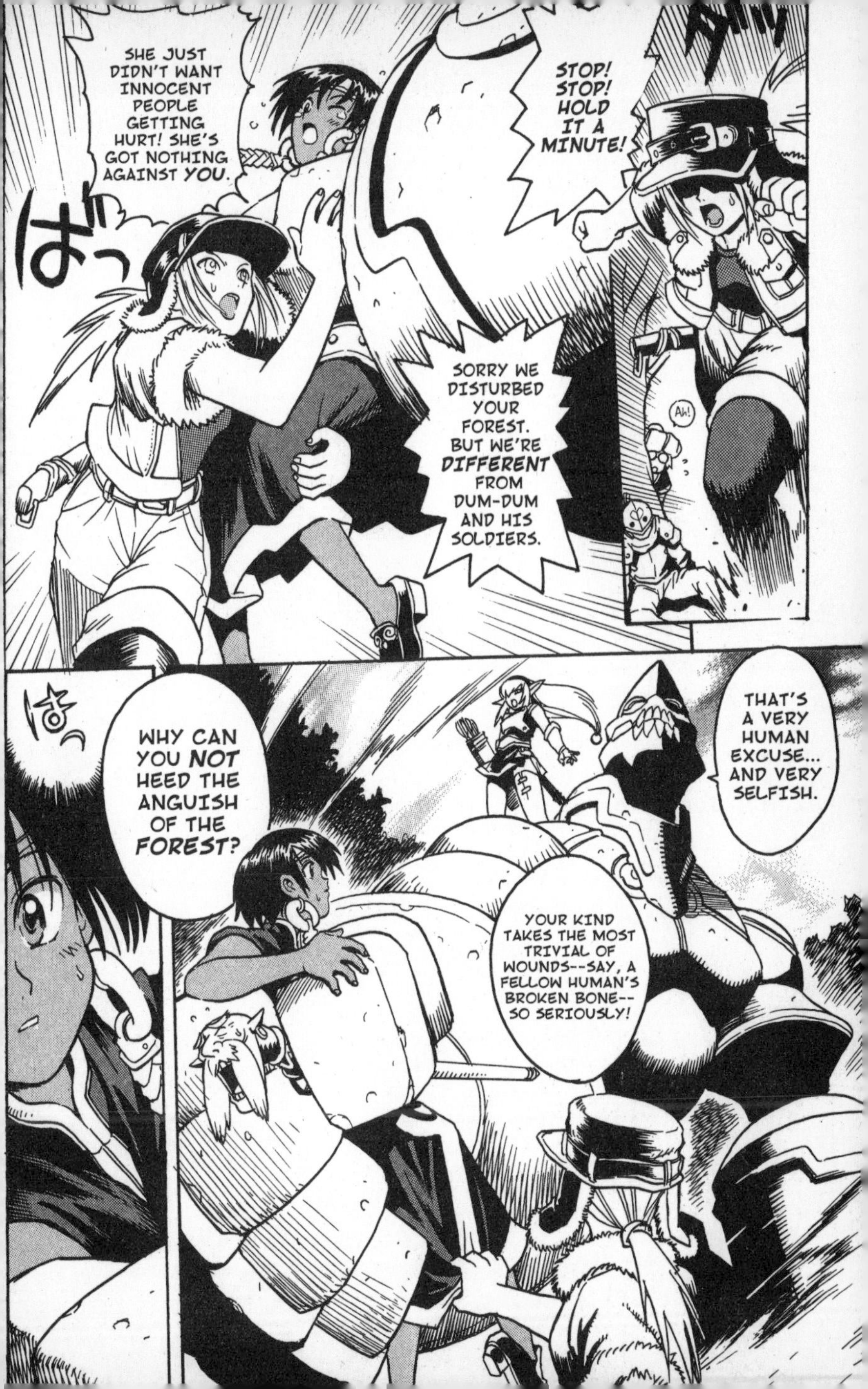

STOP! STOP! HOLD IT A MINUTE!
AH!
SORRY WE DISTURBED YOUR FOREST. BUT WE'RE *DIFFERENT* FROM DUM-DUM AND HIS SOLDIERS.
SHE JUST DIDN'T WANT INNOCENT PEOPLE GETTING HURT! SHE'S GOT NOTHING AGAINST *YOU*.
ばっ
THAT'S A VERY HUMAN EXCUSE... AND VERY SELFISH.
YOUR KIND TAKES THE MOST TRIVIAL OF WOUNDS--SAY, A FELLOW HUMAN'S BROKEN BONE--SO SERIOUSLY!
WHY CAN YOU *NOT* HEED THE ANGUISH OF THE *FOREST*?
はっ

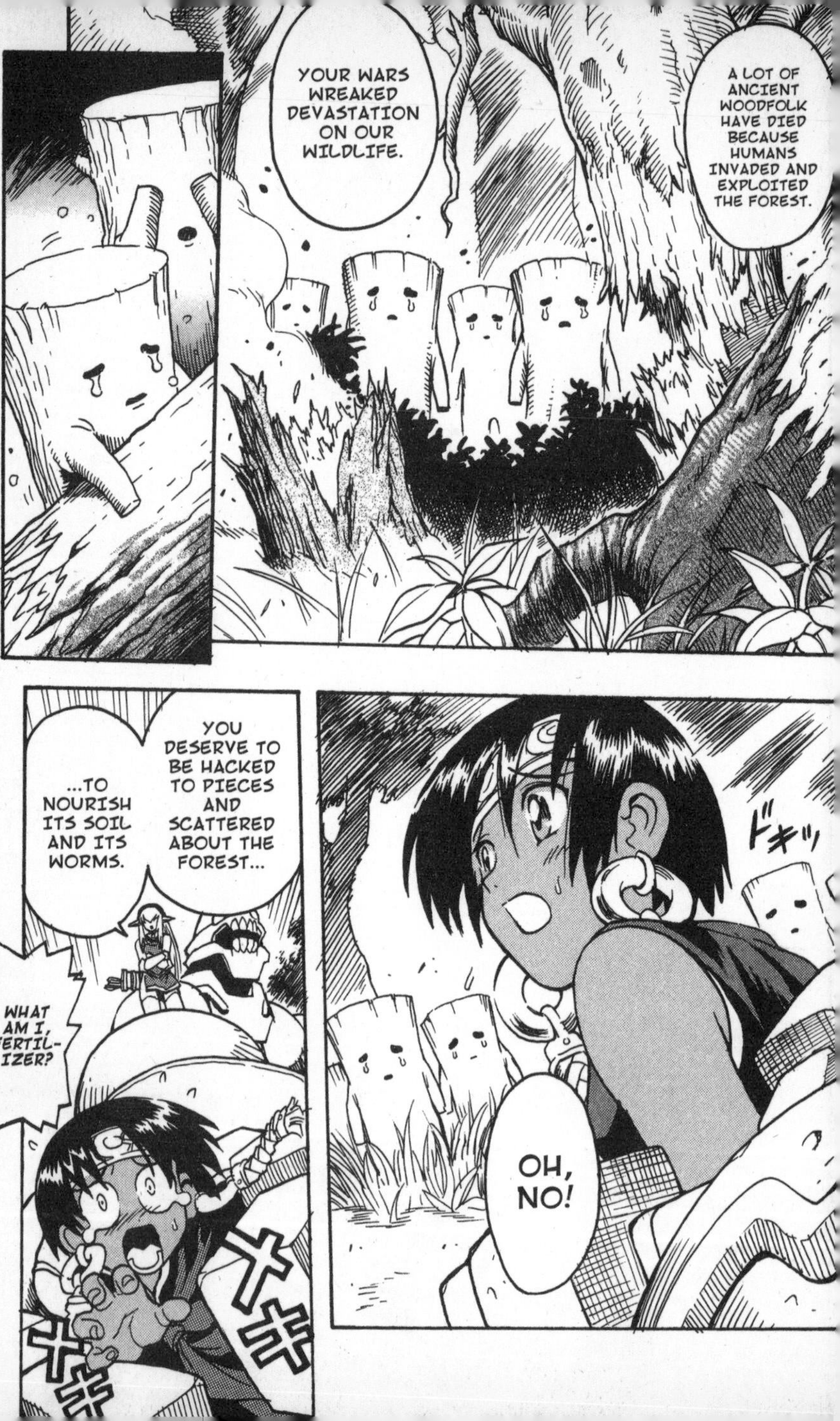
A LOT OF ANCIENT WOODFOLK HAVE DIED BECAUSE HUMANS INVADED AND EXPLOITED THE FOREST.
YOUR WARS WREAKED DEVASTATION ON OUR WILDLIFE.
ドキッ
OH, NO!
YOU DESERVE TO BE HACKED TO PIECES AND SCATTERED ABOUT THE FOREST...
...TO NOURISH ITS SOIL AND ITS WORMS.
WHAT AM I, FERTIL-IZER?

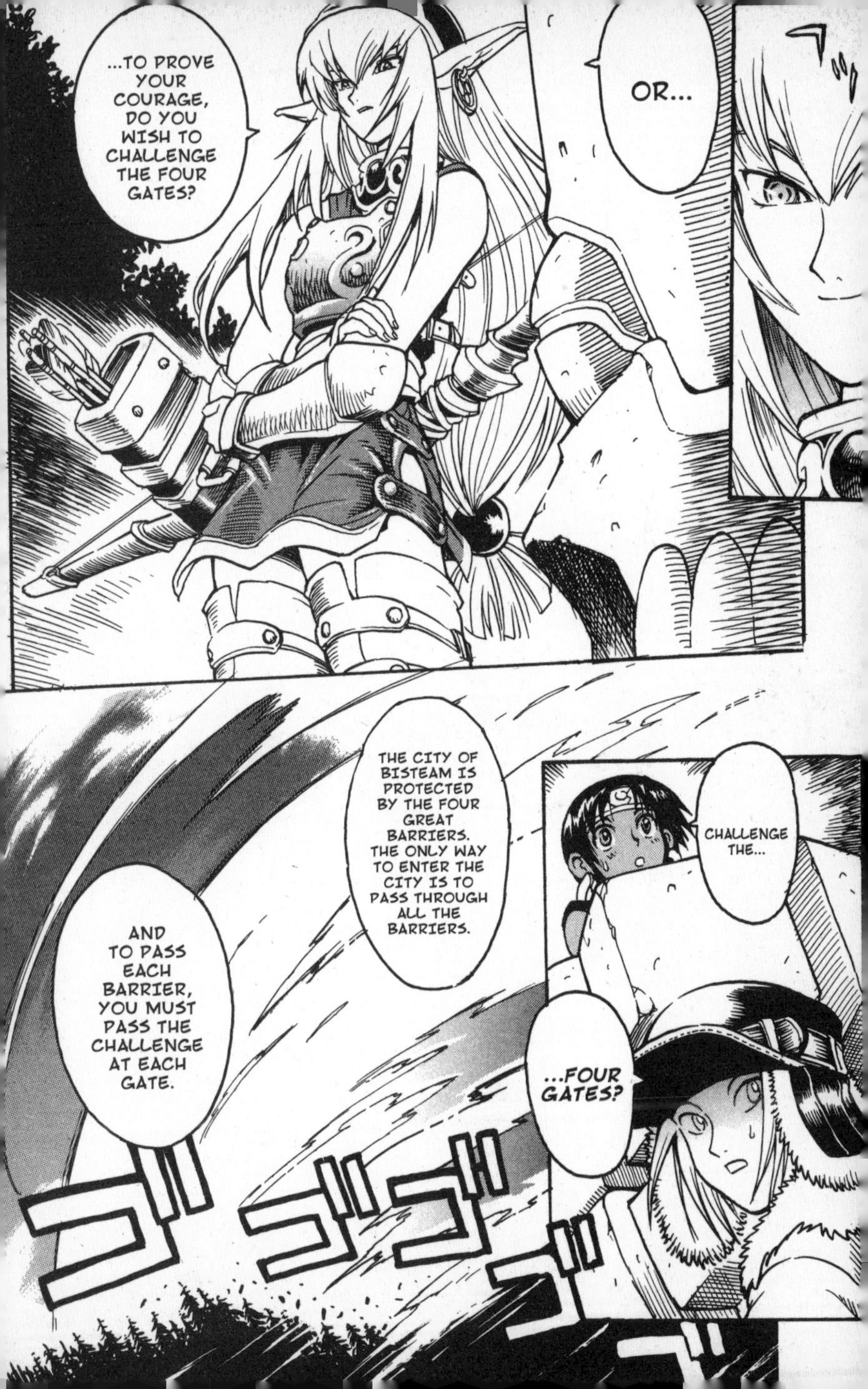
OR...
...TO PROVE YOUR COURAGE, DO YOU WISH TO CHALLENGE THE FOUR GATES?
CHALLENGE THE...
...FOUR GATES?
THE CITY OF BISTEAM IS PROTECTED BY THE FOUR GREAT BARRIERS. THE ONLY WAY TO ENTER THE CITY IS TO PASS THROUGH ALL THE BARRIERS.
AND TO PASS EACH BARRIER, YOU MUST PASS THE CHALLENGE AT EACH GATE.
ゴゴゴゴ

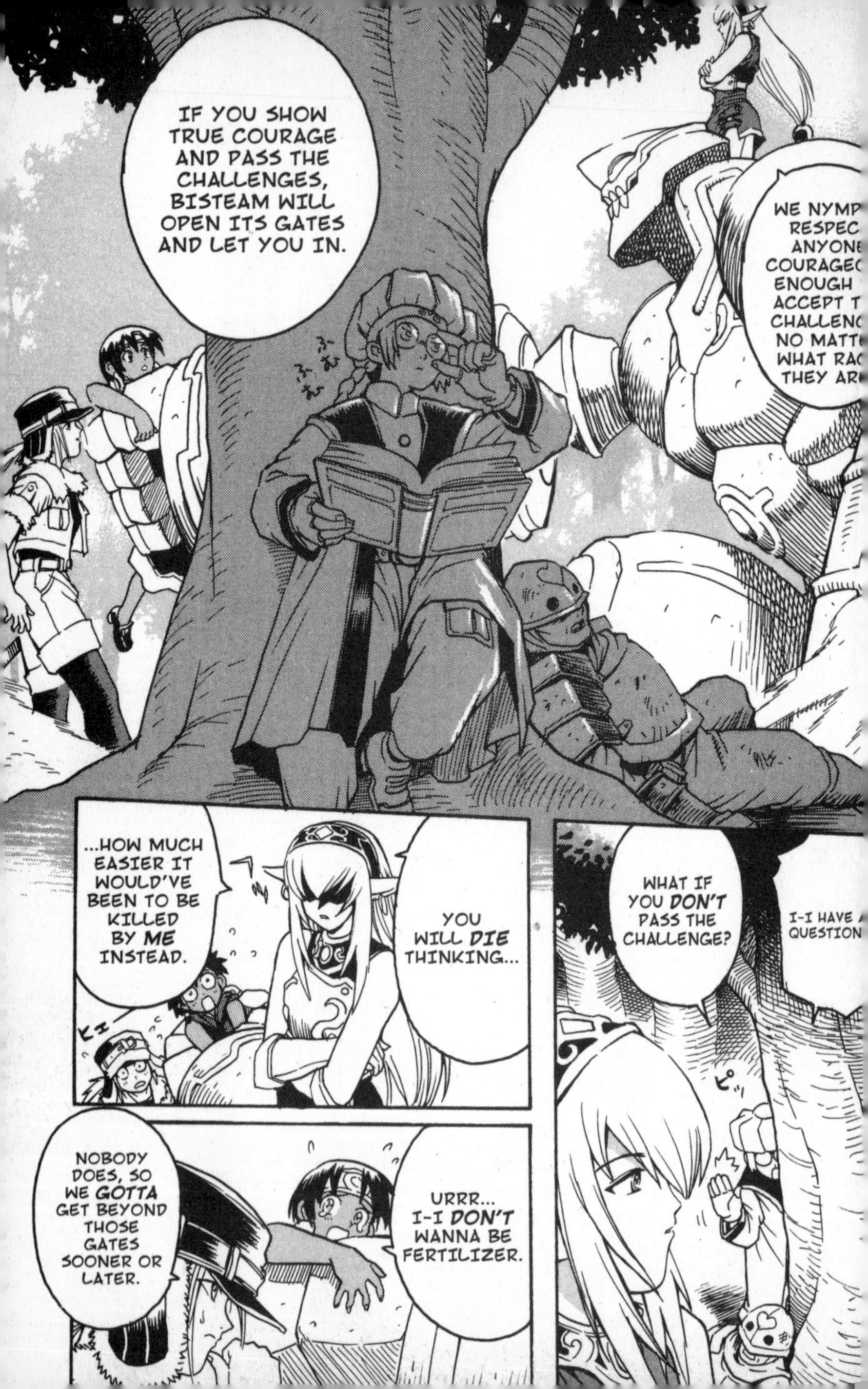
WE NYMP RESPEC ANYONE COURAGEO ENOUGH ACCEPT T CHALLENG NO MATTE WHAT RAC THEY AR
IF YOU SHOW TRUE COURAGE AND PASS THE CHALLENGES, BISTEAM WILL OPEN ITS GATES AND LET YOU IN.
I-I HAVE A QUESTION
WHAT IF YOU DON'T PASS THE CHALLENGE?
YOU WILL DIE THINKING...
...HOW MUCH EASIER IT WOULD'VE BEEN TO BE KILLED BY ME INSTEAD.
URRR... I-I DON'T WANNA BE FERTILIZER.
NOBODY DOES, SO WE GOTTA GET BEYOND THOSE GATES SOONER OR LATER.

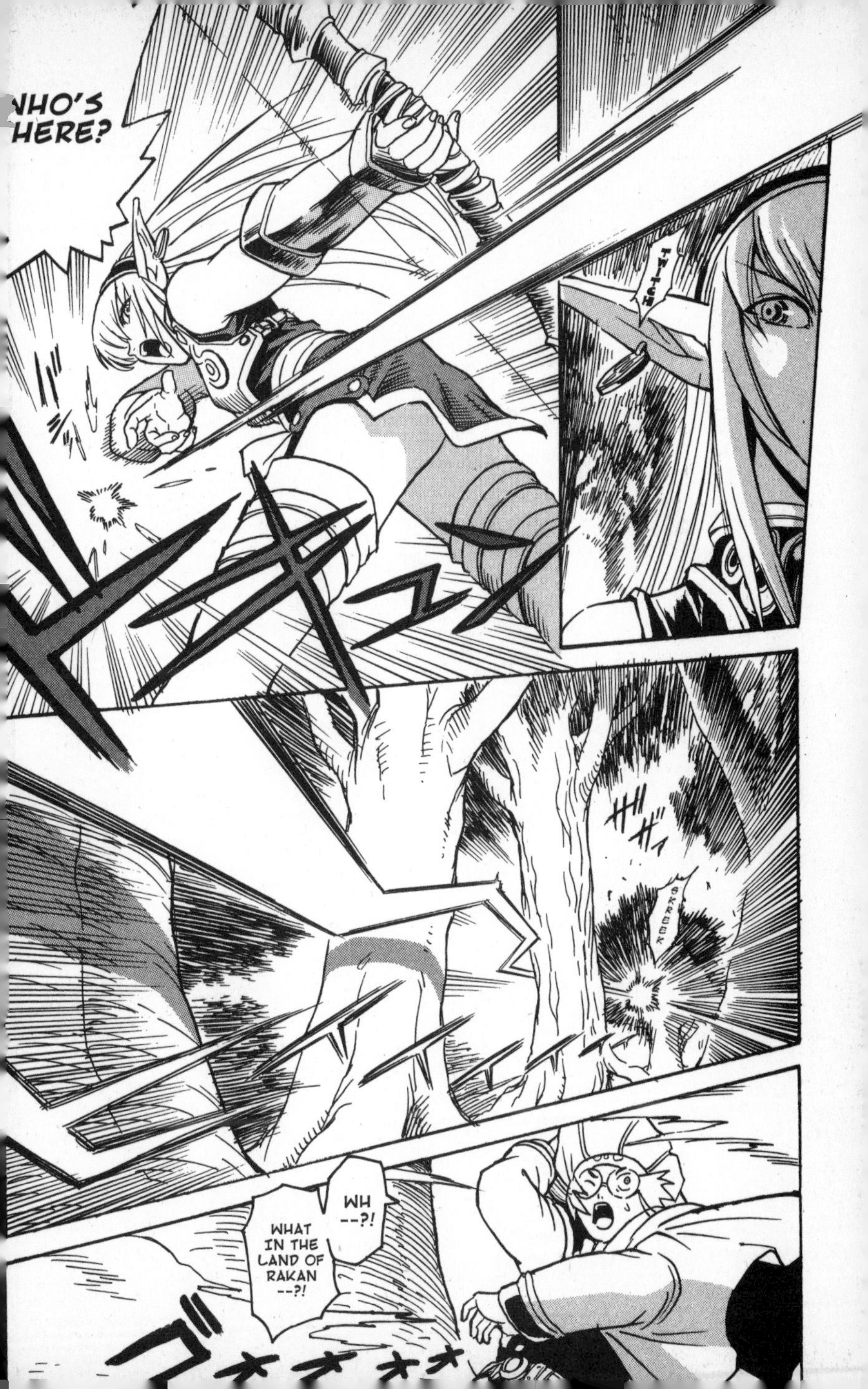
WHO'S
HERE?
TWITCH
SKREEK
WH
--?!
WHAT
IN THE
LAND OF
RAKAN
--?!

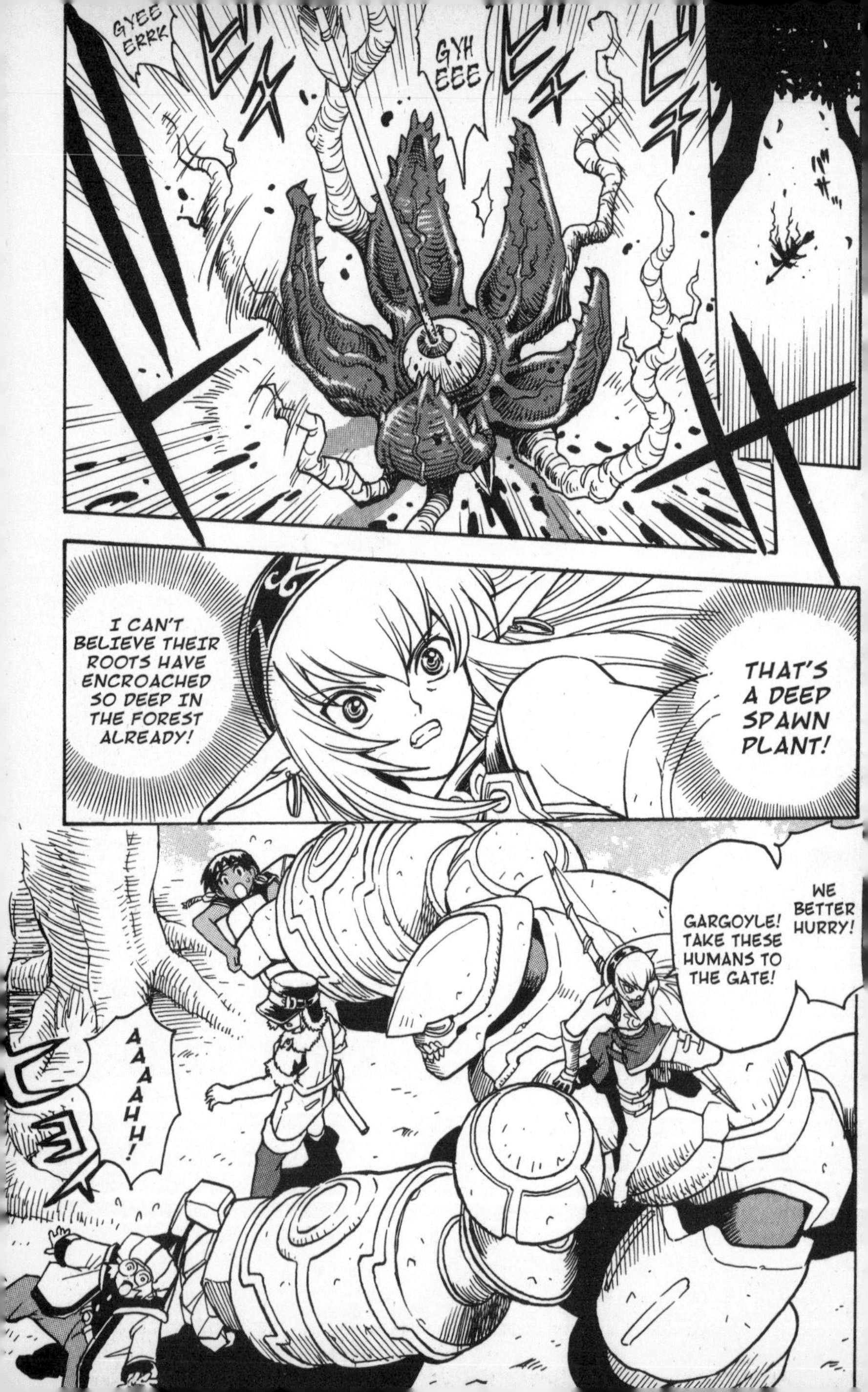
GYH EEE
GYEE ERRK
THAT'S A DEEP SPAWN PLANT!
I CAN'T BELIEVE THEIR ROOTS HAVE ENCROACHED SO DEEP IN THE FOREST ALREADY!
WE BETTER HURRY!
GARGOYLE! TAKE THESE HUMANS TO THE GATE!
AAAAAHH!

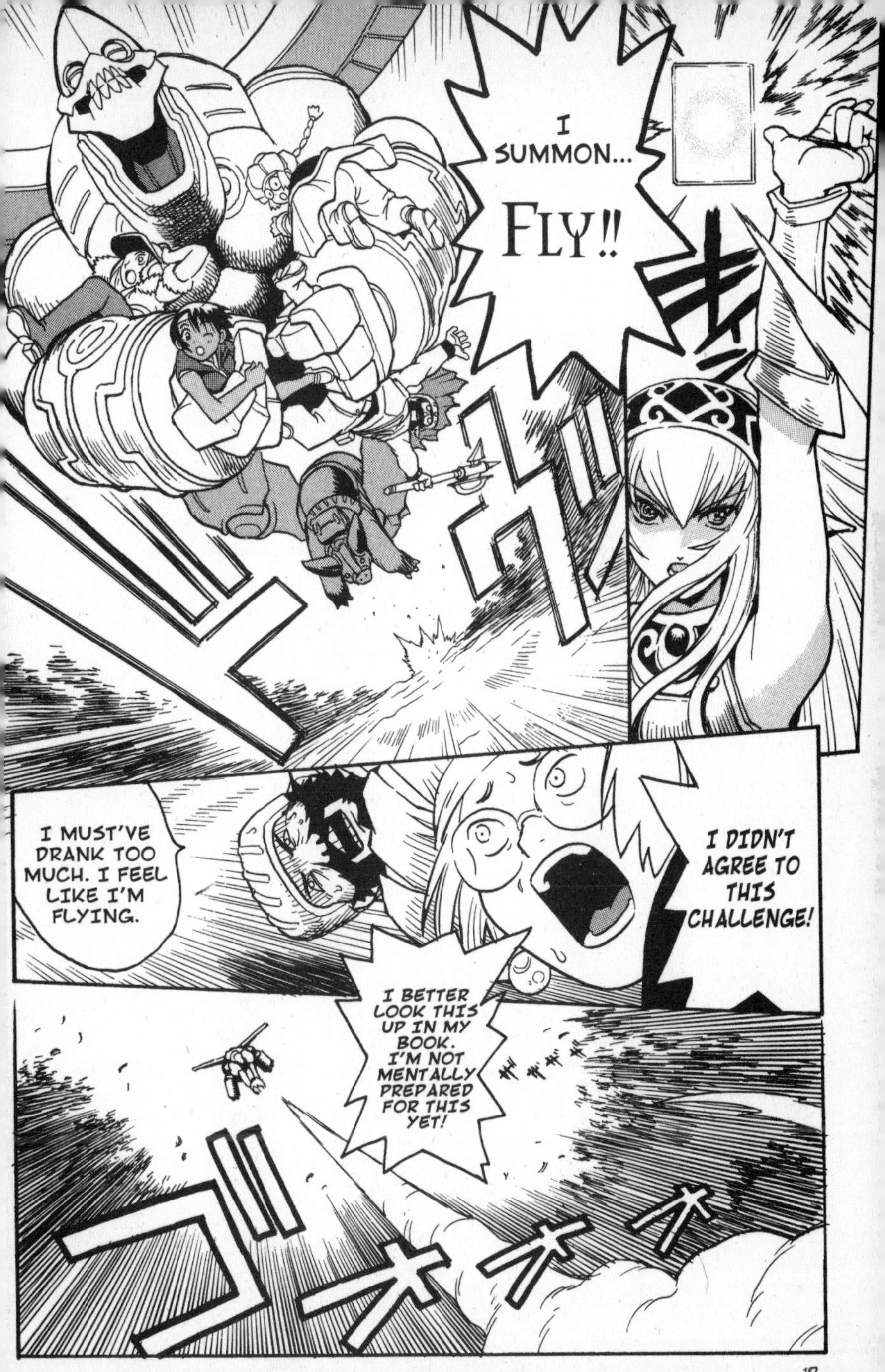
I SUMMON...
FLY!!
I DIDN'T AGREE TO THIS CHALLENGE!
I MUST'VE DRANK TOO MUCH. I FEEL LIKE I'M FLYING.
I BETTER LOOK THIS UP IN MY BOOK. I'M NOT MENTALLY PREPARED FOR THIS YET!

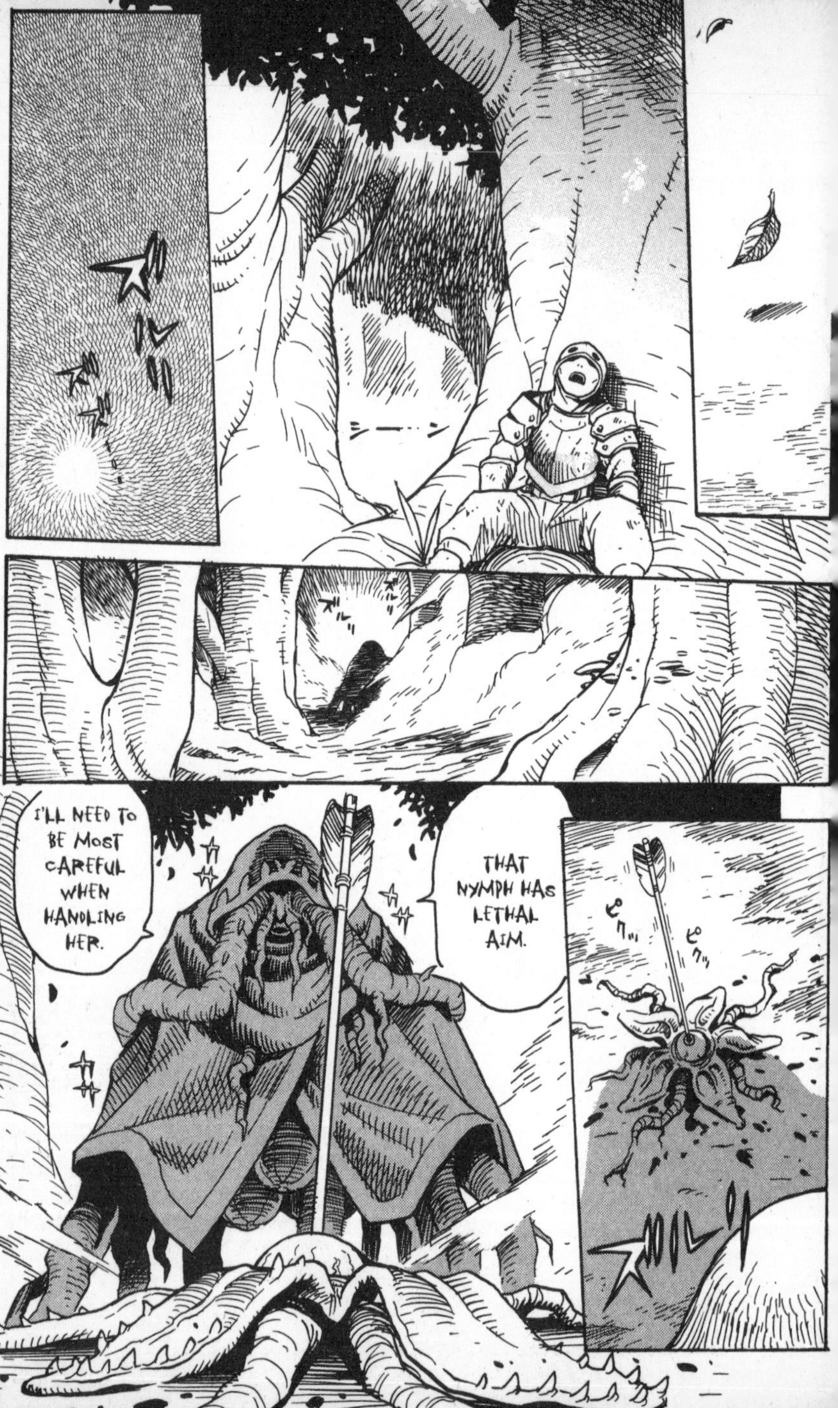
THAT NYMPH HAS LETHAL AIM.
I'LL NEED TO BE MOST CAREFUL WHEN HANDLING HER.

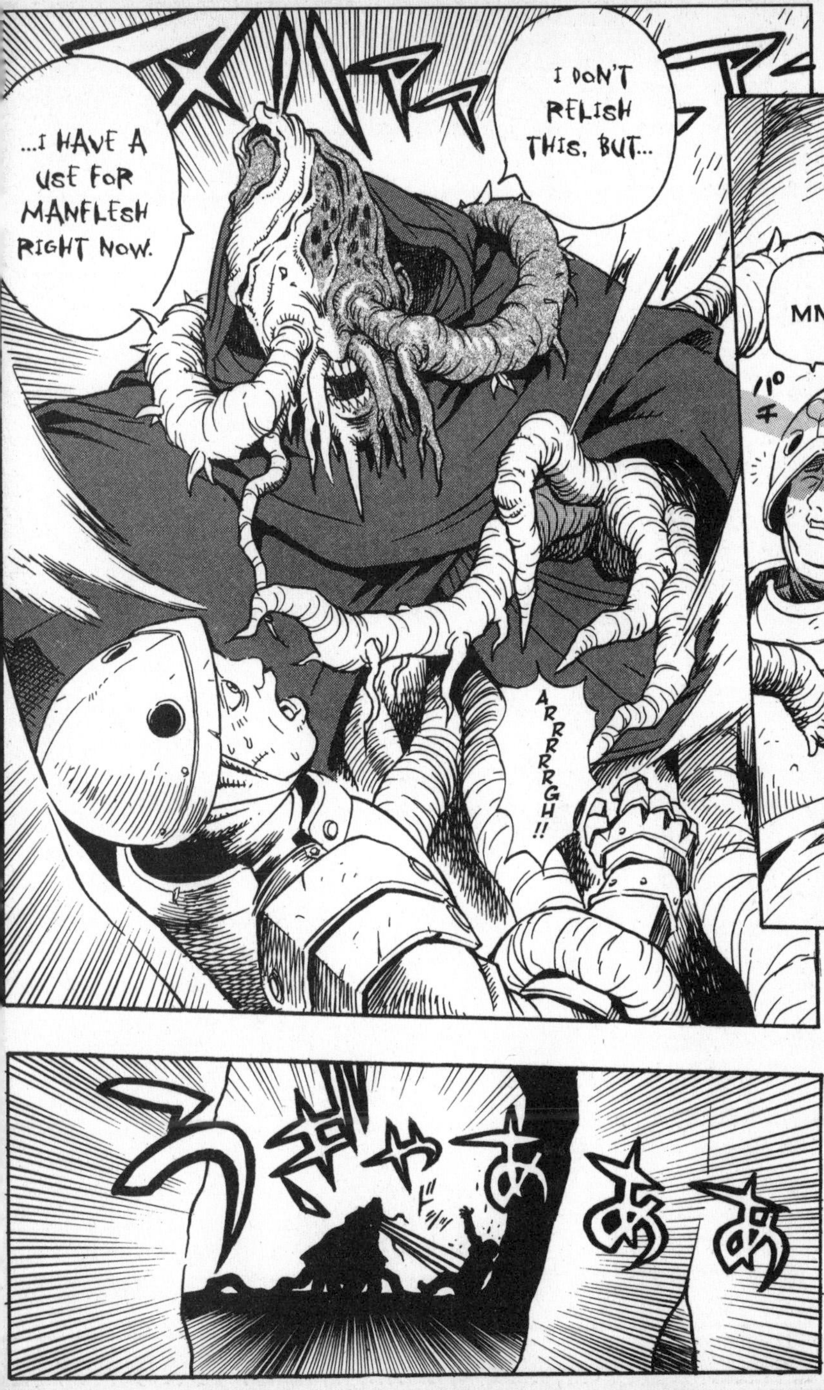
MM?
I DON'T RELISH THIS, BUT...
...I HAVE A USE FOR MANFLESH RIGHT NOW.
ARRRRRGH!!

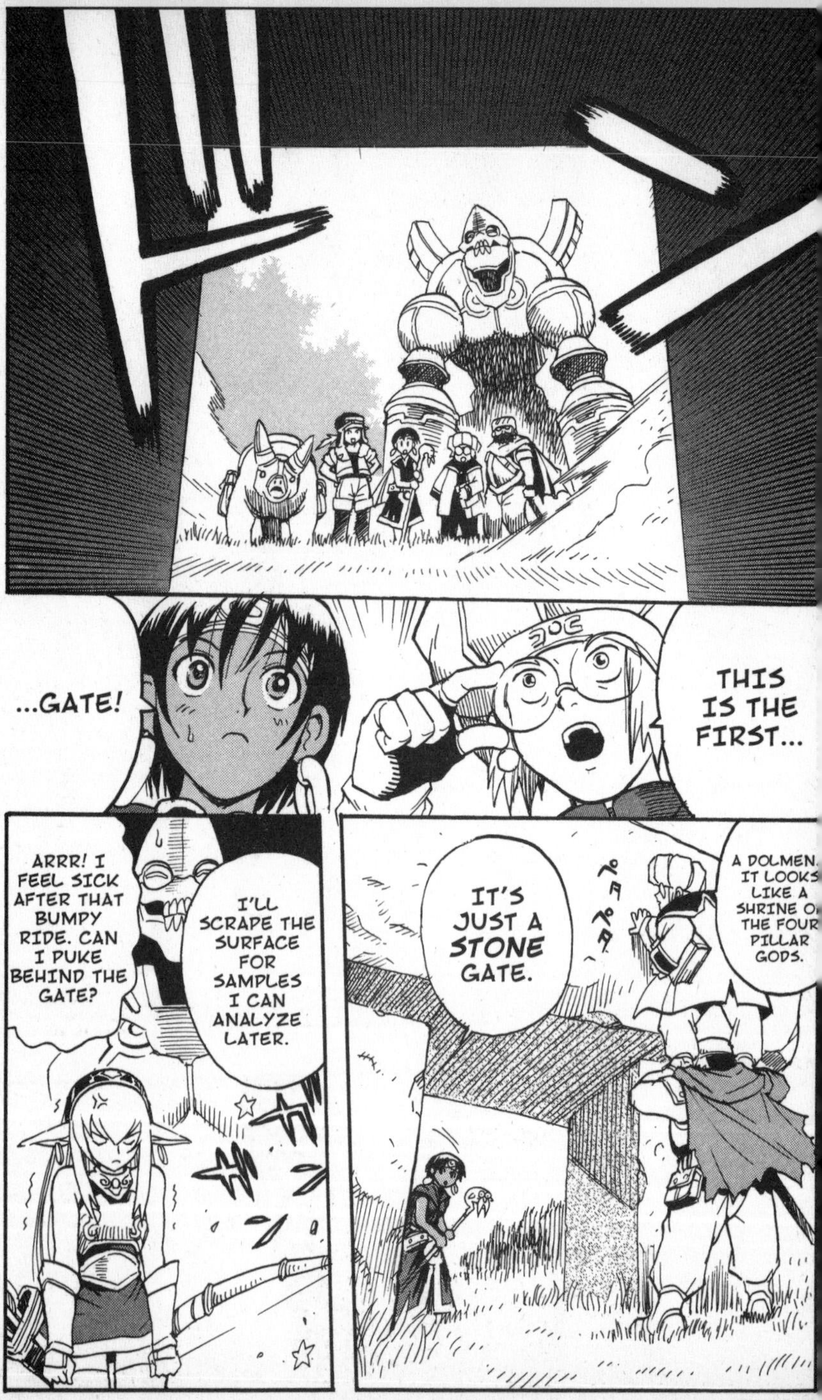
THIS IS THE FIRST...
...GATE!
A DOLMEN. IT LOOKS LIKE A SHRINE O THE FOUR PILLAR GODS.
IT'S JUST A STONE GATE.
ペタペタ
I'LL SCRAPE THE SURFACE FOR SAMPLES I CAN ANALYZE LATER.
ARRR! I FEEL SICK AFTER THAT BUMPY RIDE. CAN I PUKE BEHIND THE GATE?

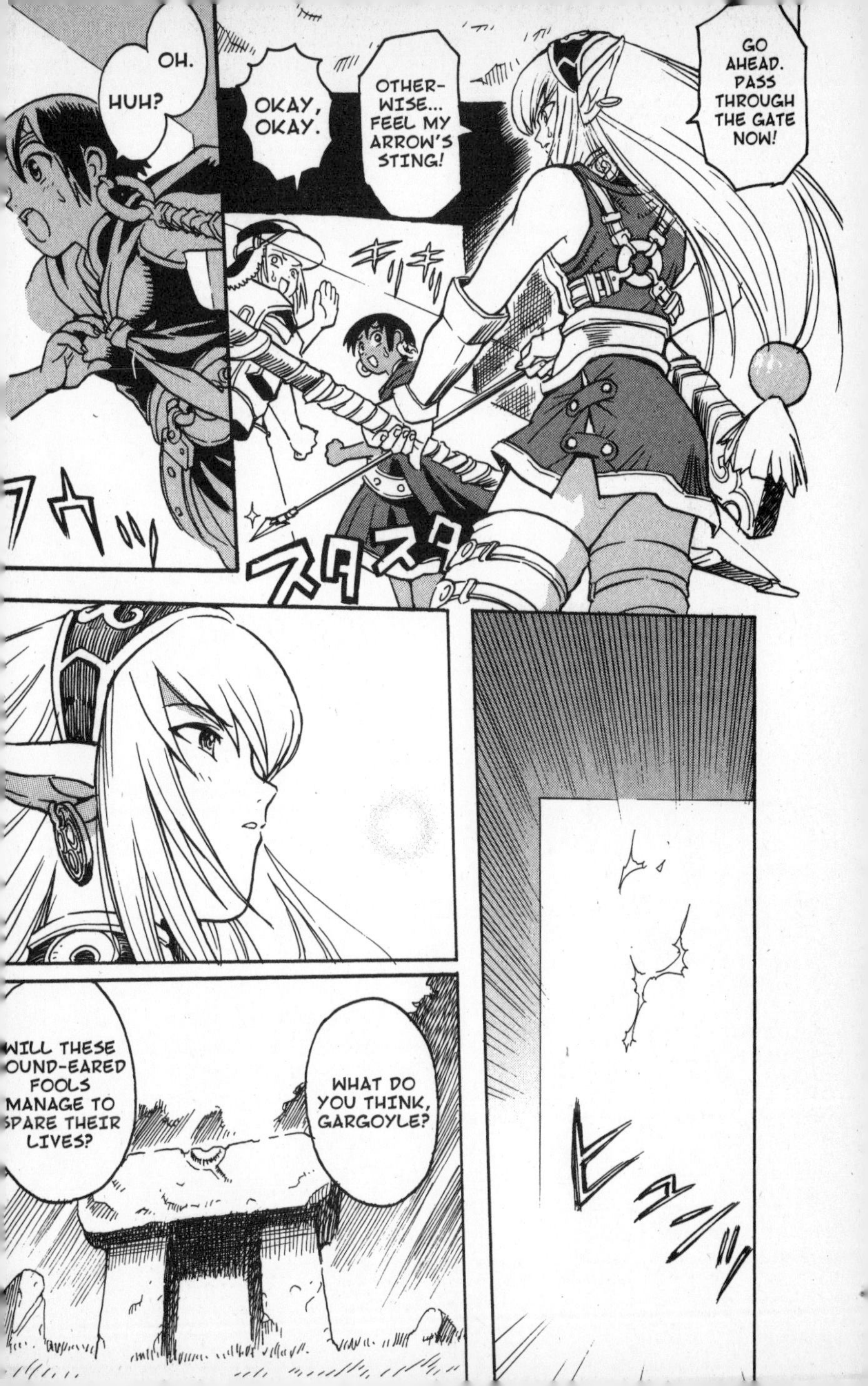
GO AHEAD. PASS THROUGH THE GATE NOW!
OTHER-WISE... FEEL MY ARROW'S STING!
OKAY, OKAY.
OH.
HUH?
WHAT DO YOU THINK, GARGOYLE?
WILL THESE OUND-EARED FOOLS MANAGE TO PARE THEIR LIVES?

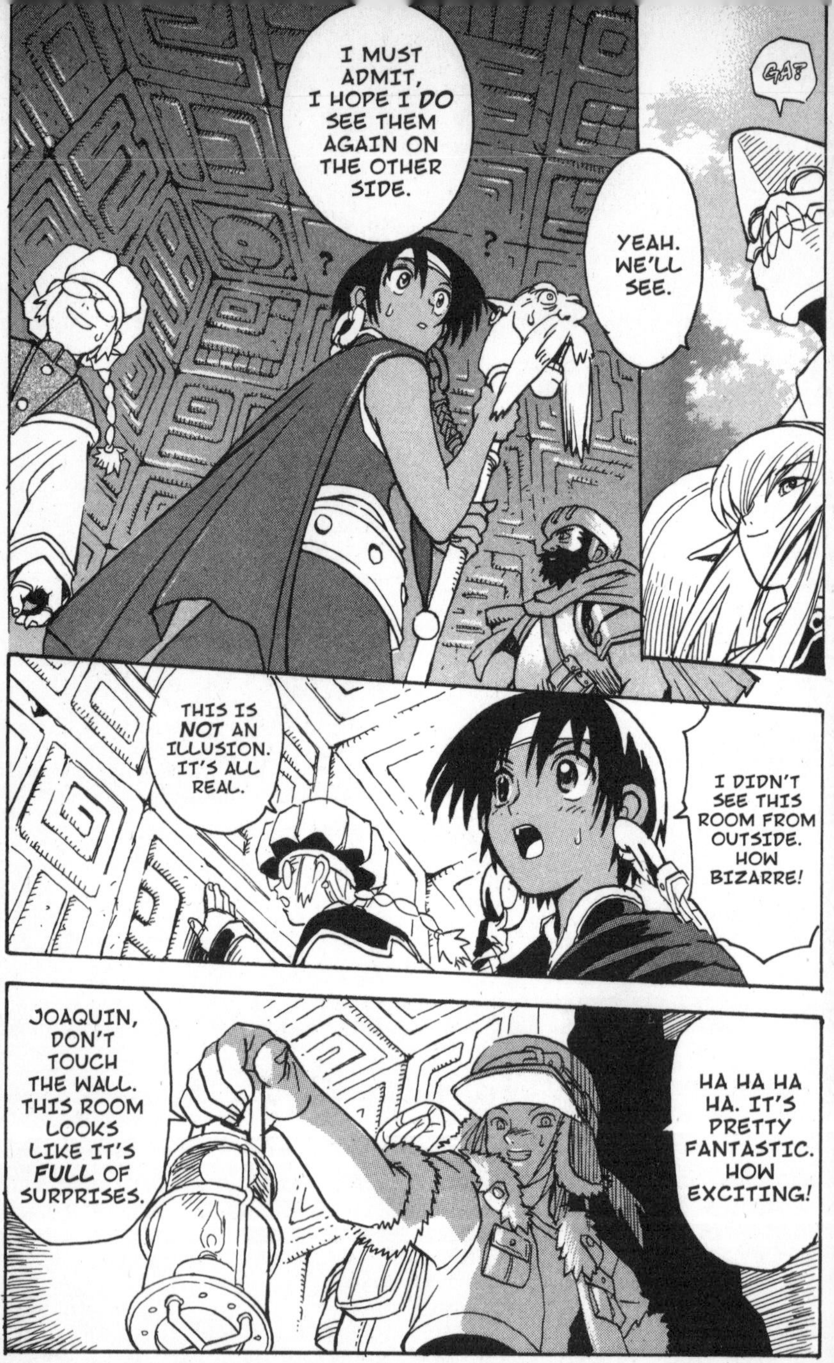
GA?
I MUST ADMIT, I HOPE I DO SEE THEM AGAIN ON THE OTHER SIDE.
YEAH. WE'LL SEE.
I DIDN'T SEE THIS ROOM FROM OUTSIDE. HOW BIZARRE!
THIS IS NOT AN ILLUSION. IT'S ALL REAL.
HA HA HA HA. IT'S PRETTY FANTASTIC. HOW EXCITING!
JOAQUIN, DON'T TOUCH THE WALL. THIS ROOM LOOKS LIKE IT'S FULL OF SURPRISES.

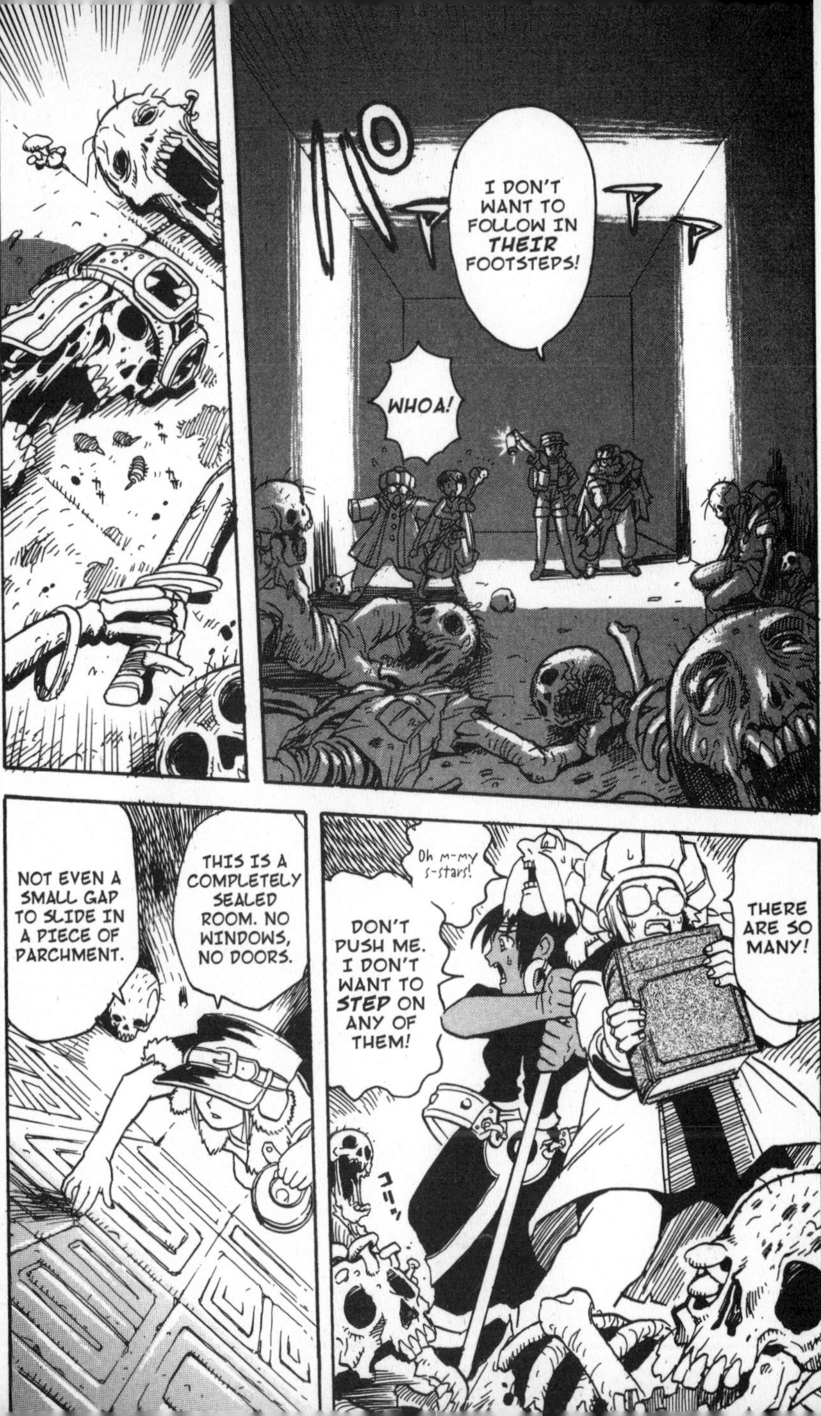
I DON'T WANT TO FOLLOW IN *THEIR* FOOTSTEPS!
WHOA!
THERE ARE SO MANY!
Oh m-my s-stars!
DON'T PUSH ME. I DON'T WANT TO *STEP* ON ANY OF THEM!
THIS IS A COMPLETELY SEALED ROOM. NO WINDOWS, NO DOORS.
NOT EVEN A SMALL GAP TO SLIDE IN A PIECE OF PARCHMENT.

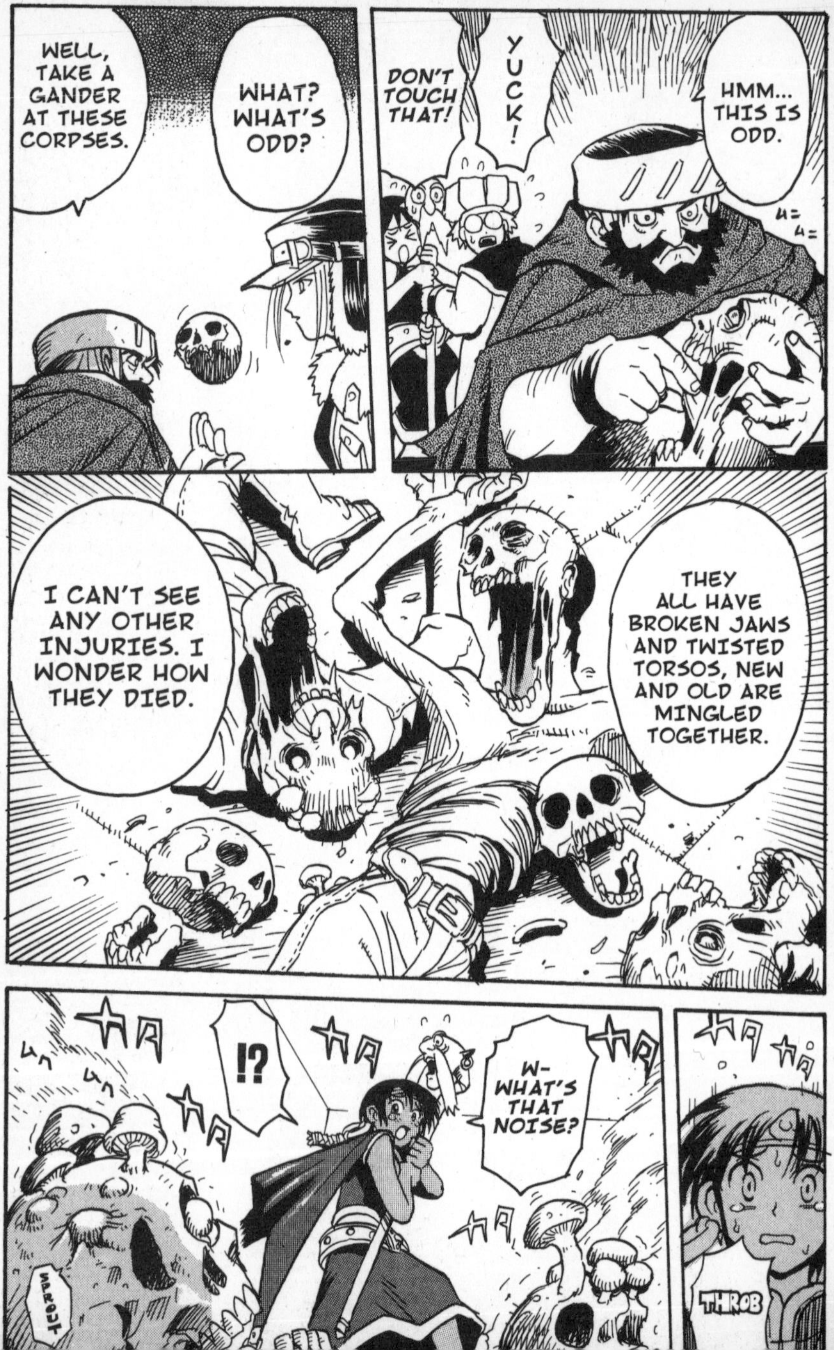
HMM... THIS IS ODD.
YUCK!
DON'T TOUCH THAT!
WHAT? WHAT'S ODD?
WELL, TAKE A GANDER AT THESE CORPSES.
THEY ALL HAVE BROKEN JAWS AND TWISTED TORSOS, NEW AND OLD ARE MINGLED TOGETHER.
I CAN'T SEE ANY OTHER INJURIES. I WONDER HOW THEY DIED.
HA HA
THROB
HA HA
W- WHAT'S THAT NOISE?
!?
HA HA
SPROUT

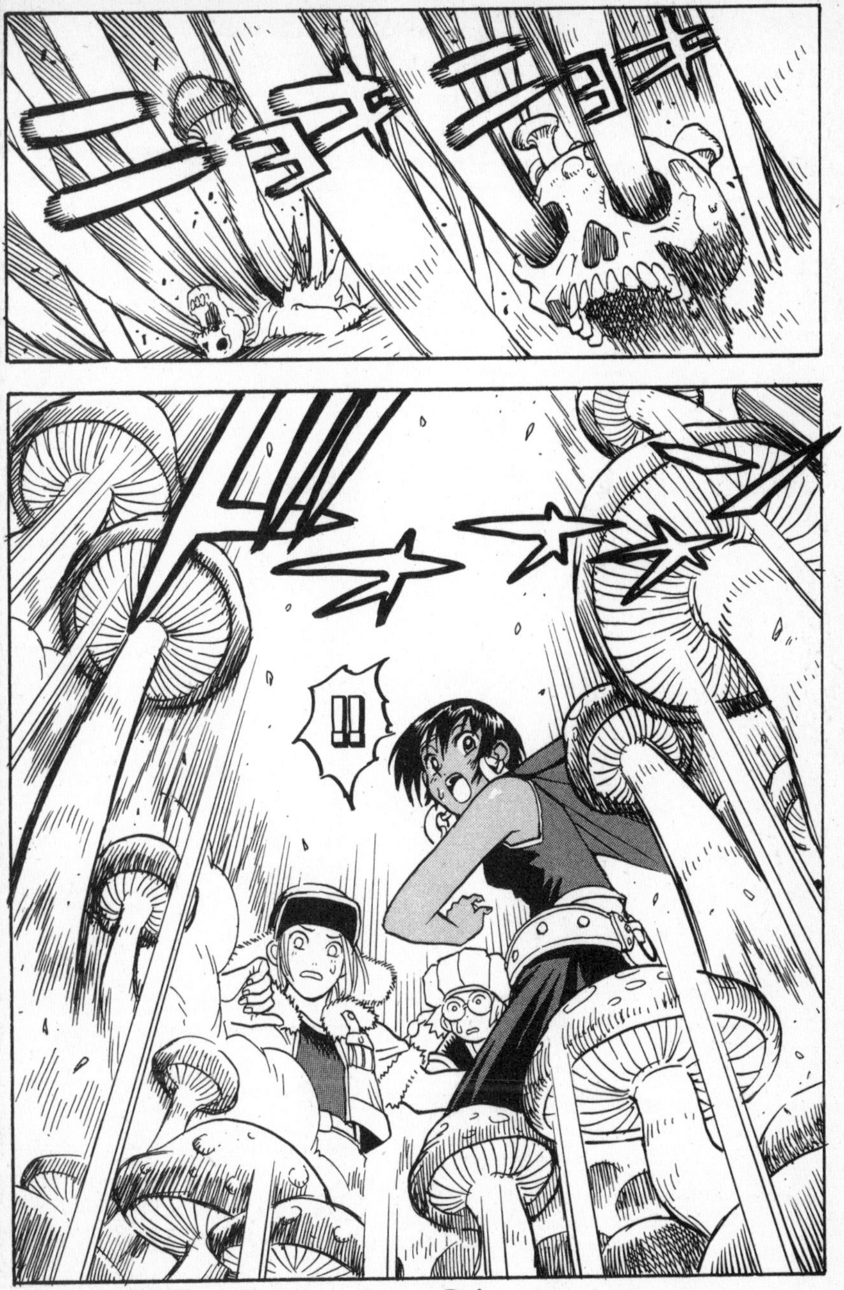
ニョキニョキ
!!

Round 21 Challenge of the First Gate - End

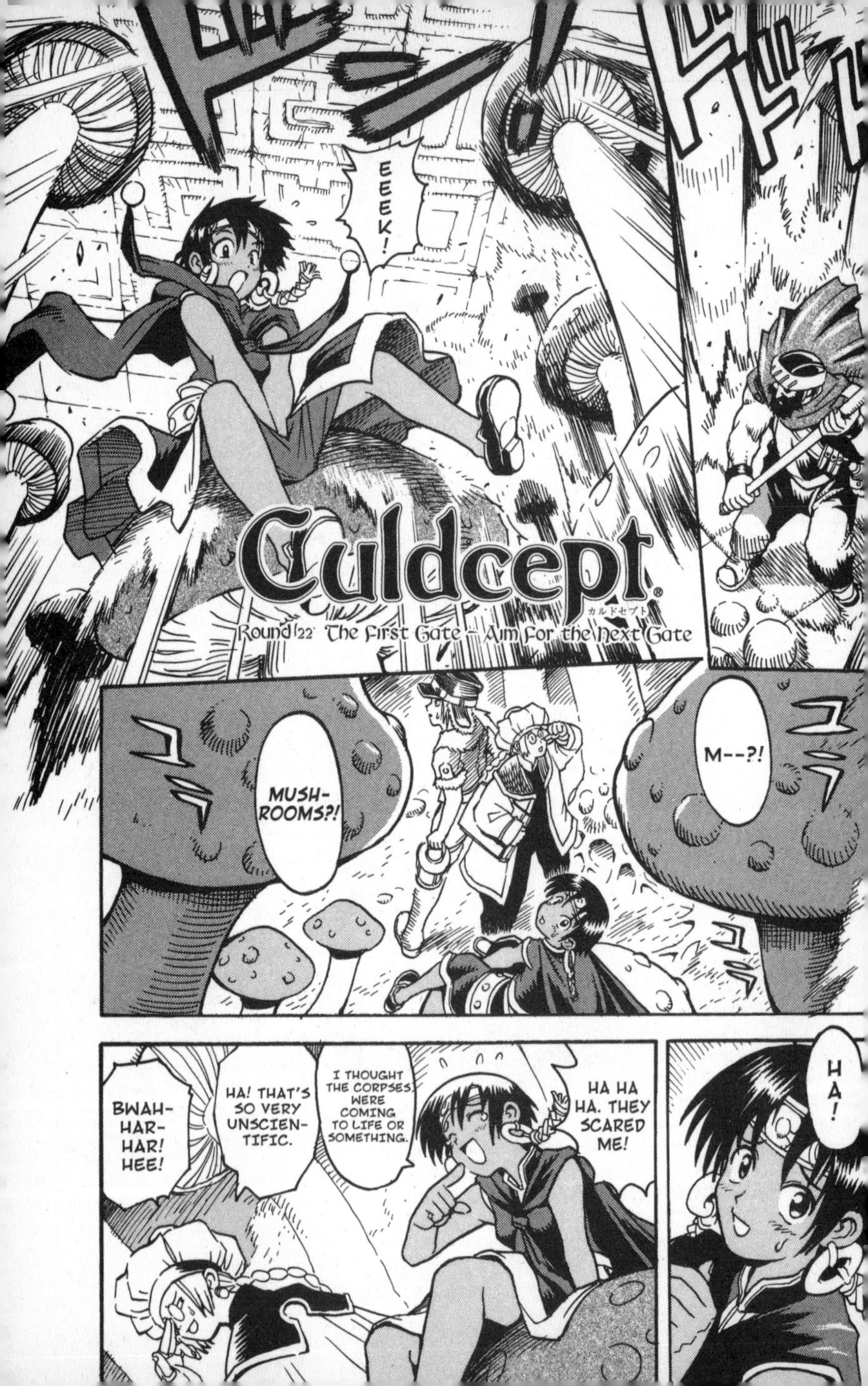
EEEK!
Culdcept®
カルドセプト
Round 22 The First Gate - Aim for the Next Gate
M--?!
MUSH-ROOMS?!
HA HA!
HA HA HA. THEY SCARED ME!
I THOUGHT THE CORPSES WERE COMING TO LIFE OR SOMETHING.
HA! THAT'S SO VERY UNSCIENTIFIC.
BWAH-HAR-HAR! HEE!

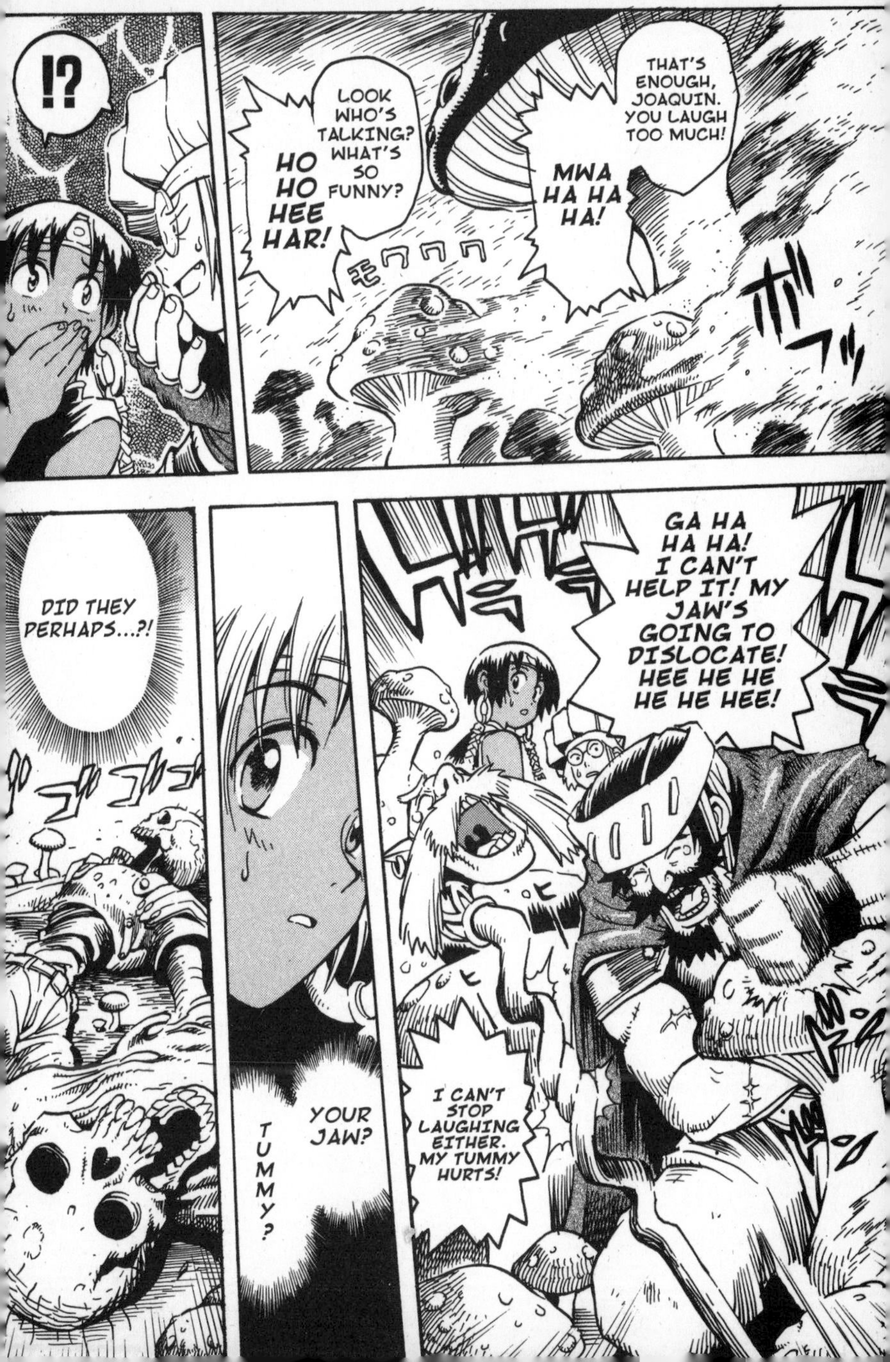
THAT'S ENOUGH, JOAQUIN. YOU LAUGH TOO MUCH!
MWA HA HA HA!
LOOK WHO'S TALKING? WHAT'S SO FUNNY?
HO HO HEE HAR!
!?
GA HA HA HA! I CAN'T HELP IT! MY JAW'S GOING TO DISLOCATE! HEE HE HE HE HE HEE!
I CAN'T STOP LAUGHING EITHER. MY TUMMY HURTS!
TUMMY?
YOUR JAW?
DID THEY PERHAPS...?!

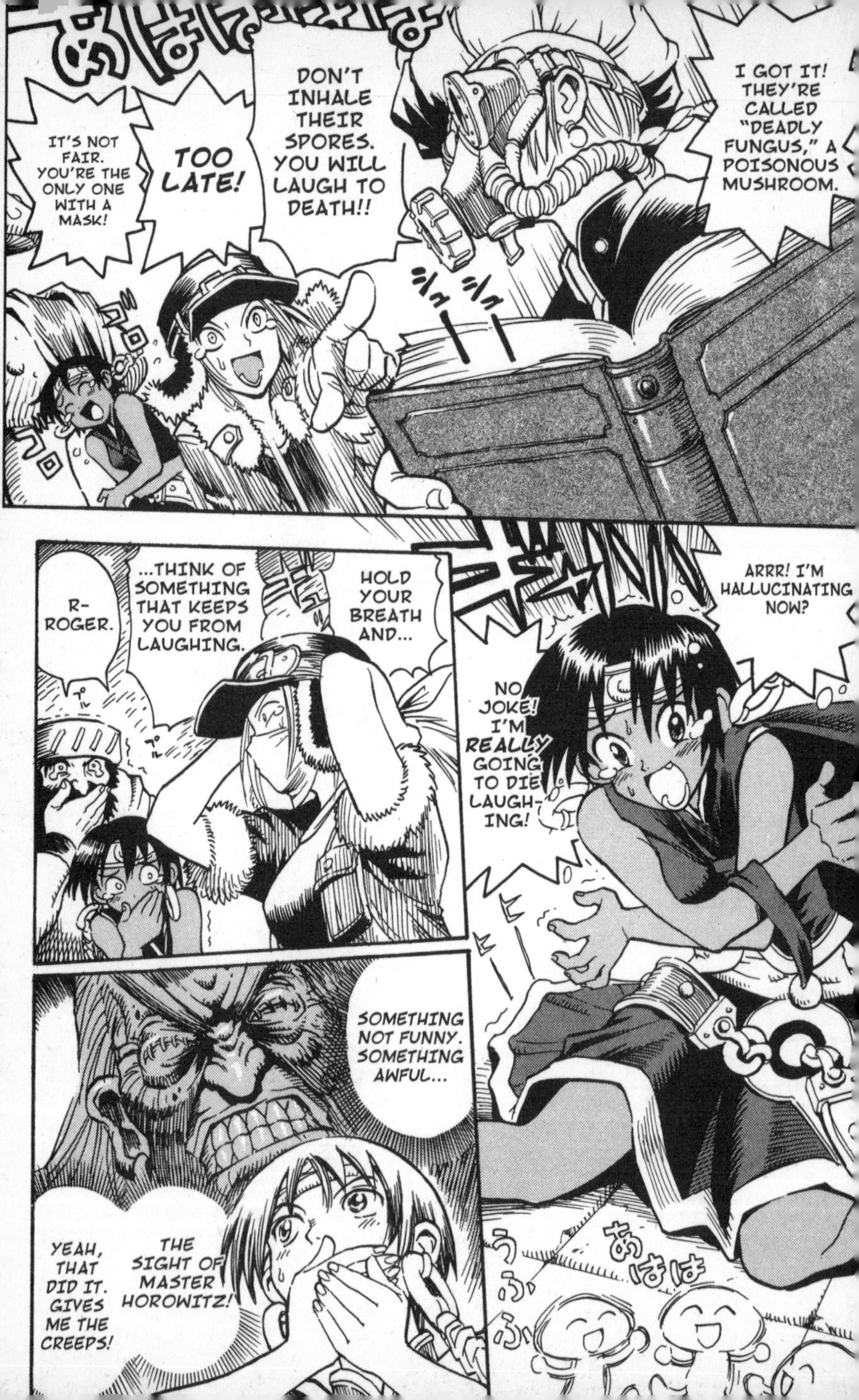
I GOT IT! THEY'RE CALLED "DEADLY FUNGUS," A POISONOUS MUSHROOM.
DON'T INHALE THEIR SPORES. YOU WILL LAUGH TO DEATH!!
TOO LATE!
IT'S NOT FAIR. YOU'RE THE ONLY ONE WITH A MASK!
ARRR! I'M HALLUCINATING NOW?
NO JOKE! I'M REALLY GOING TO DIE LAUGHING!
あはは
うふふ
HOLD YOUR BREATH AND...
...THINK OF SOMETHING THAT KEEPS YOU FROM LAUGHING.
R-ROGER.
SOMETHING NOT FUNNY. SOMETHING AWFUL...
THE SIGHT OF MASTER HOROWITZ!
YEAH, THAT DID IT. GIVES ME THE CREEPS!

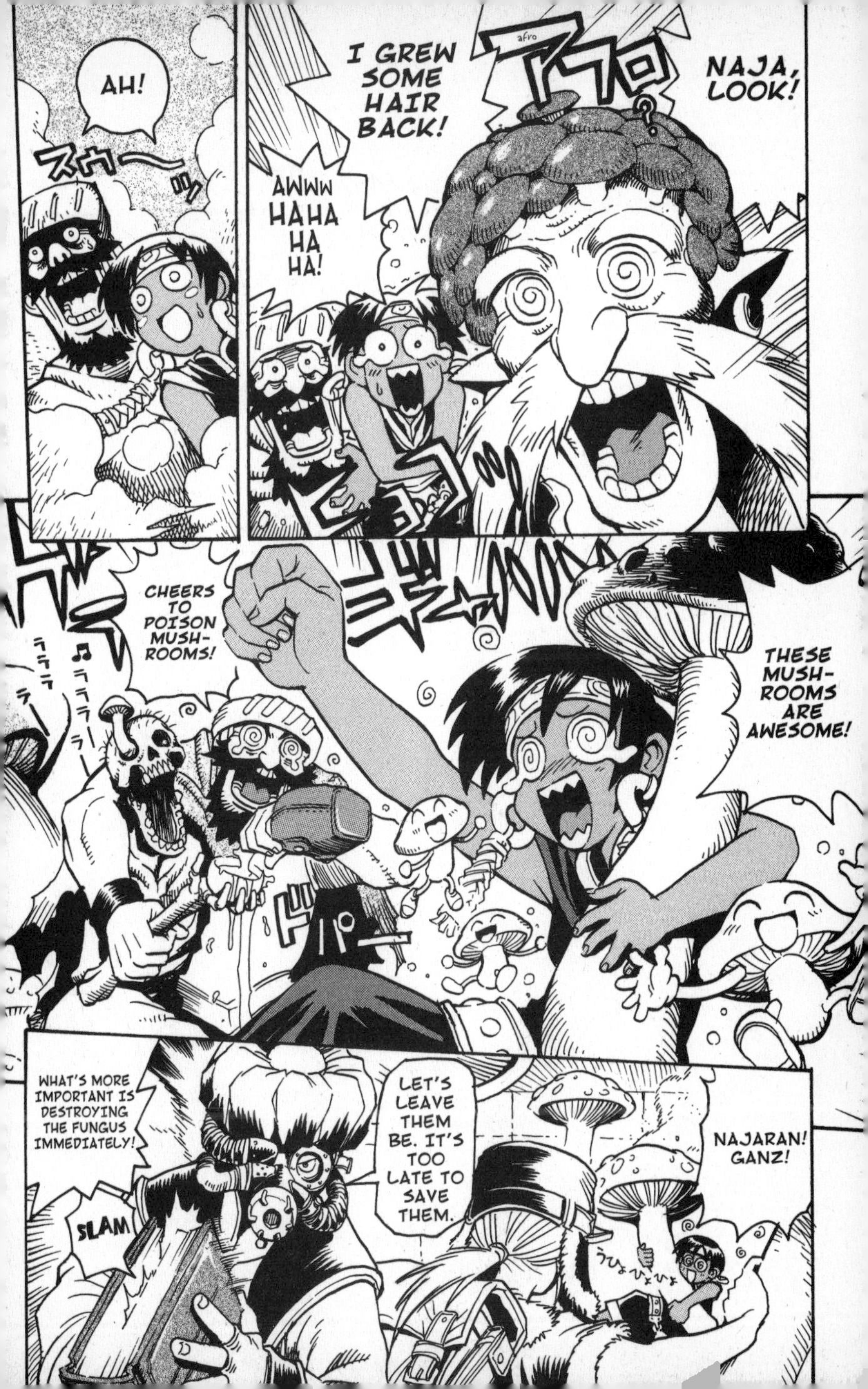
NAJA, LOOK!
afro
I GREW SOME HAIR BACK!
AWWW HAHA HA HA!
AH!
THESE MUSHROOMS ARE AWESOME!
CHEERS TO POISON MUSHROOMS!
NAJARAN! GANZ!
LET'S LEAVE THEM BE. IT'S TOO LATE TO SAVE THEM.
WHAT'S MORE IMPORTANT IS DESTROYING THE FUNGUS IMMEDIATELY!
SLAM

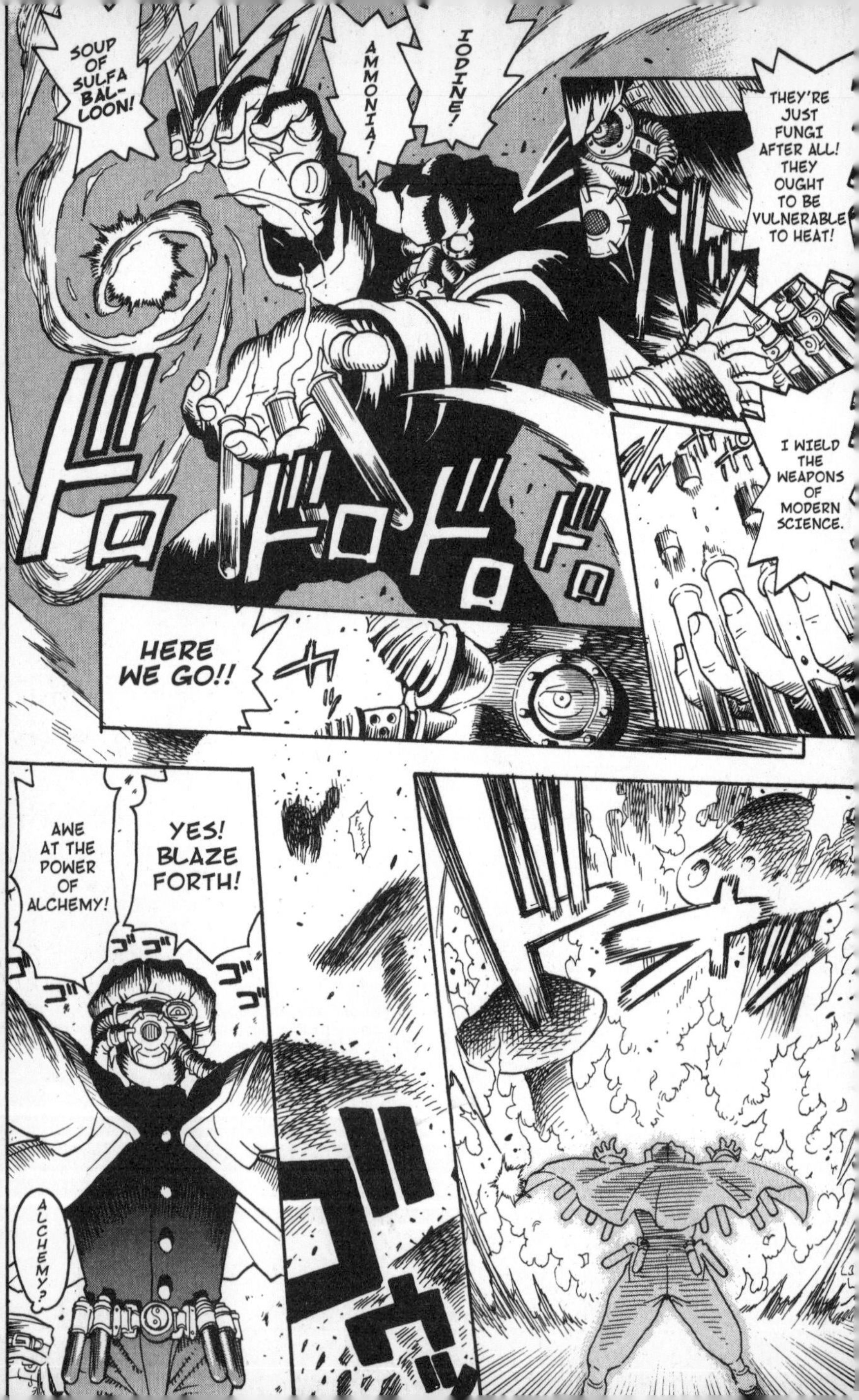
THEY'RE JUST FUNGI AFTER ALL! THEY OUGHT TO BE VULNERABLE TO HEAT!
IODINE!
AMMONIA!
SOUP OF SULFA BAL-LOON!
ドロ ドロ ドロ ドロ
I WIELD THE WEAPONS OF MODERN SCIENCE.
HERE WE GO!!
YES! BLAZE FORTH!
AWE AT THE POWER OF ALCHEMY!
ALCHEMY?

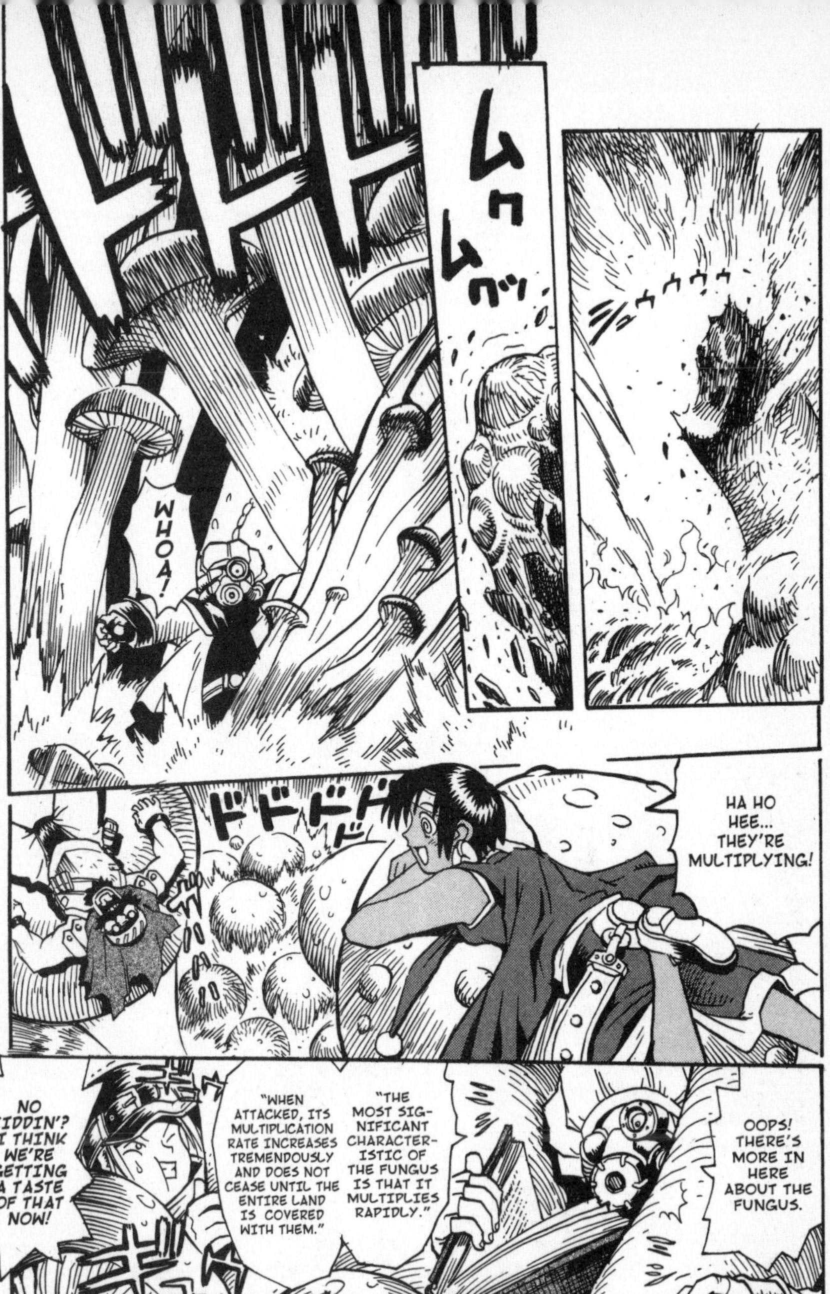
WHOA!
HA HO HEE... THEY'RE MULTIPLYING!
OOPS! THERE'S MORE IN HERE ABOUT THE FUNGUS.
"THE MOST SIGNIFICANT CHARACTERISTIC OF THE FUNGUS IS THAT IT MULTIPLIES RAPIDLY."
"WHEN ATTACKED, ITS MULTIPLICATION RATE INCREASES TREMENDOUSLY AND DOES NOT CEASE UNTIL THE ENTIRE LAND IS COVERED WITH THEM."
NO KIDDIN'? I THINK WE'RE GETTING A TASTE OF THAT NOW!

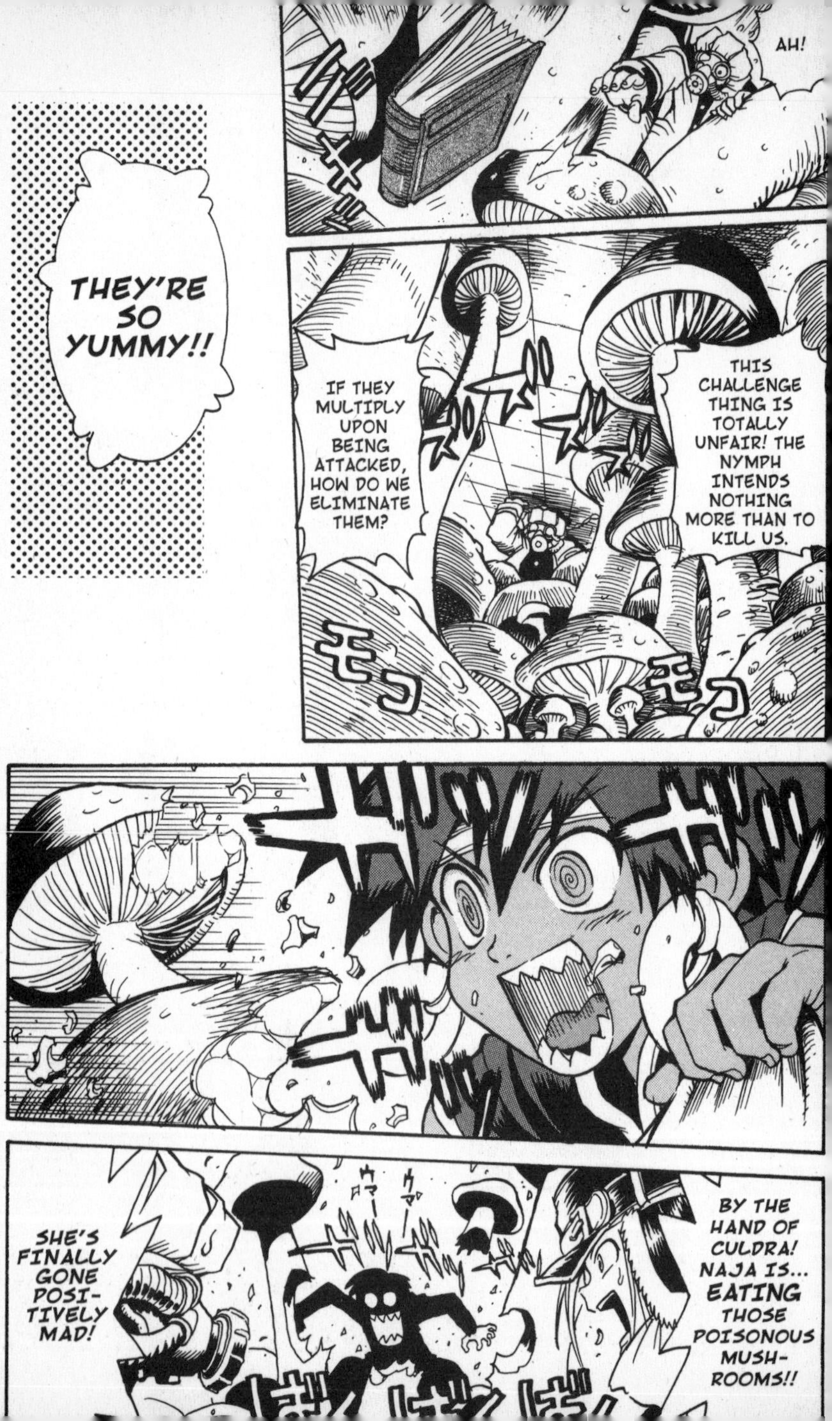
AH!
THIS CHALLENGE THING IS TOTALLY UNFAIR! THE NYMPH INTENDS NOTHING MORE THAN TO KILL US.
IF THEY MULTIPLY UPON BEING ATTACKED, HOW DO WE ELIMINATE THEM?
モッ
モッ
THEY'RE SO YUMMY!!
BY THE HAND OF CULDRA! NAJA IS... EATING THOSE POISONOUS MUSH-ROOMS!!
SHE'S FINALLY GONE POSI-TIVELY MAD!

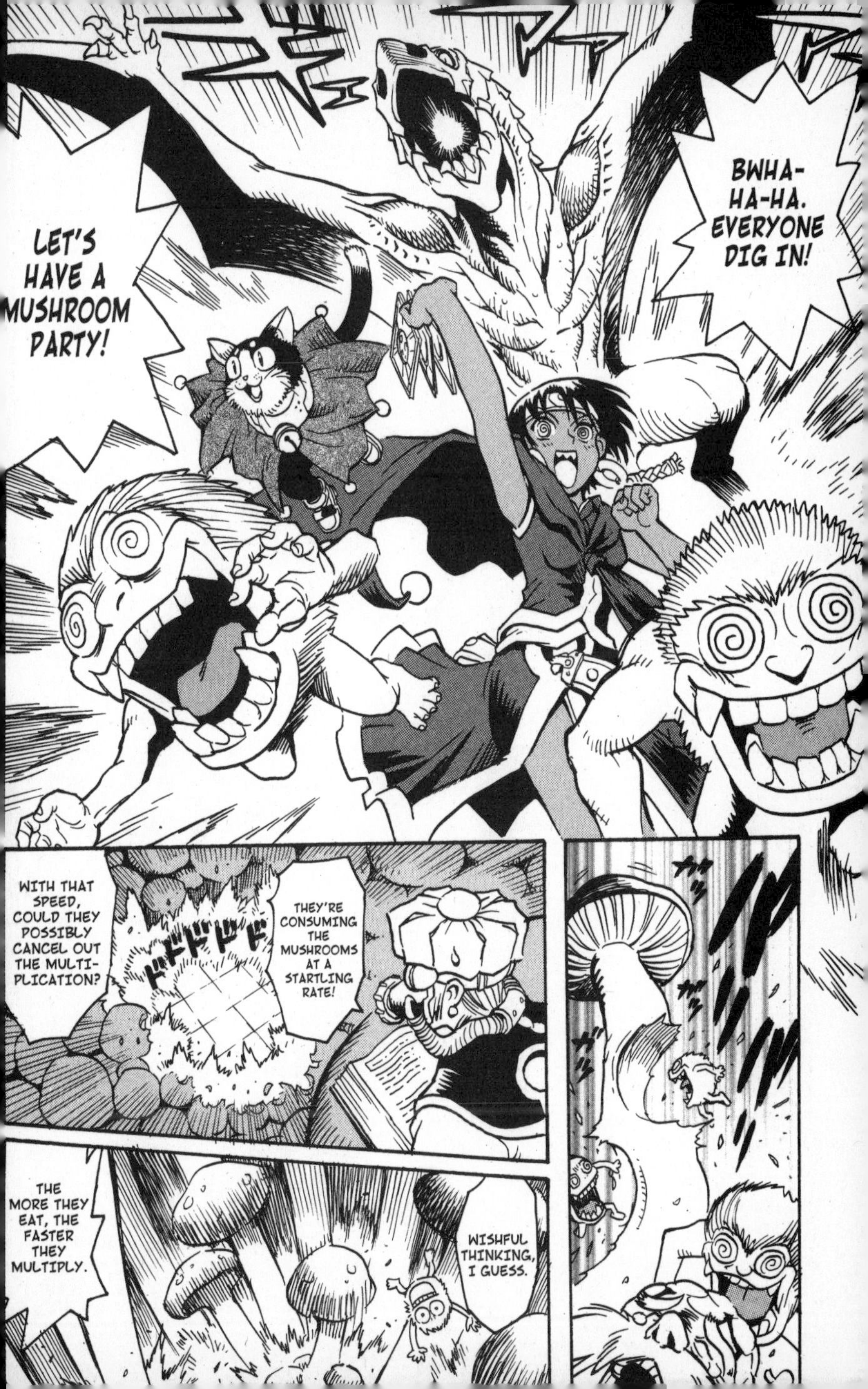
BWHA-HA-HA. EVERYONE DIG IN!
LET'S HAVE A MUSHROOM PARTY!
THEY'RE CONSUMING THE MUSHROOMS AT A STARTLING RATE!
ドドドドド
WITH THAT SPEED, COULD THEY POSSIBLY CANCEL OUT THE MULTI-PLICATION?
WISHFUL THINKING, I GUESS.
THE MORE THEY EAT, THE FASTER THEY MULTIPLY.

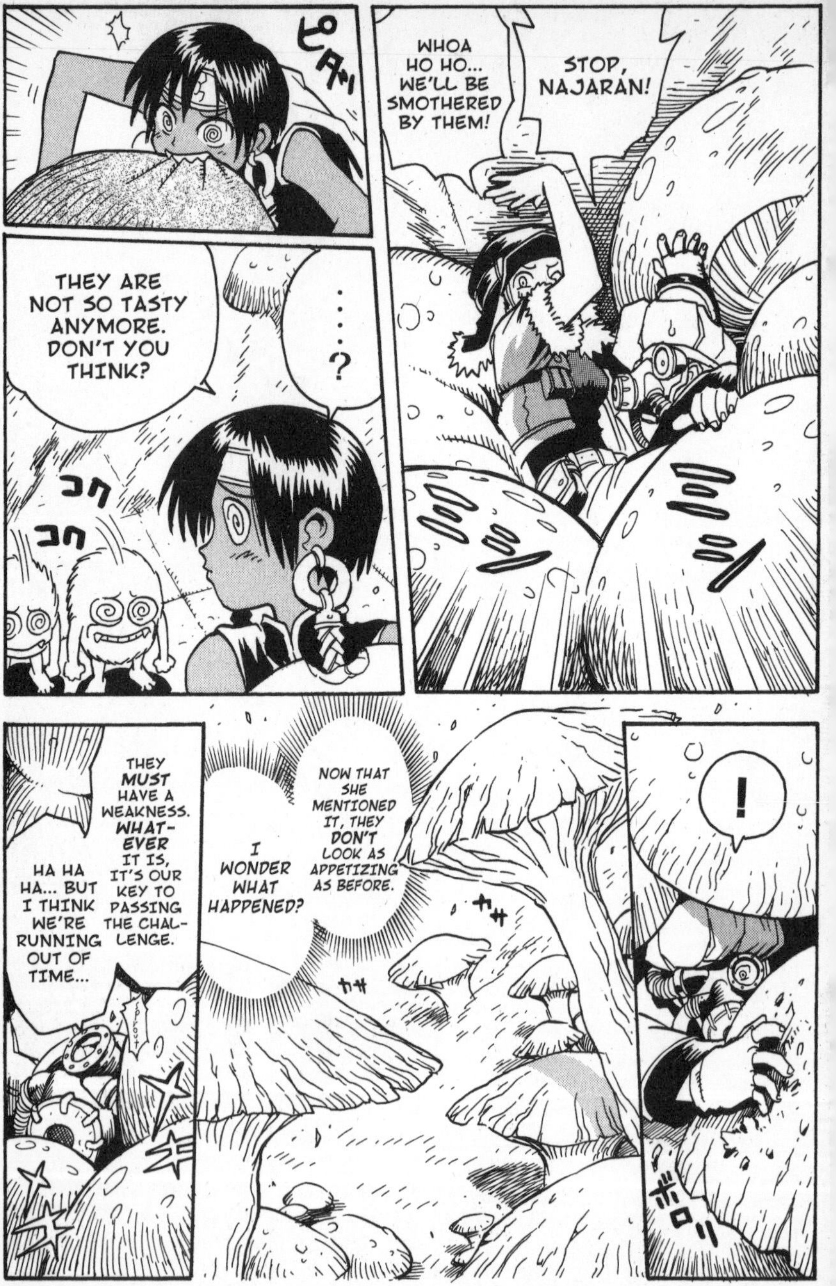
STOP, NAJARAN!
WHOA HO HO... WE'LL BE SMOTHERED BY THEM!
ミシミシ
ミシミシ
ピタッ
...?
THEY ARE NOT SO TASTY ANYMORE. DON'T YOU THINK?
コク
コク
!
ボロッ
NOW THAT SHE MENTIONED IT, THEY DON'T LOOK AS APPETIZING AS BEFORE.
I WONDER WHAT HAPPENED?
THEY MUST HAVE A WEAKNESS. WHATEVER IT IS, IT'S OUR KEY TO PASSING THE CHALLENGE.
HA HA HA... BUT I THINK WE'RE RUNNING OUT OF TIME...
カサ
カサ
sprout

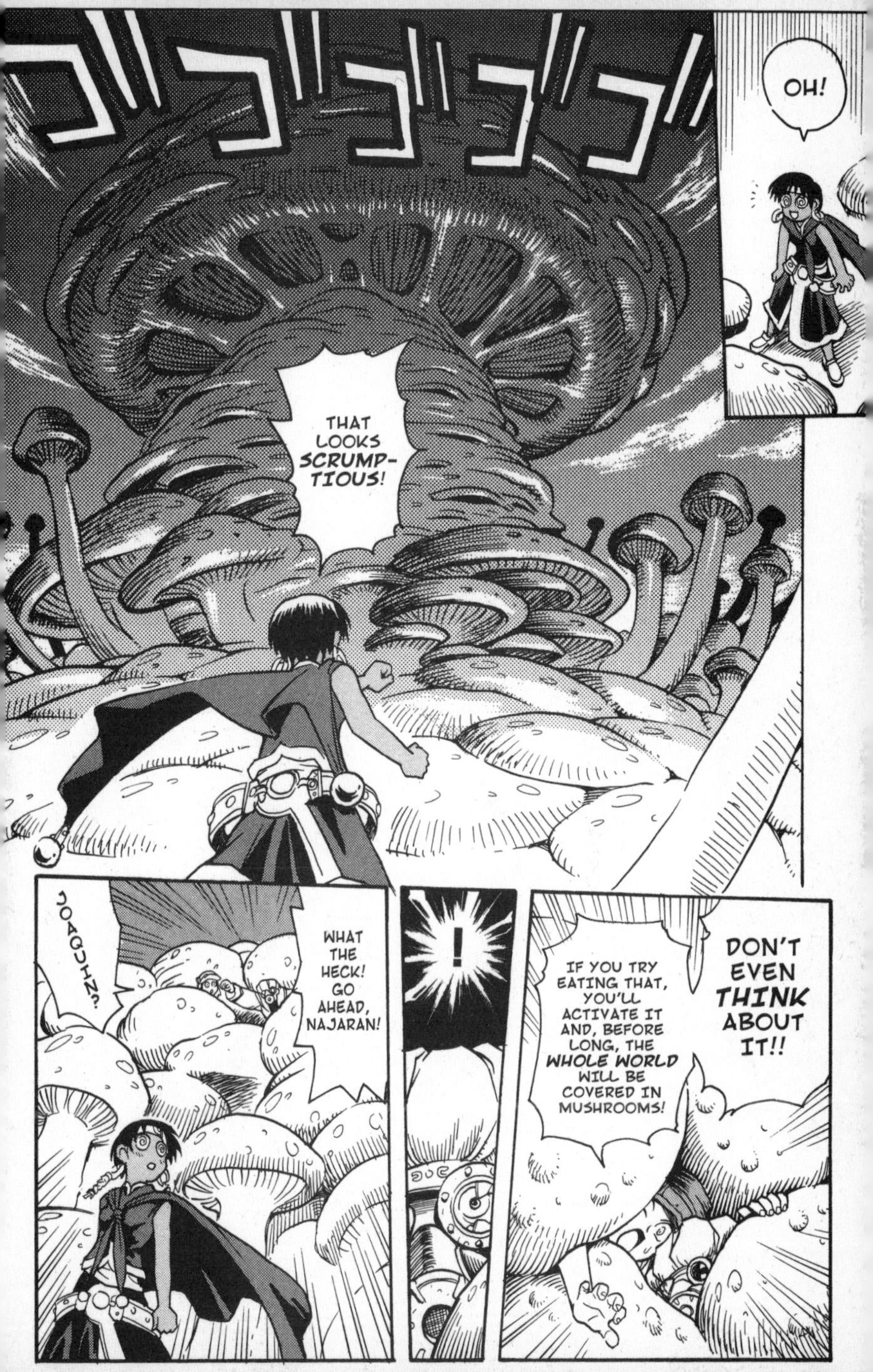
OH!
ゴゴゴゴゴ
THAT LOOKS SCRUMPTIOUS!
DON'T EVEN THINK ABOUT IT!!
IF YOU TRY EATING THAT, YOU'LL ACTIVATE IT AND, BEFORE LONG, THE WHOLE WORLD WILL BE COVERED IN MUSHROOMS!
!
WHAT THE HECK! GO AHEAD, NAJARAN!
JOAQUIN?

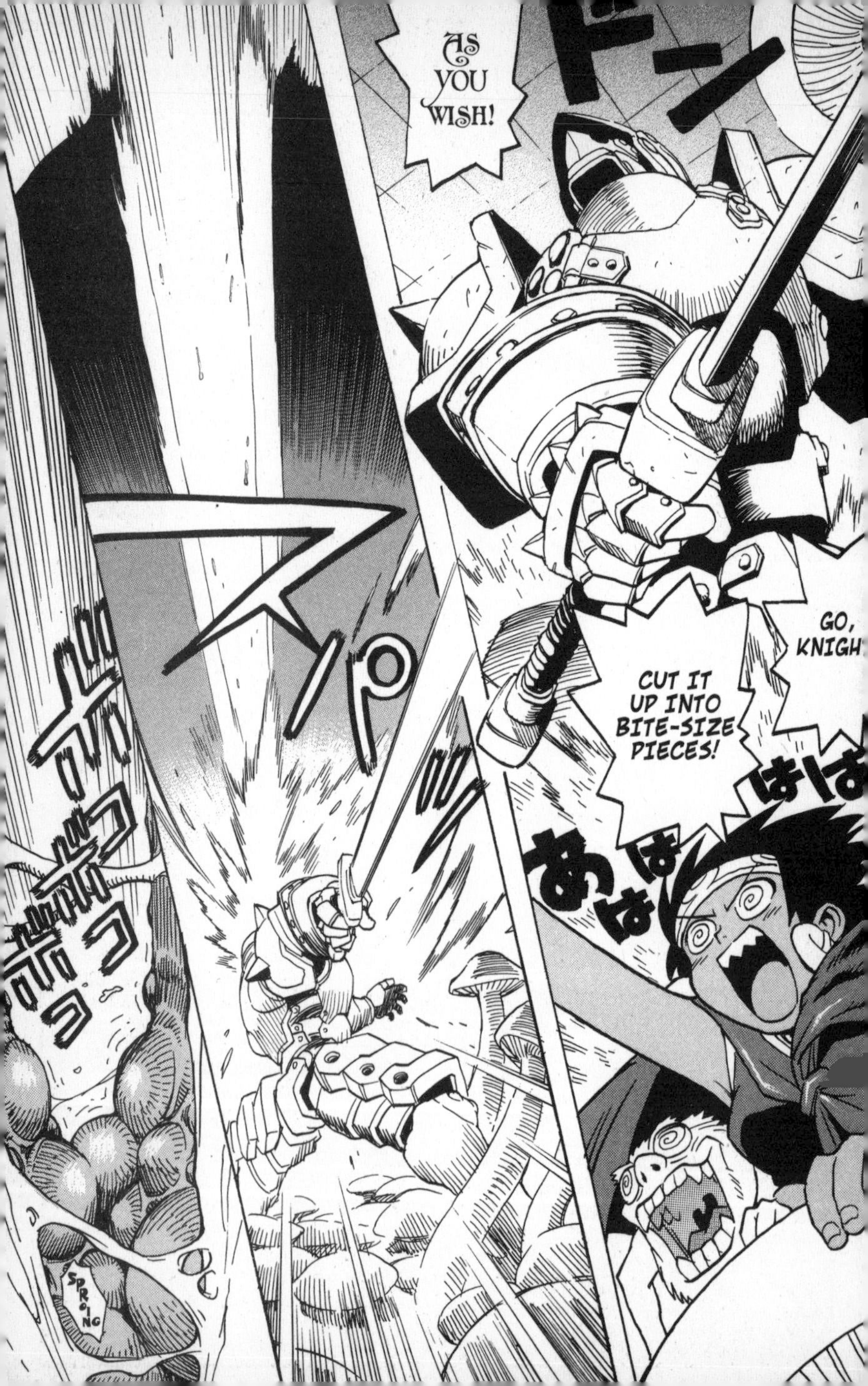
AS YOU WISH!
GO, KNIGH
CUT IT UP INTO BITE-SIZE PIECES!
SPROING

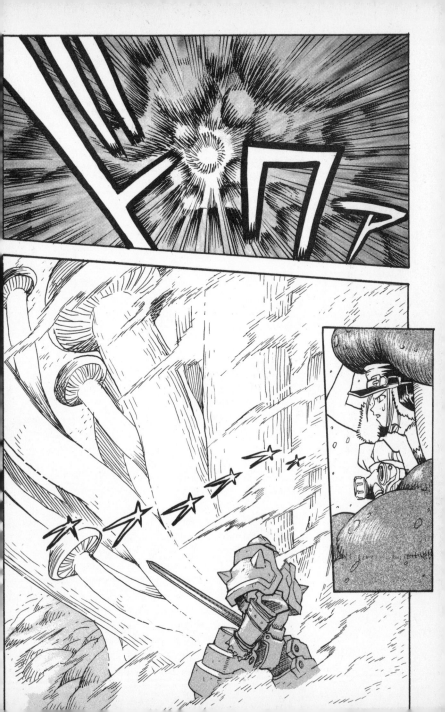

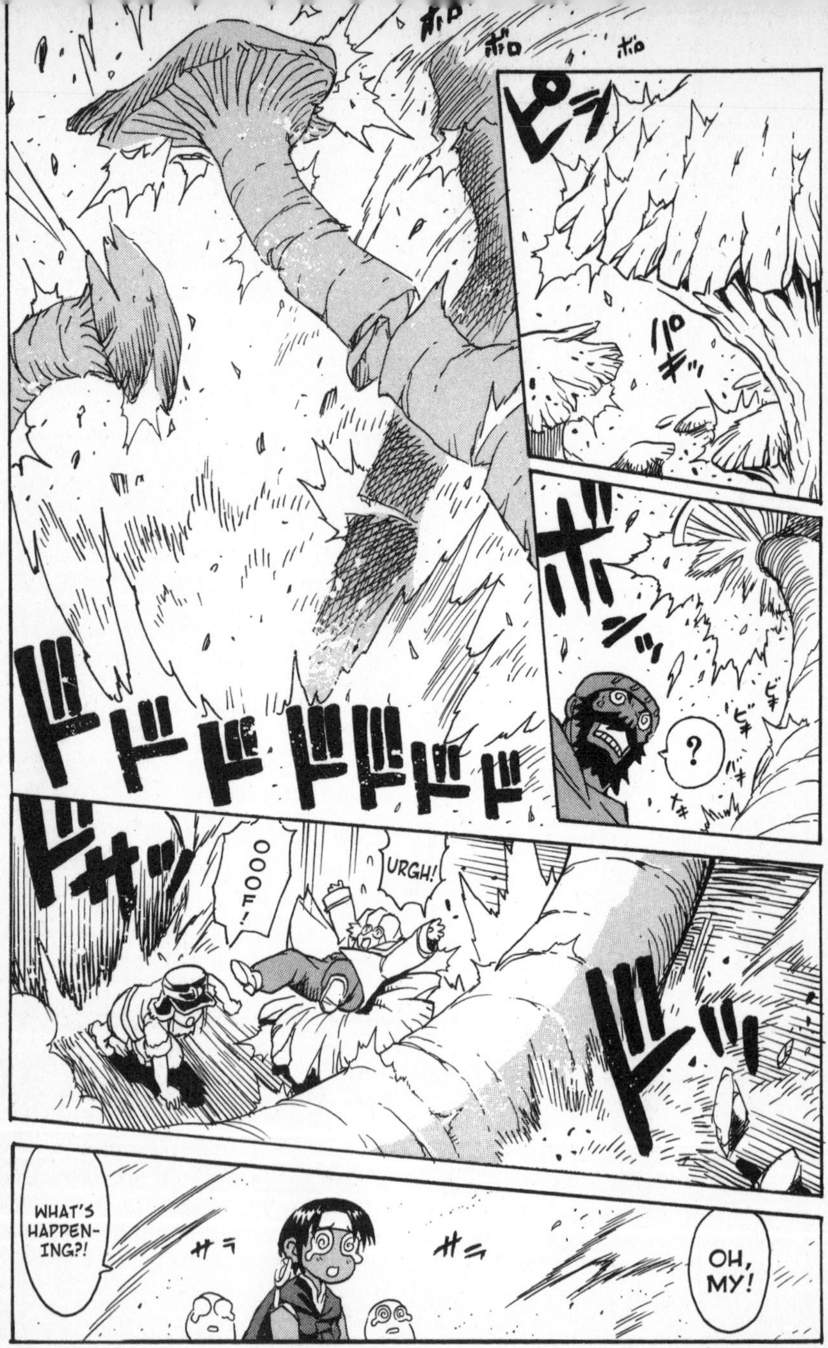
ピラ
パキッ
ボンッ
?
ボロ
ボロ
ボロ
ドドドドドドドド
URGH!
OOOF!
ドサッ
ドッ
OH, MY!
サラ
サラ
WHAT'S HAPPENING?!

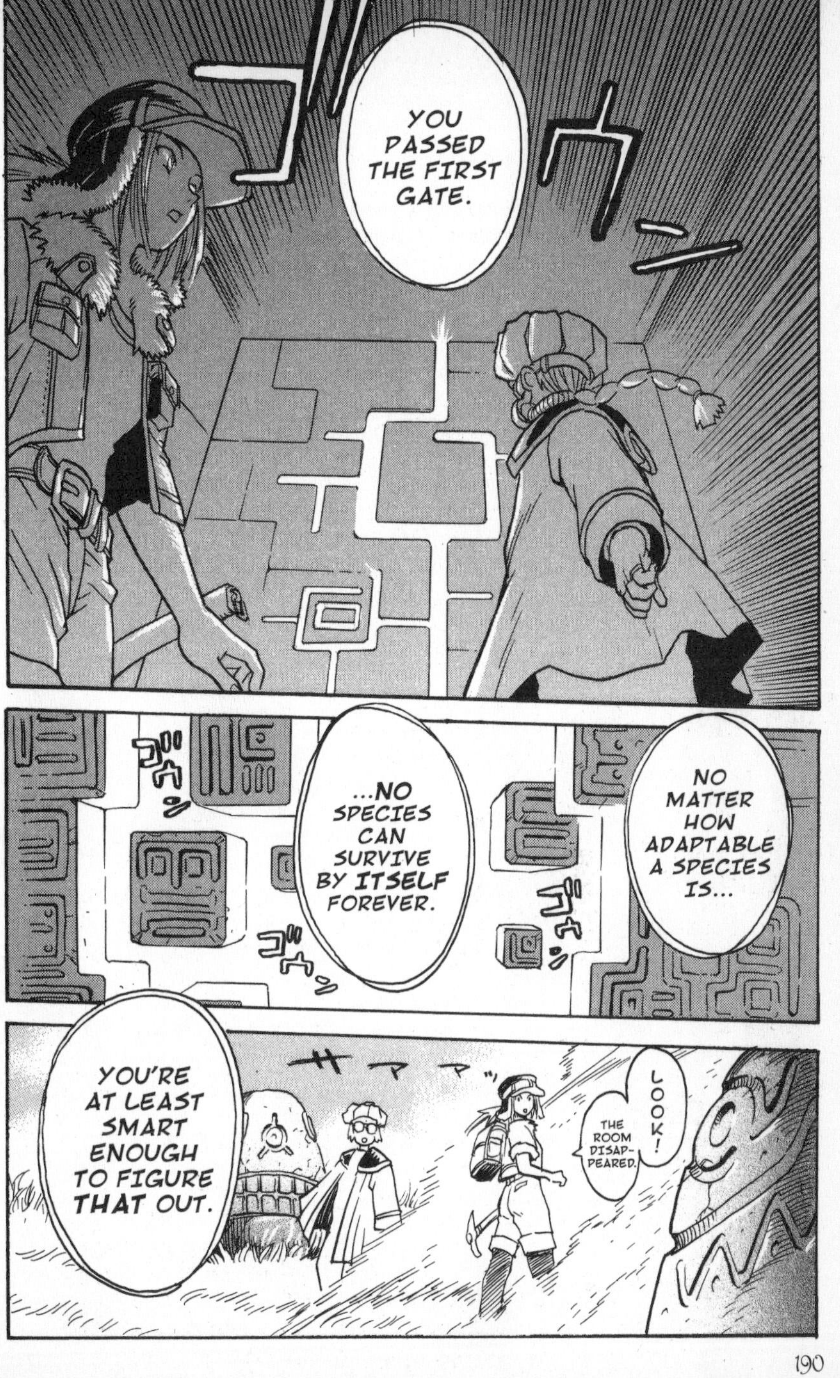
YOU PASSED THE FIRST GATE.
NO MATTER HOW ADAPTABLE A SPECIES IS...
...NO SPECIES CAN SURVIVE BY ITSELF FOREVER.
LOOK!
THE ROOM DISAPPEARED.
YOU'RE AT LEAST SMART ENOUGH TO FIGURE THAT OUT.

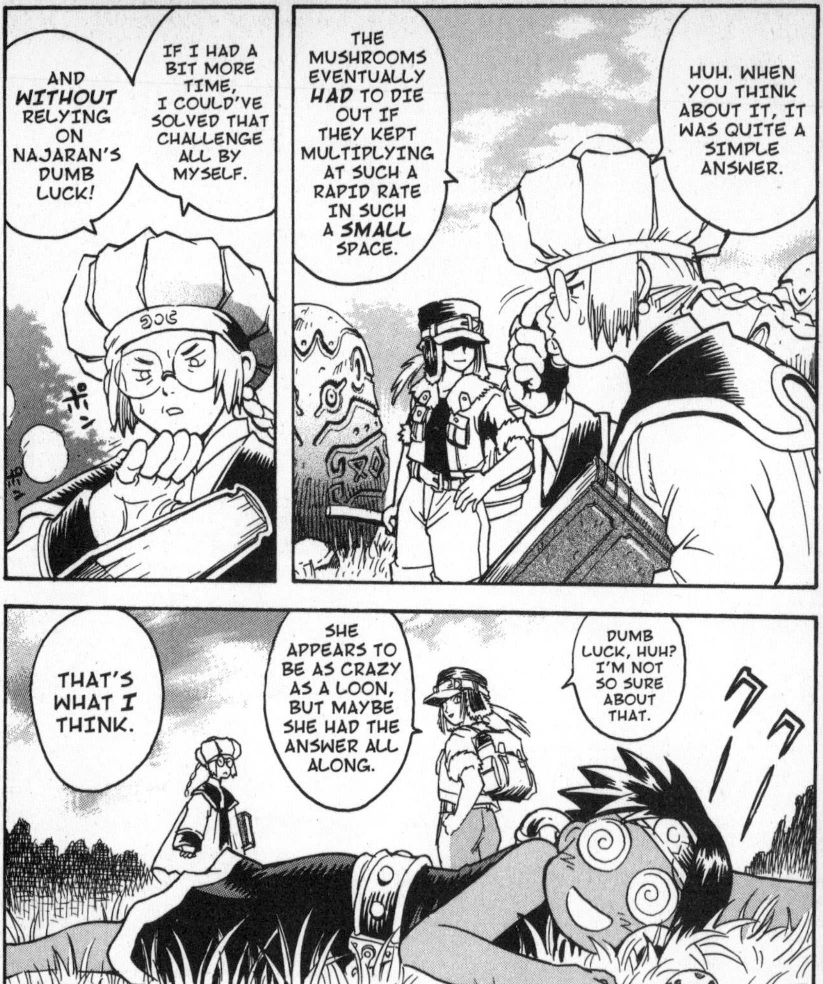
HUH. WHEN YOU THINK ABOUT IT, IT WAS QUITE A SIMPLE ANSWER.
THE MUSHROOMS EVENTUALLY **HAD** TO DIE OUT IF THEY KEPT MULTIPLYING AT SUCH A RAPID RATE IN SUCH A **SMALL** SPACE.
IF I HAD A BIT MORE TIME, I COULD'VE SOLVED THAT CHALLENGE ALL BY MYSELF.
AND **WITHOUT** RELYING ON NAJARAN'S DUMB LUCK!
DUMB LUCK, HUH? I'M NOT SO SURE ABOUT THAT.
SHE APPEARS TO BE AS CRAZY AS A LOON, BUT MAYBE SHE HAD THE ANSWER ALL ALONG.
THAT'S WHAT **I** THINK.

Round 22 The First Gate - Aim For the Next Gate - End

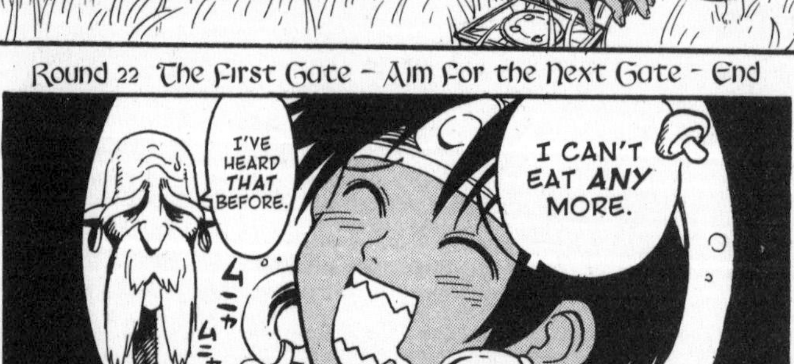
I CAN'T EAT **ANY** MORE.
I'VE HEARD **THAT** BEFORE.

Continued In Volume 3!

Special Lecture: The Culdcept and Alchemists

CEPTERS ARE NOT THE ONLY ONES WHO BENEFIT FROM CARDS. ALCHEMISTS CAN ACTUALLY HAVE A BETTER UNDERSTANDING OF THE CHARACTERISTICS OF CARDS.

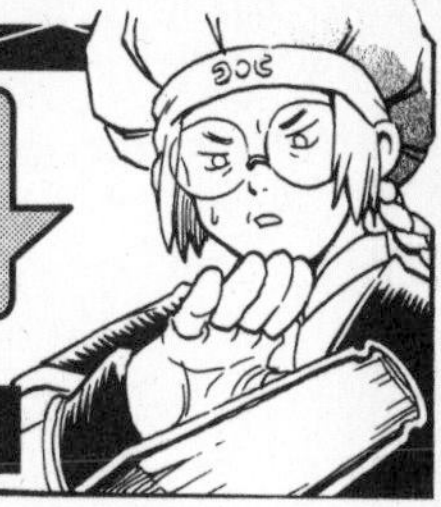

JOAQUIN

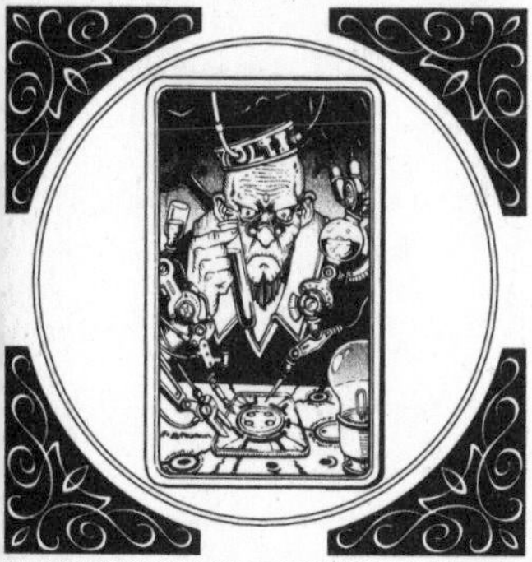

THE RELATIONSHIP BETWEEN THE ALCHEMISTS AND THE CARDS IS AN OLD ONE. IT WAS AN ALCHEMIST WHO FIRST DISCOVERED THAT THE PIECES OF THE CARDS ORIGINATED FROM THE CULDCEPT, THE BOOK OF CREATION. ALCHEMISTS ARE MORE KNOWLEDGEABLE THAN CEPTERS IN TERMS OF HOW THE CARDS ACTUALLY WORK!

Future Technology That Research of the Cards Will Bring

IN THE CULDCEPT, THERE IS A DESCRIPTION OF FUTURE CIVILIZATIONS. BY STUDYING THE CARDS THAT CORRELATE WITH A PARTICULAR SECTION OF THE CULDCEPT, ALCHEMISTS CAN FIGURE OUT WHAT KIND OF SPECIAL ATTACKS AND WEAPONS THEY WILL COME UP WITH IN THE FUTURE!!

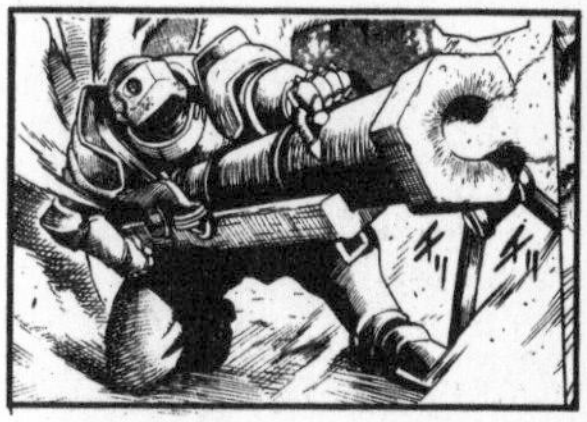

DUM-DUM STUDIED THE CARDS AND CREATED FIREARMS AND SEARCH INSTRUMENTS LONG BEFORE FUTURE CIVILIZATIONS CAME TO EXIST. SEE HOW IMPORTANT ALCHEMY IS?

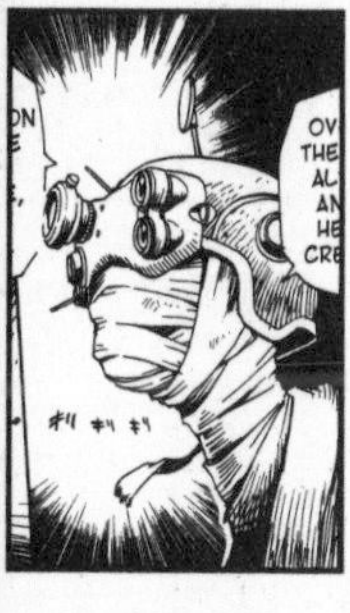

I WANT TO CREATE A HUMAN-LIKE MACHINE THAT MOVES LIKE A LIVING CREATURE, AND I'M CONDUCTING RESEARCH TO ACHIEVE THAT GOAL. IT'S GOING TO BE GREAT!

THE PROTOTYPE I MADE WAS USED AS A JUDGE MACHINE IN THE CEPTER COMPETITION AT SORON.

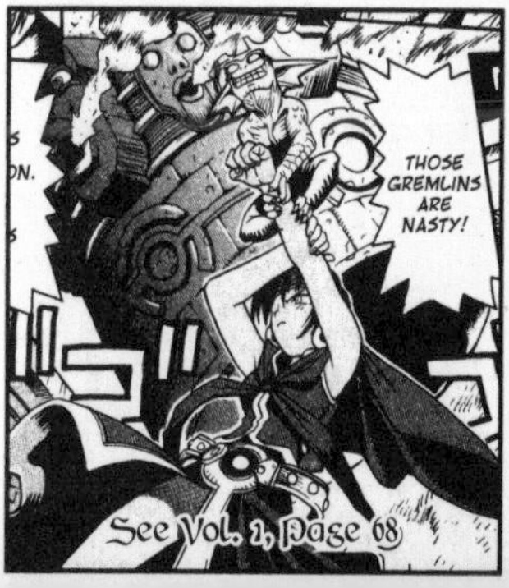
THOSE GREMLINS ARE NASTY!

See Vol. 1, Page 68

SORRY! I BROKE TWO OF THEM DURING BATTLES IN VOLUME ONE!

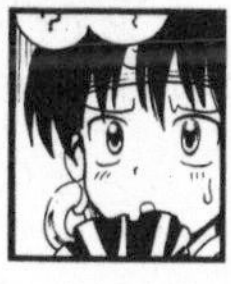

YOU WHA-A-A-A-A-A-T!?

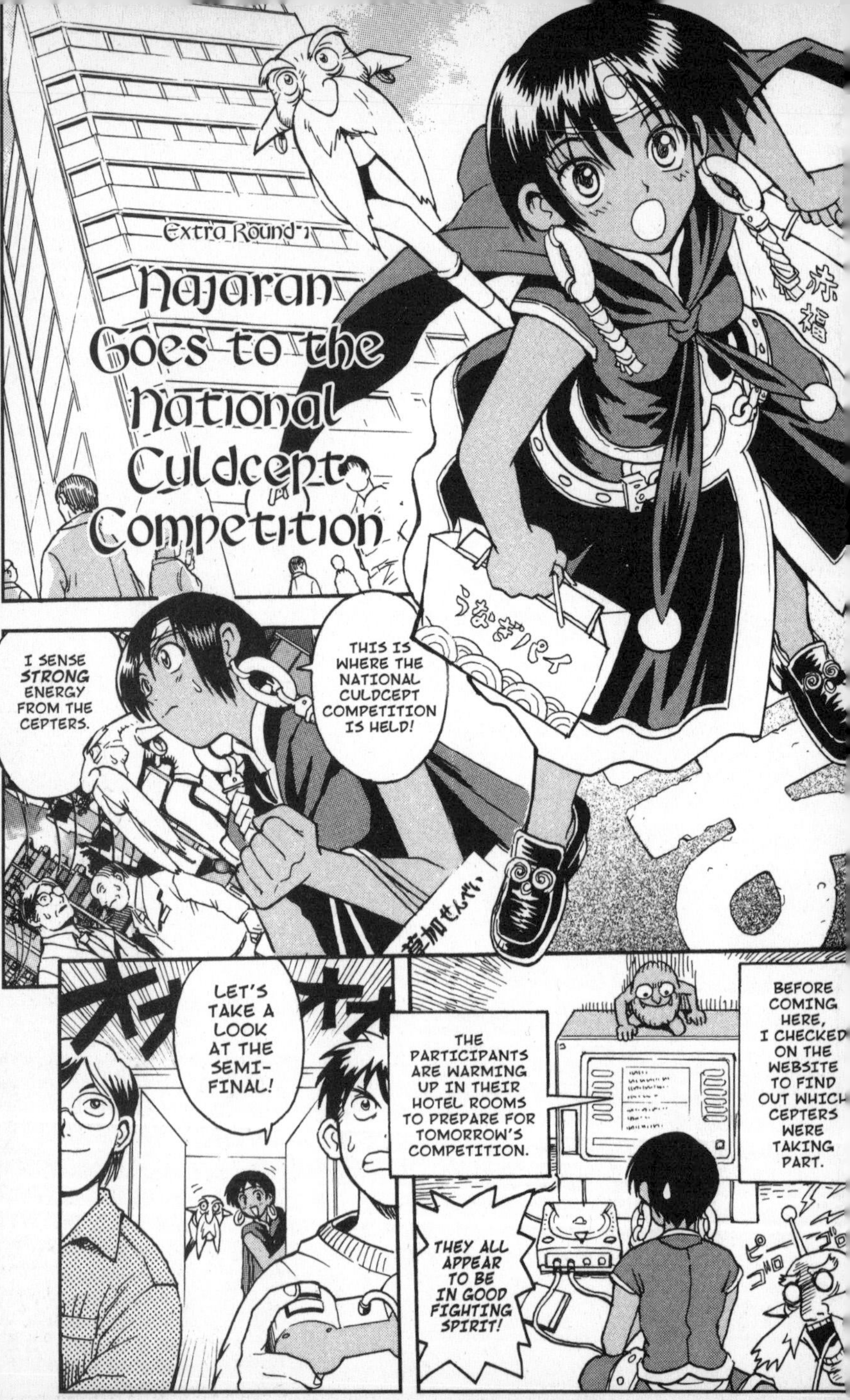
Extra Round 1
Najaran Goes to the National Culdcept Competition
赤福
うなぎパイ
THIS IS WHERE THE NATIONAL CULDCEPT COMPETITION IS HELD!
I SENSE STRONG ENERGY FROM THE CEPTERS.
草加せんべい
BEFORE COMING HERE, I CHECKED ON THE WEBSITE TO FIND OUT WHICH CEPTERS WERE TAKING PART.
THE PARTICIPANTS ARE WARMING UP IN THEIR HOTEL ROOMS TO PREPARE FOR TOMORROW'S COMPETITION.
ピーゴロゴロ
THEY ALL APPEAR TO BE IN GOOD FIGHTING SPIRIT!
LET'S TAKE A LOOK AT THE SEMI-FINAL!

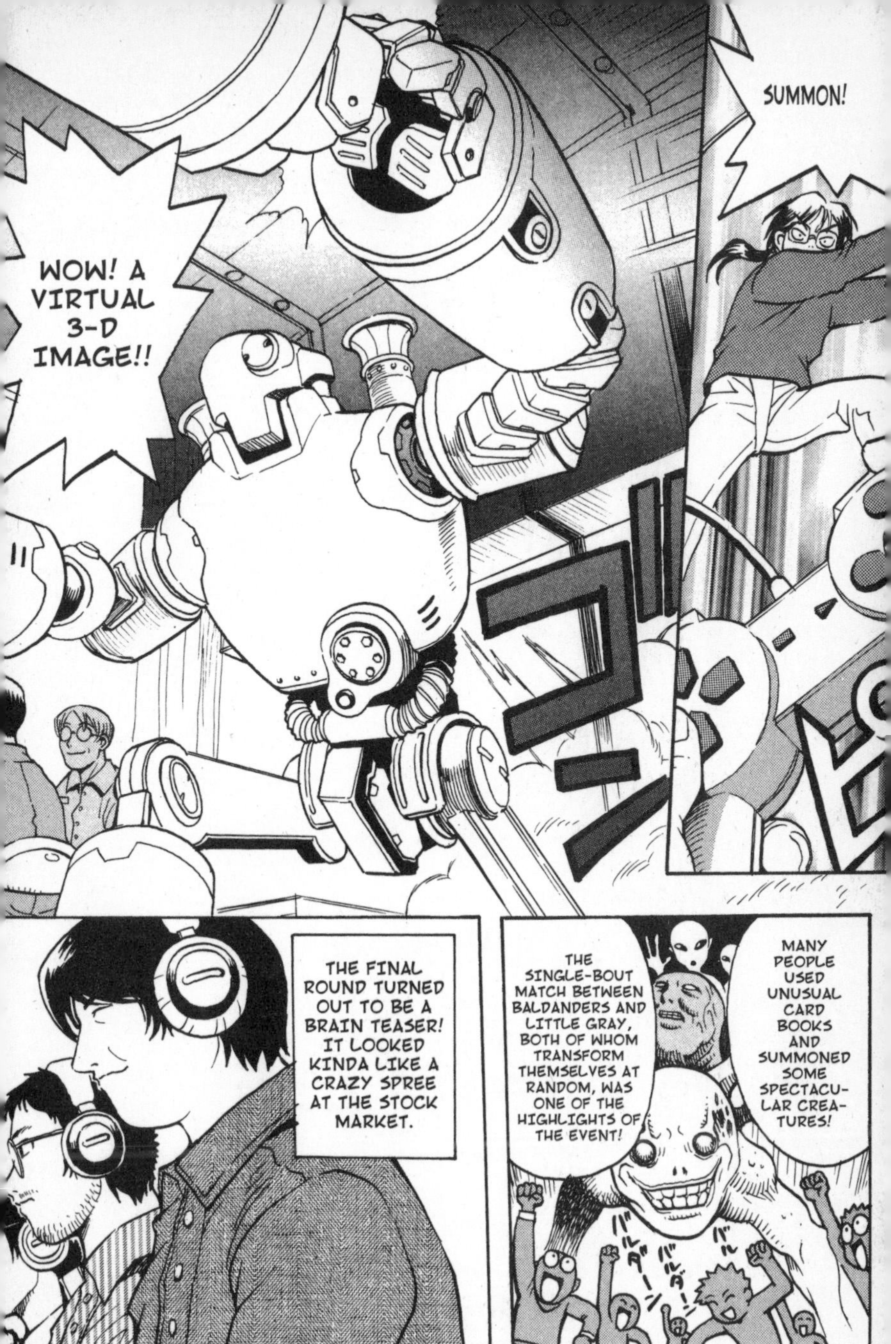
SUMMON!
WOW! A VIRTUAL 3-D IMAGE!!
MANY PEOPLE USED UNUSUAL CARD BOOKS AND SUMMONED SOME SPECTACULAR CREATURES!
THE SINGLE-BOUT MATCH BETWEEN BALDANDERS AND LITTLE GRAY, BOTH OF WHOM TRANSFORM THEMSELVES AT RANDOM, WAS ONE OF THE HIGHLIGHTS OF THE EVENT!
バル
バルダー!
バルダー!
THE FINAL ROUND TURNED OUT TO BE A BRAIN TEASER! IT LOOKED KINDA LIKE A CRAZY SPREE AT THE STOCK MARKET.

* Spectators cheering for Baldanders

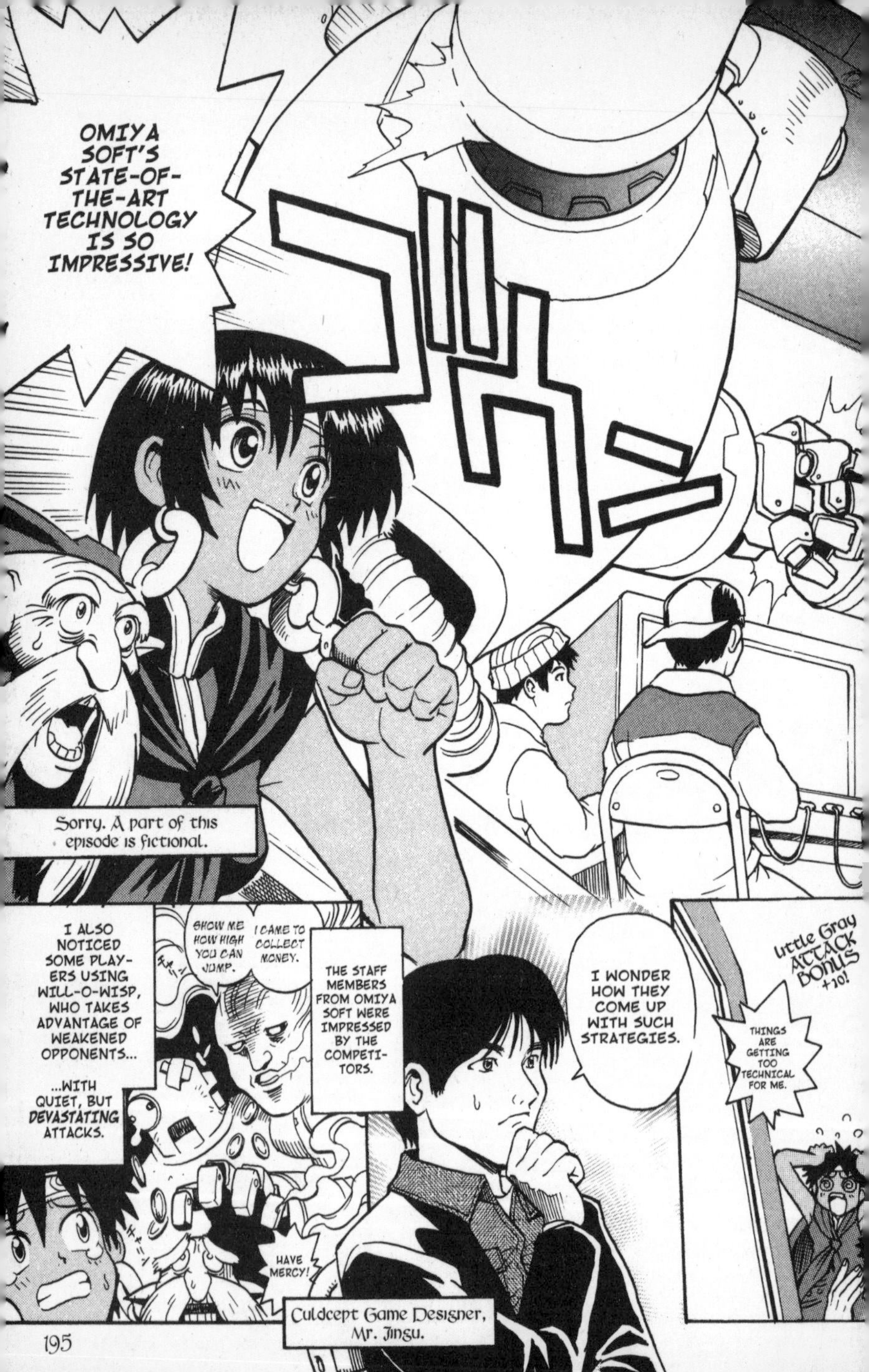

OMIYA SOFT'S STATE-OF-THE-ART TECHNOLOGY IS SO IMPRESSIVE!
ゴウン
Sorry. A part of this episode is fictional.
Little Gray ATTACK BONUS +10!
THINGS ARE GETTING TOO TECHNICAL FOR ME.
THE STAFF MEMBERS FROM OMIYA SOFT WERE IMPRESSED BY THE COMPETITORS.
I WONDER HOW THEY COME UP WITH SUCH STRATEGIES.
Culdcept Game Designer, Mr. Jingu.
I CAME TO COLLECT MONEY.
SHOW ME HOW HIGH YOU CAN JUMP.
I ALSO NOTICED SOME PLAYERS USING WILL-O-WISP, WHO TAKES ADVANTAGE OF WEAKENED OPPONENTS...
...WITH QUIET, BUT DEVASTATING ATTACKS.
HAVE MERCY!

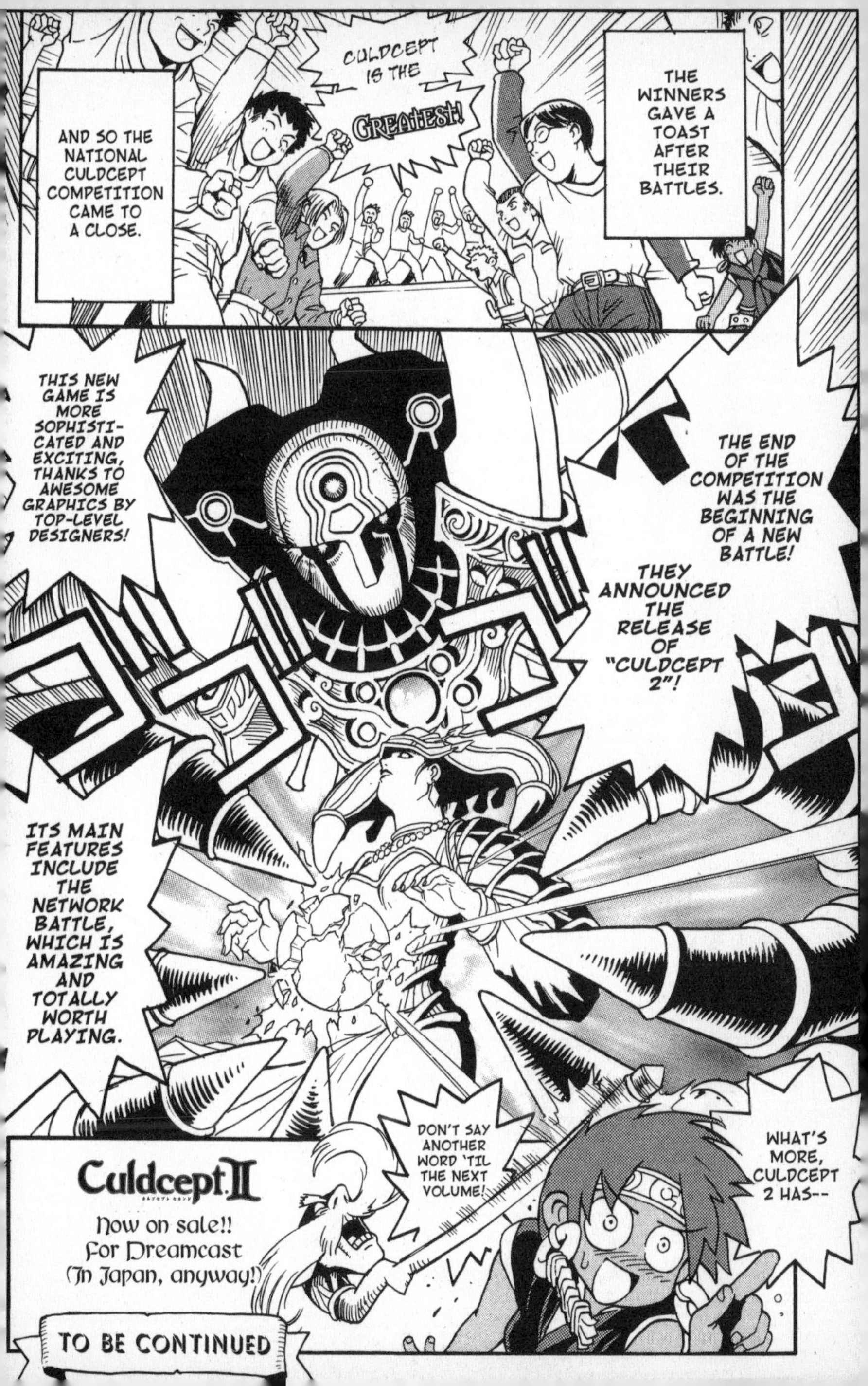
THE WINNERS GAVE A TOAST AFTER THEIR BATTLES.
CULDCEPT IS THE GREATEST!
AND SO THE NATIONAL CULDCEPT COMPETITION CAME TO A CLOSE.
THE END OF THE COMPETITION WAS THE BEGINNING OF A NEW BATTLE!
THEY ANNOUNCED THE RELEASE OF "CULDCEPT 2"!
THIS NEW GAME IS MORE SOPHISTICATED AND EXCITING, THANKS TO AWESOME GRAPHICS BY TOP-LEVEL DESIGNERS!
ITS MAIN FEATURES INCLUDE THE NETWORK BATTLE, WHICH IS AMAZING AND TOTALLY WORTH PLAYING.
WHAT'S MORE, CULDCEPT 2 HAS--
DON'T SAY ANOTHER WORD 'TIL THE NEXT VOLUME!
Culdcept II
Now on sale!!
For Dreamcast
(In Japan, anyway!)
TO BE CONTINUED

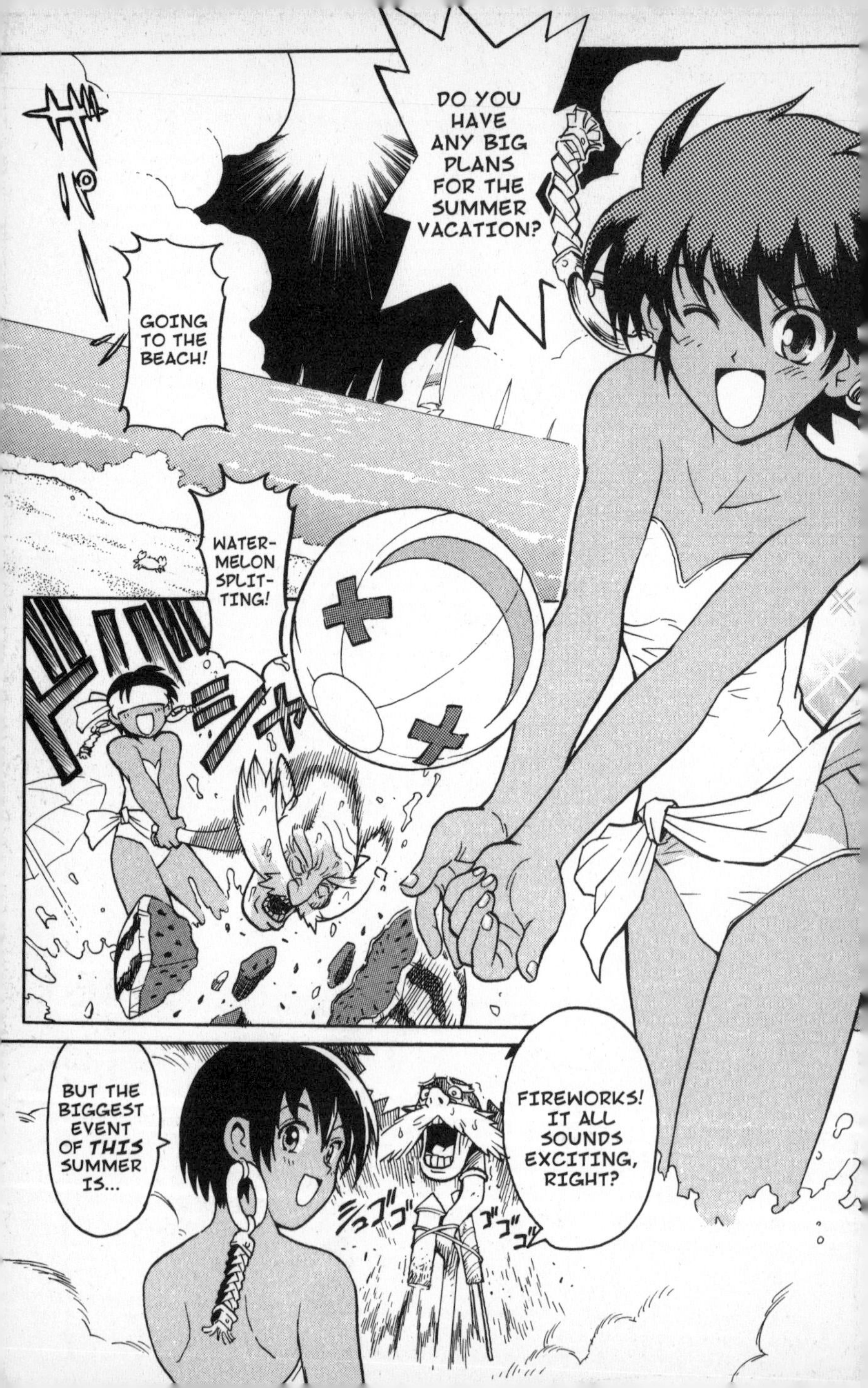
DO YOU HAVE ANY BIG PLANS FOR THE SUMMER VACATION?
GOING TO THE BEACH!
WATER-MELON SPLIT-TING!
FIREWORKS! IT ALL SOUNDS EXCITING, RIGHT?
BUT THE BIGGEST EVENT OF *THIS* SUMMER IS...

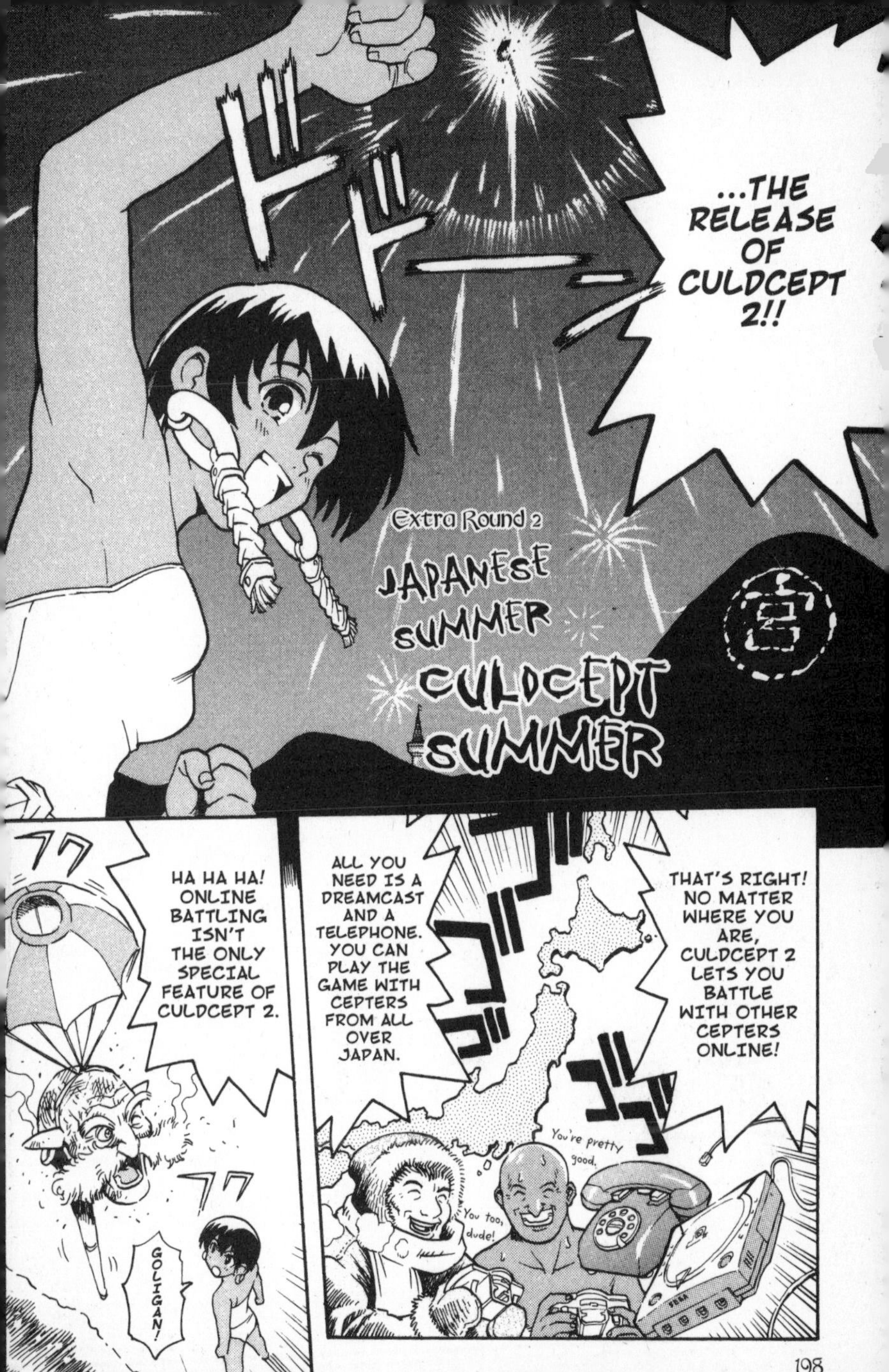
...THE RELEASE OF CULDCEPT 2!!
Extra Round 2
JAPANESE SUMMER
CULDCEPT SUMMER
THAT'S RIGHT! NO MATTER WHERE YOU ARE, CULDCEPT 2 LETS YOU BATTLE WITH OTHER CEPTERS ONLINE!
ALL YOU NEED IS A DREAMCAST AND A TELEPHONE. YOU CAN PLAY THE GAME WITH CEPTERS FROM ALL OVER JAPAN.
You're pretty good.
You too, dude!
HA HA HA! ONLINE BATTLING ISN'T THE ONLY SPECIAL FEATURE OF CULDCEPT 2.
GOLIGAN!

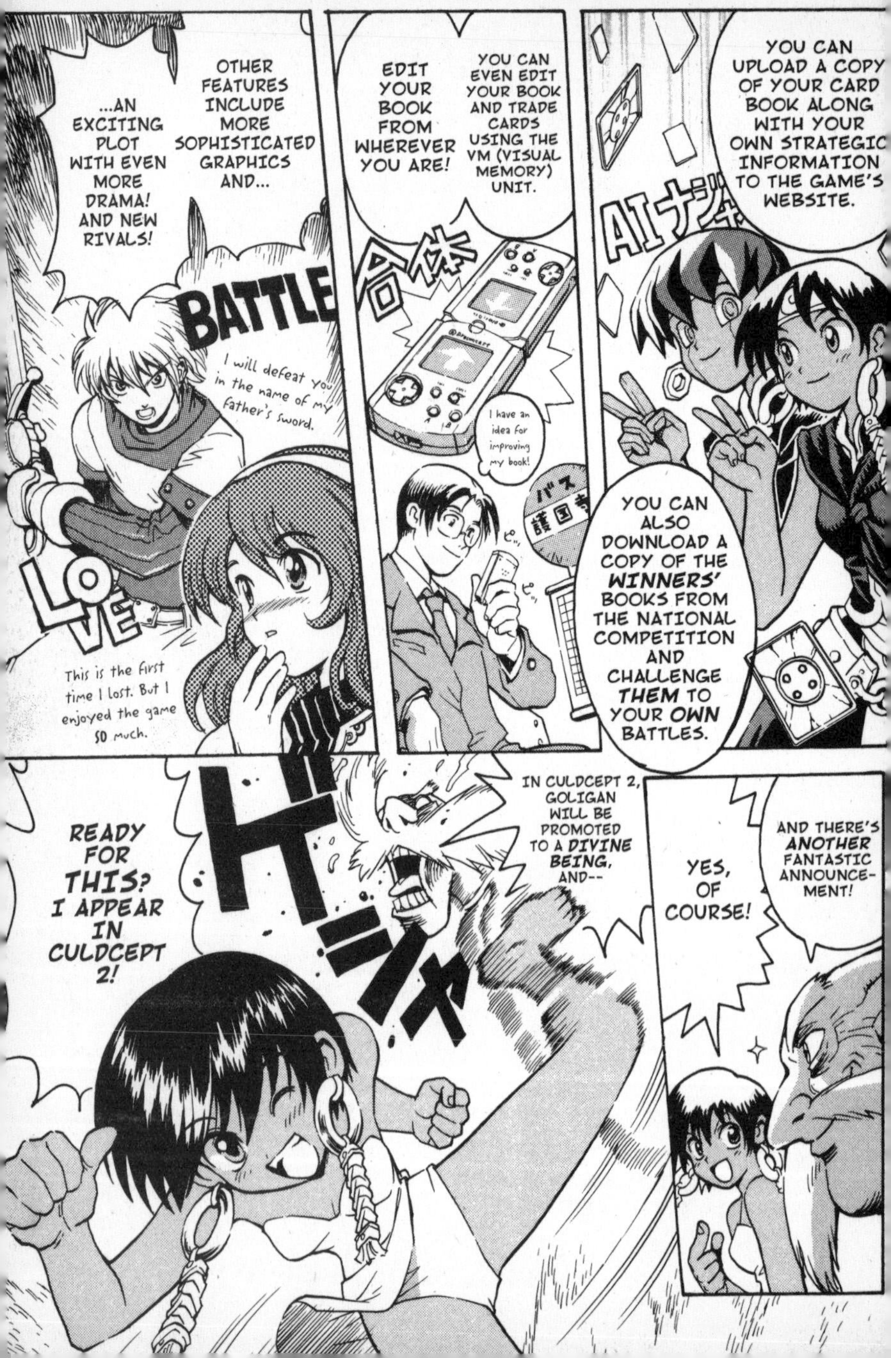
YOU CAN UPLOAD A COPY OF YOUR CARD BOOK ALONG WITH YOUR OWN STRATEGIC INFORMATION TO THE GAME'S WEBSITE.
YOU CAN ALSO DOWNLOAD A COPY OF THE WINNERS' BOOKS FROM THE NATIONAL COMPETITION AND CHALLENGE THEM TO YOUR OWN BATTLES.
YOU CAN EVEN EDIT YOUR BOOK AND TRADE CARDS USING THE VM (VISUAL MEMORY) UNIT.
EDIT YOUR BOOK FROM WHEREVER YOU ARE!
合体
I have an idea for improving my book!
バス
護国寺
OTHER FEATURES INCLUDE MORE SOPHISTICATED GRAPHICS AND...
...AN EXCITING PLOT WITH EVEN MORE DRAMA! AND NEW RIVALS!
BATTLE
I will defeat you in the name of my father's sword.
LOVE
This is the first time I lost. But I enjoyed the game so much.
AND THERE'S ANOTHER FANTASTIC ANNOUNCEMENT!
YES, OF COURSE!
IN CULDCEPT 2, GOLIGAN WILL BE PROMOTED TO A DIVINE BEING, AND--
READY FOR THIS? I APPEAR IN CULDCEPT 2!

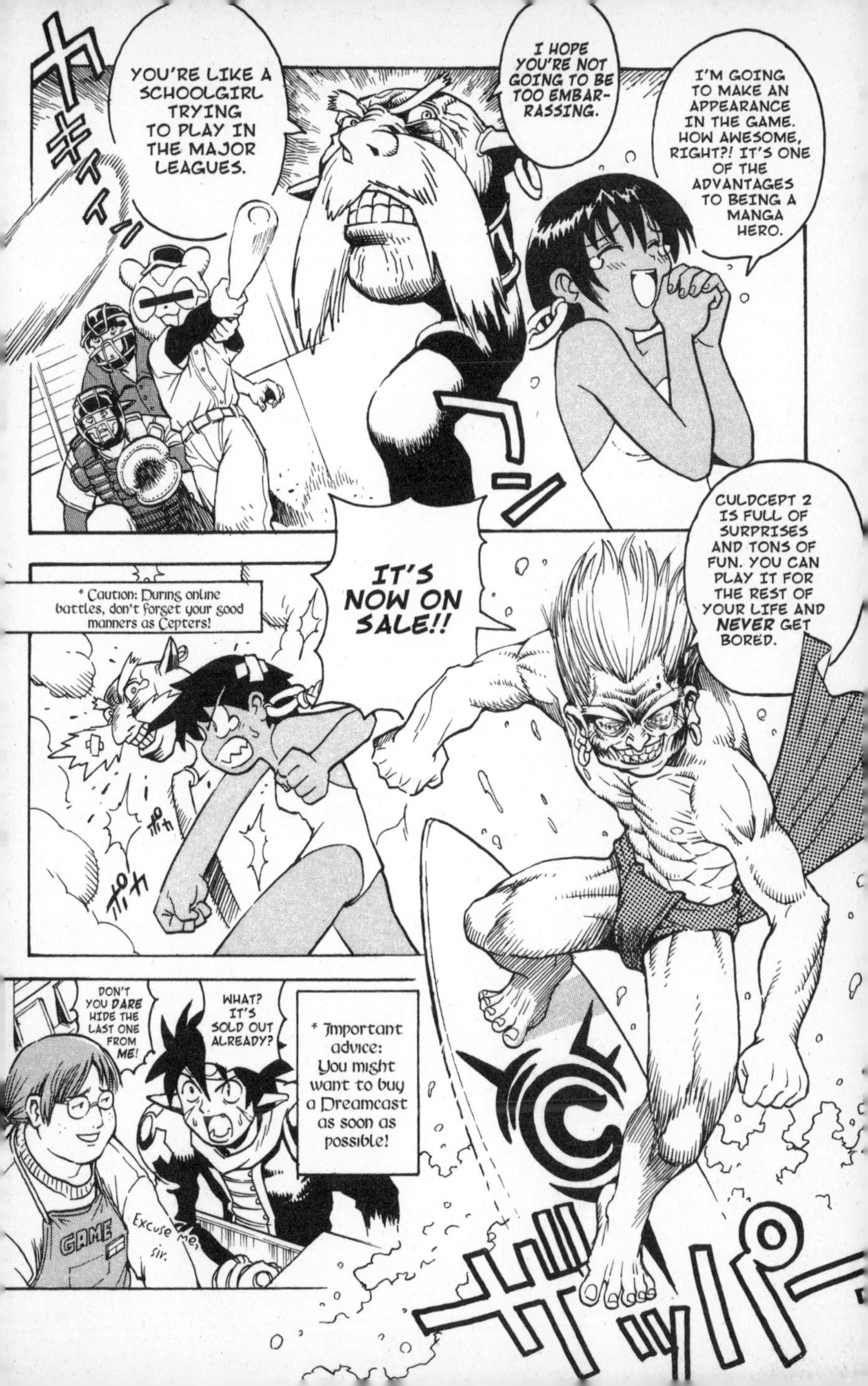
I'M GOING TO MAKE AN APPEARANCE IN THE GAME. HOW AWESOME, RIGHT?! IT'S ONE OF THE ADVANTAGES TO BEING A MANGA HERO.
I HOPE YOU'RE NOT GOING TO BE TOO EMBARRASSING.
YOU'RE LIKE A SCHOOLGIRL TRYING TO PLAY IN THE MAJOR LEAGUES.
CULDCEPT 2 IS FULL OF SURPRISES AND TONS OF FUN. YOU CAN PLAY IT FOR THE REST OF YOUR LIFE AND NEVER GET BORED.
IT'S NOW ON SALE!!
* Caution: During online battles, don't forget your good manners as Cepters!
* Important advice: You might want to buy a Dreamcast as soon as possible!
WHAT? IT'S SOLD OUT ALREADY?
DON'T YOU DARE HIDE THE LAST ONE FROM ME!
Excuse me, sir.
GAME

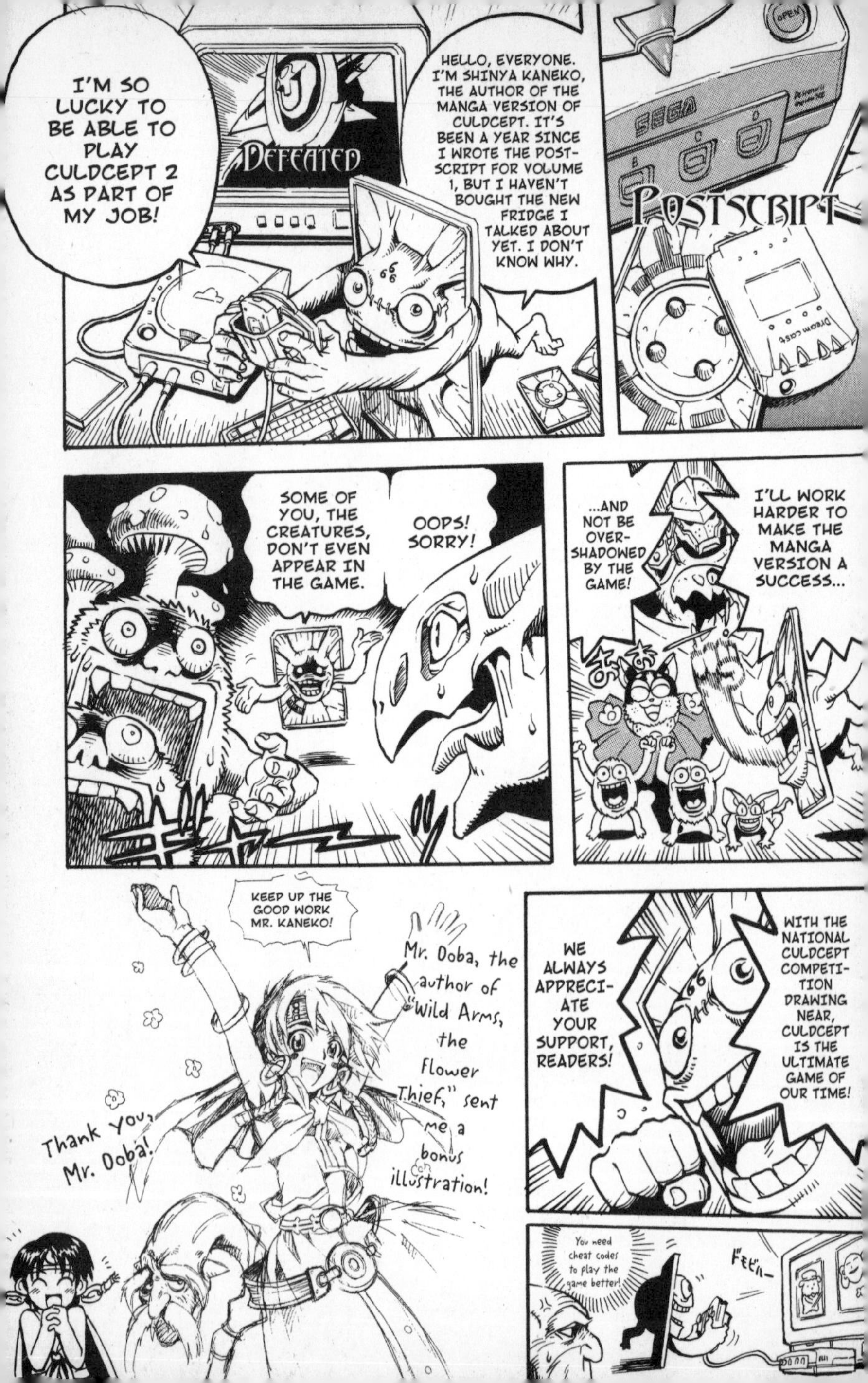
OPEN
SEGA
POSTSCRIPT
Dreamcast
DEFEATED
HELLO, EVERYONE. I'M SHINYA KANEKO, THE AUTHOR OF THE MANGA VERSION OF CULDCEPT. IT'S BEEN A YEAR SINCE I WROTE THE POST-SCRIPT FOR VOLUME 1, BUT I HAVEN'T BOUGHT THE NEW FRIDGE I TALKED ABOUT YET. I DON'T KNOW WHY.
I'M SO LUCKY TO BE ABLE TO PLAY CULDCEPT 2 AS PART OF MY JOB!
I'LL WORK HARDER TO MAKE THE MANGA VERSION A SUCCESS...
...AND NOT BE OVER-SHADOWED BY THE GAME!
OOPS! SORRY!
SOME OF YOU, THE CREATURES, DON'T EVEN APPEAR IN THE GAME.
WITH THE NATIONAL CULDCEPT COMPETI-TION DRAWING NEAR, CULDCEPT IS THE ULTIMATE GAME OF OUR TIME!
WE ALWAYS APPRECI-ATE YOUR SUPPORT, READERS!
You need cheat codes to play the game better!
KEEP UP THE GOOD WORK MR. KANEKO!
Mr. Ooba, the author of "Wild Arms, the Flower Thief," sent me a bonus illustration!
Thank You, Mr. Ooba!

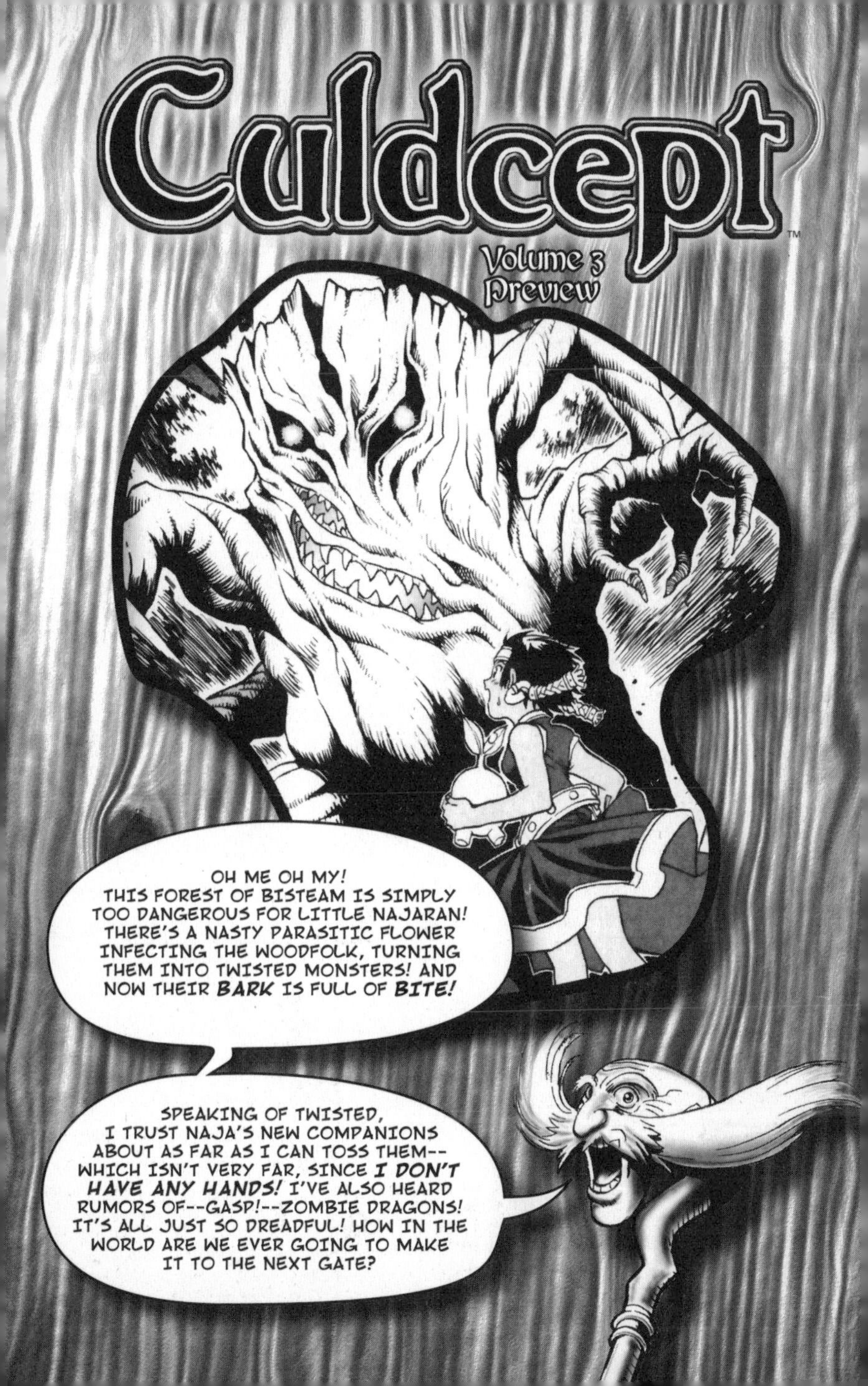
Culdcept™
Volume 3 Preview
OH ME OH MY! THIS FOREST OF BISTEAM IS SIMPLY TOO DANGEROUS FOR LITTLE NAJARAN! THERE'S A NASTY PARASITIC FLOWER INFECTING THE WOODFOLK, TURNING THEM INTO TWISTED MONSTERS! AND NOW THEIR **BARK** IS FULL OF **BITE!**
SPEAKING OF TWISTED, I TRUST NAJA'S NEW COMPANIONS ABOUT AS FAR AS I CAN TOSS THEM--WHICH ISN'T VERY FAR, SINCE ***I DON'T HAVE ANY HANDS!*** I'VE ALSO HEARD RUMORS OF--GASP!--ZOMBIE DRAGONS! IT'S ALL JUST SO DREADFUL! HOW IN THE WORLD ARE WE EVER GOING TO MAKE IT TO THE NEXT GATE?

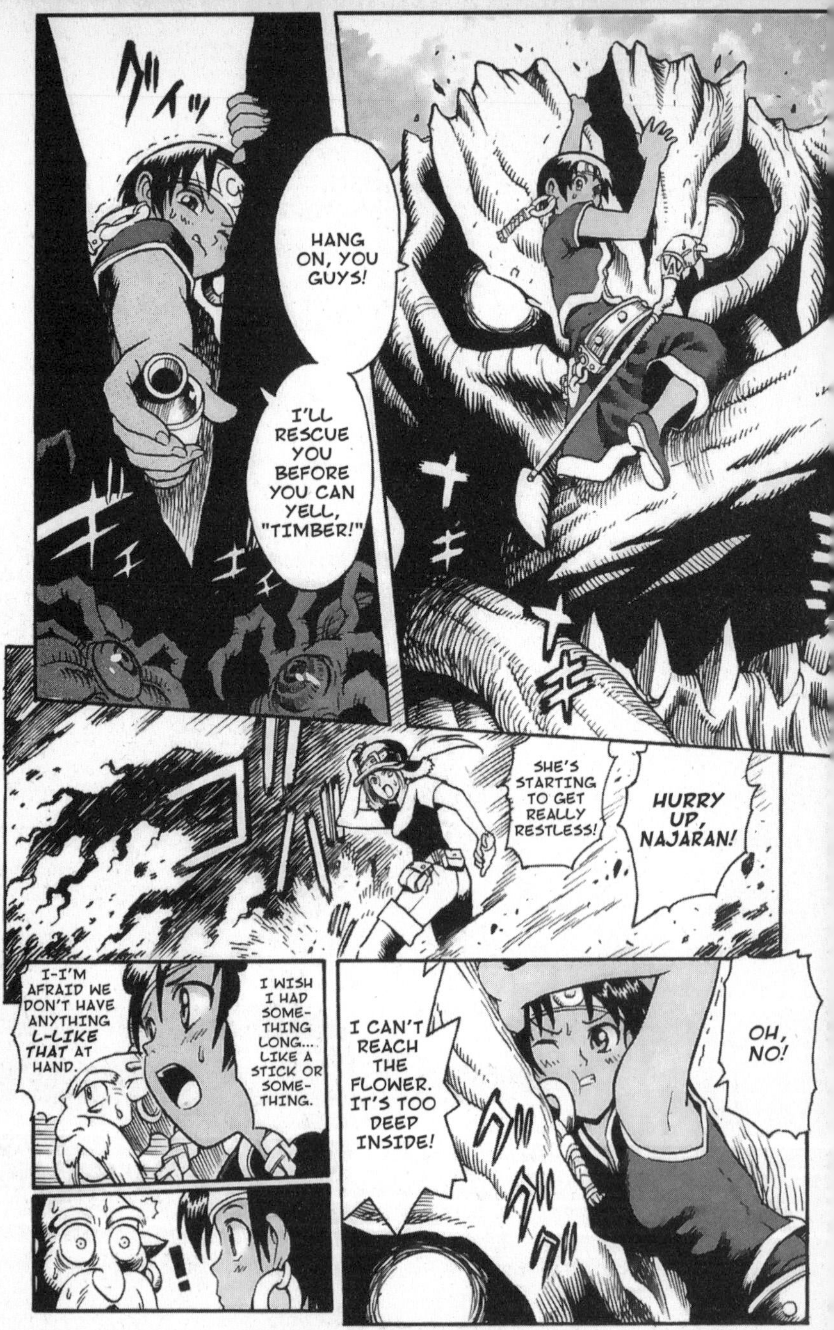
HANG ON, YOU GUYS!
I'LL RESCUE YOU BEFORE YOU CAN YELL, "TIMBER!"
グイッ
HURRY UP, NAJARAN!
SHE'S STARTING TO GET REALLY RESTLESS!
OH, NO!
I CAN'T REACH THE FLOWER. IT'S TOO DEEP INSIDE!
I WISH I HAD SOME-THING LONG... LIKE A STICK OR SOME-THING.
I-I'M AFRAID WE DON'T HAVE ANYTHING *L-LIKE THAT* AT HAND.
!

ALSO AVAILABLE FROM  TOKYOPOP®

SHUTTERBOX
SKULL MAN, THE
SUIKODEN III
SUKI
THREADS OF TIME
TOKYO BABYLON
TOKYO MEW MEW
VAMPIRE GAME
WISH
WORLD OF HARTZ
ZODIAC P.I.

CINE-MANGA™

ALADDIN
CARDCAPTORS
DUEL MASTERS
FAIRLY ODDPARENTS, THE
FAMILY GUY
FINDING NEMO
G.I. JOE SPY TROOPS
GREATEST STARS OF THE NBA: SHAQUILLE O'NEAL
GREATEST STARS OF THE NBA: TIM DUNCAN
JACKIE CHAN ADVENTURES
JIMMY NEUTRON: BOY GENIUS, THE ADVENTURES OF
KIM POSSIBLE
LILO & STITCH: THE SERIES
LIZZIE MCGUIRE
LIZZIE MCGUIRE MOVIE, THE
MALCOLM IN THE MIDDLE
POWER RANGERS: DINO THUNDER
POWER RANGERS: NINJA STORM
PRINCESS DIARIES 2
RAVE MASTER
SHREK 2
SIMPLE LIFE, THE
SPONGEBOB SQUAREPANTS
SPY KIDS 2
SPY KIDS 3-D: GAME OVER
TEENAGE MUTANT NINJA TURTLES
THAT'S SO RAVEN
TOTALLY SPIES
TRANSFORMERS: ARMADA
TRANSFORMERS: ENERGON

NOVELS

CLAMP SCHOOL PARANORMAL INVESTIGATORS
SAILOR MOON
SLAYERS

ART BOOKS

ART OF CARDCAPTOR SAKURA
ART OF MAGIC KNIGHT RAYEARTH, THE
PEACH: MIWA UEDA ILLUSTRATIONS

ANIME GUIDES

COWBOY BEBOP
GUNDAM TECHNICAL MANUALS
SAILOR MOON SCOUT GUIDES

TOKYOPOP KIDS

STRAY SHEEP

**You want it? We got it!
A full range of TOKYOPOP
products are available now at:
www.TOKYOPOP.com/shop**

07.15.04Y

ALSO AVAILABLE FROM TOKYOPOP®

MANGA

07.15.04Y

GETBACKERS™
They get back what shouldn't be gone...
most of the time.
EXPLICIT CONTENT
PARENTAL ADVISORY
EXPLICIT CONTENT
OT
OLDER TEEN AGE 16+
©1999 Yuya Aoki and Rando Ayamine ©2004 TOKYOPOP Inc. All rights reserved.
www.TOKYOPOP.com

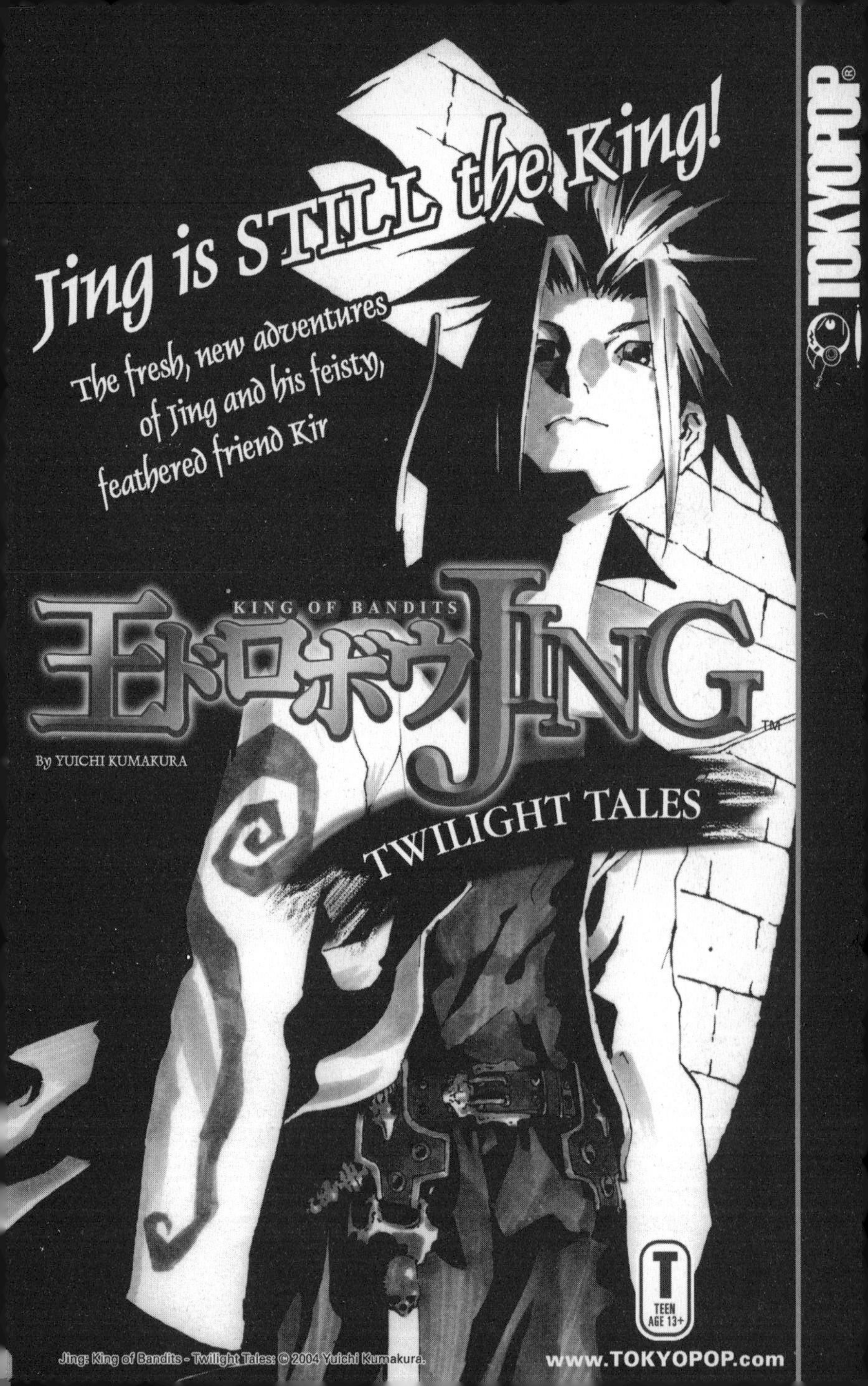
Jing is STILL the King!
The fresh, new adventures of Jing and his feisty, feathered friend Kir
KING OF BANDITS
JING
TM
By YUICHI KUMAKURA
TWILIGHT TALES
TOKYOPOP
T
TEEN AGE 13+
Jing: King of Bandits - Twilight Tales: © 2004 Yuichi Kumakura.
www.TOKYOPOP.com

S0-AKM-758

STOP!

This is the back of the book.
You wouldn't want to spoil a great ending!

This book is printed "manga-style," in the authentic Japanese right-to-left format. Since none of the artwork has been flipped or altered, readers get to experience the story just as the creator intended. You've been asking for it, so TOKYOPOP® delivered: authentic, hot-off-the-press, and far more fun!

DIRECTIONS

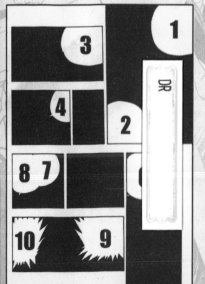

If this is your first time reading manga-style, here's a quick guide to help you understand how it works.

It's easy... just start in the top right panel and follow the numbers. Have fun, and look for more 100% authentic manga from TOKYOPOP®!